Hither Shore

Interdisciplinary Journal
on Modern Fantasy Literature

Jahrbuch der
Deutschen Tolkien Gesellschaft e. V.

Literary Worldbuilding

Interdisziplinäres Seminar der DTG
27. bis 29. Oktober 2017, Augsburg

Herausgegeben von:
Thomas Fornet-Ponse (Gesamtleitung),
Thomas Honegger, Julian T.M. Eilmann

SCRIPTORIUM OXONIAE

Bibliografische Information der Deutschen Bibliothek

Die Deutsche Bibliothek verzeichnet diese
Publikation in der Deutschen Nationalbibliografie;
detaillierte bibliografische Daten sind im
Internet über http://dnb.ddb.de abrufbar.

ISBN 978-3-9818313-2-0

Hither Shore, DTG-Jahrbuch 2017
veröffentlicht im Verlag »Scriptorium Oxoniae«

Deutsche Tolkien Gesellschaft e. V. (DTG)
E-Mail: anfrage@tolkiengesellschaft.de

Scriptorium Oxoniae im atelier für TEXTaufgaben e. K.
Brehmstraße 50 · 40239 Düsseldorf · Germany
E-Mail: rayermann@scriptorium-oxoniae.de

Hither Shore, Gesamtleitung: Thomas Fornet-Ponse
E-Mail: hither-shore@tolkiengesellschaft.de

Vorschläge für Beiträge in deutscher oder englischer Sprache (inklusive
Exposé von ca. 100 Wörtern) werden erbeten an o.g. E-Mail-Adresse.

Abwicklung: Susanne A. Rayermann, Düsseldorf
Layout/Design: Kathrin Bondzio, Solingen
Umschlagillustration: Anke Eißmann, Herborn
Druck und Vertrieb: Books on Demand, Norderstedt

Inhalt

Conference Scholarship 2017

Reviews/Rezensionen

Preface

The 14th Tolkien Seminar of the German Tolkien Society (DTG), held from the 27th to the 29th October 2017 in Augsburg, was dedicated to the topic of "Literary Worldbuilding". The breadth and variety of the theme invited not only contributions on Tolkien, but also on numerous other authors. It was the biggest Tolkien Seminar of the DTG so far, with over 30 scheduled presentations, which sadly did not all get submitted for publication.

This extraordinarily strong resonance yielded a great variety of insights, considerations, theoretical approaches, etc. and demonstrated impressively how advantageous it is for the analysis of individual authors to examine their respective ways of literary worldbuilding in a contrastive manner; or how different perspectives onto the same work can benefit from each other. Not surprisingly, Tolkien's well-established position as a theorist and practitioner of secondary world creation was reaffirmed by the presentations and discussions.

Even so it should be said that in this conference—despite the large amount of contributions—the topic could not be covered in its whole entirety, which is partially due to the wide spectrum of the works and authors examined.

The 20th anniversary of the DTG furthermore offered the opportunity to award for the first time the newly established 'Travel Grants for Junior Researchers', which enabled the contributions by Laura Selle, Germany, and Andoni Cossio, Spain. The grants are designed to cover travel and accommodation costs of promising up-and-coming scholars who would like to present their research at the Tolkien Seminar. The conference scholarship has its roots in one of the central concerns of the DTG: the promotion of new talents, especially in the field of academic research.

Another novelty was the venue, the University of Augsburg. Thanks to the highly successful cooperation with Stephan Köser and Sebastian Streitberger the Tolkien Seminar found a strong resonance. For all that I would like to thank you and everyone else who helped on-site, as well as *Walking Tree Publishers* for the cordial and active assistance and finally to the publisher's team Susanne A. Rayermann and Kathi Bondzio, with the assistance of Larissa Zöller, Marcel Aubron-Bülles and Frank Weinreich.

Thomas Fornet-Ponse

On No Magic in Tolkien: Resisting the Representational Criteria of Realism

Gergely Nagy (Budapest)

I t is very convenient to see things in either/or distinctions. But as Frank Herbert says, "the beginning is the time for taking the most delicate care that the balances are correct" (Herbert 3)—it would be too easy to say there certainly is magic in Tolkien, and it would be equally too easy to say there certainly is not. Magic is itself an either/or thing: it either works or it does not, in which case you are doing something wrong. Critics always feel the need to qualify their statements about this kind of magic in Tolkien: they say that there is 'very little' or 'relatively few occurrences' of it. But ever since I read the *Silmarillion*, I have believed there is actually none at all. Going through the *History of Middle-earth* later made me qualify my conviction, too: *there used to be, but by the time Tolkien got to write his most complete and most popular works, it dwindled and disappeared*—like the fairies, or elves that he wanted to write about originally. But then there is another sort, which critics often also see as an either/or phenomenon: the tale is either *marvellous*, in which case there is magic (of a fairly undefined kind), or *uncanny*, in which case there is not. There is either magic, in which case the tale is fantasy, or there is technology, in which case it is science fiction. Happily, these divisions are not any more the unchallenged standard in the criticism of the fantastic, and in any case the argument was called into question both by Tolkien, for whom technology *is a kind of magic*, and by Arthur C. Clarke, who claimed that "any sufficiently advanced technology is indistinguishable from magic" (Clarke 21). This (fairly undefined) 'critical magic' derives from another either/or: either there is something in the tale that we do not believe possible and is not explained by technology, or not. So, saying "there is no magic in Tolkien", one needs to take that Herbertian delicate care for the balances, and reflect (somewhat trivially) that it all depends.

The question to ask is rather: What sort of magic *is* or *is not there* in Tolkien? There are concepts of magic that are certainly there, at least at the beginning, and others that are not; and towards the end, there is less and less of any sort, and this is inextricably bound up with history, cultural and textual, with the evolving of Middle-earth and its framework, and also with texts, their genres and moods. Some Victorian fairy tale magic is undeniably present in the *Book of Lost Tales* and even in the verse 'Lay of Leithian'; the very common 'fantasy magic', the *Dragons of the Something Something* kind that some theorists apparently expect from 'fantasy' seems to me not to be there at all. And the magic that Tolkien himself talks about in *On Fairy-stories* is certainly there, but it is very different from either of these. Which is why one needs to take care for the balance, but even more importantly for the definitions: there are *several magics* that critics talk about, and these are not very well differentiated.

The first kind of either/or magic is the cultural historical or anthropological understanding: the coercion of the 'supernatural' (itself a function of what any given cultural period understands as 'natural') by means of ritual actions, objects, or words, which, if performed correctly, unfailingly give results. Tolkien's own usage in *On Fairy-stories, enchantment,* has a philological connection to this, since the word comes ultimately from Latin *incantare,* "to cast under a spell, to bewitch" (FS 112), formed from *cantare,* 'to sing' (which Tolkien would have been very conscious of). This kind of magic has a long history, going back to antiquity and quite certainly beyond, with a lot of interesting developments in the Middle Ages (which, again, Tolkien would have been very aware of). 'Natural magic' and the interference of Christianity aside, there is still a lot in the "common tradition of magic", as Richard Kieckhefer calls it (Kieckhefer 56f.): part of this is the traditional magic of the Germanic tribes, which survives for example in the Anglo-Saxon charms or the fact that in the Norse pantheon, Odin is explicitly the god of magic, runes and hidden knowledge (see Kieckhefer 43-55). This is the kind that survives most in fairy tales, in the most unreflected form: no one ever questions how magicians or witches perform their magic, whether it is 'natural', 'supernatural', or 'demonic'. One of the greatest problems of medieval theoreticians of magic was whether all magic is demonic or not (Kieckhefer 182-6)—they came to the conclusion that "many types of magic might be natural [but] virtually all types might be demonic" (Kieckhefer 184), and that conveniently solved the question, since it rerouted it into religion and theology. But there is no Thomas Aquinas in fairy tales, and therefore their magic remains non-theological and even non-religious (even when there is something like a 'default religion' in the tale itself, like in medieval romance). It is also this kind of simple either/or spellwork in much fantasy literature, without any attempt at explaining the background. *Harry Potter* works perfectly well without once asking the question "what sort of power is drawn on in all this performance?" But for Tolkien the source of power is always a relevant question, a question of background, which he cannot leave unsolved. And so, he solved it, I believe, by getting rid of this kind of magic altogether.

But when critics of the fantastic expect magic in a fantasy text, this is not what they mean. Things in the story are either explainable in everyday scientific terms or not: if not, *that* is 'magic'. Ultimately this leads to sometimes declaring the fantastic to go back to the *Iliad,* since there are no gods, it could not *really* have been Aphrodite who saved Paris in Book 3. But for the Greeks, the gods were part of nature, and in this sense not 'supernatural' at all. 'Magic' in this sense is not a matter of ritual or performance, not even of story or events: it is a question of background, the basic presuppositions about the world of the fiction, and assumptions about the real world. If the two sets of assumptions do not match, the subtle differences of fictional worlds from the 'real' one all just register as this: as 'magic'. 'In *Strategies of Fantasy*,' Brian Attebery argued that what the critics of the fantastic, from Todorov on, somewhat uncritically apply to fantastic texts are in fact the criteria of *realism*. It is not only that we read with a contemporary understanding of what *can* happen in the world and what *cannot*, but also that we read with the interiorised criteria of *how* the world is to be described and written about. Attebery, therefore, examines elements of narrative like character, story, or time, and shows how 'fantastic' texts' usage of these differ from what we have learnt to expect in good solid down-to-earth realist novels. But he additionally shows how it is also the question of *language* in the fantastic: all these narratological concepts are abstractions, and they are always manifested in actual text. The fantastic, as Attebery treats it, is basically a *different narrative language* from that of realism: and that is what seems to confuse critics to identify 'magic' as its definitive ingredient. But the criteria of realism are also frustrated in fantastic works because they construct a *radically fictitious* secondary world—a world that is fundamentally *different* from what critics like to call 'consensus reality'. When Tolkien, in *On Fairy-stories*, insists that a fairy story's world, Faërie, cannot be connected with the primary world by means of some spatial or temporal machinery (FS 33f.) or even by that of dreams (FS 35), it is this he advocates in embryonic form. A fictional world that is explicitly and radically different from the real one obviously cannot be written about in 'mimetic' terms and language. But the interesting thing is that *within* these radically fictitious worlds, fantastic texts (some of Tolkien's own, for instance) actually preserve much of the realistic logic, and often proceed exactly by the criteria of 'realistic description', if not those of character or plot. For one thing, they keep the *novel* as their (at least nominal) genre of reference.

We can more or less say that Tolkien himself excised 'cultural historical magic' from his world, and that 'theoretical magic' is sought in his works largely because he himself used the term, and because of the still somewhat prevalent, partly ideological assumption that anything that is not 'realist' must be 'magical'. These two lacks of magic are what I would like to explore in this paper: how Tolkien progressively got rid of the ritualistic magical descriptions that appeared as late as the 'Lay of Leithian', and how his type of 'fantastic' writing in fact goes against the realist ideology that supposes 'magic' to be there whenever something is 'too fictional'. The first line of inquiry is, one could say, philological, since it involves texts, their details and language. The second one is theoretical, for it is based on Tolkien's own and others' theoretical considerations of what constitutes 'magic' in 20th century narrative. I think we would all be better off if the question of magic in Tolkien was resolved in these two areas; we could then concentrate on how Tolkien handles the concept of power (which largely came to stand in for early magic) and how his work integrates into (even stands at the beginning of) a particular type of 20th century narrative that is not explicitly realistic, but not explicitly and post-modernly theoretical either.

Tolkien is usually seen to draw most of his inspiration, at least at the beginning, from medieval works; but there is more to it than this. Richard C. West has explored in depth how the *Kalevala,* with its shamanistic magic songs, "set the rocket off in story" (L 214, #163; see West), and Dimitra Fimi has shown how the Victorian and Edwardian fairy tradition was also influential in Tolkien's early writings (Fimi 28-61). It is therefore not surprising to find fairy magic all over the place in the *Book of Lost Tales*, which would not qualify as a fairy story anyway by Tolkien's later standards, since it uses both the machinery of the dream and that of spatial travel, and is anyway clearly connected to the primary world. The connecting character of Eriol and later Ælfwine ties the fairy isle not just to the primary world, but a very explicit locality, England; and the fairies, if not diminutive, are definitely closer to Victorian fairies than to Tolkien's own later elves. Even the *Qenya Lexicon* shows, as Fimi argues, that Tolkien "not only 'liked' [flower-fairies], but also considered them part of his nascent mythology" (Fimi 34). The very device of the Cottage of Lost Play, with "old tales, old songs, and elfin music" (LT 1 9) is fairy-tale-like, even connected to children, and so are the countless references to magic isles, seas, cars, conches, and so on.[1] But as early as the *Lost Tales*, Tolkien also associated magical 'functions' with his Valar and elves. Palúrien (Yavanna) is called "mother of magic", and several of the Valar are said to have their own magic.[2] The Valar as a group are said to have their magic, too (LT 1 137, 200, 236; cf. SM 16). When there is any actual magic done, it is often associated with *songs* (perhaps a nod to the *Kalevala*): even Ilúvatar "sang into being the Ainur first" (LT 1 49), and it is by "songs of utmost enchantment" (LT 1 104) that Palúrien starts growth in Middle-earth. To revive the Trees, Lórien sings "most wistful songs of magic and enchantment" and Vána "old golden songs" (LT 1 199). Yavanna attempts this with "songs of unfading growth and a song of resurrection after death and withering" (LT 1 205). Much of Lúthien's magic is also done by songs (as it still is in the *Silmarillion*). *Enchantment* and *spell* seem to be hardly separable from these, and there are countless examples of the Valar performing some kind of spell. Ulmo even connects his to "the great word that Ilúvatar said to me" (LT 1 241). There are spells that bind stones together,[3] and Melko is said to cast "the spell of bottomless dread... upon his slaves".[4] There is Thû the Wizard,

---

1   See in particular LT 1 9, 10, 198 (Ulmo's "magic car"), 238, 240, 242 ("magic conches").
2   LT 1 76; Aulë: LT 1 132, 206, 208; Ulmo: LT 1 68, 242, LT 2 5 (as "ancient mariner");
    Palúrien: LT 1 76, 113, 206, 207, 213; Lórien: LT 1 199; Kémi: LT 1 236; Oromë: LT 1
    239; Vána: LT 1 199.
3   Tevildo: LT 1 28, 29; Thû: LB 303, SM 134.
4   LT 1 272, 274, 276; LT 2 78, 159, 161: "so that he seemed ever nigh them".

whom Melko taught "much black magic" (LT 1 266). The Silmarils are said to have "a fierce and holy magic" (LT 2 33), the dragon can cast a "binding spell" (LT 2 87), and the "magics" of Gwendeling (Melian) the fay are well-known (becoming an alliterative formula in the alliterative *Húrin*: "the magic mazes of Melian the Queen"[5]). But most often these 'magics' are just a matter of course, reported without any concern to *how* they work.

There are, however, some few occasions when it *is* said how they work. Common with these is that they all occur relatively early in Tolkien's writings, and then subsequently diminish or are excised altogether. A good example for this is the Valar's creation of the Two Trees: the 'Tale of the Coming of the Valar' has them dig "two great pits" (LT 1 71) and do elaborate physical preparations, then Palúrien weaves "spells about these two places, deep enchantments of life and growth and putting forth of leaves, blessing and yielding of fruit" (LT 1 71). In a note, Christopher Tolkien remarks that "the preparations of the Valar… with all the detail of physical 'magic', were afterwards abandoned" (LT 1 92); and in the 'Sketch of the Mythology', the Trees are indeed said merely to "grow under [Yavanna's] songs" (SM 12; cf. commentary, SM 49, 50), and the 'Qenta' even says the Trees were "planted" (SM 97). Both versions of the 'Annals of Valinor' simply state that the Valar "brought into being" the Trees (SM 312; LR 123[6]). The version in the *Silmarillion* arose in the 'Quenta Silmarillion' (LR 229), and only preserved the element of song. The making of the Silmarils is another case: where the *Lost Tales* version describes a complicated process (LT 1 138) and the commentary again adds that all this was "abandoned" (LT 1 151), later accounts simply call the Silmarils "magic" or "holy", fashioned with "spells of the Gods and Gnomes" (LT 2 33). "Thrice-enchanted" occurs twice in the poems of the 1920s (LB 162, the 'Flight of the Noldoli' fragment; LB 254, Leithian Canto VI.1642) and surfaces again in the later 'Annals of Valinor' as "thrice-renowned" (LR 125). Even the introduction of the early 'Annals of Beleriand' calls them "magic gems" (SM 352), but by the 'Quenta Silmarillion', even Fëanor's "subtle magic" ('Qenta', SM 106) is modified to "subtle skill" (LR 249, which is the wording of the *Silmarillion*). Sometimes a magical ritual pops up in an already established story, like Beleg's "whetting spell" in the alliterative *Húrin* (LB 51-2, 'Húrin' 2.1203-1223): "an entirely new element," says Christopher Tolkien, "and without a trace later", but "in style reminiscent of Lúthien's 'lengthening spell'" (LB 63).

Lúthien's 'lengthening spell' is perhaps the most detailed account of actual cultural historical magic in all of Tolkien's works. This has distinct ingredients

---

5 LB 12; even in the Old English translation of the 'Annals of Valinor': 'Vala-geal-drum begól' (SME 343).
6 The Old English version of the earlier 'Annals' uses the verb "awehtan" (SM 335) and "gescópon 7 onwehtan" (SM 340).

with detailed instructions: the "clearest water of the stream below," for example, "must be drawn at midnight in a silver bowl, and brought to my hand with no word spoken" (LT 2 17)—like in a medieval manual of magic, the instructions are detailed and clear, suggesting that the spell works only if they are followed to the letter. There are other ingredients, and then, alone, "singing a very magical song", Tinúviel mixes the substances and sings "another song [with] the names of all the tallest and longest things upon Earth" (LT 2 17). Much of this survives into the verse 'Lay of Leithian' (LB 245-47), with a long list of the longest things; but in the 'Sketch', she simply "escapes" without any magic mentioned (SM 27, cf. 'Qenta', SM 132), and in *The Silmarillion* she only "put[s] forth her arts of enchantment" (S 172). However, by the time of writing the poems, Tolkien already built up quite a lot of background about his fictional world. Some late revisions for the poems, in Christopher Tolkien's opinion, show how he was trying to downsize magic in them, even dispensing with the word altogether.[7] Tolkien also got rid of the primary connection of Eriol/ Ælfwine, although in the 1930s the concept was still strong enough for him to start translating Annals to Old English where he used the word "gealdrum" for Melian's magic (SM 343). Tolkien's early creative period is important in 'magical' terms at least partly because he wrote in rather different genres: 'tales', poems, annals, condensed sketches of the mythology—kinds of text that make very clear that realistic criteria cannot possibly apply.

This is what changed radically with *The Hobbit*. However unwillingly and un-foreseen, here Tolkien embarked on a quite different project when he undertook to present his tale in the form of a children's book, a form of the novel. It was not in any way a *realistic* novel, as children's books very rarely are, and it still had remnants of the fairy tale magic in the figure of Gandalf, the Dwarves and the Elves, too. Gandalf's ineffectiveness against the wolves ("wizard though he was": H 95) is often commented on, while of the Wood-elves it is said that "their magic was strong" (154; the Elvenking even boasts about his "magic doors", 158), and Beorn is said to be "under no enchantment but his own" (108). Perhaps the Dwarves have closest associations with magic, as already in the *Lost Tales*.[8] They put "a great many spells" (41) over the Trolls' gold, are credited with inventing the Moon-letters (50), and even they cannot do anything against "the magic that had shut" (192) the side-door into the Mountain (not even with "fragments of broken spells of opening", 190f.). The inside of the Mountain and the treasure

---

7   See n. to 'Leithian' Canto XIII.3969, LB 360 and n. to the second version of Canto III.131, LB 422.

8   Seen primarily in the figure of Mîm (LT 2 113-4, 224), which survived into the 'Sketch' (SM 36) and the 'Qenta' (SM 158f.). See Rateliff 54f.

tempts even Bilbo with the "dragon-spell" (206)[9], and the Arkenstone's 'enchantment' draws his arms towards it (217). And there is the "magic ring" (80), too, which Bilbo can hardly believe he found by accident: an object that works automatically, irrespective of who is using it, to produce a well-defined effect: make its wearer invisible. Again, magic seems much more an inherent power made use of by those who have it, and not a codified, manualised technique. It comes closest to that, ironically, in the ring (such as it is in *The Hobbit*), and when 'spells' are mentioned, but there is nothing like Lúthien's "lengthening spell". Perhaps the most sinister detail is the "Necromancer", a "black sorcerer" about whom even Bilbo had heard (129; see Rateliff 81-4). This is an interesting use: necromancy is definitely a term for medieval magic, one that originally meant telling the future by conjuring and asking the dead, but also demons, until "the conjuring of demons came to be known as necromancy; this was the ordinary meaning of the term in later medieval Europe" (Kieckhefer 152f.). You would think there *is* magic in a fictional world that has a 'Necromancer'. But we do not know what he does, only that the "great council of the white wizards, masters of lore and good magic" drove him out of Mirkwood (270).

By this time, the overarching story that later became the 'Silmarillion' and its background had already been written. Tolkien has worked through stories (early ones like 'Kullervo' and the 'Lost Tales') to systematically build up his secondary world (complete with detailed languages), and that secondary world had less and less to do with the primary one, until finally the whole Eriol/ Ælfwine frame fell away, stories like 'The Fall of Númenor' rose and were integrated, and *The Hobbit* had a more or less already 'constructed' world to find its place in. This world was, however, different from that of the 'Lost Tales' and even the longer poems, the only previous texts of some length. The world of *The Hobbit* is, for lack of a better word, *Northern*: the use of dwarf-names from the 'Dvergatal' (Völuspa), the Norse concept of the dragon guarding the treasure (also in *Beowulf*), the Germanic feud that the dwarves take up against Smaug, the shape-changing Beorn and the forest of Mirkwood all infuse the story with a Northernness that some critics (C.S. Lewis, for one) recognised and which Tolkien himself used later, when he worked out properly the fiction of translation in *The Lord of the Rings*. But that device, even when it maintains a very flimsy connection to the primary world, also serves to distance the text from it. By the time of *The Lord of the Rings* (certainly the revised edition), the only explicit connection Tolkien left between Middle-earth and the primary world was the fiction of the translator/editor. And even that is a mere practicality, also mirroring the activities of figures within the fiction.

---

9   Cf. Mîm's spells on the gold in LT 2 226, 227, 230, 242, and Christopher Tolkien's commentary at LT 2 247.

It says a lot about this process that the very starting premise of *The Lord of the Rings* is a bit of eliminated magic from *The Hobbit*: providing an explanation for the either/or 'magic' ring that Bilbo found. For it turns out the Ring does not work irrespective of its user: it does matter who uses it, and its power is certainly not simply that of invisibility. Tolkien steadily shifts the focus from the effects of hidden knowledge (which could come out as 'magic') to knowledge itself, its various sources and uses; and to power, in its various manifestations. In explaining to Frodo, Gandalf says Rings of Power are "magic rings as you call them" (LotR I I.ii.45), and this exemplifies the approach of *The Lord of the Rings* perfectly: Tolkien seems to say magic is a matter not of knowledge but of ignorance. People who know little (about the world, history, other people) will see some things as magic. This is evident in the reactions to Lórien: while Boromir just calls it "perilous" (LotR I II.vi.329), others like Éomer accuse Aragorn and his companions of being "net-weavers and sorcerers" (LotR II III.ii.422) if they have Galadriel's favour. Wormtongue claims "webs of deceit were ever woven" (LotR II III.vi.502) there; and only Faramir admits simply he does not know much about it: "long now it has lain beyond the knowledge of Men" (LotR II IV.v.651-2). But Wormtongue's accusation is just an inversion: in a much-quoted passage, Galadriel remarks about her Mirror that "this is what [hobbits] would call magic, I believe; though I do not understand clearly what they mean; and they seem to use the same word of the deceits of the Enemy" (LotR I II.vii.353). Early critics again often felt the need to remark on Gandalf's ineffectuality as a 'wizard': he tries to open the gates of Moria by 'spells' (and varies his delivery and formula when they do not work: LotR I II.iv.299), shuts the door against the Orcs with a "shutting-spell" and when the Balrog comes, a "word of Command" (LotR I II.v.319), and is not very successful at either. Other characters are said to use 'spells', too, more or less metaphorically: Old Man Willow, Tom Bombadil, the Barrow-wight. Saruman's voice is described as an "enchantment" and the hearers fall "under the spell" (LotR II III.x.564). It is also a "spell that knit [the Witch-king's] unseen sinews to his will" (LotR III V.vi.826).

Again, some of this undoubtedly seems like cultural historical magic: a word is spoken, and the gates of Moria open; Gandalf says something and his staff begins to glow; Galadriel breathes on the water and the Mirror shows images. But even in these instances, the reader has been warned: Gandalf and Galadriel had been consistently described as 'different', and even though the reader has no clear idea about what the source of their power is, it is clear that what they do is no simple ritual and command. Is Sauron's "let[ting] a great part of his own former power pass into" (LotR I I.ii.50) the Ring an instance of the magical motif that Tolkien mentions in *On Fairy-stories* as 'The Monkey's Heart' (FS 37f)? Are Galadriel's Mirror or the *palantíri* 'magical'? Tom Shippey has pointed out how both can be related to the original meaning of *speculatio*, "looking in a *speculum*—a mirror, a glass, a crystal ball" (Shippey, 'Another Road' 380), but also to being deceived and coming to the wrong conclusion: the dangers of another meaning of 'speculation' (382). Is this an instance of magic?

What happens in *The Lord of the Rings* is that Tolkien sets his story in a fictional world that has a very clearcut hierarchy of power, not just military, political or historical, but theological. The theological hierarchy of Middle-earth had more or less been there in the sketches of the mythologies and 'lost tales', while *The Hobbit*, at least at its writing, was a tangent: it did not necessitate much reference to that hierarchy. *The Lord of the Rings* did, but Tolkien deliberately withheld this reference: his much-quoted letter says it is a "fundamentally religious and Catholic work; unconsciously so at first, but consciously in the revision. That is why I have not put in, or have cut out practically all references to anything like 'religion,' to cults or practices, in the imaginary world" (L 172, #142). The discourse he wanted to avoid is, surprisingly, that of religion: but since magic and religion have always had quite blurry boundaries (see Kieckhefer 8-17), the less explicit the religious discourse, the hazier and therefore more 'magical' the doubtful elements will seem. The only more or less clear references to the theological structure of Middle-earth in *The Lord of the Rings* are Gandalf's "naked I was *sent back*" (LotR II III.v.491; italics mine) and "Olórin I was in my youth in the West that is forgotten" (LotR II IV.v.655); Faramir's "that which is beyond Elvenhome and will ever be" (LotR II IV.v.661); and the cry of Faramir's men at the sight of the Mûmak: "May the Valar turn him aside!" (LotR II IV.iv.646). The reader (and apparently most people in Middle-earth) simply does not know about the theological structure of the fictional world (as Frodo does not know about Rings of Power)—and so in ignorance interprets (as most Men in Middle-earth) these instances as 'magic'. And as long as there is no context, they may well be.

But once one reads *The Silmarillion,* one knows they are not, and sees the pattern, too: how Tolkien systematically made his secondary world more and more discrete, distinct, disconnected from the primary world, constructed and consolidated its theological structure, and so supplied a context for the stand-alone stories that completely reinterpret them. But of course, it was not an unknown context *for Tolkien*, and this undoubtedly formed part of why he so desperately wanted to publish *The Silmarillion* together with *The Lord of the Rings*: it is not just the 'story context' that he wanted to supply. He had been working and reworking the group of texts that are referred to as the 'Silmarillion' corpus, and he kept doing it after *The Lord of the Rings* was finally published. When after his death, *The Silmarillion* became his first posthumously published work, readers could get a glimpse of that context, and that glimpse alone was enough to validate the conclusion that there is no cultural historical magic in Tolkien at all. But readers had to wait for the whole *History of Middle-earth* series to be able to see the *process*, to appreciate the subtle workings of Tolkien's fictional world and his endless reworkings of the texts. *The Hobbit* and *The Lord of the Rings*, however, introduced two aspects into the creative history that Tolkien was not very used to: the genre of the novel, and fixity (cf. Fimi 119f.). "The transition from myth to history, from writing a mythology to writing a 'pseudo-historical' or fantasy novel, made Middle-earth more 'realistic'", as Fimi suggests (Fimi 189). Tolkien could never finish *The Silmarillion* because he never discovered how he could possibly put it in even remotely novelistic form—"what he could not finish was the post-*Lord of the Rings* 'Silmarillion'" (Fimi 194). This had the very important effect on the theological/magical: even *The Lord of the Rings* was stretching the genre for a lot of critics, and the theology of Middle-earth would simply have exploded the form. Tolkien's compulsive rewritings were also checked by the fact that *The Hobbit* and *The Lord of the Rings,* being published, were supposed to be fixed, and the rest was supposed to be coherent with them. Tolkien could not even bear this, and tinkered even with the fixed texts (and then even *incorporated the fact that he changed The Hobbit* into the story as an illustration for the Ring's effect on Bilbo). Both these factors contributed to his getting lost in the conceptual and other details of the 'Silmarillion' corpus, clarifying and refining points but not changing the story or the conceptual framework. The theological structure of Middle-earth had taken shape and consolidated even before *The Hobbit*; it went through further changes of story but relatively little of concept during the writing of *The Lord of the Rings,* which meant that there was literally *no room for magic* in it.

The theological hierarchy of Middle-earth, as evolved in the early 'Silmarillion' writings, in fact goes a long way to explain away every bit of what looks like magic in Tolkien. In these texts, Tolkien evolved a world much to his liking: one similar to the medieval world model insofar as there is a metaphysical centre to it, the creator Ilúvatar. Everything else is his work: the Valar, the Ainur, the Maiar, the Children of Ilúvatar, Elves and Men, the children of Aulë, Dwarves, and the totally unforeseen Hobbits, too. Ilúvatar functions in Middle-earth much as God functioned in the medieval world: the guarantee that each and every bit of his created world *has a meaning.* Following Yuri Lotman's typology of cultures (see Lotman), I will call this a *pansemiotic world model*, one where everything is a sign, and ultimately refers back to the Creator. Just like in the medieval 'great chain of being', everyone has their place in descending order, and with these places come knowledge and innate power. Ilúvatar is the totality of meaning, knowledge, and power. The Ainur each "comprehended only that part of the mind of Ilúvatar from which [they] came" (S 15) and are asked to interpret the themes of music expounded to them "each with his own thoughts and devices, if he will" (S 15). The Valar are then given power over Arda, the physical world, about which they know much more than anyone else; within Arda, the Children and adopted children of Ilúvatar are also arranged in a hierarchy. The Elves have primacy, and Dwarves have special skills and knowledge from Aulë; Men and Hobbits are down towards the bottom. This structure, Fimi says, was already in place in the early writings (Fimi 48, 141-44), but is eventually put in a historical perspective: by the time of *The Hobbit* and *The Lord of the Rings*, the end of the Third Age, the Elves had mostly left, Men are losing their ancient knowledge, and the Valar are all but forgotten. This contributes to that often remarked-on quality of depth in Tolkien, too: because it creates the overwhelming and pervasive sense of something lost, of knowledge to be unearthed, and of ignorance. But it is there, and that is made clear, too: Théoden recognises the Ents from old stories when he sees one; the tales of Ioreth about the King's healing hands or the virtues of athelas prove true; Gandalf finds Isildur's long-forgotten manuscript in Minas Tirith. Knowledge is lost but can be recovered; power is veiled but can still be used: Gandalf and Aragorn occasionally rise to an image of majesty and power, Galadriel is revealed to all of the Fellowship as clearly very powerful, and of course there is Sauron, a massive and threatening locus of power.

In this world there is and can be no cultural historical magic. Gandalf's 'magic' is things he does by his 'angelic' power: Gandalf is a Maia, rather high up in the hierarchy compared to everyone else (except for Sauron and to some extent, the Balrog). Sauron does not perform demonic magic as his *Hobbit* nickname 'the Necromancer' suggests: he is a Maia, too, in the terminology of the medieval theologians, himself a demon, and no one does any magic to coerce Sauron to do anything. Galadriel is a Noldorin elf, one of the last on Middle-earth: she does things by her innate power. Elrond is half-elven, a son of Eärendil, while Aragorn is the heir to the other line of Eärendil's children, to Elros and the Númenóreans. The reader can be excused if he or she does not see or understand this: most people in Middle-earth do not either. Maybe it is not surprising that Sam takes Galadriel's acts as 'magic'. Wormtongue even calls her a "Sorceress" (LotR II III.vi.502), and even Boromir, who as a Gondorian could be expected to know better, is also wary of Galadriel. She herself only says that she does not clearly see the distinction: after all, 'magic' is the word that some "seem to use… of the deceits of the Enemy" (LotR I II.vii.353). But all this is in fact a function of the character's place in the theological hierarchy. They influence the world with their innate power, not by some other power harnessed through ritual, object or incantation. We can find any number of parallels in primary world literature and religion: Zeus does not 'do magic', he is a god. God does not create the world by a 'word of power': his word is powerful because He is God. Jesus does not raise Lazarus by saying it, but by being Jesus. Even the apostles do not heal people by magic, but by the power granted to them by Jesus. And even though early Christians did have problems arguing this (Kieckhefer 33-6), it all depends on the kind of world we are talking about. In a way, early Christians had to argue exactly the same thing: that in a pansemiotic world, where their God is the ultimate metaphysical centre and the guarantee of meaning and power, He grants them power to do what they do. A late antique pagan or early Anglo-Saxon might have had his doubts, especially seeing the highly ritualised liturgy of the Christian church, their dogma of transubstantiation (even though it was codified later), and so on. But for a medieval theologian, and so for Tolkien, well-versed in both medieval culture and Christian theology, this would have been easy enough to accept. I think Tolkien is even playing a philological joke here, giving another clue that what might seem magic in the rather implicitly pansemiotic world of *The Lord of the Rings* are actually manifestations of theological power: this is the very word 'spell' used for example for some of Gandalf's 'magic'. Even though this word is commonly used for magical incantations or commands (even in fantasy where there certainly is magic), Tolkien subverts its meaning by Gandalf's status, which he points out in a letter: "I wd. venture to say that he was an *incarnate* 'angel',," he explains to Robert Murray, SJ, "an emissary from the Lords of the West, sent to Middle-earth" (L 202, #156), and with this, immediately brings into play some Old English meanings. Clark Hall's *Concise Anglo-Saxon Dictionary* defines 'spell' as meaning "narrative, history, story, fable; speech, discourse, homily; message, news, statement, observation" (Clark Hall 315; cf. Wormtongue calling Gandalf *Láthspell*, LotR II III.vi.502), and lists compounds such as *spellboc* 'book of sermons', *spellboda* 'messenger' (the original meaning of the Greek word 'angelos'), and of course there is *godspel* 'gospel, glad tidings' (158), the exact translation of Greek *euangelion*. When Tolkien uses 'spell' for Gandalf's 'magic', he plays on this meaning: these acts are Gandalf's way of manifesting his power, of bearing and communicating the 'glad tidings', that the power of Ilúvatar is there and it endures. There is no Christ in Middle-earth to bring tidings of, so the good news is that there is at least a god who wields, guarantees and delegates power.

But there was another factor in this process that also came into play roughly after *The Hobbit* and before *The Lord of the Rings*: this was *On Fairy-stories*, where Tolkien systematically expounded his views on the writing of the kind of stories he liked to write—part of which was his views on 'magic'. Here he talked about "Faërie" as the subject of fairy stories, which for him, as he explained, meant a historically layered, more or less traditional *fiction*: "a parallel reality tangential in time and space to the ordinary world" (FS 85), as editors Flieger and Anderson comment. As mentioned earlier, he maintained that this fiction should be unconnected to the primary world: so unconnected, in fact, that he called it a "Secondary World" (FS 52, 64). To (sub-)create such a fiction, the author needs a kind of "elvish craft" (FS 63) which Tolkien calls, instead of Magic, Enchantment (FS 64). He says that the 'magic' of Faërie is "of a peculiar mood and power, at the furthest pole from the vulgar devices of the laborious, scientific, magician" (FS 32f.). Magic 'proper' "produces, or pretends to produce, an alteration in the Primary World. It does not matter by whom it is said to be practiced, fay or mortal…; it is not an art but a technique; its desire is *power* in this world, domination of things and wills" (FS 64). Tolkien's use of *enchantment* I have already commented upon: his word choice underscores even philologically his argument that the primary medium of fairy stories is literature, language, since it comes ultimately from Latin *incantare*, a use of language to bewitch. He even comments on *spell*, underscoring my point that he uses this word, too, with an eye to its origin: "*spell* means both a story told, and a formula of power over living men" (FS 48). But in *On Fairy-stories*, Tolkien's use of "magic" (or "enchantment", even "glamour": FS 29) is somewhat off the mark for the either/ or magic that we are now after. He uses it as a metaphor for the *effect* of fairy stories: this kind of enchantment, he argues, is necessary for the creation of a successful Secondary World. It is the Art, the "elvish craft" that lends the fiction "the inner consistency of reality" (FS 59), so that within that world, its story "is 'true': it accords with the laws of that world"—it produces "literary belief" (FS 52). It thus appears that in this essay Tolkien merely touches upon the theme of magic, and mentions 'magic as technique' only in passing, and not very favourably, as something he is not really interested in. How would it appear in his work if he barely just mentions it in his theoretical manifesto?

But in his letters, mostly after *The Lord of the Rings*, he does treat magic in a bit more detail, and even introduces distinctions: his well-known differentiation between 'magia' and 'goeteia' (notice his uses of Greek terms). Despite how much is sometimes made of these in criticism, even the evidence of the letters bears out my contention that there is no either/or, automatic, cultural historical magic in Tolkien. The most important quote is "a difference in the use of 'magic' in this story is that it is not to be come by by 'lore' or spells; but is in an *inherent power* not possessed or attainable by Men as such" (L 200, #155; italics mine). Both *magia* and *goeteia* Tolkien sees as manifestations of one's 'inherent power': the position in the theological hierarchy that assigns that power. It is never a question of just 'knowledge', knowing the right formula or incantation. This should by itself be enough to close the argument for ever. The explanations that the letters affix to these aspects ('magic' as Art, 'goetic' as the Machine) match the shorter remarks that we have seen in *On Fairy-stories*: there, he wrote that an "essential power of Faërie is thus the power of making immediately effective by the will the visions of 'fantasy'" (FS 42) and that magic "produces, or pre-tends to produce, an alteration in the Primary World" (FS 64). In the letters, he says that the "basic motive for *magia*… is immediacy: … reduction… to a minimum (or vanishing point) of the gap between the idea or desire and the result or effect" (L 200, #155). In the famous Milton Waldman letter, he is more careful and accurate: by 'magic', he means "all use of external plans or devices (apparatus) instead of development of the inherent inner powers or talents—or even the use of these talents with the corrupted motive of dominating" (L 145f.,

#131). Again, he simply refers to 'inherent inner powers' instead of any either/ or magic, and declares that "Neither [magia or goeteia] is, in this tale, good or bad (per se), but only by motive or purpose or use" (*Letters* 199, #155). Indeed, he even explains some of the instances that *seem like* magic in *The Lord of the Rings*: "Their *magia* the Elves and Gandalf use (sparingly): a *magia,* producing real results (like fire in a wet faggot) for specific beneficent purposes" (L 200, #155), and remarks that in Eregion, "Elves came their nearest to falling to 'magic' and machinery. With the aid of Sauron's lore they made *Rings of Power...* [which] enhanced the natural powers of a possessor—thus approaching 'magic'" (L 152, #131). It thus seems that Tolkien's own arguments in *On Fairy-stories* and more familiarly expressed in his letters are the strongest argument for my initial either/or claim—that *there is no magic in Tolkien at all.* What even he calls 'magic' or 'magia' is not what cultural history and anthropology, and by extension much fantasy literature mean by it.

Why then should we even bother, I ask after 14 pages? I think primarily because this needed to be said. And also, because it might be clear, but it is not at all evident from reading *The Hobbit* and *The Lord of the Rings,* but only after reviewing the thousands of pages of the textual history that became *The Silmarillion.* And finally, we should bother because despite the evidence, the question of magic in Tolkien just does not go away; and that is because of the other sort of magic that I referred to: the 'critical magic' in the fantastic. Shippey says Tolkien's problem was that he was not 'in' with the moderns (Shippey, *Author* 315f.); but he was not 'in' with the overwhelmingly dominant mode of literature, realism, and its critical backing either. So, while critics approached him and the fantastic from such a standpoint, it always became the question of how these relate to 'consensus reality'. Todorov's either/or distinction is emblematic: if there is something in the story that is 'impossible' in reality, and is not explained somehow, it is *the marvellous*—magic (Todorov 41f.). The Aristotelian dictum that art is imitation, and the purpose of literature is to show the world, 'human nature', *as they are,* had led to 'mimetic' considerations overwhelming all others, to the point that an unreflected point of reference (like Todorov's) does not even register. Through its history leading back through modernism, rationalism, and ultimately Christianity (all having their reasons to privilege the 'real' and "denigrat[e] the non-real", Hume 3, see also 5-7 and 33-9), realism had become ideological: it tells you how things are, and does not ask your opinion. It is this ideologically entrenched critical orthodoxy that Tolkien (and the fantastic) upset. In *On Fairy-stories,* he says that "creative Fantasy is founded upon the hard recognition that things are so in the world as it appears under the sun"—a basically mimetic system of reference; but then he continues: "on the recognition of fact, but not a slavery to it" (FS 65). While critical and readerly practice assumes mimesis, and declares all non-mimetic elements 'magical', Tolkien insists on a different framework:

on the *independence of fictional worlds*. His Secondary Worlds are not 'mimetic with some fantastic elements', but *radically different*, radically *fictitious* worlds that do not claim to be representations of the actual one.

But nothing *ever can be that* anyway: whatever you put in language will not *iconically* represent 'the world', because the world is 'out there', a non-linguistic reality—*any way of putting it* is just more or less conventional discourse about the world and the events in it. *All* literature is set in a fictitious world (insofar as it is a linguistic construct), but realistic literature purposely strives for it to be (or to be perceived as) *isomorphous* with the real one. This verisimilitude, however, is always an illusion: just one set of conventions that had been judged 'appropriate' to represent the world, in which readers (now trained mostly in the realistic tradition) can easily recognise what concepts of personality or motivation or interaction they hold in the real world (see Hume 37-9). *Magic* is something that is excluded, something that is by definition *cannot* be part of verisimilitude, since, as we well know, it does not exist. But Tolkien's (and other fantastic) Secondary Worlds do not claim verisimilitude, in fact quite the opposite: "the fantasy world and the axioms that underlie it are *radically* unlike our own" (Attebery 110; italics mine). The author, says Tolkien, "makes a Secondary World which your mind can enter. Inside it, what he relates is 'true': it accords with the laws of that world" (FS 52). Here he foreshadows the theory of possible worlds, or its use in literary studies, in expecting not 'correspond-ence' (to the real world: mimesis), but 'consistency' (within the fiction). *And 'critical magic' simply makes no sense here*, since the frame of reference is the Secondary World and its own logic, not the Primary World and an ideologically prescribed mimetic logic. Not unless it can be described by another definition, like the cultural historical one I have been using, if that can be applied within the fiction. It then looks like there is no 'magic' in Tolkien at all: the either/ or magic of cultural history he excised himself as the theological hierarchy of Middle-earth came to be more established; and the other has simply no business *being called* magic, when that simply signifies 'impossible in the real world, thus subverting realist convention'.

In actual practice, of course, one can probably never subvert *all* aspects of representing a world in language, and for other aspects one is not interested in one will fall back more or less on the conventions of realism. This is why fantastic works, Tolkien included, in some respects fit the requirements of the realistic ideology perfectly well. Descriptions, geography, some of the handling of time—most authors have no interest in going all the way to *Finnegans Wake* (an emblematically modernist text) and abandon language itself. Brian Rosebury, for example, argued persuasively that *The Lord of the Rings* in fact passes quite easily for a novel, if not a prominently realistic one. Significantly, about magic he says that it is "largely avoided... in favour of a putatively consistent system of powers and 'lore'" (Rosebury 115). Even the representation of the world and the story he finds tolerable by novelistic standards; one is reminded of Tom Shippey who said that *The Lord of the Rings*, like *Ulysses*, is "engaged in deep negotiation with the ancient genres of epic and romance" (Shippey, *Author* 311). And other worldviews, one could add: Tolkien's choice of a pansemiotic world certainly is quite unfitted for realism, because it presupposes meaning everywhere, while realism infuses with meaning (by the characters, their actions, their thoughts) a world that is otherwise meaningless. This all-pervasive meaning, if we will, is then also 'critically magical', since there is nothing like it in the Primary World. As John Garth put it in the discussion after this paper was originally delivered, it is "either no magic or all magic." Seeing this un- or even anti-realist 'magic' in Tolkien is exactly like reading *Beowulf* in the way he so disapproved of—not at all on its own terms, not at all in the way it *works*.

Criticism has no problem with postmodernist experimentation, magical realism, or metafiction, often classed as 'fantastic', all of which resist the realist ideology and subvert realistic criteria of representation. Tolkien does that, too, but in another way: he creates a huge, historical fiction which examines the ways language, knowledge, narrative and its various different forms are layered in a system across cultures, and together constitute the world and its past. Being a philologist, he does that in *texts,* so for Tolkien 'world-building' is really 'text-building': this is why he insists in *On Fairy-stories* that literature is their prime medium, and that the art, the 'elvish craft' needed for it is not to be called 'magic'. It is not, because the term invokes cultural historical phenomena that are not there (after a while), and because it is defined by reference to an ideology of representation that fairy stories by nature circumvent and subvert. Tolkien is certainly not a postmodernist, nor is his work 'postmodern' in this subversion. But that does not mean that the entire corpus cannot be seen from this perspective. For Tolkien, very much as for postmodernists, *the world is in a text*, and so his work "is always metafictional" (Attebery 41), questioning discourses of culture, negotiating between them, in the end showing how even the ultimate knowledge is only a matter of discourse, of privileged text. In this sense, he even queries his own theological hierarchy, representing that as merely one set of traditions, assigned the most authority. And that is even further from magic than a pansemiotic fictional world. It's not magic, it's philology; or maybe we should say *glamour*, and point everyone to the etymology.

Bibliography

Attebery, Brian. *Strategies of Fantasy.* Bloomington/Indianapolis: Indiana University Press, 1992

Clark Hall, John R. *A Concise Anglo-Saxon Dictionary.* 4th ed. Cambridge: Cambridge University Press, 1960

Clarke, Arthur C. *Profiles of the Future: An Inquiry into the Limits of the Possible.* New York: Harper and Row, 1973

Fimi, Dimitra. *Tolkien, Race and Cultural History. From Fairies to Hobbits.* London: Palgrave Macmillan, 2010

Herbert, Frank. *Dune.* New York: Berkley, 1977

Hume, Kathryn. *Fantasy and Mimesis. Responses to Reality in Western Literature.* New York/London: Methuen, 1984

Kieckhefer, Richard. *Magic in the Middle Ages.* Cambridge: Cambridge University Press, 1989

Lotman, Yuri. 'Problems in the typology of culture.' In: *Soviet Semiotics: An Anthology.* Ed.: Daniel P. Lucid. Baltimore, MD: Johns Hopkins University Press, 1977, 213-21

Rateliff, John D. *The History of* The Hobbit, *Vol. 1. Mr. Baggins.* Boston/New York: HoughtonMifflin, 2007

Rosebury, Brian. *Tolkien. A Cultural Phenomenon.* London: Palgrave Macmillan, 2003

Shippey, Tom. 'Another Road to Middle-earth: Jackson's Movie Trilogy.' In: *Roots and Branches. Selected Papers on Tolkien.* Zurich: Walking Tree Publishers, 2007, 365-86

---. *J.R.R. Tolkien, Author of the Century.* Boston/New York: Houghton Mifflin, 2001

Todorov, Tzvetan. *The Fantastic. A Structural Approach to a Literary Genre.* Transl.: Richard Howard. Ithaca: Cornell University Press, 1975

Tolkien, J.R.R. *Tolkien On Fairy-stories.* Eds.: Verlyn Flieger, Douglas A. Anderson. London: HarperCollins, 2008

---. *The Hobbit.* Boston/New York: HoughtonMifflin, 2007

---. *The Silmarillion.* Boston/New York: HoughtonMifflin, 1999

---. *The Lost Road and Other Writings.* New York: Ballantines, 1996

---. *The Shaping of Middle-earth.* New York: Ballantines, 1995

---. *The Lays of Beleriand.* New York: Ballantines, 1994

---. *The Book of Lost Tales, Vol. 1.* New York: Ballantines, 1992

---. *The Book of Lost Tales, Vol. 2.* New York: Ballantines, 1992

---. *The Fellowship of the Ring.* London: HarperCollins, 1991

---. *The Two Towers.* London: HarperCollins, 1991

---. *The Return of the King.* London: HarperCollins, 1991

---. *The Letters of J.R.R. Tolkien.* Edited by Humphrey Carpenter, with the assistance of Christopher Tolkien. London: George Allen & Unwin; Boston: HoughtonMifflin, 1981

West, Richard C. 'Setting the Rocket Off in Story: The *Kalevala* as the Germ of Tolkien's *Legendarium*.' In: *Tolkien and the Invention of Myth. A Reader.* Ed.: Jane Chance. Lexington: University Press of Kentucky, 2004, 285-94

Apologie der Phantastik

Christian und Sophie Lemburg (Aachen, Göttingen)

Ziel

»Du liest Fantasy? Das ist doch voll die Weltflucht! Lies lieber mal etwas Vernünftiges.« Diese oder vergleichbare Aussagen haben sich sicherlich schon viele Leser der phantastischen Literatur gefallen lassen müssen. Aber sind dieser Vorwurf des Eskapismus oder ähnliche Vorwürfe überhaupt berechtigt?

Das Ziel des vorliegenden Essays ist es, diesem Vorwurf zu begegnen, indem aus der Wirkungsweise der Phantastik spezifische individuelle und gesellschaftliche Nutzenpotentiale abgeleitet werden. Hierbei spielt das phantastische *Worldbuilding* eine entscheidende Rolle.

Gegenstand

Gegenstand dieser Apologie ist die Phantastik, d.h. phantastische Schöpfungen in verschiedenen Medien wie Literatur, Film, Computerspiel usw.; der oben genannte Vorwurf wird schließlich auch all diesen Medien gegenüber erhoben. Wenn im Folgenden von Genres oder literarischen Formen gesprochen wird, sind – soweit nicht anders erwähnt – auch andere Medien wie Film und Computerspiel mit gemeint.

Allen diesen Schöpfungen ist gemeinsam, dass sie abweichend von einfachen Beschreibungen der »realen« Welt neue Elemente enthalten, die in der »realen« Welt in dieser Form nicht gegeben sind: die »phantastischen« Elemente im eigentlichen Sinne. Je nach Art und Grad der »Möglichkeit« dieser neuen, phantastischen Elemente ergeben sich verschiedene Unterformen, die z.T. literarischen Genres direkt entsprechen (Wolf 17ff). Für die Zwecke dieser Untersuchung gehen wir damit von einer »weiten« Definition der Phantastik im Sinne von Weinreich (Weinreich 10ff) aus.

Tolkien (FS) folgend unterscheiden wir im Folgenden weiterhin zwischen der sog. *Primary World* (der »realen« Welt) und der vom Autor neu geschaffenen *Secondary World*, in der die phantastische Schöpfung mit ihrer Handlung spielt. Jede Form der *Secondary World* enthält eine bestimmte Menge an Fiktion (Wolf 25). So ergibt sich ein Kontinuum literarischer Genres von der »reinen Realität« (*Primary World*) hin zur »reinen Phantasie« (*Secondary World*) (Wolf 27ff). Die Art und die Qualität des Aufbaus der *Secondary World* wird dabei als *Worldbuilding* bezeichnet. Das *Worldbuilding* einer phantastischen Schöpfung ist für die Rezeption des Werks von hoher Bedeutung (Wolf 48ff).

Philosophisch interessant ist hier – vor allem vor dem Hintergrund moderner Medien und Begriffe wie »Fake News« und »Alternative Wahrheiten« –, dass streng genommen jegliche Berichterstattung inklusive festgehaltener eigener Erinnerungen als *Secondary World* mit mehr oder weniger fiktionalen Elementen aufgefasst werden kann. »Wahrheit in einer Geschichte« erweist sich philosophisch als fundamental andere logische Kategorie verglichen mit der Wahrheit von Tatsachenaussagen (Zalta).

Für unsere Betrachtung besonders relevant sind Fantasy, Science-Fiction, Utopie, Dystopie und Satire als die »eigentlichen« phantastischen Literaturformen, deren *Secondary Worlds* im Folgenden betrachtet werden, sowie »Pure Worlds« wie z.B. die »Open World Games« der Virtual-Games-Industrie, die im Unterschied zu literarischen Werken kaum noch eine Handlung im eigentlichen Sinne aufweisen.

Der Vorwurf

Der Vorwurf des Eskapismus bzw. der Weltflucht ist sicherlich einer der häufigsten, wenn es um die phantastische Literatur geht. Der Vorwurf ist, dass sich der Leser in eine Scheinwelt flüchtet, in der alles schöner und besser zu sein scheint, anstatt sich mit der realen Welt und ihren Problemen zu beschäftigen. Doch ist dem wirklich so? Flüchtet sich der Leser, oder liegt dahinter vielleicht eine andere Motivation?

J.R.R. Tolkien, einer der führenden Autoren der Fantasy-Literatur, geht folgendermaßen auf diesen Vorwurf ein (B): Er behauptet, dass der Begriff des Eskapismus eine Konnotation mit Mitleid und Verachtung trägt, die er so nicht akzeptieren möchte. Er streitet nicht ab, dass das Lesen solcher Literatur eine Art der Flucht darstellt, jedoch missbilligt er die negative Konnotation dieses Wortes. Er wirft im Zusammenhang mit der Flucht das Beispiel auf, warum ein Mann, der in einem Gefängnis sitzt, nicht versuchen darf zu fliehen, bzw., wenn das nicht möglich ist, sich mit anderen Themen zu beschäftigen als seiner momentanen Situation (Wolf 33): »The world outside has not become less real because the prisoner cannot see it.« Wir haben hier also weniger eine Erklärung, warum das Lesen solcher Literatur keine Flucht ist, sondern vielmehr eine Bestätigung der Fluchtthese, und diesbezüglich dann eine Erläuterung, warum eine solche Flucht nicht negativ zu bewerten sein sollte.

Ein anderer Autor der phantastischen Literatur, Michael Ende, gibt dazu eine andere Antwort. Als er seinen Bestseller-Roman *Die unendliche Geschichte* schrieb, galt (in Deutschland) phantastische Literatur als »Fluchtliteratur«, nur sozialkritische und politisch erziehende Bücher wurden ernstgenommen (Hocke 432ff). Die Fantasy war ins Kinderzimmer verbannt worden! Mit der *Unendlichen Geschichte* wollte sich Ende darüber klarwerden, was phantastische

Literatur für ihn bedeutet. Dieses Buch war Endes Antwort auf den Vorwurf der Weltflucht. Ende vertritt die These, dass Phantasie, und so auch phantastische Literatur, keine Weltflucht ist:

> Die Gefahr besteht (wenn man nicht mehr aus Phantásien heraus-findet). Aber wenn man wieder zurückkehrt, hat man der Welt Relevanteres zu geben als nur das unmittelbar Nützliche... Wir brauchen Phantasie, weil sie uns hilft, uns selbst und damit auch die Welt zu verstehen, in der wir leben: uns ein Bild, eine Vorstellung von ihr zu machen... Außerdem finden wir in Phantásien Orientierung: Werte wie Freundschaft oder Liebe.   (Hocke 437)

Diese Idee einer positiven Wertevermittlung und der Phantasie als kreativer Quelle, die das rationale, nüchterne Wissenschaftsbild ergänzt, ist für Ende unabdingbar.

Wir haben nun zwei Antworten berühmter Autoren auf den Vorwurf des Eskapismus. Einer, der zugibt, dass das Lesen phantastischer Literatur eine Art der Flucht ist, dies aber nicht als etwas Negatives oder zu Verachtendes betrachtet. Ein anderer, der davon spricht, dass Phantasie unbedingt für das eigene Selbstverständnis und das der Welt benötigt wird, auch um ein Gegengewicht für die rationale, wissenschaftliche Betrachtung zu schaffen.

Um den Vorwurf des Eskapismus bzw. der »Zeitverschwendung« hinsichtlich der Beschäftigung mit der Phantastik bewerten zu können, muss man Wirkungsweise und Folgen der Beschäftigung mit der Phantastik verstehen. Im Folgenden wird untersucht, wie Phantastik und insbesondere Fantasy funktioniert, um hier zu einem besseren Verständnis zu gelangen.

Wie funktioniert Phantastik? Wie funktioniert Fantasy?

Das definierende Merkmal der Phantastik allgemein sind bewusste Abweichungen in der Abbildung der Primärwelt. Die so geschaffene Sekundärwirklichkeit weist neue Eigenschaften und Handlungsmöglichkeiten auf, die in der Primärwelt nicht gegeben sind, z.B. veränderte geographische Gegebenheiten, neue Wesen wie Warge, Einhörner oder Drachen, neue Handlungsmöglichkeiten wie die Fähigkeiten zu fliegen, magische Fähigkeiten zu erlangen, Gedanken zu lesen und vieles mehr.

Interessant ist in diesem Zusammenhang, dass die erwähnten Abweichungen **in der Regel additiv** sind, d.h., es kommen Dinge, Wesen oder Möglichkeiten zur Wirklichkeit der Primärwelt hinzu. Nur selten gibt es subtraktive Abweichungen – z.B. in der Science-Fiction-Story *Flatland* (Abbott), in der die Haupthandlung nur in zwei Dimensionen spielt.

Weiterhin sind die Abweichungen oft besonders **auffällig und spektakulär** gestaltet. Riesige Gebirge mit ungeheuren Höhlensystemen, zusätzliche Gestirne, prächtige Schätze, farbenprächtige Fabelwesen in prunkender Gestaltung, ungeheure Machtzuwächse durch magische Fähigkeiten, rasante Karrieren vom dahergelaufenen Landstreicher zum König – die Veränderungen in der Sekundärwirklichkeit fallen dem Leser in der Regel sofort ins Auge und ziehen ihn in ihren Bann.

Fabelwesen weisen dabei oft eine Konstruktion auf, die durch **gezielte Übertreibungen** gekennzeichnet ist. Spezielle Merkmale werden überhöht dargestellt, um so ein neues Wesen zu beschreiben. Warge als Riesenwölfe, nahezu unendlich lang lebende Elben, riesige Trolle als nahezu unverletzliche Panzerwesen – man könnte die Liste noch lange weiterführen. Besonders interessant ist natürlich der Fall des Drachen, der als Amalgam der existierenden Tiergattungen Vierbeiner, Reptilien die Flugfähigkeit der Vögel und das Feuer des Menschen in sich vereint.

Die in der Regel additive, spektakuläre und übertriebene Natur der Abbildungsabweichungen deutet darauf hin, dass hier das psychologische Prinzip der Salienz Anwendung findet. Die Salienz, also die Auffälligkeit eines Reizes, beeinflusst stark, wie leicht Personen diesen wahrnehmen bzw. aus der Erinnerung abrufen können. Weiterhin spielt die Salienz auch eine entscheidende Rolle bei der Ursachenzuschreibung (Attribution) in komplexen Situationen. Saliente, d.h. auffällige Reize werden eher als Ursachen für Veränderungen in der Situation wahrgenommen bzw. erinnert (Taylor & Fiske).

Interessant ist hier – vor allem vor dem Hintergrund der Phänomene der »Saturation« und »Absorption« (Wolf 48ff), die ja maßgeblich zum Lesevergnügen und damit zur Motivation der Konsumption von Texten beitragen –, die **Verbindung zwischen der Vorstellung der Sekundärwirklichkeit während bzw. nach dem Lesevorgang und dem modernen Mentaltraining**, wie z.B. im Sport verwendet, zu betrachten. Gängige Anleitungen zum mentalen Training[1] weisen immer wieder darauf hin, sich die vorgestellte Situation möglichst hell, farbenprächtig, detailliert und auffällig vorzustellen, um so die Vertiefung in die vorgestellte Situation und damit den Trainingseffekt zu erhöhen. Auch Techniken der Mnemotechnik, also der Kunst, sich Inhalte zu merken, schärfen dem Übenden ein, sich die zu merkenden Inhalte möglichst farbig, bewegt, auffällig, ungewöhnlich und unterhaltend bzw. lustig vorzustellen, da sie so besser behalten und wieder abgerufen werden können, z.B. die Technik des »Gedächtnispalasts« bzw. Memory Palace, eine Erweiterung der alten römischen Loci-Methode (Buzan).

Es liegt also nahe, dass die spezifischen phantastischen Abbildungsabweichungen der Sekundärwirklichkeit von der Primärrealität eine erhöhte Satu-

---

1   Vgl. z.B. Baum & Trubo.

ration, Absorption und Retention der erzählten Geschichten bzw. der Gestalt und Elemente der Sekundärwirklichkeit selbst bewirken.

Die Phantastik zieht ihre Leser stärker in den Bann (Saturation und Absorption) und wird auch besser von diesen behalten als andere Literatur (Retention).

Weiter verstärkt wird dieser Effekt besonders in der Fantasy, in deren Handlungen und Sekundärwirklichkeiten gern **bekannte Handlungsmuster und vorgegebene Gattungen** verwendet bzw. aufgegriffen werden. Es handelt sich hierbei zum Teil um echte **Archetypen** im Sinne C.G. Jungs (Jung), z.B. das Handlungsmuster der Suche[2] mit der darin eingebundenen Entwicklung, Prüfung und Initiation des Jünglings zum Mann, zum Teil aber auch um vorgegebene **Themenkreise, Topoi oder Motive** (Schneidewind 9ff) der jeweiligen Erzählkultur, wie Zwerge, Drachen oder Vampire, oft in kulturspezifischer Ausgestaltung. **Die Bekanntheit dieser Muster führt dazu, dass auch große Handlungsbögen und komplizierte Abläufe leicht antizipiert, mit vielen Details behalten und korrekt wiedergegeben werden können.** Die Retention des Gesamtzusammenhangs und der Relationen zwischen den einzelnen Elementen der Sekundärwirklichkeit wird so noch einmal deutlich gestärkt.

Sichtbar wird dies vielfach in den erstaunlichen Gedächtnisleistungen von Fans der verschiedenen Sekundärwirklichkeiten, wenn sie scheinbar endlose – und für Nicht-Fans auch belanglose – Details und Zusammenhänge der jeweiligen imaginären Welten wiedergeben und diese auch mit viel Freude erlernen und diskutieren.

Die starke Fähigkeit der Phantastik, sich sozusagen in die Hirne ihrer Lesen einzunisten, stellt die Voraussetzung für einige erstaunliche weitere Folgen ihres Konsums dar. Zum einen ist hier der offensichtlich **extrem hohe Unterhaltungswert der Phantastik** zu nennen. Der stete Umgang mit der imaginierten Sekundärwirklichkeit bereitet den Lesern bzw. Fans Freude, und wird für viele zur steten Gewohnheit, bis hin zur Sucht. Dies wäre ohne die hohen Retentionsleistungen der Konsumenten schlicht nicht möglich, die Geschichten wären schnell vergessen, Neues würde das Bekannte verdrängen.

Die stete Wiederholung der Beschäftigung mit den phantastischen Inhalten führt bei vielen Fans zu einer hohen Identifikation mit den dargestellten Themen sowie der Gruppe der ebenfalls an diesen Themen Interessierten. **Es bilden sich moderne »Stämme« heraus mit den jeweiligen Inhalten als konstituierenden »Mythen«.** Vielfach werden auch »Stammestreffen« abgehalten. Zum Teil werden die konstituierenden »Mythen« kanonisiert und von privilegierten Stammesmitgliedern »rein« erhalten. Hier beginnen die Inhalte der Sekundärwirklichkeit der Phantastik im echten Sinne auf die Primärrealität einzuwirken, der Übergang zu klassischen Mythen oder Religionen wird z.T. fließend, wie

---

2   Die sogenannte Quest.

man gut am Beispiel der Romane von Marion Zimmer Bradley – besonders der Serien um Avalon und Darkover – sehen kann, die nach Ansicht einiger einen erheblichen Einfluss auf die Entwicklung neuheidnischer religiöser Bewegungen sowie auf den Feminismus hatten (Sadovsky).

Die Phantastik, und hier besonders die Fantasy, führt über Retention und Repetition **bei ihren Fans zu einer hohen Identifikation mit den dargestellten Themen, zur Bildung von Stämmen und z.T. zu echten Mythen.**

Dadurch bietet sie ihren Fans die Möglichkeit einer **alternativen Sinnfindung und Identitätsstiftung, auf der individuellen Ebene und in der Gruppe.** Sie bietet Menschen eine Alternative, die an der Sinnfindung im gesellschaftlichen Normalkonstrukt scheitern bzw. mit diesem unzufrieden sind, und stellt so eine **geistige Heimat** für viele Suchende dar. Dies ist sicherlich im Kern das, was der Phantastik von ihren Gegnern als Eskapismus vorgeworfen wird. Doch wie oben dargestellt geht dieser Vorwurf fehl, denn ähnlich wie klassische Mythen oder Religionen übt die Phantastik über ihre Inhalte durchaus eine Wirkung auf die Primärrealität aus. Jeder Besucher einer der größeren Conventions wird dies nach kurzer Reflektion nicht mehr leugnen können.

Auf der individuellen Ebene bietet die Phantastik durch die veränderten bzw. oft erweiterten Handlungsmöglichkeiten in der Sekundärwirklichkeit die Möglichkeit, alternative Problemlösungen zu simulieren, neue Handlungsmöglichkeiten und Rollen in der imaginären Welt auszuprobieren bzw. einzuüben und so neue Problemlösungen zu finden und einzuüben.

Die Simulation möglicher Handlungsabläufe mittels Identifikation mit einem verfolgten Tier im Rahmen des Jagens steht vermutlich am Anfang des bewussten Denkens der Menschheit (Liebenberg). Hier wird der **direkte evolutionäre Nutzen des** Worldbuildings so deutlich wie selten. Bis in heutige Zeiten stellen sich Jäger vor, wie sich das verfolgte Wild verhalten würde, indem sie sich in dieses in ihrer Phantasie hineinversetzen, und suchen dann in der *Primary World* nach Anzeichen bzw. Spuren, ob sie mit ihrer »Zweitschöpfung« richtiglagen. Sicherlich wurden auch Jagdabläufe und Strategien durch phantastische Identifikation mit dem Jagdwild beeinflusst bzw. eingeübt. Reste dieser Vorstellungen überleben vielfach in Mythen und Phantastik, z.B. die Gestalt des »Gehörnten« im Werk von Marion Zimmer Bradley (Zimmer Bradley).

Aus technischer Sicht ist dies das klassische Feld der Science-Fiction. Kaum eine neue Entwicklung, die nicht schon mehrfach in der Literatur durchprobiert und in ihren Folgen untersucht wäre – der Science-Fiction-Leser ist auf viele gesellschaftliche Diskussionen, die für den Normalbürger noch Überraschungs- bzw. Alarm-Charakter haben, bereits bestens vorbereitet. Künstliche Intelligenzen, autonome Fahrzeuge, klimatische und gentechnische Veränderungen unserer Umwelt, ihre gesellschaftlichen Folgen und Gefahren – für Science-Fiction-Fans ist das alles seit Langem wohlbekannt. Hier sehen wir einen **klaren individuellen und gesellschaftlichen Nutzen der Phantastik –**

sie bietet einen präventiven Simulationsraum für Probleme, ihre Folgen und mögliche Lösungen. Dies gilt natürlich insbesondere für die politischen phantastischen Genres: die Satire, die Utopie und die Dystopie.

Ein besonders gutes Beispiel für diesen Nutzen der Phantastik ist das Projekt *Future Life* der Phantastischen Bibliothek in Wetzlar[3]. In diesem Projekt werden »aus dem Ideenreservoir der Science-Fiction-Literatur Zukunftsszenarien sowie technische und systemische Innovationen exzerpiert und für Unternehmen aufbereitet« (LeBlanc 28). In Workshops und Seminaren werden Projektstudien, Produktideen und Technologiefolgenabschätzungen durch kreativen Input auf Basis der gesammelten Science-Fiction-Literatur befördert. Die einführende Publikation der Phantastischen Bibliothek (LeBlanc) zeigt in über 20 Porträts konkrete Beispiele für Technologien auf, die in der Science-Fiction-Literatur sozusagen »vorgedacht« wurden, z.B. das Unterseeboot, das Mobiltelefon, Roboter, künstliche Intelligenz, die Kreditkarte und das eBook.

Aber auch in der Fantasy ist die Simulation alternativer Problemlösungen ein gängiges Thema, hier jedoch oft in psychologischer Hinsicht, im Sinne der individuellen Entwicklung. Von der klassischen *Erdsee*-Saga von Ursula K. Le Guin (Le Guin) bis hin zu *Harry Potter* beschäftigen sich Fantasy-Erzählungen mit dem archetypischen Thema der **Individualentwicklung** und bieten vor dem Hintergrund spektakulärer Konflikte und neuer Möglichkeiten dem Individuum Gelegenheit zu mancher Einsicht und Übertragung auf den eigenen Lebensverlauf. Ähnlich wie Märchen (Estes) stehen hier die Stoffe der Fantasy als farbige Bilder symbolisch für psychologische Entwicklungsprozesse und befördern diese durch bewusste und unbewusste Identifikationsprozesse[4]. Die stete Beschäftigung mit den phantastischen Inhalten der imaginären Welt ähnelt hier in verblüffender Weise dem modernen Mentaltraining und Therapieformen wie Phantasiereisen oder gegenständlicher Meditation.

Schließlich ist auch festzustellen, dass die Beschäftigung mit den Inhalten der Phantastik und den einzelnen imaginären Welten bzw. ihrer spezifischen Sekundärwirklichkeiten zu erheblichen Anteilen der **reinen Befriedigung eines starken Explorationstriebes bzw. starker Neugier sowie der Freude am »Puzzle«** dienen kann. Dies wird in verblüffender Weise in den »Open World Games« der Virtual-Games-Industrie deutlich. Hier bezahlen riesige Communities von Fans erhebliche Summen, um ihre Neugier auf die simulierten Online-Welten zu stillen, vielfach ohne jede zusammenhängende Story im klassischen Sinne.

Und sicherlich hat diese Art imaginärer bzw. virtueller Erkundung neuer Welten einen **Trainingseffekt**. Ähnlich wie die stete Wiederholung von Inhalten fördert auch stete Exploration die geistigen Fähigkeiten und erhält sie bis ins

---

3　Vielen Dank an Friedhelm Schneidewind für den Hinweis auf dieses Projekt!
4　In der modernen Filmindustrie ist sicherlich die TV-Serie *Buffy* eines der besten Beispiele.

hohe Alter – das sagen heutzutage sogar die Experten bei Krankenkassen und Ministerien: »Denn das menschliche Gehirn braucht Reize und Anstöße, um leistungsfähig zu werden und zu bleiben« (Website zur Demenzprävention[5]).

Schlussfolgerungen

Im Effekt ermöglicht Fantasy dem Individuum:
  (1) die Simulation von neuen Handlungsalternativen im Rahmen eines alternativen moralischen und/oder gesellschaftlichen Handlungsrahmens mit erweiterten Handlungsmöglichkeiten;
  (2) die Identifikation mit der »Botschaft« der Inhalte der Sekundärwirklichkeit bzw. einer durch diese geprägten Gruppe (»Stamm«);
  (3) eine alternative Sinnstiftung analog zum literarischen Beispiel der Sekundärwelt;
  (4) die Antwortfindung auf persönliche Probleme durch Extrapolation dieser in die Sekundärrealität;
  (5) Unterhaltung und persönliche Weiterentwicklung durch das mentale Erleben bzw. das mentale Training von Handlungen und Zusammenhängen, die in der Primärwelt so nicht möglich bzw. nicht wahrscheinlich sind.
Hierin liegt gerade für weniger angepasste bzw. weniger anpassungswillige Individuen ein großer Mehrwert gegenüber normalen Erzählungen, die stärker an die Primärwelt angelehnt sind. Die Eigenschaft der Stärkung und Verbindung sowie Sinn- und Gruppenstiftung (z.B. Tolkien Thing) wird dabei von der umgebenden sozialen Norm-Gesellschaft sowohl als befremdlich bzw. rebellisch oder aufrührerisch als auch als gelegentlich unterhaltsam, belebend und anregend empfunden.

Aus Sicht des gesamtgesellschaftlichen Konstrukts unterstützt bzw. bildet die Phantastik so geistige Potentiale, Individuen und Gruppen, die verstärkt an zum sozialen Hauptkonstrukt alternativen Problemlösungen, Interpretationen und Sinnstiftungen interessiert sind und für das gesellschaftliche Normalkonstrukt eine »Notfallreserve« bzw. ein »Innovationspotential« relativ zu den Möglichkeiten der Verwirklichung des sozialen Hauptkonstrukts darstellen. Phantastik bewahrt uns vor der Stagnation!

---

5   Bundesministerium für Familie, Senioren, Frauen und Jugend: https://www.wegweiser-demenz.de/informationen/medizinischer-hintergrund-demenz/vorbeugung-und-praevention.html

Bibliographie

Abbott, Edwin. *Flatland: A romance of many dimensions.* London: Seeley, 1884

Baum, Kenneth & Trubo, Richard. *The Mental Edge.* New York: The Berkeley Publishing Group, 1999

Buzan, Tony. *The Memory Book: How to remember anything you want.* London: BBC Active, 2009

Ende, Michael. *Die unendliche Geschichte.* Stuttgart: K. Thienemanns Verlag, 1979

Estes, Clarissa Pinkola. *Die Wolfsfrau. Die Kraft der weiblichen Urinstinkte.* München: Heyne, 1997

Hocke, Roman. »Von dem Zauberbuch, das die Welt eroberte. Eine kleine Entstehungsge-schichte«. Nachwort zu: Ende, Michael. *Die unendliche Geschichte.* München: Piper, 2009.

Jung, Carl. *Man and his Symbols.* New York: Doubleday, 1964

LeBlanc, Thomas (Hg.). *Die Zukunftsideen der Science Fiction Literatur.* Wetzlar: Phantastische Bibliothek Wetzlar, 2014

Le Guin, Ursula K. *Erdsee.* München: Heyne, 1999

Liebenberg, Louis. *The Art of Tracking: the Origin of Science.* Claremont: David Philip Publishers, 1990

Sadovsky, Sonja. *The Priestess & the Pen: Marion Zimmer Bradley, Dion Fortune & Diana Paxson's Influence on Modern Paganism.* Woodbury: Llewellyn Worldwide, 2014

Schneidewind, Friedhelm. *Mythologie und phantastische Literatur.* Essen: Oldib Verlag, 2008

Taylor, S.E. & Fiske, S.T. "Salience, attention, and attribution: Top of the head phenomena". In: *Advances in experimental social psychology. Vol. 11.* Ed.: L. Berkowitz. New York: Academic Press, 1978. 249-288

Tolkien, John R.R. "On Fairy-stories." (As published in: *Tree and Leaf.* Oxford, 1964). In: *The Monsters and the Critics and Other Essays.* Ed.: Christopher Tolkien. New York: Harper-Collins Publishers, 1997

Weinreich, Frank. *Fantasy – Eine Einführung.* Essen: Oldib Verlag, 2007

Wolf, Mark J.P. *Building Imaginary Worlds: The Theory and History of Subcreation.* New York: Routledge, 2012

Zalta, Edward. *Intensional Logic and the Metaphysics of Intentionality.* Cambridge: MIT Press, 1988

Zimmer Bradley, Marion. *Die Nebel von Avalon.* Frankfurt: Fischer, 1987

How to Distinguish Secondary from Primary Creations?

A Leibnizian Elucidation of a Distinction by J.R.R. Tolkien

Jan Levin Propach[1] (Augsburg)

Introduction

Tolkien uses the terms "primary creation" and "secondary creation" in his works with reference to divine and human creation respectively. In the first part of this paper, I argue that one criterion to distinguish the former from the latter is their completeness or incompleteness. The primary creation is complete because it is thought of and created by God. The secondary creations like human fictions are incomplete since the human intellect is finite and does not have the capacity to grasp the entire structure of its own creation. In the second part, I examine this distinction in relation to Tolkien's Christian background, and reformulate and systematise it in the metaphysical framework of G.W. Leibniz. Finally, I offer a definition of a human fiction as a part of a divine fiction, i.e. as a part of a possible world in a Leibnizian sense.

1. Completeness and Incompleteness

Let us examine the following sentences:
(1) 3 is less than 5.
(2) Donald Trump is the 45th President of the
United States of America.
(3) Drogo Baggins was married to Primula Baggins.
(4) Elrond has 104,774 hairs on his head.

Among the propositions above, (1), (2) and (3) are considered to be true. However, each of these propositions pertains to a different type of truth. The truth expressed in (1) is a necessary truth, the negation of which is simply a contra-

---

1   I extend my thanks to the Deutsche Tolkien Gesellschaft for enabling me to present my paper in their 14th Conference in Augsburg. I am also grateful to Steve Roy for very helpful discussions considering my paper and to Aysenur Ünügür Tabur and Sören Frickenhaus for proofreading this article.

diction. We cannot conceive of any situation or any world in which number 3 exists and lacks the property of being lesser than 5. Suppose there is a God. Even for him it is logically impossible to create number 3 without it having the property of being lesser than 5. Therefore, the essence of 3 entails the property of being lesser than 5. With Immanuel Kant we can say that (1) expresses an analytic truth (cf. KrV A 148-153).

The truth of (2), however, does not entail any necessary relation between Donald Trump and the property *being the 45th President of the United States of America.*[2] If something in Donald Trump's life had been otherwise, he might have become, for example, a circus clown instead of a president. We can conceive of many other possible worlds, in which Donald Trump is not the 45th President of the United States of America. Obviously, it is not impossible for Trump to be the 45th President of the United States of America, but at the same time this is not necessary for him, either. The essence of Donald Trump does not entail the property *being the 45th President of the United States of America.* The state of affairs expressed by (2) obtains only contingently. So, (2) is contingently true and it could have been wrong if our actual world had been different.

Unlike (1) and (2), the truth of (3) depends neither on necessary reasons nor on any state of affairs in the actual world. (3) has its truth value in respect of a fiction, or in Tolkien's terms, in relation to a secondary creation (cf. LotR 67). It is the fiction which is conceived of and generated by the mind of an artist that makes (3) true.

(4) is totally different from the other three propositions. While the other three have to possess a truth value, that is, they have to be either true or false, (4) is neither true nor false. A fiction F, created by a human mind, is incomplete because there are infinitely many sentences about F that are neither true nor false. Let F be Sir Conan Arthur Doyle's *Sherlock Holmes*. There are a lot of sentences about that fiction which are clearly true or false. Even like (3), (4) is a proposition about a secondary creation but it seems to be impossible to decide whether (4) is true or false or whether the state of affairs expressed in (4) obtains or not, because (4) is underdetermined and hence, incomplete. "Sherlock Holmes is a green frog" is clearly a false statement about Doyle's fiction and "Sherlock Holmes lives in Baker Street 221b" is clearly true. But a statement like "Sherlock Holmes has a great interest in Ikebana, but he hides it" can be considered neither as true nor false. Doyle leaves us completely in the dark

---

2   There would be a necessary relation between them if one accepted some kind of necessitarianism. An example of such necessitarianism can be found in Baruch de Spinoza (cf. E I p 29). However, necessitarianism has an adverse consequence that the difference between necessary and contingent states of affairs is removed, which does not seem to be compatible with our everyday intuition. Some states of affairs seem to obtain necessarily, such as mathematical truths, while seems to obtain contingently, like writing this article.

about a possible interest of Sherlock Holmes in Ikebana. So, a human fiction seems to be like a holey carpet that has not yet been fully completed. But what do sentences like (4) have to do with Tolkien's theory of secondary creation?

2. Tolkien's Christian Background

(4) shows us that human fictions are characterised by their incompleteness. This characterisation fits perfectly with Tolkien's Christian perspective on human beings and their knowledge, which is expressed in the following quote from Mythopoeia: "The heart of Man is not compound of lies, but draws some wisdom from the only Wise, ... Though now long estranged, man is not wholly lost nor wholly changed... and keeps the rags of lordship once he owned, his world-dominion by creative act..." (My 87). Fictions created by a human mind must be incomplete because our wisdom, our intellectual capacity is only an image of the original and unsurpassable divine wisdom and intellect. The intellectual capacity of a human intellect is finite, while God's intellect is infinite. To be more precise, only God can be called wise in its truest sense. Moreover, God is not only wise, but he is wisdom itself.[3] The wisdom of human beings is only an image of this archetype of wisdom. The creativity of human beings expressed in arts, literature, technology, etc., is an image of the original creativity of God as well, which he expresses in his creation of the world. The doctrine of the God-likeness of human beings,[4] which is expressed in their creative capacities, plays an essential role in Tolkien's theory of fictions. This point is remarkable because in the Christian tradition, the God-likeness of human beings was not only exhibited in their creativity, but also in their various other capacities like volition and rationality, or in the relational character of human beings.[5] But the Second Vatican Council in the Pastoral Constitution *Gaudium et spes* clearly speaks about the creativity of human beings as an expression of their God-likeness:

> Throughout the course of the centuries, men have laboured to better the circumstances of their lives through a monumental amount of individual and collective effort. To believers, this point is settled: considered in itself, this human activity accords with God's will. For man, created to God's image, received a mandate to subject to himself the earth and all it contains, and to govern

---

3   Cf. S. Th. I, q. 3, a. 4. resp.
4   Cf. "Then God said, 'Let us make man in our image, after our likeness...'" (Gen. 1, 26-27).
5   Because God is intellect, human beings are intellects as well in a weaker sense. Because, in respect to the Christian doctrine of the Trinity, God Himself is relational, human beings are relational as well, because one's existence is due to others, i.e. to his parents.

the world with justice and holiness; a mandate to relate himself and the totality of things to Him Who was to be acknowledged as the Lord and Creator of all. Thus, by the subjection of all things to man, the name of God would be wonderful in all the earth... Thus, far from thinking that works produced by man's own talent and energy are in opposition to God's power, and that the rational creature exists as a kind of rival to the Creator, Christians are convinced that the triumphs of the human race are a sign of God's grace and the flowering of His own mysterious design.   (GS 34)

Tolkien's Christian background needs to be further specified to understand the relevance of Christian faith to his way of thinking. After the conversion of his mother to the Catholic faith in 1900, Tolkien was raised Catholic. Since then, Catholicism played an important role not only in his life, but also in shaping his theories. For example, Tolkien's denial of the complete corruption of the God-likeness of human beings through the original sin is in complete accordance with the doctrine of the Roman Catholic Church (cf. My 87). The Council of Trent issued the following dogmatic decree on the original sin:

For, in those who are born again, there is nothing that God hates; because, there is no condemnation to those who are truly buried together with Christ by baptism into death; who walk not according to the flesh, but, putting off the old man, and putting on the new who is created according to God, are made innocent, immaculate, pure, harmless, and beloved of God, heirs indeed of God, but joint heirs with Christ; so that there is nothing whatever to retard their entrance into heaven.   (Waterworth 23)

The original sin distorted the image of God-likeness in human beings. For those who are baptised, the original condition, i.e. the God-likeness of human nature, is reconstituted; that is, every human nature participates in the divine nature and even without being baptised not all human capacities were destroyed through original sin. The rationality of human beings, for example, is much weaker than it was originally created, but human beings still are capable of rationality. For Christians, such capacities, which originate in the God-likeness of human beings, enable to establish a relation between God's creativity and creativity of human beings. This relation is not a relation of identity, but of similarity between the divine and the human nature. But what exactly is this similarity? In *On Fairy-stories*, Tolkien characterises the creativity of human beings in the following way:

> When we can take green from grass, blue from heaven, and red from blood, we have already an enchanter's power—upon one plane; and the desire to wield that power in the world external to our minds awakes. It does not follow that we shall use that power well upon any plane. We may put a deadly green upon a man's face and produce a horror; we may make the rare and terrible blue moon to shine; or we may cause woods to spring with silver leaves and rams to wear fleeces of gold, and put hot fire into the belly of the cold worm. But in such "fantasy," as it is called, new form is made; Faerie begins; Man becomes a sub-creator. (FS22)

According to Tolkien, human beings act as sub-creators and generate secondary creations by doing arts, literature, music or technology.[6] However, there is a significant distinction between secondary creations of human beings and the primary creation, i.e. God's creation of the world. God's primary creation is a *creatio ex nihilo*, i.e. a creation out of nothing and therefore, God alone has the power to create unconditionally. However, the secondary creations of human beings require something as their constitutive parts since the secondary creations, as Tolkien states in *On Fairy-Stories*, are nothing more than a recombination of already existing "material" (cf. Fornet-Ponse 370). As *Gaudium et spes* and classical theism claim, there should not be an opposition or rivalry between the primary creation and different secondary creations. Tolkien draws a beautiful picture of the connection between God's creativity and that of human beings, in *The Silmarillion*:

> And it came to pass that Ilúvatar called together all the Ainur and declared to them a mighty theme, unfolding to them things greater and more wonderful than he had yet revealed; and the glory of its beginning and the splendour of its end amazed the Ainur, so that they bowed before Ilúvatar and were silent. Then Ilúvatar said to them: 'Of the theme that I have declared to you, I will now that ye make in harmony together a Great Music.' (S15)

Eru, the One—a name for Ilúvatar—hands over the Ainur a theme, a present of his own creativity. This theme is the requirement for the generation of the Great Music, and through it "the echo of the music went out into the Void, and it was not void" (S 15).[7] The "material" of the Ainur is the primordial theme

---

6   It is a bit more complicated in photography, film, painting, music, sculpting, and theatre than in literature because in the former the primary creation is involved into the secondary creation necessarily.

7   The relation of the text to classical theological topics additional to the doctrine of creation like to eschatology is remarkable: "Never since have the Ainur made any music like

given by Eru. Similar to the secondary creation of human beings, the Ainur's secondary creation is not unconditional but is a development of the original "material" which is originated from Eru's creation out of nothing. This picture from literature can be systematised within a Leibnizian setting as will be argued in the following chapter.

3. A Leibnizian Systematisation

In Leibniz's depiction, God can be compared to a storyteller, but in contrast to a human storyteller, God's fictions are complete and so rich, that any statement about his fictions has to be either true or false. But what exactly is a divine fiction?

For Leibniz, God is primarily an intellect. And there cannot be an intellect that does not think of something; that is, there must be some content of thinking. The content of the divine thinking is the ideas. The divine intellect contains an infinite number of ideas which are conceptual entities like *being even*, or *being taller than...* (cf. A 2.1 117). The ideas are the basal entities the divine intellect contains and the divine intellect combines the ideas into richer conceptual structures, into so-called *conceptus completi*. A *conceptus completus* consists of an infinite number of ideas. But not all infinite collections of ideas form *conceptus completi*. To form a *conceptus completus*, these ideas must be maximal-consistent. A set of ideas I is maximal-consistent, if (i) for any idea i, I contains i or the complement of i and (ii) I does not entail i and ¬i (cf. A 6.4 1374). We can consider a *conceptus completus* as a single figure in a divine fiction. Leibniz's term for a divine fiction as a compossible sequence of figures is 'possible world'. A sequence of *conceptus completi* W is compossible, if all *conceptus completi* in W are realisable together without any contradiction. A possible world W which contains the *conceptus completi* c and d, both of them containing the idea *being the wisest man at a time t*, would not be realisable together at the same time, because there can only be one wisest man at a time t. There are an infinite number of possible worlds in the divine intellect, each consisting of an infinite number of *conceptus completi*, and each consisting of an infinite number of ideas. The divine fictions are ideal or mental structures and

---

to this music, though it has been said that a greater still shall be made before Ilúvatar by the choirs of the Ainur and the Children of Ilúvatar after the end of days" (S 15). And the relation to the doctrine of the original sin is also noteworthy: "But as the theme progressed, it came into the heart of Melkor to interweave matters of his own imagining that were not in accord with the theme of Ilúvatar; for he sought therein to increase the power and glory of the part assigned to himself" (S 16).

only one of them, the best of all possible worlds, was realised by divine creation.[8] The argument for the realisation of the best of all possible world is as follows:

(1) God is benevolent. [Theistic premise]

(2) If God is benevolent, he prefers the existence over non-existence. [Principle of Existence > Non-Existence]

(3) God prefers to realise a possible world. [modus ponens from (1) and (2)]

(4) God needs a sufficient reason to realise a unique possible world. [Principle of Sufficient Reason]

(5) The axiological status of the best of all possible worlds, is the sufficient reason to realise that world. [Principle of the Best]

(6) God realises the best of all possible worlds and created the actual world [from (3), (4) and (5)][9]

Between the best possible world as an ideal structure within the divine intellect, consisting of an infinite number of *conceptus completi*, and the created concrete actual world, consisting of an infinite number of individual substances—in his later period Leibniz calls them monads—, there is a one-to-one relation of correspondence. In Leibniz's *Discourse on Metaphysics*, written in 1686, he says:

> Since this is so, we can say that the nature of an individual sub-stance or of a complete being is to have a notion so complete that it is sufficient to contain and to allow us to deduce from it all the predicates of the subject to which this notion is attributed... God, seeing Alexander's individual notion or haecceity sees in it at the same time the basis and reason for all the predicates which can be said truly of him, for example, that he vanquished Darius and Porus; he even knows a priori (and not by experience) whether he died a natural death or whether he was poisoned, something we can know only through history.   (AG 41)

---

8   It seems to be more adequate to consider the realm of possible worlds, i.e. the primary creation, as blueprints for possible universes. The actual world would be the second creation as its existence requires the primary creation. In this case, arts, literature, etc. would be third creations, they require the primary and secondary creation. Nevertheless, it seems to be accurate to consider both, viz. the ideal realm and the actual world, as primary creation since in Leibniz there is no temporal subordination of the ideal struc-tures or possible worlds and our actual world, but only a logical one. Both together can be called primary creation.

9   Whether this argument works, is still controversial. See: Strickland 141-157, Plantinga 539-552, Blumenfeld 163-177 and Rescher 129-162.

A *conceptus completus* is like a blueprint which is designed in a way to contain each one of the properties that its corresponding individual substance will ever exhibit.[10] Therefore, both individual substances and their corresponding *conceptus completus* are completely determined. Leibniz's theory of complete concepts and their relation to individual substances brings about a severe consequence which is called Hyperessentialism (cf. Mondadori 162-190). Philosophers traditionally make a distinction between accidental and essential properties. An essential property E is a property of an entity x that x cannot exist without having E. The property of being identical with oneself, for example, could be an essential property, given that every entity must exemplify this property not to lose its own identity and existence. An accidental property A is a property which x does not have to exemplify necessarily. For example the property *being the 45ᵗʰ President of the United States of America* is an accidental property of Donald Trump because he would not cease to exist, had he lost that property. In Leibniz's theory, an individual substance has all its properties essentially because its corresponding *conceptus completus* is completely determined by the combinatorial "procedure" of the divine intellect.

Even though some statements in human fiction might lack a truth value, that is, they might be neither true nor false, all statements in a divine fiction have to be either true or false because divine fictions are totally determined. But the truth or falsehood of all statements about a divine fiction is not knowable by finite human intellects because a divine fiction is an infinite plurality of ideal structures.[11] Based on the distinction between completeness and incompleteness, Leibniz's metaphysical system allows for a clear distinction between God's fictions, i.e. the possible worlds as ideal structures in the divine intellect and human fictions. A comparison between Leibniz and Tolkien seems to be appropriate for two reasons: (a) Tolkien, like Leibniz, believes that reality has a two-part structure: ideal and actual, the former being superior than the latter. (b) Both are theists and believe in the absolute sovereignty of God over the world, according to which the reality as a whole (the primary creation and secondary creations) depends ontologically on God.

---

10 The real difference between an individual substance and its corresponding *conceptus completus* is not fully clear in the writings of Leibniz. On the one hand, the quotation from the *Discourse of Metaphysics* suggests that there is a radical ontological difference between the two, for example, between the idea of a sculpture in the mind of a sculptor and the concrete sculpture. On the other hand, Leibniz says in *Genera Terminorum Substantiae* from 1685(?): "S u b s t a n t i a est Terminus completus" (A 6.4 568). Hence, the relationship between an individual substance and its corresponding *conceptus completus* remains as a question of interpretation.

11 In *De Contingentia* (1689) and *Origo Veritatem Contingentium* (1689) Leibniz argues that something is contingent if its corresponding *conceptus completus* is analysable in an infinite number of steps, cf. A 6.4 1649-1652.

3.1 The Two-part Structure of Reality

Even though the distinction between an individual substance and its corresponding *conceptus completus* in Leibniz's theory of modality has been stated in the previous section, the relation between these two levels does not still seem to be entirely clear. In the *Principles of Nature and Grace, Based on Reason*, Leibniz says that monads are capable of action (cf. GP VI 598). Therefore, there is a fundamental difference between *conceptus completi* and monads. The concepts are in some sense "dead" entities, the monads living and spontaneous beings. Tolkien seems to make a similar distinction between something that is thought and something that is living. There are a few passages from the *Ainulindalë* which express this distinction obviously:

> But for a long while they sang only each alone, or but few together, while the rest hearkened; for each comprehended only that part of the mind of Ilúvatar from which he came, and in the understanding of their brethren they grew but slowly.   (S 15)
>
> In that time the Valar brought order to the seas and the lands and the mountains, and Yavanna planted at last the seeds that she had long devised.   (S 35)
>
> As yet no flower had bloomed nor any bird had sung, for these things waited still their time in the bosom of Yavanna; but wealth there was of her imagining, and nowhere more rich than in the midmost parts of the Earth, where the light of both the Lamps met and blended.   (S 35)
>
> … [M]oving when thou thinkest to move them, and if thy thought be elsewhere, standing idle…   (S 43)

3.2 Theism as a Shared Premise

In this paper, I interpret a human fiction as a part of a divine fiction which is not completely discovered by a finite human intellect, but only partially. Since human intellectual capacities are limited and finite, they capture only fragmentary parts of the complete divine fictions. In a letter, Tolkien wrote "They [the fictions] arose in my mind as 'given' things, and as they came, separately, so too the links grew… yet always I had the sense of recording what was already 'there', somewhere: 'not of inventing'" (L 145). In a Leibnizian setting, the secondary creator records some parts of a fully determined divine fiction. However, if divine fictions are possible worlds in a Leibnizian sense, it is clear that a part of a divine fiction is still integrated into a greater structure and this greater structure is "mirrored" by the part—the picture of a mirror which Leibniz uses in many cases (cf. AG 42, PNG 5 and M 57). A divine fiction is linked to all other divine fictions, because they are all part of the whole of the divine intellect. Therefore, the secondary creator gets connected to the whole divine intellect mediately when he gets connected to a divine fiction. By recording a part of a divine fiction, i.e. a possible world, the whole reality, as it is thought and unified by the divine mind, is mirrored. To regard a part of a divine fiction as a reflection of the whole divine intellect makes a fiction to a good one. A human fiction seems to be "far" away from the actual world—that is the point which makes the fiction fascinating—but it is still one unique divine intellect that unifies not only all divine fictions, but also all human fictions. Thus, every possible world is connected with each other. If this moment of unity is not foreshadowed in a fiction, it should be considered as a bad fiction.

A human fiction could be interpreted as a recorded part of a divine fiction, wherein the unity of the divine intellect appears. But there are many divine fictions that are so unlike our world that they might not have any relevance for the reader in our actual world. For example, a world without any free agents or without any kind of change, or a world without any physical, logical or moral laws would be so different that an author would not be interested in recording it. On the other side, a human fiction needs to be different from the real world in order to be fascinating. So, a human fiction could be interpreted as a part of a divine fiction as being originally thought by the divine intellect. Such part of a divine fiction must be sufficiently similar to our actual world to be relevant and it must be sufficiently dissimilar to our world to be fascinating. A relation of similarity is already problematic because of its internal structure (i.e. its transitivity). But in this case, there is another misunderstanding that should be eliminated. The similarity between our actual world and a part of a divine fiction does not just refer to obvious similarities like the similarities between the physiognomy of dwarves and human beings (cf. Kölzer 118-120). It is primarily a deeper or a more serious similarity: a similarity regarding existential questions and human nature like "What significance do relationships have for our lives?", "What is the purpose and meaning of our existence?", "What is a good life?", "How do I deal with the tragic in my life?", etc. A fiction has no obligation to our actual world, but at the same time it has an existential implication for our world (cf. Kölzer 43).

The reconstruction of secondary creations in a Leibnizian setting seems to fulfil the theistic thesis of God's sovereignty: both the primary creation and the secondary creations depend on God alone (cf. Schult 20).

4. Conclusion

In a Leibnizian setting, a human fiction can be interpreted as a part of a divine fiction with the recognition that it is a unique intellect who is thinking of the whole of reality—God's intellect. The distinction between human and divine fictions is that the former are incomplete while the latter are complete. Tolkien's distinction between human and divine fictions can be systematised in Leibniz's metaphysics because they share strikingly similar theistic premises in their theological assumptions.

Bibliography

Primary literature

A =   Deutsche Akademie der Wissenschaften (ed.). *Gottfried Wilhelm Leibniz, Sämtliche Schriften und Briefe*. Darmstadt: 1923 ff., quoted according to series and volume

AG =   Leibniz, Gottfried Wilhelm. *Philosophical Essays*. Transl.: Roger Ariew, Daniel Garber. Indianapolis/Cambridge: Hackett, 1989

E =   Spinoza, Baruch de. *Ethica Ordine Geometrico demonstrata et in quinque Partes distincta*. Ed.: Wolfgang Bartuschat, Hamburg: Felix Meiner Verlag, 2015

FS =   Tolkien, John Ronald Reuel. "On Fairy-stories". In: *Tree and Leaf*. London: HarperCollins Publishers, 2001, 1-82

GP =   C.I. Gerhardt (ed.), *Die philosophischen Schriften von G.W. Leibniz*, 7 volumes, Berlin 1875-1890, reprint Hildesheim: Olms, 1978

KrV =   Kant, Immanuel. *Kritik der reinen Vernunft*. Ed.: Jens Timmermann. Hamburg: Felix Meiner Verlag, 1998

LotR =   Tolkien, John Ronald Reuel. *The Lord of the Rings. The Fellowship of the Ring*. London: HarperCollins Publishers, 1994

M =   Leibniz, Gottfried Wilhelm. *Monadologie*. Transl.: Artur Buchenau. Ed.: Herbert Herring. Hamburg: Felix Meiner Verlag, 1956

My =   Tolkien, John Ronald Reuel. "Mythopoeia". In: *Tree and Leaf*. London: HarperCollins Publishers, 2001, 85-90

PNG =   Leibniz, Gottfried Wilhelm. *Principes de la Nature et de la Grace fondes en Raison*. Transl. Artur Buchenau. Ed.: Herbert Herring. Hamburg: Felix Meiner Verlag, 1956

S =   Tolkien, John Ronald Reuel. *The Silmarillion*. London: George Allen & Unwin, 1977

S.Th. =   Aquinas. *Summa Theologiae, Vol. XVI*. Transl. and ed. by Thomas Gilby, O.P. London/ New York: Blackfriars, Eyre and Spottiswoode, 1969

Secondary literature

Blumenfeld, David. "Is The Best Possible World Possible?". In: *The Philosophical Review 84* (1975): 163-177

Carpenter, Humphrey, ed. with assistance of Christopher Tolkien. *The Letters of J.R.R. Tolkien*. London: HarperCollins Publishers, 2006

Fornet-Ponse, Thomas. "Kunst als Zweitschöpfung. Oder: Müssen Theologen Tolkien lesen?". *Münchener Theologische Zeitschrift 60* (2009): 367-376

Kölzer, Christian. *'Fairy tales are more than true'. Das mythische und neomythische Weltdeutungspotential der Fantasy am Beispiel von J.R.R. Tolkiens* The Lord of the Rings *und Philip Pullmans* His Dark Materials. Trier: WVT, 2008

Mondadori, Fabrizio. "Understanding superessentialism". *Studia Leibnitiana 17* (1985): 162-190

Plantinga, Alvin. *"Which World Could God Have Created?"*. Journal of Philosophy 70 (1973): 539-552

Rescher, Nicholas. "Leibniz on Possible Worlds". *Studia Leibnitiana 28/2* (1996): 129-162

Schult, Stefanie. *Subcreation: Fictional World Construction from J.R.R. Tolkien to Terry Pratchett and Tad Williams*. Berlin: Logos Verlag, 2017

Strickland, Lloyd. "God's Problem of Multiple Choice". *Religious Studies 42/2* (2006): 141-157

Waterworth, James (ed.). *The Council of Trent. The Twenty-Fifth Session. The canons and decrees of the sacred and oecumenical Council of Trent*. London: Dolman, 1848

We are Middle-earth: Transmedia World-building and Media Convergence

Helmut W. Pesch (Köln)

The term 'worldbuilding' has been applied to "the creation of an imaginary world and its geography, biology, cultures, etc." (Prucher 270) since the mid-1960s but has recently gained a new significance in the context of exploitation of content across different media. Here the focus is no longer on the work as such, but on merchandising, tie-ins, prequels, sequels and spin-offs extending the value-added chain of a successful product.

The emphasis on the storyworld rather than on the story itself is viewed rather sceptically by some critics, and novelists in particular. M. John Harrison, formerly a champion of the "New Wave" science fiction writers' movement in the 1960s, who, in his *Viriconium* fantasy cycle, eschews the demand for internal consistency, takes worldbuilding to task most severely in a much-discussed blog post of 2007:

> Above all, worldbuilding is not technically necessary. It is the great clomping foot of nerdism. It is the attempt to exhaustively survey a place that isn't there. A good writer would never try to do that, even with a place that is there. It isn't possible, & if it was the results wouldn't be readable: they would constitute not a book but the biggest library ever built, a hallowed place of dedication & lifelong study. This gives us a clue to the psychological type of the worldbuilder & the worldbuilder's victim, & makes us very afraid. (n. pag.)

In his response, his fellow writer, China Miéville, tries to put this into perspective, but for him, there are also some questions begging answers:

> Why does the 'internal consistency' of a world matter to us? What does that even mean? How can we map every corner of a non-existent place? Why do we want to? Why are we so anxious when writers contradict their canon statements? What is going on? What kind of urges are these? (n. pag.)

At this stage, J.R.R. Tolkien's *The Lord of the Rings* was already a benchmark of worldbuilding, a hindrance rather than an advantage in terms of its critical acceptance. From early on, the author had to defend himself against the contention that his novel was just an excessive hobby of an Oxford don (L 219), and in one of his letters he writes:

> Nobody believes me when I say that my long book is an attempt to create a world in which a form of language agreeable to my personal aesthetic might seem real… [I]t was an effort to create a situation in which a common greeting would be *elen síla lúmenn' omentielmo*, and … the phrase long antedated the book. (L264f.)

At that time, little was known of his long years of preparatory work, including the unpublished "Silmarillion", a conglomeration of unfinished texts of various kinds, sketches, and notes. Looking at Tolkien's creation, the immense multi-modal and multi-semiotic effort immediately strikes the eye. In the published versions of *The Hobbit* and *The Lord of the Rings* alone, there are self-designed covers, illustrations, calligraphic samples of invented writing systems in imaginary languages, maps in diverse modes of presentation, and forewords and appendices of various text types. In the end, the act of reading requires a reader versed in the interpretation of sign systems, while the additions both supplement and challenge the narrative text. As Wolfgang Hallet notes:

> In the multimodal novel, it is even possible to present the specific capacity that cartographic and other visualisations supposedly have to represent and express the physicality and sensuality of space and motion and simultaneously to question and critique it on a meta-semiotic level.   (167)

The journey of the heroes may be double-checked on the map, which in turn contains information irrelevant to the plot—an exemplary case of overdesign.

Multi-modal or multi-semiotic worldbuilding is much older than the advent of digital media. The underlying mechanisms are rather basic cultural techniques. The Abrahamic religions, for instance, operate on the basis of a central text and a symbolism partly derived from the text itself, partly developed independently, which is communally accessible in ritual. On the other end of the spectrum, there are idiosyncratic symbolic creations such as the work of William Blake (1757-1827), multi-talented as a visual artist and poet, whose illuminated prints combine texts with hand-coloured etchings based on an invented personal mythology. As examples of the "literary prehistory of virtual reality" Michael Saler cites the literary worlds of Arthur Conan Doyle (1859-1930), H.P. Lovecraft (1890-1937) and J.R.R. Tolkien (1892-1973), due to their persistence and public accessibility as well as to the "double consciousness of the ironic imagination" (22) they invite. Readers may pretend that the narrative world and the characters exist in real life—as proposed by the Baker

Street Irregulars, a readers' organisation founded in the USA in 1934—while being fully aware that this isn't true. Similarly, it is possible to playfully reduce the role of the author to that of an editor and to regard the narrator Dr Watson as the "real" author, just as Tolkien later employs an editorial fiction in *The Lord of the Rings*.

The systematic creation of non-fictional material for the background of a complex narrative world blossomed fully after the beginning of the 20th century. Besides Tolkien, his older contemporary, Edgar Rice Burroughs (1875-1950), ought to be mentioned here, whose first novels *Tarzan of the Apes* and *A Princess of Mars* were published in 1912. For the sake of internal consistency, he drew maps of his fantastic narrative worlds such as Mars, Venus, or Pellucidar, the land at the earth's core, but not of Tarzan's Africa, the dark continent, where vague descriptions of the locations of lost civilisations seemed sufficient. The linguistic aspects of worldbuilding were limited to word lists with a rudimentary morphology. While Burroughs' series initially existed independently of each other, they evolved over the years by crossover elements into an "interdependent heterocosmos" (Pesch 115), in which a *persona* of the author appears as a witness. Burroughs was also very interested in commercial media exploitation and tried to exert some control over it. The "Tarzan" of the movies has only the basic concept in common with the literary character, while the comic strip artists came closer to the original text. But in all cases, it was just a secondary text. A copyright shared by the author and the illustrator, as in the case of L. Frank Baum and W.W. Wenslow's *The Wonderful Wizard of Oz* (1900), was exceptional and has only established itself in the media with the rise of the graphic novel in recent years.

While in a written novel the primacy of the narrative text, irrespective of all additional elements, is undisputed, a "medium" more often than not encompasses a reciprocal relationship between different modalities and semiotic categories: language, image, and sound (Ryan 26). The construction of a narrative by the interaction of images and written language as in graphic novels, or from moving images, spoken language, and music as in films does not yet produce a multimedia product unless all technological media are understood as "mixed media" (Mitchell 95; cf. Ryan 26).

The parallel exploitation of the story—e.g., through novels and audio-books—may best be labelled by the term 'crossmedia'. The standard definition of transmedia storytelling goes back to Henry Jenkins' widely cited study, *Convergence Culture: Where Old and New Media Collide* (2006). Jenkins understands this as a narrative extending across several media, "with each new text making a distinctive and valuable contribution to the whole" (97 f.), the term "text" here referring to all forms of media products. In addition, factors such as branding, adaptation, seriality, and intertextuality may be taken into consideration. As Dan Hassler-Forest puts it:

> Transmedia worldbuilding thereby articulates a fundamental
> element of convergence culture: boundaries between media have
> blurred to the point at which it makes little sense to foreground
> fundamental distinctions between contemporary media. Instead
> the term helpfully foregrounds the fact that our immersion in ima-
> ginary storyworlds takes place not within but across media. (8)

Genuine transmediality presupposes a deconstruction of the narrative coherence of the text in the various media forms so that views are opened through "media windows" (Wolf 247) on different parts of a larger whole. This overarching context of meaning, even if it suggests a totality, is by nature incomplete. It may even be hypothetical or subject to continuous evolution, as in the case of *Star Trek* or *Star Wars*. While knowledge of the superstructure is not indispensable for the participant's understanding, it confers an additional "depth" (Shippey 259) and synergy.

In Jenkins' ideal conception, a transmedia narrative allows entry equally via each media window. Instances of indetermination, which in Wolfgang Iser's aesthetics of literary reception (5-7) are a central condition for literary validity, are restricted to the boundaries of individual texts since they may be resolved in the transmedia context. On the one hand, the recipient is requested to obtain a valid interpretation by collecting and exploiting new information; on the other hand, the different entry points and paths of reception do not offer any definitive criteria for how and whether this point may be reached. While Jenkins emphasises that conventional literary and film criticism cannot provide a valid model for such transmedia reception strategies, he concedes that such a model has not yet been established.

Criticism of this approach emphasises two aspects which counteract this postulated undifferentiated flow:

On the one hand, there is an effort towards controlling the order of reception to a certain degree by "moving the story world *(sic!)* calculated across media" (Bordwell, n. pag.). Not all ways of reception are equal, but some are preferred for various reasons. Mark J.P. Wolf names six types of sequences that may change the experience of a storyworld: order of *appearance*, of *creation*, of *internal chronology*, of *canonicity*, of *media preference,* and of *age adequacy* (265). All these strategies come into play in the reception of Tolkien's literary works and their media adaptations.

By order of appearance, *The Hobbit* (1937) and *The Lord of the Rings* (1954/55) precede *The Silmarillion* (1977), which is prior both by order of creation and of internal chronology, and the "History of Middle-earth". *The Hobbit*, on the other hand, is considered a children's book and should be read first under the aspect of age adequacy. The movies, on the other hand, reverse the sequence: The *Lord of the Rings* trilogy is followed by the *Hobbit* trilogy. Consequently, the characters appearing in both film trilogies had to appear younger—or, in the case of the immortal Elves, at least unchanged—in the later movies, while the actors had aged. A chronological or age-appropriate order, reversing the sequence of reception, would for its part raise a problem with visual quotations, since the *Hobbit* movies contain allusions to their predecessor, and thus interchange original and quote.

The internal chronology of the texts themselves is far more complex and requires frequent alternation between several books. There is, in fact, no definite sequence in which these books are supposed to be read; although readers are usually advised to start with *The Lord of the Rings*, which is considered not only as the central work but also as the most significant narrative achievement.

Works published during the author's lifetime are considered canonical in the strict sense. With Tolkien, the posthumously published *The Silmarillion*, assembled from original texts written over a period of several decades and completed by his son Christopher, is also numbered among them since the author had in fact intended to finish it but had failed to do so due to the complexity of the text and the troubles of old age. The posthumously published books, in particular, *Unfinished Tales* and the volumes of the "History of Middle-earth", comprise aside from the *Book of Lost Tales*, a precursor to *The Silmarillion*, mostly discarded manuscript versions as well as other texts which were never intended to be published in this form by the author. They are therefore considered as non-canonical or auxiliary.

"Media franchising" (Johnson), the commercial exploitation of an overarching narrative world on a variety of platforms, multiplies the number and type of texts contingent on the storyworld. Within a span of just three months prior to and immediately following the launch of *The Return of the King* in Britain, there were at least some 2,500 articles with a "sign value": news items, advertisements, reviews, essays, DVD extras, interviews, merchandising articles, etc. (Barker/Egan/Jones/Mathijs 17). We may safely assume that such paratexts also have an influence on the reception of the text itself. While marketing had only a limited effect on those potential viewers who had already read the books, it increased the attention of the general cinema audience (113). The book readers grudgingly accepted certain aspects of the film adaptations, such as its horror film aesthetics and extensive battle scenes, as concessions to the commercial nature of a blockbuster movie. These elements, on the other hand, were a major attraction for the young media generation, which in turn had difficulties in following the storyline.

On the other hand, the world in which the story takes place provides a spatio-temporal framework. As David Herman notes:

> Interpreters do not merely reconstruct a sequence of events and a
> set of existents, but imaginatively (emotionally, viscerally) inhabit

> a world in which things matter, agitate, exalt, repulse, provide
> grounds for narrative participants and interpreters of the story.
> (570; cf. Schmidt 11)

The different transmedia roads of exploration only reinforce this effect. By exploring the narrative world, the traveller inevitably foregrounds its construction. The producer fosters this process by publishing supplementary material on the essential background. However, by doing so, he is not only providing a service to the consumer but also trying to maintain his prerogative of interpretation.

This idea is already apparent in Christopher Tolkien's compilation of background material on his father's work. When he compiled the first collation of texts in 1981, he wrote in a letter to the publisher: "It is done partly for my own satisfaction in getting things right, and because I wanted to know how the whole conception did in reality evolve from the earliest origins" (9). But he also stated: "I want to make as sure as I can that any later research in JRRT's 'literary history' is not turned into nonsense by mistaking the actual course of its evolution" (10). Even then, he was aware of the fact that there are various possible ways of presenting the material, and that the editorial decisions inevitably have an impact on the subsequent interpretation.

The same notion applies to the "appendices" to the extended version of the cinema films. While deliberately echoing Tolkien's appendices in *The Lord of the Rings*, they deal both with the content and with the cinematic implementation of the story world. They "function as arguments for the value of the films. They justify its outcomes." (Egan/Barker 101). In fact, the creators of the film attempt to amend perceived faults in Tolkien's writings and subject the books to a "*friendly criticism*" (92, emphasis by authors):

> By consistently positioning the films as mediator between the
> books themselves and the extratext that is Tolkien's life, thematic
> preoccupations, and wider Middle-earth mythology, the films thus
> become almost an *homage to what Tolkien really meant to do* or
> should have done if he'd been able to stand back and analyse his
> story from a distance, or at least *might have wanted to do*, if he
> had only known what we now know.   (95, emphasis by authors)

It is also revealing that Tolkien's ideological convictions are not an issue in the supplementary material: it neither addresses the author's conservatism nor his attitudes towards women and reinterprets his Catholicism in terms of a general morality (91).

The film claims to be more canonical than the book, at least for our time. For this reason, it surrounds itself with the appearance of authenticity. In Susan Collins' *The Hunger Games*, a novel pervaded by a media-critical subtext, the heroine, Katniss Everdeen, is advised to "Be yourself" (148), so that she may provide an effective media image. In the *Lord of the Rings* and *Hobbit* movies, the impression of authenticity is reinforced by the overdesign of the total project. Clothing and objects were made using traditional techniques, an expenditure which is to some extent lost on the moviegoer since the material quality is only of limited relevance to its visual appearance. Artists and manufacturers also designed and produced a lot more weapons and equipment than ever appear on the screen. This material, in turn, functions, for example in merchandising and public relations, as a kind of parallel narrative to the overdesign of Tolkien's work.

The subsequent "extended version" of the movies, which claims an even higher degree of true representation than the cinematic version, forms an integral part of the reception chain. The collective cinema experience is supplemented by a private viewing. The viewer is guided from a passive to a self-directed exploration of the subject. The induced and partially controlled active participation is continued in the tertiary texts derived from the film, e.g., video games. Generally, the successful adaptation of existing media forms is considered more difficult than the creation of original interactive game worlds since derived games must both meet the expectations of those familiar with the source material and function apart from the original (Wolf 261f.). In the *Lord of the Rings* games, we find not only a stronger emphasis on elements that have the greatest appeal for the media generation—action and special effects—but also a development of parallel storylines. In *Middle-earth: Shadow of War* (2017) the Elven smith Celebrimbor forges another ring of power to defeat Sauron, and in the end, his spirit merges with that of the Dark Lord. Besides, the games are moving away from the traditional idealism that characterises Tolkien's work towards a "cynical reason" (Hassler-Forest 74), which also reflects a general tendency within the fantasy genre.

Active involvement on the readers' side does not necessarily require a transmedia approach. The literary storyworld as such creates "an environment in which a potentially unlimited number of narratives can take place" (Hassler-Forest 8), but the transmedia "multitext" raises this experience to a new level. To quote Hassler-Forest once again: "[I]n terms of content, these popular fantastic storyworlds offer immersive, participatory and endlessly expansive environments" (15f.). He also maintains that the model of "nostalgic" fantasy as "the kind of depthless play with empty signifiers that makes up postmodern pastiche" (16), is no longer valid for such contents since they allow an escapist immersion into the storyworld as well as critical reflection, both of which are playfully negotiable. They are also "highly accessible to casual audiences but deliberately layered to offer rewards to 'fannish' groups willing to invest more time and energy" (16).

On the one hand, the paratexts encourage the creative participation of the recipient; on the other hand, they channel it into particular directions. The visual impression of the film has proved immensely dominant. Tolkien himself already expressed some reservations about adapting the material for the theatre because he thought its special effects would restrict the imagination (FS 62f.). The fan art of Middle-earth after the release of the films differs significantly from earlier paintings and drawings. Nowadays, hardly any other visual representation of the characters and the world seems possible. Fan fiction either fills gaps in the narrative, also in the sense of providing prequels or sequels, or contrasts it with deviating interpretations, up to erotic-pornographic stories including ones with homosexual themes ("slash fiction"), which Tolkien presumably would find horrifying. In any case, they are not considered canonical.

The Lord of the Rings is also the first blockbuster cinema project in which the producers deliberately liaised with the fan community as a multiplier, going as far as to take advantage of the free work of fan clubs and include fans' names in the credits of the extended version. Here, too, the dilemma between collaboration and control is evident. In legal terms, the work enjoys protection and may only be reproduced or adapted in public by permission of the proprietor. The Tolkien Estate states on its website under the heading "Permissions and Requests":

> **Can I / someone else write / complete / develop my / their own version of one of these unfinished tales? (or any others)**
> The simple answer is NO.
> You are of course free to do whatever you like for your own private enjoyment, but there is no question of any commercial exploitation of this form of "fan-fiction".
> Also, in these days of the Internet, and privately produced collectors' items for sale on eBay, we must make it as clear as possible that the Tolkien Estate never has, and never will authorise the commercialisation or distribution of any works of this type.
> The Estate exists to defend the integrity of J.R.R. Tolkien's writings. Christopher Tolkien's work as his father's literary executor has always been to publish as faithfully and honestly as possible his father's completed and uncompleted works, without adaptation or embellishment.

In recent years, the Tolkien Estate has successfully taken legal action against commercial derivative works on a case-by-case basis. But so far, no attempts have been made to stop the spread of non-commercial fan fiction. Here, too, the desire for interpretative governance overlaps with the wish for economic control.

It is interesting to note that Peter Jackson and some of the actors have declared themselves Tolkien fans. In a kind of parallel narrative, the group of actors, who had the word "nine" tattooed in Elvish script, was portrayed as a community of friends, a real-world Fellowship of the Ring. While this may even be true to some extent, the narrative is also exploited by the marketing campaign. As Janet Wasko writes in "*The Lord of the Rings*: Selling the Franchise":

> It seems clear… that the companies that control these films and attempt to control the events that surround them ultimately make decisions based on the potential for profit, not necessarily for artistic, creative, or communicative goals. (36)

Similarly, as a parallel narrative blurring the boundaries between the fictional and the real world, an extensive body of fiction has emerged about the Inklings, the literary group comprising J.R.R. Tolkien, C.S. Lewis, and their friends. The authors themselves started the fictionalisation during their lifetime. The biographies on Tolkien and the Inklings by Humphrey Carpenter, each of them with a scenic chapter, and biopics such as the stage play *Shadowlands* (subsequently filmed twice) continued this strategy. By now, "Inklings" novels ranging from fantasy stories to mysteries and thrillers almost constitute a genre of its own, while most of them would most probably not be noticed to the same extent if they didn't avail themselves of this modern myth.

As far as fannish works are concerned, tertiary texts derived from the film do not necessarily move ever further away from the original. On the contrary, the "fan edits" of the films, for example, constitute an attempt to break New Line Cinema's interpretational sovereignty and to fall back on the original story (Pérez-Gómez 37). There is, for example, an unofficial "Tolkien version" of the *Hobbit* movies shortened to about four hours runtime and trying to dispose of everything that is not in the book but has been added by the scriptwriters.

Even though there may be consumers today who know Tolkien's work from film or computer games only and have never read the novels, it has now become accepted in the theoretical considerations of transmediality that not all media approaches to a story world are to be ranked the same. Especially in the case of *The Lord of Rings*, the book has the function of a thematic core, due to its worldwide distribution and cult status. Its characters and themes have long since become a cultural phenomenon, and through the filming, they have now gained a face. The films and the film experience, enhanced by re-enactment (Turnbull 182), create a communicative interface by establishing a greater sense of connection with others who share this experience and knowledge and therefore also have a community-building function. In this way, everybody joining in this discourse is a part of Middle-earth.

Bibliography

Barker, Martin, Kate Egan, Stan Jones & Ernest Mathijs. "Introduction: Researching *The Lord of the Rings:* Audiences and Contexts." In: Barker/Mathijs, 1-20

Barker, Martin & Ernest Mathijs (eds.). *Watching* The Lord of the Rings: *Tolkien's World Audiences.* New York et al.: Peter Lang, 2008

Bordwell, David. "Now Leaving from Platform One." *David Bordwell's Website on Cinema*, 19.08.2009. http://www.davidbordwell.net/blog/2009/08/19/now-leaving-from-platform-1/ (25.10.2017)

Collins, Susan. *The Hunger Games.* 2008. London: Scholastic, 2009

Egan, Kate, & Martin Barker. "The Books, the DVDs, the Extras, and their Lovers." In: Barker & Mathijs, 83-102

Harrison, M. John. "very afraid". In: *Uncle Zip's Window* (January 27, 2007), archived under: http://web.archive.org/web/20080410181840/http://uzwi.wordpress.com/2007/01/27/very-afraid/ (25.10.2017)

Harvey, Colin. *Fantastic Transmedia: Narrative, Play and Memory Across Science Fiction and Fantasy Storyworlds.* Basingstoke: Palgrave Macmillan, 2015

Hallet, Wolfgang. "The Rise of the Multimedial Novel: Generic Change and its Narratological Implications." In: *Storyworlds across Media: Towards a Media-Conscious Narratology.* Eds.: Maria-Laure Ryan, Jan-Noël Thon. Lincoln, NE/London: University of Nebraska Press, 2014, (Frontiers of Narrative Series) 151-172

Hassler-Forest, Dan. *Science Fiction, Fantasy, and Politics: Transmedia Worldbuilding Beyond Capitalism.* London: Rowman and Littlefield, 2016

Herman, David. "Storyworlds." In: *Routledge Encyclopedia of Narrative Theory.* Eds.: David Herman, Manfred Jahn, Marie-Laure Ryan. London: Routledge, 2005, 569-570

Iser, Wolfgang. *Die Appellstruktur der Texte: Unbestimmtheit als Wirkungsbedingung literarischer Prosa.* Konstanz: Universitätsverlag, 1970

Jenkins, Henry. *Convergence Culture: Where Old and New Media Collide.* New York/London: New York University Press, 2006

Johnson, Derek. *Media Franchising: Creative License and Collaboration in the Media Industries.* New York: New York Univ. Press, 2013

[Miéville, China.] "Mind Meld Make-Up with China Miéville on World-Building." Interview by John De Nardo. In: *SF Signal.* May 5, 2011. http://www.sfsignal.com/archives/2011/05/mind_meld_make-up_with_china_miville_on_world-building/ (25.10.2017)

Mitchell, P.J.T. *Picture Theory: Essays on Verbal and Visual Representation.* Chicago: Univ. of Chicago Press, 1994

Pérez-Gómez, Miguel Ángel. "Walking Between Two Lands, or How Double Canon Works in The Lord of the Rings Fan Films." In: *Fan Phenomena: The Lord of the Rings.* Ed.: Lorna Piatti-Farnell. Bristol & Chicago, IL: Intellect Books, 2015, (Fan Phenomena Series) 36-46

Pesch, Helmut W. *Fantasy: Theorie und Geschichte einer literarischen Gattung.* Phil. Diss. Univ. Köln 1981. Norderstedt: Twentysix, 2017

Prucher, Jeff (ed.). *Brave New Words: The Oxford Dictionary of Science Fiction.* New York et al.: Oxford Univ. Pres, 2007

Saler, Michael. *As If: Modern Enchantment and the Literary Prehistory of Virtual Reality.* New York: Oxford Univ. Press, 2012

Schmidt, Hanns Christian. "Origami Unicorn Revisited. 'Transmediales Erzählen' und 'transmediales Worldbuilding' im *The Walking Dead*-Franchise." In: *Image*, Ausg. 20, Themenheft *Medienkonvergenz und Transmediale Welten (Teil 1)*, 07/2014, 5-24

Shippey, Tom. *The Road to Middle-earth.* 1982. Revised and expanded edition. London: HarperCollins, 2005.

Tolkien, Christopher. "Preface." In: J.R.R. Tolkien, *Beren and Lúthien*. Ed.: Christopher Tolkien. London: HarperCollins, 2017, 9-17

Tolkien, J.R.R. *The Letters of J.R.R. Tolkien*. Ed.: Humphrey Carpenter, with the assistance of Christopher Tolkien. Boston: Houghton Mifflin, 1981

---. "On Fairy-stories." 1947. *Tolkien On Fairy-stories: Expanded Edition, with Commentary and Notes*. Eds.: Verlyn Flieger, Douglas A. Anderson. London: HarperCollins, 2008

[Tolkien Estate, The.] "Permissions and Requests": http://www.tolkienestate.com/en/paths/faq/permissions-requests.html (25.10.2017.)

Turnbull, Sue. "Beyond Words? *The Return of the King* and the Pleasures of the Text." *Watching The Lord of the Rings: Tolkien's World Audiences*. In: Barker/Mathijs, 181-190

Wasko, Janet. "*The Lord of the Rings:* Selling the Franchise". In: Barker/Mathijs, 21-36

Wolf, Mark J.P. *Building Imaginary Worlds: The Theory and History of Subcreation*. New York/London: Routledge, 2012

Worldbuilding and Mythopoeia in Modern Fantasy Literature[1]

Massimiliano Izzo (Oxford)

Worldbuilding, the construction of imaginary worlds, has acquired a preeminent role in contemporary fantasy literature. Nowadays, a majority of fantasy novels come not only with a map, but fully equipped with details on history, politics, economics, heraldry, cultures, warfare logistics, and complex magical systems. J.R.R. Tolkien's *The Lord of the Rings*, first published in three volumes in 1954-55, represents the ur-example of high fantasy novel set in an extensively developed Secondary World. Even if fantasy novels with maps[2] and timelines had been published before—such as *The Worm Ouroboros* (1922) and *Mistress of Mistresses* (1935) by E.R. Eddison—Tolkien's opus was unprecedented in its breadth and scope, with extensive chronicles spanning over two ages of his world, annals and lineages of four kingdoms and peoples, and long dissertations on language and calendars. Tolkien was not only a practitioner of the genre, but a theorist and apologist as well. He wrote a manifesto of sorts—the essay *On Fairy-stories,* originally presented as a lecture in honour of Andrew Lang at the University of St. Andrews in 1939—to defend the legitimacy of fantasy. In this essay he coined the term *sub-creation*, which describes the fantasist's creative process as subordinate to the existence and experience of the Primary World.

In the last decade worldbuilding has gained interest as a subject of study among scholars. In 2012, Mark J.P. Wolf published *Building Imaginary Worlds: the Theory and History of Subcreation,* the first book-length comprehensive study on worldbuilding across multiple media, with an emphasis on literature and gaming. Not surprisingly, both Tolkien's Secondary World and 'On Fairy-stories' are discussed at length (Wolf 22-25, 130-34, 202-05). At the beginning of his book, Wolf draws a parallel between the concepts of worldbuilding and sub-creation, to the point that the latter appears in the title rather than the former, and the sub-creator is equated with the builder of imaginary world: "Thus, a 'subcreator' is a specific kind of author, one who very deliberately builds an imaginary world, and does so for reasons beyond that of merely providing a backdrop for a story" (Wolf 23). Afterwards Wolf states that "secondary worlds that are geographically distinct from the Primary World" and "those that are

1   Special thanks to Giovanni Carmine Costabile and Claudio Testi for providing feedback on the paper's subject. Very special thanks to Davide Chiarella for proofreading and discussion on contemporary fantasy literature, and to Milo Thurston and Bethan Jenkins for providing precious revisions and suggestions to the final draft.
2   For a detailed account on maps in fantasy literature see Ekman 14-68.

used for stories whose action occurs mainly within a secondary world" are "the ones that contain the most subcreation" (Wolf 28) and that these will be the subject of his study. Throughout the book he proceeds to examine various imaginary worlds, with a particular focus on trans-medial worlds such as the world of Oz, the *Star Wars* and *Star Trek* universes, and the Myst franchise world. Popular contemporary fantasy worlds such as Randland from Robert Jordan's *The Wheel of Time*, Roshar and the entire Cosmere universe from Brandon Sanderson's *The Stormlight Archive*, and Westeros from George R.R. Martin's *A Song of Ice and Fire* would perfectly fit Wolf's definition of worlds containing "the most sub-creation". However, I am not convinced that Tolkien was discussing this type of imaginary worlds when he first introduced the concept of sub-creation. I think that this approach of considering worldbuilding and sub-creation as two equivalent concepts that proceed alongside each other is misleading and overlooks some fundamental differences between the two. The main thesis exposed in this paper is that the two concepts—even if complementary to some extent—do not really proceed hand in hand, but rather they often find themselves at odds with. The concept of sub-creation—and the cognate term sub-creator—first appears in the section 'Origins' of the afore-mentioned essay *On Fairy-stories*, where the origins of fairy and folk tales are considered. It must be noted that fairy tales are a type of narrative with little or no worldbuilding as currently understood. They are usually set "long ago in a place far away" and this is as much as we know in most cases. In 'Origins', Tolkien defines sub-creation as the faculty of the human mind ("endowed with the powers of abstraction and generalisation") to produce images and concepts not present in the Primary World through the use of language. He offers the use of the adjective as the best example of the sub-creative power of language:

> When we can take green from grass, blue from heaven, and red from blood, we have already an enchanter's power—upon one plane; and the desire to wield that power in the world external to our minds awakes. It does not follow that we shall use that power well upon any plane. We may put a deadly green upon a man's face and produce a horror; we may make the rare and terrible blue moon to shine; or we may cause woods to spring with silver leaves and rams to wear fleeces of gold, and put hot fire into the belly of the cold worm. But in such 'fantasy', as it is called, new form is made; Faërie begins; Man becomes a sub-creator. (FS 41)

Tolkien goes on to state that "This aspect of mythology—sub-creation—(…) is, I think, too little considered" (FS 42). Sub-creation is therefore considered by Tolkien as an aspect of mythology, and moreover more present in the so-called "lower mythology"—referring to legends, fairy tales, and folk tales, usually transmitted orally—rather than in the "higher", the written body of works relating the accounts of divine or supernatural beings (FS 42). Even if in the section 'Fantasy' of *On Fairy-stories* the concept of sub-creation is broadened to encompass the act of inventing Secondary Worlds, the chief image used by Tolkien—the "green sun"—remains still purely linguistic. To make a green sun believable in the Primary World, Tolkien states that some kind of elvish craft is required (FS 61) rather than the tools of a scientist or an engineer: a skill that preserves the enchantment, the sense of wonder that is the key to gaining a glimpse of Faërie. The sub-creator, for Tolkien, was a maker of myths. Tolkien borrowed from the Ancient Greek the term "mythopoeia" to better emphasise how the sub-creative process works with mythological sources to produce new myths. He also used the term as a title for a poem with strong Christian undertones where he defends the value of myth and the right of Man to produce new myths through sub-creation, in the image of God's creation.

In order to analyse sub-creation as myth-making, however, a proper definition for mythology is required. A mythology is usually defined as a collection of myths. Now, as we have seen above, it can be inferred from the *Letters* (such as the famous Letter 131 to Milton Waldman) that Tolkien does use the word "myth" in a broad context encompassing higher myths, legends, fairy tales, and folk tales. This definition essentially puts all of his literary output—the whole legendarium as well as the short works unrelated to it (*Smith of Wootton Major, Farmer Giles of Ham, Roverandom*) and poems like *The Fall of Arthur* and *The Lay of Aotrou and Itroun*—under the umbrella of myth. In this broader view, myth can be defined as a narrative that explains "why the world is as it is". Its goal is to provide meaning to the world, a unified picture of it. This definition is borrowed from the work of Margaret Hiley and builds on the work of the French structuralist school (Hiley 839f.). As it has been argued by Claude Levi-Strauss and Roland Barthes, myth is a language construct that artificially constructs the illusion of being natural. The key aspect of myth is its aura of truth and timelessness. Myth claims universal validity, aiming to encompass everything that exists[3]. In doing this it goes against the grain of "science", as it is currently understood. In the last four centuries, the sciences have acted as demythologisers, providing evidence-based explanation for, or falsifying, the accounts of ancient myth. Tolkien, however, did not share the belief that myths are lies, and he devoted the poem *Mythopoeia* to defend his position. In the letter to Milton Waldman he stated that "legends and myths are largely made of 'truths' and indeed present aspects of it that can only be received in this mode"

---

3   Attebery challenges Levi-Strauss's interpretation of myth and its timelessness (Attebery 31f.). But his view of myth as ever evolving and self-transforming (just as language is) in the Primary World does not invalidate the claim of universal validity and timelessness within the frame of the story itself (i.e. the Secondary World).

(Letters 147). This firm conviction, together with the desire to go back to the original meaning of terms of mythical significance, is the foundation of Tolkien's sub-creative approach. In Tolkien's Secondary World(s) history and myth are the same. Tolkien wrote his major novels—*The Hobbit* and, in particular, *The Lord of the Rings*—against the backdrop of his independently conceived and, as we have seen before, long established body of mythologies, the legendarium. Among the most effectively sub-created scenes in the two books are the descriptions of events from past ages and times, when narrated or referred to in the main narrative. These sub-creative pieces of Tolkien's writing have the best qualities of fairy tales: to "open a door to Other Time, and for a moment maybe to be outside Time altogether" (FS 48). This is the effect produced, for instance, by the account of the various peoples of the Elves in the chapter 'Flies and Spiders' of *The Hobbit* (H 154) and by the short tale of Beren and Lúthien as narrated to the hobbits by Aragorn at Weathertop in the chapter 'A Knife in the Dark' (LotR I 193f.). Mythological sub-creation is eminently used in *The Lord of Rings*, but Tolkien demonstrates his theory by applying it to other contexts: in his fairy tales *Roverandom* and *Smith of Wootton Major*. In the former while describing all the dangerous creatures that inhabit the Moon (R 29f.), and in the latter especially when describing the excursions and the encounters of Smith in Faery (SWM 258–60). Other powerful examples can be found in the unfinished "scientifiction" thriller *The Notion Club Papers*, when Ramer relates various fragments from his "vivid dreams" (SD 194, 198-99).

Mythological sub-creation mostly coexisted with a more encyclopaedic and "scientific" worldbuilding. This became more prominent in *The Lord of the Rings* and in the later rewritings of the 'Silmarillion'. Tolkien was extremely careful in multiple aspects of his worldbuilding, from history and geography to genealogy and astronomy. In *The Lord of the Rings* the encyclopaedic and "scientific" worldbuilding is brought to the fore mostly in the *Appendices*, but it often emerges in the narrative. However, this produces some demythologising effects: Orcs and Trolls, for instance, once systematised as corruptions of the Enemy, become less the stuff of fairy tales than they were in *The Hobbit* and more akin to a degenerate life form. This process becomes even more pronounced in the final rewritings of the 'Silmarillion' where Tolkien felt the urge to modify some long-established mythological concepts to make its Secondary World more believable to modern readers (see *Myths Transformed*, MR 370-94). The tension between mythopoeia and worldbuilding in Tolkien's work became even more marked in the works of the authors that came after him and who drew inspiration from his work.

Fantasy after Tolkien

It took the literary and publishing world at least two decades to absorb the import of *The Lord of the Rings*. In 1977, the commercial success of Terry Brooks's *The Sword of Shannara* and Stephen Donaldson's *Lord Foul's Bane*—together with the long-awaited publication of *The Silmarillion*—demonstrated the viability of high fantasy as a commercial genre. These books codified the genre for over a decade afterwards, and denoted a change in worldbuilding strategies. Rather than using Tolkien's mythopoeic approach of re-construction from fragments, more and more writers were drawn into using the whole that he sub-created as a template, and proceeded to fill the gaps and systematise it. Terry Brooks, for instance, always admitted his admiration for *The Lord of the Rings* and the influence it exerted on him, but he stressed that did not share Tolkien's "interest in cultural studies". Therefore, he omitted from his own novel "the poetry and songs, the digressions on the ways and habits of types of characters, and the appendices of language and backstory that characterised and informed Tolkien's work" (Brooks, *Magic* 188). Brooks discarded altogether Tolkien's mythopoetic approach; however, the influence of Tolkien on him was so strong that he ended up using Middle-earth as a template for the Four Lands and *The Lord of the Rings* as a blueprint for *The Sword of Shannara*. The shadow of Tolkien is also discernible in *Lord Foul's Bane*'s worldbuilding, even though Stephen Donaldson still offers us some glimpses of mythical poetry. This worldbuilding practice proved so successful that in the following years numerous writers took the easier road, and, rather than sub-create their own fantasies from the Primary World myths, felt drawn into using Tolkien's own world and narrative as a template for their imaginary stories. As a result, they failed to tap into what Tolkien referred to as the "reservoir of power" that lies behind Faërie (FS 270), and their novels lacked this mythological quality while keeping the adventure story traits and epic scope of *The Lord of the Rings*. Successful authors such as David Eddings and Dennis L. McKiernan reused to varying extents the building blocks of Tolkien's Secondary World. At almost the same time a new factor, which was to become another great influence for worldbuilding, came into play. *Dungeons & Dragons* (D&D), the table-top role-playing game (RPG), was invented by E. Gary Gygax in 1974 drawing inspiration from various fantasy and horror authors, who were duly acknowledged in the famous 'Appendix N' of the *Advanced D&D Dungeon Master's Guide* in 1977. By the beginning of the eighties, many shared worlds had been built as settings for D&D or similar RPGs, notable examples being Midkemia, developed by a group of students at the University of California, and the *Dragonlance* world conceived by Laura and Tracy Hickman. In the first half of the 1980s, authors started to publish works set in such worlds: Raymond E. Feist's *Magician* came out in 1982, while Margaret Weis and Tracy Hickman's

Dragons of Autumn Twilight was published in 1984. Both books garnered great commercial success and were followed by a slew of sequels. The closure of the feedback loop between fantasy literature and RPGs had profound consequences on worldbuilding, more so than on other aspects of the narrative. In games, the main objective of building a Secondary World is not artistic, but aimed at controlling the game and the options available to players in order to make it enjoyable, fair, reliable, and reproducible. This requires, among other things, providing extensive details of multiple aspects of the world. These aspects may not be needed to move forward a narrative in a novel, but once they have been developed (for gaming purposes, at least initially), they are used in the book to put more "flesh" on the world, in a sense to make it more realistic.

The ubiquitous reuse of Tolkien's tropes in fantasy worldbuilding without drawing inspiration from his original sources, and the success thereof, produced a reaction around the middle of the 1980s. This is best exemplified by Canadian author Guy Gavriel Kay, who explains the origin of his *Fionavar Tapestry* high fantasy trilogy as a conscious reaction to the flood of commercial fantasy. The *Fionavar Tapestry* achieved a modest commercial success, but it proved unable to inspire other writers in bringing back to the core of high fantasy novels the myth-making and sub-creative approach theorised and used by Tolkien. Most of the writers of this period who were interested in going back to the Cauldron of the Story and the sub-creative power of language—authors like Patricia A. McKillip, Charles De Lint, Peter S. Beagle, Ursula K. Le Guin and others—turned their backs on high fantasy, focusing on a variety of other sub-genres from science fiction romance to small scale fantasy novels far from the grandiose scope of *The Lord of the Rings* and its slew of imitators. As a consequence, these writers moved away from detailed and extensive worldbuilding and went to explore the numinous possibilities of magic in more familiar and rustic environments (consider for instance McKillip's *The Changeling Sea*, Le Guin's *Tehanu*, or Ellen Kushner's *Thomas the Rhymer*), in contemporary urban settings (such as Ottawa in De Lint's *Moonheart*), or in loosely described imaginary worlds rich in sub-created invention (such as in Tanith Lee's *Tales from the Flat Earth* series or in Diana Wynne-Jones's *Howl's Moving Castle*).

At the end of the 1980s, the Tolkien-inspired worldbuilding which still retained the format of trilogies and most of the metaphysical binary oppositions that constituted the basis of those fantasy worlds (good/evil, light/dark, hero/villain, material/spiritual) began to show fatigue. Readers who had fallen into the genre at the beginning of the eighties had grown up in the meantime and were now demanding more "realistic" fantasy, and more careful worldbuilding. Tad William's *Memory, Thorn, and Sorrow,* represented an early tentative attempt to broaden the scope of the world, adding detail at the level of political machinations and the number of factions and cultures depicted in the Secondary World. At the same time, while still moving in a Tolkienesque trajectory, he tried to deconstruct some of the formulae of the established narrative, such as the return of an ancient Evil from the past, here recast as a kind of deranged tragic hero. In the following two decades worldbuilding in high fantasy evolved along two lines: (1) increase in detail, and (2) deconstruction of (allegedly) established tropes. More often than not, these two aspects proceeded alongside one another, and the overall effect was a further demythologisation of the Secondary Worlds. The trailblazer in this scenario was Robert Jordan; the success of *The Wheel of Time* brought new life to the high fantasy genre and opened the gates for the multi-volume series of doorstoppers that would expand the scope of worldbuilding at an unprecedented level. *The Eye of the World*, the first book in the series, starts by adopting many of the defaults of Tolkien's world and narrative, but Jordan devotes a good deal of his novels to describing the various cultures and factions in his world, putting in the narrative far more worldbuilding detail than anybody before him. While these do not necessarily help in moving the story forwards—a multiplication of storylines and side-quests sidestep the main confrontation between the protagonist and the Dark Lord—they help to make the world more complex than many of his predecessors'. Jordan, as most of the worldbuilders who came after him, does not accept Tolkien's theory that going back in time history will become more mythical; rather, the opposite happens[4]. Even figures who might seem inspired by Primary World legends, such as the king Artur Paendrag (an obvious reference to Arthur Pendragon), are developed as purely historical figures within the Secondary World without trying to use the mythical motifs that were at the root of their Primary World sources of inspiration. The legendary characters of the series, such as the evil Forsaken or the immortal heroes like Paendrag or Birgitte the archer, come to appear quite mundane when they interact with the protagonists of the series. Detailed explanations of the magical system (which is referred to as One Power, rather than magic, but acts as such) are also provided throughout the novels. Finally, Jordan's worldbuilding, even in its multi-faceted complexity, is entirely subordinate to the story and not an independent endeavour of years if not decades, as was Tolkien's. The consequence is that any element of worldbuilding has its raison d'être in the framework of the final battle between the protagonist Rand Al'Thor and the Dark One. The characteristics of Jordan's worldbuilding here outlined can be applied to many subsequent high fantasy writers, from Brandon Sanderson[5], to Steven Erikson,

---

4   The theory for which mythology arises from real history and deities originate from men whose stature has been magnified by the lens of Time is called euhemerism, after the Greek mythographer Euhemerus (IV century BC). In relation to the Norse mythology it has been adopted in the XII–XIII century by Snorri Sturluson in the *Ynglinga Saga* and the prologue to *Edda* and by Saxo Grammaticus in *Gesta Danorum* (Simek 75f.).

5   On the subordination of worldbuilding to the story in Branderson's *The Stormlight Archive*, see Givens.

to R. Scott Bakker. The worldbuilding approach is more and more "scientific", reliable rules govern magical systems, and the invented creatures and races are "naturalised". None of these authors construct a mythical past: when there are myths or legends, they arise through a collective loss of memory from original historical events. The other path followed in the last twenty years—even if its seeds can be traced in Tolkien himself, considering the 'Narn i Chîn Húrin', especially the converse of Húrin with Morgoth (UT 66-8)—can be defined a "deconstructive" approach in the sense that it tries to dismantle from within some of the assumed tropes and metaphysical conventions of the fantasy literature that *The Lord of the Rings* popularised. This deconstructionist approach goes further than merely taking a disenchanted look into history. The lines between good and evil, hero and villain are blurred, so that the worlds become in most if not all aspects morally grey and teleologically bleak. If there are divinities, or supernatural beings, they usually range from being amoral to utterly immoral and lack any salvific qualities. Most of these narratives subscribe a materialistic worldview: the demythologisation of the world entails the lack of a spiritual dimension, with no possibility of salvation, damnation, or redemption. Hence, evil manifests itself purely on a physical basis: physical abuse, mutilation, and sexual violence are used extensively and explicitly, often to shock the reader, and provide a tool to identify the "wicked" characters. The most popular among the 'deconstructive' sub-currents of fantasy is "Grimdark", which boasts authors such as R. Scott Bakker, Joe Abercrombie, and Mark Lawrence. As we have seen from this survey, the main two trends of worldbuilding in fantasy have sidelined the mythopoeic approach that was at the basis of Tolkien's theory of sub-creation. This has clearly survived in other currents of fantasy that, as described before, had already flourished in the 1980s. Some genre authors kept on working with material and themes from fairy and folk tales, either setting their stories in small-scale and unmapped Secondary Worlds (such as Patricia McKillip in *The Book of Atrix Wolfe*, *Ombria in Shadow*, and *In the Forests of Serre*), or, to some extent, the Primary World with an access to the Otherworld (Peter Beagle's *Tamsin*, Neil Gaiman's *Stardust,* or Juliet Marillier's *Wildwood Dancing),* while in some cases the placeless and timeless quality of fairy stories is preserved (Grace Lin's Where the *Mountain meets the Moon*, for instance). Other authors have dabbled and experimented to greater extent with literary currents, especially postmodernism and magical realism, to bring new life to ancient myths. Within this current, the term "mythpunk" has been coined by Catherynne Valente to describe her work and those of fellow writers such as C.S.E. Cooney, Amal El-Mohtar, and Theodora Goss. All the mythopoeic authors share some common strategies of worldbuilding. They do not provide a map of their world, and often their world (or the Faërie part of it) resists any such mapping: the borders are not clearly defined, places shift locations. Faërie remains a perilous realm, as Tolkien postulated in his essay, but the danger is more in losing one's self (or soul), rather than physical peril. Magic has a subtle quality, and it is more directly related to the sub-creative possibilities offered by language. One, or more, of the fairy tale's functions posited by Tolkien are satisfied: recovery, escape, and consolation. More than that, they are still "faërie tales" according to Tolkien's definition, as they are concerned with humans who are offered some access to the world of Faërie and the wonders therein. The writers from this second category tend to be more appreciated by critics and are often recipients of literary awards such as the Nebula, the World Fantasy, or the Mythopoeic Award. However, with few notable exceptions—Neil Gaiman stands out—they are usually outsold by writers of worldbuilding-reliant high fantasy. The lack of commercial success and recognition among readers may be a factor behind the criticism that more literary and mythopoeic-oriented writers have aimed at worldbuilding for the role it has played in disenchanting fantasy literature.

Critiques of Worldbuilding

The incompatibility—or strain—between worldbuilding and mythopoiesis has been observed by various critics in the recent years. The first comes from M. John Harrison, author of the *Viriconium* quartet, who famously dubbed worldbuilding "the clomped foot of nerdism" in an essay published on his personal weblog (Harrison, *Afraid*). That essay was actually a continuation of a previous short piece, entitled *What It Might Be Like to Live in Viriconium*. Here, as we can see, his critique is more aimed at post-Tolkienian worldbuilding, rather than at Tolkien's sub-creation itself:

> … the moment you begin to ask (or rather to answer) questions like, "Yes, but what did Sauron look like?"; or, "Just how might an Orc regiment organise itself?"; the moment you concern yourself with the economic geography of pseudo-feudal societies, with the real way to use swords, with the politics of courts, you have diluted the poetic power of Tolkien's images. You have brought them under control. You have tamed, colonised and put your own cultural mark on them.   (Harrison, *What*)

Harrison's main concern regarding worldbuilding is related to the impulse of the author to control the Secondary Worlds, a sentiment that curiously mirrors a central theme of Tolkien's legendarium: that sub-creators may desire to become masters of their little worlds, leading to rebellion against the only Creator and consequent effort to tyrannise the Primary World itself. Harrison does not share Tolkien's Catholic faith and his motivations are different. However, the concern is the same, with ethical implications in the real world. Similar concerns, but from authors more actively engaged in reusing Tolkien's mythopoeic method, have been raised in two recent lectures in honour of Tolkien at Pembroke College in Oxford. The first one was from Lev Grossman, literary critic of the *Time* magazine and author of the *Magicians* trilogy, who pointed out the increasing mundanity of imaginary worlds in fantasy:

> And you write about these worlds differently. You do not treat them as fantastic, you write them in the same way that you would write about the mundane world, using the ordinary tools and conventions of realism. Narnia has no economy that I am aware of, but more and more fantasy worlds do, and not only that. They have ecology and geology... Magic has rules now.
> (Grossman 20:24-21:02)

An even more radical rebuttal against worldbuilding was pronounced by Terri Windling, an author and editor firmly rooted in the mythopoeic side:

> If we could map Narnia, or Middle-earth, or Prydain, or the great Earthsea Archipelago so that every detail is defined, every alleyway known, ...it would no longer be Fantasy for the mystery would be gone, and when mystery is dead, Fantasy is dead.
> (Windling 6:29-6:58)

Most of these critiques, as honestly felt as they are, betray some kind of literary contempt towards (most of) contemporary high fantasy, seen as commercial and facile. However, they also reveal the need for a new generation of authors, able to tap again into the sources that Tolkien used (or to similar ones), the reservoir of power from which Faërie draws sustenance.

Conclusions or: Is there a Way Back?

This paper aimed to show evidence of a fundamental difference between mythopoeia and worldbuilding. The first operates through language and its goal is to provide access to or at least a glimpse at the realm of Faërie, while the second uses a variety of "scientific" (including human sciences) disciplines to construct imaginary worlds that obey reliable rules, as the Primary World does. The inner consistency of reality is achieved through language alone in mythopoeic worlds, while it relies on an additional layer of rules that govern the invented elements in immersive Secondary Worlds. Obviously in practice there is no clear-cut difference, but after Tolkien high fantasy has relied more and more on worldbuilding and less on mythopoeia. Fragmentation is an un-avoidable consequence of an established genre; however, one wonders whether the sundered paths of mythopoeia and worldbuilding can come back together in the future. Looking at the past 40 years this would not seem easy, as there are only a handful of works that tried to bring back a mythopoeic approach to high fantasy[6], and the majority were not successful, either artistically or commercially. However most of the criticisms come from "myth-makers" regarding the loss of numinous magic and mystery in the contemporary high fantasy worlds. High fantasy writers accept the current status quo and it is unlikely that they will go back and try to adopt Tolkien's mythopoeic approach, which is fraught with perils and pitfalls. I would argue that, rather than tending their little garden, it is up to mythopoeic writers to "reach out", and write stories that can satisfy both desires: to provide a glimpse of Faërie as well as an immersive experience in a massive story.

---

6   The few works that come to my mind are the already mentioned *The Riddle-master* trilogy by Patricia A. McKillip, and *A Gathering of Heroes* and *Ingulf the Mad* by Paul Edwin Zimmer, and they were written well over two decades ago.

Bibliography

Attebery, Brian. *Stories about Stories: Fantasy and the Remaking of Myth*. electronic ed. New York: Oxford University Press, 2014

Brooks, Terry. *The Sword of Shannara*. [1977]. 5th ed. London: Orbit, 2006

---. *Sometimes the Magic Works*. London: Simon & Schuster UK, 2003

Donaldson, Stephen. *The Chronicles of Thomas Covenant, the Unbeliever*. London: HarperCollins, 1996

Ekman, Stefan. *Here Be Dragons: Exploring Fantasy Maps and Settings*. Middletown: Wesleyan University Press, 2013

Givens, Nathaniel. "Failing Tolkien: the Fall of High Fantasy." *Difficult Run*. 19 Aug. 2014, http://difficultrun.nathanielgivens.com/2014/08/19/failing-tolkien-the-fall-of-high-fantasy/

Grossman, Lev. "Fear and Loathing in Aslan's Land." *Tolkien Lecture on Fantasy Literature*. 13 May 2015, https://youtu.be/EcIWgPvx41c

Harrison, M. John. "Very Afraid." 27 Jan. 2007, http://web.archive.org/web/20080410181840/http://uzwi.wordpress.com/2007/01/27/very-afraid/

---. "What It Might Be Like to Live in Viriconium." 15 Oct. 2001, https://www2.warwick.ac.uk/fac/arts/english/currentstudents/undergraduate/modules/en361fantastika/bibliography/2.7harrison_mj._2001what_might_it_be_like_to_live_in_viriconium.pdf

Hiley, Margaret. "Stolen Language, Cosmic Models: Myth and Mythology in Tolkien." *MFS Modern Fiction Studies* 50.4 (2004): 838-860

Jordan, Robert. *The Fires of Heaven* [1993]. London: Orbit, 2014

Simek, Rudolph. *Dictionary of Northern Mythology*. Cambridge: D.S. Brewer, 1993

Tolkien, J.R.R. *The Hobbit*. London: HarperCollins, 1995

---. *The Letters of J.R.R. Tolkien*. Edited by Humphrey Carpenter, with the assistance of Christopher Tolkien. London: George Allen & Unwin, 1981

---. *The Lord of the Rings*. 50th anniversary ed. London: HarperCollins, 2005

---. *Morgoth's Ring* (The History of Middle-earth 10). Ed.: Christopher Tolkien. London: HarperCollins, 1993.

---. *On Fairy-stories*. Eds.: Verlyn Flieger, Douglas A. Anderson. London: HarperCollins, 2008

---. *Sauron Defeated* (The History of Middle-earth 9). Ed.: Christopher Tolkien. London: HarperCollins, 1992

---. *Tales from the Perilous Realm*. London: HarperCollins, 2009

---. *Unfinished Tales of Númenor and Middle-earth*. Ed.: Christopher Tolkien. London: HarperCollins, 2010

Windling Terri. "Reflections on Fantasy Literature in the Post-Tolkien Era." *Tolkien Lecture on Fantasy Literature*. 26 May 2016, https://youtu.be/SXh6oms0Kqg

Wolf, Mark J. *Building Imaginary Worlds: the Theory and History of Subcreation*. electronic ed. New York: Routledge, 2014

Points of Departure through Strange Realms—Literary Worldbuilding in Tolkien, Jordan and Williams

Patrick Schmitz (Alsdorf)

> "It was a bright cold day in April, and the clocks were striking
> thirteen"   (Orwell 3)

Many first lines in the course of literary history have taken up their place within what reader-response theorists have called our *repertoire* (cf. Nodelman/Reimer 17), i.e. our knowledge of literature and life. Upon hearing or reading these and other lines of similar significance, we are reminded of the very works and their captivating characters, their respective plots and other details and characteristics. Similar to this readers of fantasy literature are prompted to take up residence in their beloved fictional worlds (cf. Herman 112) not only when reading first lines such as "In a hole in the ground there lived a Hobbit" (H 29), but also when 'entering' the first parts of the fictional worlds. Many of these—the Shire, Winterfell, the Hundred Acre Wood, etc.—are indispensable when it comes to the imagination of an enthusiastic readership. The paper at hand is meant to shed light on the structure and function of the introductory places to be found in three major works of fantasy literature, namely Tolkien's *The Lord of the Rings*, Jordan's *Wheel of Time* and Williams's *Memory, Sorrow and Thorn*. The role of the two concepts of familiarity and strangeness, which are fundamental to the creation of imaginary worlds, shall be connected to Harshav's Approach of *Constructive Poetics*. This theoretical background is to be applied to the presentation of the Shire, Emond's Field and Hayholt in the aforementioned works of fantasy literature.

The first question that needs to be answered before analysing these fictional realms in detail refers to the exact connection between worldbuilding in general and fantasy literature as such, which shall briefly be elucidated in this context. One of many ways to examine this connection is by following up on the ongoing debate flaring up time and again. While many scholars have already taken part in this discussion (cf. Mendlesohn/James 6), the definition still "rests in a … 'fuzzy set'" (Mendlesohn XIII) of features with different emphases. However, Colin Manlove's contributions, which have been presented and developed in some of his books and articles, reveal several basic principles that might help in understanding the relation mentioned above. The literary critic defines fantasy as a "fiction evoking wonder and containing a substantial and irreducible element of supernatural or impossible worlds, beings or objects with which the mortal characters in the story or the readers come on at least partly familiar terms" (Manlove 16). Without going so far as to call this the best definition, one has to admit that his words connect fantasy with fundamental concepts as 'wonder' and 'familiarity', which are at the heart of building a fictional world, while many other definitions superficially rest on the heavily quoted "departure from consensus reality" (Ekman 15). Keeping the high importance of 'wonder' and 'familiarity' in mind, it is surprising that comprehensive and comparative approaches to worldbuilding in fantasy literature, which rest on a solid theoretical groundwork, remain rare or neglected. And this is especially astonishing since several scholars have already stressed the role of imaginary worlds as the "heart of fantasy" (Swinfen 3) as well as their creation as a key concept of literary and artificial productivity (cf. Klenke et al. 9). Literary worldbuilding indeed plays a fundamental role in 'evoking wonder' and making the reader feel at home in an imaginary realm, at the same time satisfying the readers' "thirst for otherness" (Timmermann 2)—the latter a concept that Manlove did not actively incorporate into his definition.

One scholar, who has published about this matter and simultaneously created "a marvelous example of world building" (Saler 32), is—of course—J.R.R. Tolkien. In his essay *On Fairy-stories*, the author talks about his concept of Sub-creation and connects our Primary World to imaginary Secondary Worlds as well as to additional aspects as for instance 'enchantment' and 'Secondary Belief'. For Tolkien, it is essential that an author creates an image of a world in a way that guarantees its acceptance (cf. FS 35), readability (cf. FS 52) and the enchantment of the readership (cf. FS 64). Central are furthermore the notions of familiarity and strangeness (cf. FS 60), the latter of which Tolkien e.g. adequately links to Chesterton's famous "Mooreffoc" (FS 68) and the idea of recovery, i.e. "the regaining of a clear view" (FS 59), perhaps the re-enchantment of our own reality through fantasy literature. Familiarity in works of fantasy helps to invite the reader into a secondary world by "underscoring the distance between readers and characters" (Bowman 281) in providing a firm foothold in our own horizon of experience (cf. Swinfen 76). This familiarity is most often realised by very similar natural laws (sometimes only violated by the existence of magic) or by direct references to the reader's actual-world encyclopedia (cf. Doležel 177). Strangeness, on the other hand, could be "a novum ... deviating from the reader's norm" (Suvin 80), such as talking beasts (cf. FS 36) or the depiction of a distant time (cf. FS 34), thus renewing or refreshing our impression of our own surroundings (cf. Swinfen 6). Nevertheless, the balance between both ends of a continuum should be taken into consideration, as too much familiarity might endanger the enchantment of fantasy, while too much strangeness could render entering an imaginary world difficult. Hence, a secondary world should be "familiar but not too familiar, strange but not too strange" (Kocher 147). With these fundamental thoughts and concepts kept in mind, one could venture to approach another central issue of "critical world-building" (Ekman & Taylor 15), i.e. to analyse the structure and details of a given imaginary world. In this respect, Tolkien emphasised that "the realm of fairy-story is wide and deep and filled with many things" (FS 27). Paired with the fact that "finite texts … are bound to create incomplete worlds" (Doležel 169), this leads us to the assumption that the (generic) signals and cues within a given piece of fantasy literature are—of course—deliberately chosen (cf. Doležel 170) to support a reader in reconstructing an image of the world created by its author(s) (cf. Nünning 191). This, in turn, suggests the analysis of the overall structure of a secondary world—the macro-structure—as well as that of minute textual cues navigating our imagination—the micro-structure. One first step towards analysing the structure of a fictional world has been made by Benjamin Harshav in his *Constructive Poetics*, an approach that has been taken up favourably by critics (cf. Porter). Although the approach surely has its shortcomings, especially when it comes to the terminology and application to the micro-level, as will be pointed out later, it surely helps to deduce some further assumptions about the creation of secondary worlds. Harshav underlines that a work of literature "projects … one Internal Field of Reference (IFR) to which meanings in the text are related" (Harshav 12). This network of interrelated concepts, as characters, events or dialogues, is set parallel to our real world, the External Field of Reference (ExFR) (cf. Harshav 37). Harshav further subdivides the Internal Field of Reference into a "multitude of contextual, crisscrossing, and interrelated" (Harshav 6) frames of reference (fr), i.e. a semantic continuum (cf. Harshav 5). A frame of reference could be a character, a plot, a forest or a district of London. This frame is—in turn—made up of a certain number of referents "may it be a real object, an event, an idea, or a fictional, non-existent object" (Harshav 5). Every one of these three layers is permeable as the addition of further details might transform a referent (r) into a frame of reference (cf. Harshav 5) and so on. Besides this partition, representing the structuredness of a (fictional) world, Harshav puts emphasis on the fact that referents or whole frames of reference are regularly taken from External Fields and integrated into Internal ones (cf. Harshav 29), without altering them. This indeed affects the quality of familiarity of a piece of literature. As opposed to this, some elements from the ExFr are obviously changed upon being incorporated into a fictional world increasing the level of strangeness, as it were (cf. Harshav 25). In this context, the referent 'George Washington' of the frame of reference [American politician] or [Presidents of the United States of America] could be taken from the External Field of Reference unmodified or not. Harshav, however, does not elaborate on the categorisation of fictional referents as [King Arthur]. Owing to this, we are left to decide, whether these belong to the External or a distinct Internal Field of Reference separated from the one that is currently analysed or, as a third option, if it could be used to create a third Field of Reference.

This could be called an Intertextual Field of Reference holding all those fictional referents and frames of reference that have entered our culturally shared fictional encyclopedia. Finally, the scholar points out that an actual existence is not ascribed to fictional referents through this approach (cf. Harshav 132). In putting emphasis on this circumstance, Harshav joins the ranks of other theorists (esp. classical segregationists) (cf. Pavel 13).

As to put the value and usefulness of this model to test, the approach shall be applied to Tolkien's Shire, Jordan's Emond's Field as well as William's Hayholt. The results are also to be presented within the context of the influence of familiarity and strangeness on the respective structures as elaborated on further above. Benjamin Harshav calls these first frames, the reader comes across right at the beginning of a book, "referential grounding" (Harshav 134). As a landing point (cf. Suvin 411) for the readers 'transport' into an imaginary world, they provide a "baseline reality" (Salo 25). In doing this, they also supply the readership with a familiar fundament to which later frames might be compared. They could furthermore be considered an anchor for both readers and characters after having ventured into the exotic, enchanting realms that are part of the respective secondary worlds. Hence, these referential frames serve the purpose of attracting interest—as in all types of media—, easing the crossing into the strange world and setting up a boundary to later frames, an aspect that Lotman similarly observed in the case of myths and medieval literature (cf. Lotman 305), two ingredients that surely simmer in Tolkien's *Cauldron of Story* (cf. FS 11). The Shire as the first and most famous of the three referential frames is widely thought of as the typical idyllic, pastoral, late 19th century English countryside (cf. e.g. Nagel 34; Salo 25 etc.). Although Curry incorrectly states that "Englishness is not inscribed in the text" (Curry 21), a close analysis of the material stresses the importance of this quality. Tolkien incorporated several frames of reference into his first chapters that help in modifying the level of familiarity, resulting in an easier access to his world (cf. Fimi 185). This very effect is realised by various frames as for example [names] comprising referents such as 'Baggins' or 'Took', [cultural practices], e.g. represented by the traditional concept of 'tea-time' (cf. H 36), as well as the fr [food] with referents as "porter" (H 40), "scones" (H 40) or "seed-cake" (H 38). All of these and others more or less add to the Britishness of the Shire. Apart from this, the seclusion of these regions (cf. Honegger 65) and the apparent ordinariness of its inhabitants support the readers in clearing this – admittedly very low – hurdle into Middle-earth further lowered by Tolkien's chapter "Concerning Hobbits". Especially the attitude of the Hobbits towards strangeness is significant in this respect, as they face "a strange outside world with much the same sense of alienation as the reader" (Salo 25). They are proud of calling their home region a "safe and comfortable ... foothold" (LotR I 62), where "everything seemed quiet and peaceful" (91). The Hobbits seclude themselves from the wide world outside and "meddled not at all with events" (5) outside their sheltered homes. This impression is further stressed by statements as "Elves and Dragons! … Cabbages and potatoes are better for me and you" (24), again revealing the Hobbits' plainness and earthiness (cf. Flieger XIII). In addition to that rejection of outer strangeness, the Hobbits convey their distrust of the inhabitants of the Shire every now and then. The people in Buckland "are so queer" (LotR I 22) and the Brandybucks are "a queer breed" (22). Therefore, Hobbiton—the landing point of the readership—is obviously constructed as the insular heart of the Shire, and those places closer to Faerie, which the characters and readers come across later on, are clearly 'pushed away' to their literal boundaries of perception for now. However, in order to increase the enchantment and appeal that has already been called forth by the peaceful and romantic landscapes, Tolkien added a dash of strangeness to his Shire. Yet, this quality remains all in all carefully managed. We find referents within the frame [names] that are less likely part of the pool of British names as 'Belladonna' (H 30) or even 'Tobold' (LotR I 8) and 'Sancho' (39), but still close to other names to be found in the ExFr. Still, Tolkien moves closer along the edges of the reader's encyclopedia by e.g. using Welsh terms as 'Gorhendad' (98), providing a deeper level of detail, or supplying additional pieces of information as in "Fornost, or Norbury as they called it" (9). The latter example also shows that Tolkien attempts to move some referents closer to the reader's ExFr to facilitate access into his imaginary world. He moreover actively links referents from his Internal Field to the ExFr as in the case of 'Golfimbul', the goblin leader, and 'golf', the sport (H 48), thus inducing a re-mystification at the same time. Owing to this, Tolkien's referential grounding remains acceptable to the reader, who can refer to their fictional encyclopedia (cf. Doležel 178) to cope with stranger elements as dwarves or wizards entering Tolkien's version of a "rural English landscape" (Moorcock 46). Later on, a retrieval of entries as 'Balrog' or 'Ent' may work out less easily and has to be prepared and accompanied more thoroughly.

Similar strategies may be found in Robert Jordan's referential grounding within his *Wheel of Time* series, Emond's Field. Other than in Tolkien's oeuvre, the reference to the ExFr based on [Britishness] is far less obvious and many referents to be found in the first chapters remain unmarked. Nevertheless, Jordan used the names of the inhabitants of the village to contribute to the necessary notion of familiarity. Slightly modified versions of names known from the ExFr, as for instance 'Tam' (Jordan 2), 'Abell' (92) or 'Daise' (8) and 'Bili' (40) create a contrast to stranger names as 'Aginor' (14) or 'Thakan'dar' (108) from outside these first frames. Much like the Shire, Emond's Field is secluded and described as an ordinary, peaceful place as well. So "outsiders never came into the Two Rivers" (23), which is generally regarded the "back end of forever" (29) as opposed to the "world outside … [that] is nothing like" (126) it. This character of seclusion and ordinariness is spiced up by the enrichment of different frames with stranger, but recognisable referents to mark the border to our own reality. Referents of the fr [names] such as 'Nynaeve' (8), the Irish 'Cenn Buie' (7), and Dha'vol (146) or [creatures] as for example the infamous 'biteme' (146) or the 'Draghkar' (147) are textual cues that are obviously meant to support the reader in reconstructing the image of Jordan's world. Due to their reference to our Primary World it is easier to reconstrue Emond's Field "as conforming as far as possible to our representation" (Ryan 51) of our own reality, the ExFr. This assumption is connected to Ryan's *Principle of minimal departure* (cf. Ryan 51). Again, the transition between familiarity and strangeness is fluid. Yet, similar to the Shire, Emond's Field's ordinariness, seclusion and peace are disturbed both by strange incidents as unusual winter storms or stillborn lambs (cf. Jordan 7) and the intrusion of strange referents as the Myrddraal, Thom Merilin or the Aes Sedai. These, much like the referents Gandalf or Nazgûl, suggest the idea that both works are not pure *portal-quest fantasies* (cf. Mendlesohn XIX), but a mixed form combined with an *intrusion fantasy* (cf. Mendlesohn XXI).

The last exemplary referential grounding that is to be examined within the paper at hand is that of Hayholt from Tad Williams's series of *Memory, Sorrow and Thorn*. Other than the idyllic, pastoral and secluded regions of the Shire and the Two Rivers, Hayholt is presented as the ancient, somewhat mythic centre of a big, vibrant realm that is about to change in an extreme way due to the passing away of a long-lived, benevolent king. Due to its role as the king's seat, the level of ordinariness is—compared to that of the other two groundings— much weaker. This quality is rather transported by the main characters, whom the readers accompany at the beginning, above all Seoman/Simon, the kitchen boy. Familiarity is induced by several frames of reference, e.g. the fr [names], which is made up of Biblical names such as 'Simon' (Williams 4), 'Rachel' (4), 'Shem' (19) or 'Judith' (23). These names that belong to the inhabitants of Hayholt one comes across first are part of many different cultures to be found in our ExFr. The same motivation could be attested for the fr [place names] as Hayholt, which is even 'translated' as "High Keep" (5), "Erchester" (49) or "Swertclif" (74) reveal. These remain accessible for readers and—in spite of their slight alteration—still recognizable. A very striking example of a strategy meant to generate familiarity is one not included in Tolkien's or Jordan's referential groundings. Hence, Williams connects his fr [religion] within his Internal Field with the fr [Catholicism] from the ExFr. Many different referents and aspects strengthen this significant link. The readership learns about Usires Aedon (cf. 11), the son of God (cf. 79) and the Immaculate Elysia (cf. 48), who was executed by hanging from a tree (cf. 78f.), albeit upside-down. There is a Devil (cf. 14), Heaven (cf. 79) as well as Angels (cf. 16) and Archangels (cf. 156). The church knows a lot of different saints (cf. e.g. 35), the rite of anointment of rulers (cf. 73), bishops (cf. 49), mendicant friars (cf. 53) and even familiar-sounding mottos as "Duos Wulstei" (77). Again, this quality of familiarity is modified by a carefully managed level of strangeness. The inclusion of (partly) Old English [names] as "Helfcene" (58), "Deornoth" (72) or "Fengbald" (84) and "Lofsunu" (103) as well as "Sangfugol" (85) allude to Tolkien's demand concerning an "enchantment of distance, especially of distant time" (FS 34). Referents in the fr [months] as "Jonever" (Williams 74), "Avrel" (155) or "Maia" (179) seem strange at first glance but remain accessible and add to the impression of strangeness. Readers are still capable of finding their way within Erkynland. The same certainly holds true for the slight modification of the referents within the fr [weekdays], viz. "Drorsday" (41) or "Frayday" (50). Another interesting strategy in William's work is the very slight altering of traditional proverbs as 'idle hands are the Devil's workshop' into "[an] idle mind is the Devil's seedbed" (14) and others, contributing to the little less familiar character of the secondary world. Similar to the Shire and Emond's Field, Hayholt faces a changing world (cf. 50), yet without pushing these changes away by means of seclusion on the surface, mostly due to the tidings of King Elias and his dark and powerful advisor Pryrates. The 'Other' is already there below the surface level as "older citadels … lie buried beneath … [and] have stood here since before memories of mankind" (22), sleeping and waiting to rise below the feet of "castle boys" (155). Other than the Shire or Emond's Field, Williams's referential grounding is more frequently entered by Faerie, the latter being the literal fundament of the old castle. This makes Williams's grounding a melting pot of familiarity and strangeness, of "mundane world" (Ekman 99) and "Faerie, the mysterious land" (Ekman 99) to an arguably far greater extent than the other examples mentioned before. While both authors, Tolkien and Jordan, admittedly allow glances at the "vast backcloths" (Drout 4) of their respective worlds, these seem to be much closer to the surface in William's Hayholt.

What remains to be said about the referential grounding in the three works of fantasy literature examined within this paper is that—in addition to the exemplary strategies presented above—many frames also feature a certain geographical seclusion, both reflected in the respective texts (cf. LotR I 5; Jordan 55) and the maps provided with these. An incorporation of these materials elsewhere would indeed help on differentiating the results.

Ultimately, there is no denying the fact that the notions of strangeness and—especially—familiarity play a significant role in terms of the creation of the first frames of the Internal Fields within the three works. The implementation and enhancement of both notions are attained by means of different strategies e.g. comprising linguistic and cultural referents. However, one has to distinguish between a world-internal and -external familiarity and strangeness, since many readers may be capable of resorting to their fictional encyclopedia when facing dwarves, Sithi or other magical beings. The characters inside the Internal Fields however are largely unfamiliar with these creatures, which in turn affects the seclusion and pushing away of Faerie especially regarding the first frames. Harshav's approach, especially its terminology, used to structure the analysis of the referential groundings obviously needs to be expanded and combined with other theories in order to prove more helpful. Thus, the terminology for instance is still too imprecise, as there seems to be no distinction between the frames of reference [Shire], [names] or [place names]. At which exact point does a referent become a frame? What amount of information is decisive in this respect? Thus, a more comprehensive analysis would necessitate a differentiation of the group of frames by means of the results to be found in the work of Wolf or Ryan. In resorting to these authors one could identify the referents used in the books more explicitly and categorise them into clear-cut frames still referring to each other. In doing this it e.g. becomes obvious that Tolkien based his quality of familiarity—among other things—largely on a *linguistic compatibility* (cf. Ryan 33) as in the case of names, as well as on the *identity of properties* and *of inventory* (cf. Ryan 32), for instance. Additionally, one could resort to the approach of "world-architecture" (Ekman/Taylor, *Notes*) to methodise an analysis of a secondary world. The combination and revision of these and other approaches and their application to other referential groundings and those (geographical) frames that lie further within Faerie shall be conducted elsewhere and to a larger extent.

Bibliography

Bowman, Mary R. "The Story Was Already Written: Narrative Theory in *The Lord of the Rings.*" *Narrative* 14.3 (2006): 272-293

Curry, Patrick. *Defending Middle-earth – Tolkien: Myth and Modernity.* Boston/New York: Houghton Mifflin Company, 2004

Doležel, Lubomír. *Heterocosmica.* Baltimore: Johns Hopkins University Press, 1998

Drout, Michael. "Introduction – Reading Tolkien's Poetry". In: *Tolkien's Poetry.* Eds.: Julian T.M. Eilmann, Allan Turner. Zurich/Jena: Walking Tree Publishers, 2013, 1-9

Ekman, Stefan & Audrey Isabel Taylor. "Notes Toward a Critical Approach to Worlds and World-Building." In: *Fafnir* 3.3 (2016): 7-18

---. *Writing Worlds, Reading Landscapes: An Exploration of Settings in Fantasy.* Lund: Center for Languages and Literature, 2010

Fimi, Dimitra. *Tolkien, Race and Cultural History – From Fairies to Hobbits.* London: Palgrave Macmillan, 2010

Flieger, Verlyn. *Splintered Light – Logos and Language in Tolkien's World.* Kent: The Kent State University Press, 2002

Harshav, Benjamin. *Explorations in Poetics.* Stanford: Stanford University Press, 2007

Herman, David. *Basic Elements of Narrative.* Chichester: Wiley & Sons, 2009

Honegger, Thomas. "From Bag End to Lórien: the Creation of a Literary World." *News from the Shire and Beyond – Studies on Tolkien.* Eds.: Peter Buchs, Thomas Honegger. Zurich: Walking Tree Publishers, 2004

Jordan, Robert. *The Eye of the World.* London: Orbit, 2006

Klenke, Pascal et al. "Vorwort". In: *Writing Worlds – Welten- und Raummodelle der Fantastik.* Eds.: Pascal Klenke et al. Heidelberg: Universitätsverlag Winter, 2014, 9-12

Kocher, Paul. *Master of Middle-earth – The Achievement of J.R.R. Tolkien.* London: Pimlico, 2002.

Lotman, Jurij M. *Die Struktur literarischer Texte.* München: Wilhelm Fink Verlag, 1972

Manlove, Colin N. "On the Nature of Fantasy." In: *The Aesthetics of Fantasy Literature and Art.* Ed.: Roger C. Schlobin. Brighton: Harvester Press Limited, 1982, 16-35

Mendlesohn, Farah, & Edward James. *A Short History of Fantasy.* Faringdon: Libri Publishing, 2012

Mendlesohn, Farah. *Rhetorics of Fantasy.* Middletown: Wesleyan University Press, 2008

Moorcock, Michael. *Wizardry & Wild Romance – A Study of Epic Fantasy.* Austin: MonkeyBrain, 2004

Nagel, Rainer. *Hobbit Place-names – A linguistic Excursion through the Shire.* Zurich/Jena: Walking Tree Publishers, 2012

Nodelman, Perry, & Mavis Reimer. *The Pleasures of Children's Literature.* Boston: Allyn and Bacon, 2003

Nünning, Ansgar. "Making Events – Making Stories – Making Worlds: Ways of Worldmaking from a Narratological Point of View." In: *Cultural Ways of Worldmaking – Media and Narratives.* Eds.: Vera Nünning, Ansgar Nünning, Birgit Neumann. Berlin: Walter de Gruyter, 2010, 191-214

Orwell, George. *Nineteen Eighty-Four.* London: Penguin, 2000

Pavel, Thomas G. *Fictional Worlds.* Cambridge: Harvard University Press, 1986

Porter, Laurence M. "Review". In: *SubStance* 38.1 (2009): 154-160

Ryan, Marie-Laure. *Possible Worlds, Artificial Intelligence and Narrative Theory.* Bloomington: Indiana University Press, 1991

Saler, Michael. *As If – Modern Enchantment and the Literary Prehistory of Virtual Reality.* New York: Oxford University Press, 2012

Salo, David. "Heroism and Alienation through Language in *The Lord of the Rings*." In: *The Medieval Hero on Screen: Representations from Beowulf to Buffy*. Eds. Martha W. Driver, Sid Ray. Jefferson: McFarland, 2004, 23-37

Suvin, Darko. *Metamorphoses of Science Fiction – On the Poetics and History of a Literary Genre.* Ed. Gerry Canavan. Bern et al.: Peter Lang Verlag, 2016

Swinfen, Ann. *In Defence of Fantasy – A Study of the Genre in English and American Literature since 1945.* London: Routledge & Kegan Paul, 1984

Timermann, John H. *Other Worlds – The Fantasy Genre.* Bowling Green: Bowling Green University Popular Press: 1983

Tolkien, John Ronald Reuel. *On Fairy-stories.* Eds.: Verlyn Flieger, Douglas A. Anderson. London: HarperCollins, 2004

---. *The Annotated Hobbit.* Ed.: Douglas A. Anderson. London: HarperCollins, 2003

---. *The Fellowship of the Ring. Being the First Part of The Lord of the Rings.* London: HarperCollins, 2005

Williams, Tad. *The Dragonbone Chair. Book One of Memory Sorrow and Thorn.* New York: DAW Books, 1989

The Writer as a Scribe:
Sub-creation in J.R.R. Tolkien and J.L. Borges

Natalia González de la Llana (Aachen)

To Anette, for her kindness

1. Introduction

Roland Barthes reminded us in a well-known article[1] that the author is a modern figure, the product of a society which has discovered the prestige of the individual. In primitive societies, narrative is never undertaken by a person, but by a mediator, a shaman or speaker, whose "performance" may be admired, but not his "genius".

In this paper, we would like to focus precisely on a comparative analysis of Jorge Luis Borges' and J.R.R. Tolkien's concept of the author as a transmitter or scribe. This concept turns the originality of a work into a rather unimportant issue, while leaving space for a dialogue with literary works of the past. Intertextuality can become therefore, as we shall see, an essential basis for sub-creation.

However, even though these two writers may show some parallels in their ideas about authorship and the process of creating fiction, there are also differences in the meaning or intention which they profess to attach to their stories. The last part of this essay will try to find a link between their *Weltanschauung* and their preference for low and high fantasy respectively as a means to incarnate it in literature.

2. The Writer as a Scribe

2.1. J.L. Borges

In a conference at the Collège de France in 1983 (Borges, *Conferencia*), Borges spoke about two opposing theories of poetic creativity. One of them would be Allan Poe's, who saw it as an intellectual act. Borges disagrees completely with

---

1   "… dans les sociétés ethnographiques, le récit n'est jamais pris en charge par une personne, mais par un médiateur, shaman ou récitant, dont on peut à la rigueur admirer la «performance» (c'est à dire la maîtrise du code narratif), mais jamais le «génie». L'*auteur* est un personnage moderne, produit sans doute par notre société dans la mésure où, au sortir du Moyen Age, avec l'empirisme anglais, le rationalisme français, et la foi personnelle de la Réforme, elle a découvert le prestige de l'individu, ou, comme on dit plus noblement, de la «personne humaine»." (Barthes 491)

him. The other one, which is dearer to the Argentinian author, is represented by the old idea of inspiration, the idea of the poet as a secretary, as someone who takes dictation from an unknown force; or also by what W.B. Yeats called "great memory", the belief that in each of us our ancestors' memories lie, and therefore a poet cannot be reduced to his personal reality.

The influence of the *Bible* in this sense is explicit in Borges's view, who declares in an interview with María Esther Vázquez, that he may have gained access to literature through the Holy Spirit, a translation of the Hebrew *Ruach Ha-kodesh*, which is associated with the divine inspiration of the Scriptures. As Aizenberg points out, Borges is impressed by the *Bible's* conception of the writer not as a creator, but as a scribe; not as an inventor, but as a transmitter of something which comes from the outside. In the case of the biblical writer, it is God who supplies the substance for the book. In Borges's case, it is Literature, his precursors' productions, which dictate what he must write, although his idea that writing is transcribing can be better understood as a metaphor of intertextuality. Literature is for him a palimpsest, in which the writer's individuality contributes only as the imperfect prism of that which he is passing on (Aizenberg 68-72).

This view, Aizenberg says, claims for the elimination of subjectivity as source and content of artistic creativity, because the author's main task is not to display his personality, but to produce a work of art. Borges defends also a unitary vision of literature which deals with the eternal topics of the past and is expressed through a brief and synthetic style. As those who proposed the idea of the *Ruach Ha-kodesh*, he believed in the supremacy of the written word over those who wrote it (Aizenberg 73f.).

The eternal topics for Borges's works are to be found in literature, philosophy, theology. Sometimes it is the reading of a text which induces him to write. Other times, it is a thought or an idea, like the notion of eternity (see Borges, *Conferencia*).

The *Cabbala* is known to have had a strong influence on him as well, though his interest was more aesthetic than religious. He felt attracted by the idea of a sacred book, divinely inspired, which is subject to eternal speculation and endless interpretation. Aspects of the *Cabbala* which have most clearly found an echo in Borges's fiction, as Evelyn Fishburn affirms, can be seen in stories connected primarily with the act of writing such as *The Writing of the God*, *The Library of Babel* and *The Immortal*:

> "El inmortal" concerns a narrative text, a *cento*, which is symbolic of literature in that it is made up of different extracts of previous text woven around re-enactments of the Odyssey and other tales of eternal quests. It is full of quotations, some intratextual, of other writings by Borges such as "Princess Lucinge", a reference

to a character mentioned in "Tlön"; others, intertextual, to wide-ranging allusions from Ecclesiastes to Shaw and others, unsaid, glaring from the empty spaces of suggestion, such as the absent presence of Swift's immortal Struldbruggs. An important clue to the significance of intertextuality can be found in "la tenacísima pluma del doctor Nahum Cordovero", the commentator of this enigmatic text. This choice of name is significant: Moses Cordovero was one of the most original exponents of Cabbala as a *theory of influences,* seeing every existing thing as endlessly correlated with the whole of creation. He was unique among the masters of Cabbala in seeking to explain the contradiction between a static, eternal Deity and its active worldly manifestation as a dialectical interplay between different images of God's presence. Such a "theory of influence" underpins, in a lay setting, the theme of "El inmortal" which deals with the same yet changing manifestations of an eternal author and his text. The fact that the narrator of the text should be called Joseph Cartaphilus adds meaning to this Cabbalistic (mis)interpretation. Cartaphilus was the name by which Joseph of Arimathea was known in one mediaeval legend of the Wandering Jew, according to which he taunted Christ on the way to the Cross and was condemned to roam the earth until the Second Coming. The figure of the Wandering Jew, here recalled, was itself the subject of various legends, and became the inspiration of many works of literature.

The quests in "El inmortal", that of Odysseus and of the Wandering Jew, both mirror and reinforce each other as an illustration of literature, or what Bloom calls "the always wandering meaning of all literary representations" (1975: 82), Borges has said something similar more simply: "Quizá la historia universal es la historia de la diversa entonación de algunas metáforas" and "Tengo pocas ideas, pero las disfrazo".   (Fishburn 415f.)

But, if the author is a scribe who repeats a few everlasting ideas or metaphors, and the text is composed by a myriad of other texts, what about the reader? For Borges the reader's role is that of interpreting literary works, knowing that it is impossible to find a true meaning through language, as well as it is impossible to understand the universe.

Pablo Martín Ruiz proposes precisely the Scripture and the detective story as reading models for Borges's fiction. The detective story implies rigour and a careful planning of the plot, but above all, a new way of reading which has to do with suspicion, the paranoid reading of someone who tries to avoid being deceived. Borges turns also to the *Cabbala*, as we have seen, because it leads the reading process to its limits. The identification between sacred text and literature is constant in the Argentinian author, the first one being a model for the second one as a source for different interpretations. Borges's reader must be therefore very careful not to be misled by false clues, as well as attentive for possible meanings which are not easy to apprehend.[2]

With Borges therefore, we find: the author as a scribe who transmits eternal themes in constant dialogue with the literature of the past; the *Bible* as literary model, a pluralistic and also unitary work inspired by the Spirit and inspiring never-ending interpretations; a reader who has to cooperate trying to find a hidden sense which eludes him again and again.

2.2. J.R.R. Tolkien

In his study about imaginary worlds, Mark J.P. Wolf (283f.) explains that for many authors sub-creation can be seen as a reflection of Creation, the Primary World. When writing about human creativity, they have interpreted the text from Genesis, in which God creates human beings in His own image, to indicate that our desire to create is part of what it means to be made as *imago Dei*.

Or as Tolkien puts it in *On Fairy-stories*: "Fantasy remains a human right: we make in our measure and in our derivative mode, because we are made: and not only made but made in the image and likeness of a Maker" (FS 66).

However, both creator and sub-creator are not on the same level, if we believe what Pope Johannes Paul II wrote to artists substituting the word "craftsman" for "subcreator": the creator conceives something out of nothing, a way of operating which belongs only to God, while the craftsman uses something that already exists, to which he gives form and meaning, the mode peculiar to man. Differing as it does from *ex nihilo* creation, Wolf upholds that sub-creation does not usurp the Creator's role, but is rather a cooperation and acknowledgement of it. The sub-creative desire is part of human nature, and the action and contemplation that accompanies it are both a gift and a part of a divinely-mandated vocation to carry on what God has begun (Wolf 284-286).

In his poem *Mythopoeia*, Tolkien also describes man as "subcreator, the refracted light/through whom is splintered from a single White/ to many hues, and endlessly combined/ in living shapes that move from mind to mind" (My

---

2　"A partir de esta doble experiencia en tanto lectores, podemos postular que Borges es también el inventor de un nuevo tipo de lector. Un lector que, para simplificarlo en un esquema, surge de combinar los procedimientos de la exégesis religiosa, que confieren potencialmente sentido plural a cada parte del texto, con la desconfianza y suspicacia del lector del género policial, que trata de anticiparse a las trampas que el escritor de policiales le tiende." (Martín Ruiz)

87). Human beings are therefore here described as capable of inventing worlds, functioning like a kind of prism which takes in God's light and redirects it.

Another well-known text by Tolkien which deals with the topic of sub-creation is his story *Leaf by Niggle*. In this tale, the artist Niggle paints a canvas of a great tree, investing all his time and energy in it. However, it is a huge task, and his mundane duties prevent him from finishing his work.

As a sub-creator made in the image of God, Niggle learns that he must relate to Creation as God relates to it: help and sacrifice for those around him. Only then can he follow his artistic calling. In the new country where he goes, Niggle recognises his own tree, finished and come alive, and says: "It's a gift!" and the narrator adds: "He was referring to his art, and also to the result; but he was using the word quite literally" (LN 94). In other words, Niggle's ability to paint is not merely a talent he possesses, something he can take pride in, but a true gift by God, and likewise the completed painting must be appraised (see Hammond 6f.). Tolkien had both a high estimation of the artists' worth and a humble assessment of their indebtedness. He knew that their accomplishments were a present, originating elsewhere and transmitted through themselves. An artist, however, cannot grasp more than is offered, and can become frustrated if he cannot achieve his goals. On the other side, good art has lasting value, even if an artwork may be incomplete (Hammond 10f.).

In his *Letters*, it is also possible to see this concept of the author as a mediator, for example, when he relates how someone once questioned him:

> 'Of course, you don't suppose, do you, that you wrote all that book yourself?' … I think I said: 'No, I don't suppose so any longer.' I have never since been able to suppose so. An alarming conclusion for an old philologist to draw concerning his private amusement. But not one that should puff any one up who considers the imperfections of 'chosen instruments', and indeed what sometimes seems their lamentable unfitness for the purpose.   (L 413)

And also in the same letter afterwards, when he speaks of a missive he has received from a reader:

> … but you', he said, 'create a world in which some sort of faith seems to be everywhere without a visible source, like light from an invisible lamp'. I can only answer: 'Of his own sanity no man can securely judge. If sanctity inhabits his work or as a pervading light illumines it then it does not come from him but through him. And neither of you would perceive it in these terms unless it was with you also.'   (L 413)

Tolkien understands, therefore, the ability to sub-create as a gift and as a vocation to fulfil a task (which has to be combined with other daily duties), to humbly cooperate with the real Creator as His instrument. Even if Tolkien's works do not speak about religion, the *eucatastrophe* at which he aims in his fantasy narrative may provoke in the reader a joy experienced as "a sudden glimpse of the underlying reality or truth" which may be a "far-off gleam or echo of *evangelium* in the real world" (FS 77). And this is only possible because, as he implies in the letter quoted before, there is something inside the readers which seems to resound with the stories.

3. Literary Creation and Intertextuality

3.1. J.L. Borges

As we have seen, a traditional understanding of originality does not play an essential role in Borges's vision. For him, intertextuality is at the centre of the literature he wants to write. Many of his stories quote existing references and authors, as well as false ones, mix fictional and non-fictional genres, recreate old stories or ideas. In *Pierre Menard, Author of the Quixote*, for instance, a tale which pretends to be an essay of literary criticism, a French author wants to rewrite *Don Quixote* with the exact same words as Cervantes:

> El método inicial que imaginó era relativamente sencillo. Conocer bien el español, recuperar la fe católica, guerrear contra los moros o contra el turco, olvidar la historia de Europa entre los años de 1602 y de 1918, *ser* Miguel de Cervantes. Pierre Menard estudió ese procedimiento (sé que logró un manejo bastante fiel del español del siglo XVII) pero lo descartó por fácil... Ser en el siglo XX un novelista popular del siglo XVII le pareció una disminución. Ser, de alguna manera, Cervantes y llegar al *Quijote* le pareció menos arduo —por consiguiente, menos interesante— que seguir siendo Pierre Menard y llegar al *Quijote*, a través de las experiencias de Pierre Menard.   (Borges, *Menard* 534)[3]

---

3   "Initially, Menard's method was to be relatively simple: Learn Spanish, return to Catholicism, fight against the Moor or Turk, forget the history of Europe from 1602 to 1918—*be* Miguel de Cervantes. Pierre Menard weighed that course (I know he pretty thoroughly mastered seventeenth-century Castilian) but he discarded it as too easy... To be a popular novelist of the seventeenth century in the twentieth seemed to Menard to be a diminution. Being, somehow, Cervantes, and arriving thereby at the Quixote—that looked to Menard less challenging (and therefore less interesting) than continuing to be Pierre Menard and coming to the Quixote *through the experiences of Pierre Menard*." (Borges, *Fictions* 91)

The narrator, a critic who comments Menard's work, affirms afterwards:

> ... el fragmentario *Quijote* de Menard es más sutil que el de
> Cervantes. Éste, de un modo burdo, opone a las ficciones cabal-
> lerescas la pobre realidad provinciana de su país; Menard elige
> como "realidad" la tierra de Carmen durante el siglo de Lepanto
> y de Lope.   (Borges, *Menard* 536)[4]

In other words, Menard transforms Cervantes's text without changing anything
of the original, making it richer and more interesting with its anachronism,
so the critic tells us. In this way, according to Beatriz Sarlo, Borges destroys
the idea of the fixed identity of a text, the idea of author, and that of original
writing. Meaning is constructed in a space between the moment of writing
and the moment of reading (Sarlo 78f.). The fact that Menard has written his
text in the 20th century gives his phrases, which are identical to Cervantes's, a
completely different sense than the one they have in the novel of the Spanish
author. The reader becomes the author. Each era and each reader, the story says
to us, write their own reading of a literary work.

However, what we see in this tale, this serious game with intertextuality, is
not an exception in Borges's work, but its fundament. Borges uses themes and
motifs from different literary and philosophical traditions, classical mythology,
Hebrew literature, Buddhistic thought, etc.

We find another example in *The Gospel According to Mark*, where Borges
presents one of the recurrent topics of his works, the crucifixion of Christ, and
raises the problem of a too faithful reading (of the *Bible*). Baltasar Espinosa,
the main character of the story, whose description shows reminiscences of
Jesus, goes to spend some time on a ranch where he begins reading the Gospel
to the Gutres, the foreman and his family. They listen to him attentively and,
interpreting what they hear literally, they finally decide to crucify Espinosa. In
this text, we can also find the repeatedly quoted passage that men have always
told two stories: that of a lost ship which searches the Mediterranean seas for
a dearly loved island, and that of a god who is crucified on mount Golgotha
(Borges, *Evangelio* 514), stressing again the belief in literature as rewriting.

The narrative of Jesus is at the centre of *Three Versions of Judas* as well, a
tale in the form of an essay where the theological theories of Nils Runeberg
are analysed in detail. The last one of them proposes the idea that God was
incarnate not in Jesus, but in Judas. Borges offers here a new interpretation of
the Passion, a "Christological fantasy", as he calls it, in which he uses different

---

4   "... Menard's fragmentary Quixote is more subtle than Cervantes'. Cervantes crudely
     juxtaposes the humble provincial reality of his country against the fantasies of the
     romance, while Menard chooses as his 'reality' the land of Carmen during the century
     that saw the Battle of Lepanto and the plays of Lope de Vega." (Borges, *Fictions* 93)

theological thoughts and quotes from the *Bible* to prove an absurd thesis, showing thus at the end of the story that man cannot penetrate the divine mystery (see González de la Llana 4-7).

Ana María Barrenechea is of the opinion that the conviction that the world is a chaos, impossible to reduce to any human law, is probably the most important of Borges's concerns, even if he recognises that he cannot help but try to find a meaning. More than trying to find a solution which he already knows to be condemned to failure, Barrenechea says, the Argentinian writer comments or re-elaborates the literary and philosophical solutions with greater imaginative power to communicate the drama or the magic of the human destiny (Barrenecha 39).

We can so affirm that Borges, aware of the fact that we cannot understand the universe, turns to the old (literary, philosophical, theological) stories playing with their characters, motifs and beliefs, recreating them, taking them to their last consequences. His works are based in a deep intertextuality which gives readers and their interpretations a central role, years before the literary studies about reader-reception began to originate.

Rejecting any systematic thought because it leads inevitably into a trap, to dogmatism, Borges explores the literary possibilities of philosophy or religion as an intellectual, but also as a sentimental path: "En ese cuento, y lo espero de todos mis cuentos, hay una parte intelectual y otra -más importante, según creo-, el sentimiento de la soledad, de la angustia, de la inutilidad, del carácter misterioso del universo, del tiempo, y lo que es más importante: de nosotros mismos, para decirlo de una buena vez: de mí mismo"[5] (Charbonnier 16).

3.2. J.R.R. Tolkien

In his analysis of narrative models in Tolkien's stories of Middle-earth, Jaume Albero explains that Tolkien's fiction is built on the foundations of traditional narrative forms and is far off from the literary trends of his time. The British author found inspiration in myths and sagas from the past, but never claimed any patent of originality. His search for literary models turned him into an artist who recreated more than he created, reformulating the narrative materials from tradition (Albero 20).

In *The Lord of the Rings*, for instance, we can find two kinds of intertextuality with other texts: one in which there is a connection with works by other authors who inspired and influenced Tolkien, and one which makes reference

---

5   In that tale, and I hope the same of all my tales, there is an intellectual part and another one—more important, or so I think—, the feeling of solitude, of anguish, of uselessness, of the mysterious character of the universe, of time and, what is more important: of ourselves, to say it directly: of myself. (My translation)

to his own works (*The Lord of the Rings, The Hobbit, The Silmarillion*) as part of a single worldbuilding.

Intertextuality as the basis of literary creativity appears also in his essay *On Fairy-stories*, when Tolkien speaks about the origins of fairy stories. Many investigators of folklore, says the British author, are inclined to say that any two stories that are built around the same folklore motif, or are made up of a generally similar combination of such motifs, are "the same stories". But this is not true in art or literature, because it is the individual details of a story and the general purport that really count. Quoting Dasent, Tolkien affirms: "We must be satisfied with the soup that is set before us, and not desire to see the bones of the ox out of which it has been boiled", understanding the soup as the story as it is served up by its author, and the bones as its sources or material (FS 39f.).

The Pot of Soup, Tolkien continues in his essay, the Cauldron of Story has always been boiling, and to it new bits have continually been added. The fairy-tale element does not rise or fall, but is there, in the Cauldron of Story, waiting for the great figures of Myth and History, and for the nameless people, waiting for the moment when they are cast into the simmering stew (FS 44-6).

Therefore, similarly to Borges, Tolkien's view of literary creation is not grounded in the idea of creating something completely new, which does not mean, of course, that authors are repeating the same stories again and again in a mechanical way. As Tolkien very clearly shows, many of the elements come from that cauldron of stories. They are not new nor original in this sense, but the authors play an important role: they are the cooks, and their selection is important.

In one of the many studies dedicated to Tolkien's sources, Gloriana St. Clair says:

> That Tolkien knew Norse mythology and literature is clear, that he used these works as a source of inspiration for the matter of Middle-earth is also apparent. But everything he used is changed and altered to meet the demands and needs of his original creation. Pieces of story, bits of character, descriptions of implements, themes and motifs, manners and customs are all borrowed, but nothing is left unaltered. In each instance, Tolkien changes materials to serve the needs of his own stories.   (St. Clair 3)

Tolkien, then, borrowed many elements which were already there, but he also altered them to fulfil his own literary purposes, to give his own message of hope, as for him the Consolation of a Happy Ending is one of the most important aspects of fairy tales. The *eucatastrophe* is what he even sees as the highest function of these kinds of stories. This joy, however, does not deny the existence of *dyscatastrophe*, as he explains, of sorrow and failure. What it denies is universal final defeat, and in so far is *evangelium* (FS 75).

Unlike Borges, who believed the universe to be an incomprehensible chaos, Tolkien's vision of the world is Christian, and he thinks, as we commented before, that "the peculiar quality of the 'joy' in successful Fantasy can thus be explained as a sudden glimpse of the underlying reality or truth", that in the *eucatastrophe* we can possibly see an echo of *evangelium* in the real world. The Gospels also contain in his view a fairy story, but a story which has entered History and the primary world: the birth of Christ being the eucatrastrophe of Man's history (FS 78).

As Verlyn Flieger affirms, for Tolkien the story of Christ is the greatest fairy story of them all because for him it is not fiction, but fact. It does not come from imagination, but from recorded history. It has bridged the gap between primary and secondary worlds and fulfilled in Creation mankind's desire for Escape and Consolation, with the possibility of looking forward to the final Happy Ending. This is the ultimate joyous "turn" of the eucatastrophe, the sudden grace, a kind of conversion which we experience as readers (see Flieger 29).

If Tolkien, similarly to Borges, seems to renounce the idea of originality and turns for inspiration to older stories, seeing himself as a kind of instrument of something greater, there is a very significant difference between both writers. Tolkien looks for the truth within his works, while the Argentinian author does not believe in the possibility of understanding the world, of coming to a conclusion about the truth. Tolkien tries to open a door for his readers, with the help of old myths and legends, so that they can wonder about God and his Creation. Borges plays seriously with theories, motifs and stories from the past, even if he has no answer to offer, because posing questions is the only thing that human beings can do.

4. Different Fantasies, Different Goals

Among the many theories of fantastic literature, there is a tendency to distinguish between two big categories: the fantastic (low fantasy) and the marvelous (high fantasy). Even if the presence of a supernatural phenomenon is essential in both kinds, the respective relationship between the supernatural and reality is what makes the difference.

In fantastic literature there has to be a similar room to the one that the reader inhabits, a room which will be assaulted by a phenomenon which will provoke its instability. The laws of a world similar to ours (the primary world) are therefore broken by something inexplicable and inexistent according to those laws. That is why fantastic literature always means a threat to our reality. If, on the contrary, there is no breach in the structures of our world, if a story does not include the problem of what is real and what is not, we are confronted, like in the case of fairy stories, with the marvelous (Roas 8-10).

But there is also a modern development of fantastic literature which some critics have called the neo-fantastic. David Roas explains that, for him, what characterises the contemporary fantastic is the invasion of the abnormal in an apparently normal world, in order not to demonstrate the evidence of the supernatural or the possibility that reality goes beyond rational knowledge, like in the 19th century, but to propose that reality may be abnormal. So, more than understanding the neo-fantastic as different from the traditional fantastic, this author sees in it a new stage in relation to a different notion of man and the world: while the romantics expressed the problematic of explaining the world rationally, the 20th century has evolved into a conception of the world as irreality (Roas 37-40).

This is exactly what we see in Borges, one of the classical authors of the neo-fantastic: reality is incomprehensible for the human intelligence, but that does not prevent human beings from inventing theories to explain it, be it through philosophy, religion or science. Reality is, therefore, a construct, a fiction. Many of his stories cannot but provoke uncertainty in the reader.

A good example of this can be found in *The Circular Ruins*, a short story in which a man tries to dream up another man and make him real. After a process of trial and error, he successfully creates him and gives him life with the help of the god Fire. Only the creator and the god know that the young man is not real, but just a dream. After some time, the dreamer hears about a fire spreading where his "son" is and is worried, because he could discover that he is just the projection of another one. A fire gets also to where he is, and the creator is ready to die, only to realise in the end that he too is but a dream.[6]

When speaking about the rhetoric of fantastic literature, Chen describes the typical discourse of the fantastic (what she calls mirror-discourse) as close to a nightmare. The mirror is taken metaphorically as rendering the real world seemingly unreal by the narration grounded in realism (Chen 253). On the other hand, the dream-discourse[7] includes the narrative type, i.e. myth, epic or saga. The creation of fantastic literature with dream-discourse is in essence

---

6   The confusion of dream and reality is precisely one of the themes which Borges mentions in his conferences about fantastic literature, in which he defends that there is a limited number of such themes, indicating, in his opinion, that fantastic literature cannot be arbitrary (Svensson 37-40). At his conference in Montevideo in 1949, Borges also affirms that fantastic literature does not pretend to avoid reality, but to express a deeper and more complex vision of it. This kind of fiction is destined more to offer metaphors of reality, by which the writer tries to transcend the superficial remarks of realism, than to escape to an unwarranted territory. That is why, for him, fantastic literature requires more lucidity and rigour, a greater stylistic demand than the simple copy of everyday reality (Rodríguez Monegal 188).

7   Apart from the dream-discourse and the mirror-discourse, Chen recognises a third pattern of the fantastic rhetoric: the magician's hat-discourse, which comprises stories that portray the unknown, but on a smaller and more fragmentary scale than the dream-discourse, for example, fairy tales, fantastic ballads, fables, supernatural tales, etc. (194f.)

teleological and is coupled, according to Chen, with musical imagination to harmonise into the state of *unus mundus*. In the dream-discourse, human beings dream of being attached to the Causality of all Becoming, through which all human nature and fate are related to gods/God and their/his relations with other gods or devils/Satan. Among the authors who continue this teleological depiction in modern times is, of course, Tolkien (Chen 207f.).

For Chen, works of fantasy are likely to be characterised as superficial, without psychological depth. But this is a bias generated from the intellectual and conscious stages of human conscious evolution. From the state of original participation, man perceives an existing unity with Nature. This stage arouses fantastic creation, centring on man embraced by the world and gods. A later evolution of consciousness towards science and intellect separates man from Nature, psychological literature being an outgrowth of it (Chen 231).

Tolkien tries to recover the truth which is behind the myths, where the universal memory lies, wishing at the same time to regain humanity's harmony with Nature. Through the narrative structure of an epic quest, the ideal of *unus mundus* is then accomplished. Borges, on the other hand, awakens readers from the so-called reality of the world and shows them the impossibility of understanding, leaving them in a state of hesitation.

Conclusions

In this paper, we have seen how two apparently very different authors like J.L. Borges and J.R.R. Tolkien share a similar vision about the role of the author and literary creativity. Borges was touched by the biblical idea of inspiration, the idea of the writer as a scribe, a transmitter of something greater than himself. Not being a religious man (although there are many discussions about what he believed or not), the source of his fictions is not God, but Literature, the literary works from the past. However, even if the author is just an instrument, and not a creator, he also contributes to the text. In his poem "John I, 14" (Borges, *Juan* 408), Borges says: "He encomendado esta escritura a un hombre cualquiera; / no será nunca lo que quiero decir, /no dejará de ser su reflejo",[8] proposing a very similar image to the one which Tolkien wrote in *Mythopoeia*, although the stress lies here more in the impossibility of transmitting a message through an imperfect medium. The limits of language and the inaccesibility of truth lead to a kind of literature which can only be an interpretation of theories, ideas and stories, taken to further endless interpretations.

---

8   I have entrusted this writing to the common man;/ it will never be what I want to say/ but only his reflection. (My translation)

For Tolkien, sub-creation is also a subordinate but essential role. The artist takes up this role as a consequence of his being created as *imago Dei*, and his task implies a gift and a divinely-mandated vocation to continue with God's work. The author is an instrument which can reveal an echo of the Gospels through his books, if he manages to provoke the *eucatastrophe*, a joy which resounds in the reader allowing him a glimpse of the truth.

This concept of creativity as transmission, this metaphor of the writer as a prism does not need to rely on originality to justify itself. Rewriting, rereading, reinterpreting is at the basis of Borges's stories, and plays such an important part that it is even, sometimes, the theme on which a story reflects, as is the case of „Pierre Menard, Author of the *Quixote*". Intertextualiy serves the Argentinian writer as a search for meaning in the tales of the past, although he knows that his search is in vain, as the world is incomprehensible for man. His exploration of the literary possibilities of philosophy or religion, in his understanding of them as fantastic literature, is also his way of expressing a feeling of loneliness and of the mysterious character of the universe.

Tolkien was also an author who recreated narrative materials from tradition, who selected and cooked the fairy elements that he found in the Cauldron of Story, but changing the old themes and motifs to serve the needs of his own works. Those needs have to do with a nearly religious purpose, his books being characterised by a constant which C.N. Manlove sees in fantasy in general: "its devotion to wonder at created things, and its profound sense that that wonder is above almost everything else a spiritual good not to be lost" (156).

In the previous pages, we have therefore realised that Borges and Tolkien have various important aspects in common in relation to their ideas about creativity. These ideas, however, take a very different form, which is connected to their individual *Weltanschauung*. Following his conception of the world as chaos, Borges chooses the rhetoric of the (neo)fantastic (or the mirror-discourse in Chen's terminology) to show the irreality of everything which surrounds us. Tolkien, on the other hand, develops his fantasy within the framework of the marvellous (the dream-discourse), trying to represent a state in which human beings are in harmony with Creation.

Bibliography

Aizenberg, Edna. *Borges, el tejedor del Aleph y otros ensayos*. Frankfurt am Main/Madrid, Vervuert/Iberoamericana, 1997

Albero Poveda, Jaume. "Narrative Models in Tolkien's Stories of Middle-earth." *Journal of English Studies*, volume 4 (2004): 7-20: https://publicaciones.unirioja.es/ojs/index.php/jes/article/view/84 [19.12.2017]

Barthes, Roland. "La mort de l'auteur." *Œuvres complètes*. Tome II, 1966-1973. Paris: Éditions du Seuil, 1994. 491-5

Barrenecha, Ana María. *La expresión de la irrealidad en la obra de Borges*. Buenos Aires: Centro Editor de América Latina. Bibliotecas Universitarias, 1984

Borges, Jorge Luis. *Collected Fictions*. Translation Andrew Hurley. New York: Penguin, 1999

---. "Conferencia dictada en el Collège de France en 1983." Cátedras de la Facultad de Ciencias Sociales, Universidad de Buenos Aires: http://www.catedras.fsoc.uba.ar/reale/conferencia-creacion-poetica.pdf [19.12.2017]

---. "El evangelio según Marcos." *Obras completas*. Tomo II. Buenos Aires: Emecé, 2007, 511-16

---. "Juan, I,14." *Obras completas*. Tomo II. Buenos Aires: Emecé, 2007, 407-8

---. "Pierre Menard, autor del *Quijote*." *Obras completas*. Tomo I. Buenos Aires: Emecé, 2007, 530-8

Charbonnier, Georges. *El escritor y su obra: entrevistas con Jorge Luis Borges*. México: Siglo XXI Editores, 2000

Chen, Fanfan. *Fantasticism. Poetics of Fantastic Literature*. Frankfurt am Main: Peter Lang, 2007

Fishburn, Evelyn. "Borges, Cabbala and 'Creative Misreading'." J.L. Borges Center for Studies & Documentation. (online 20.07.2001): http://www.borges.pitt.edu/bsol/evil.php [19.12.2017]

Flieger, Verlyn. *Splintered Light. Logos and Language in Tolkien's World*. Kent/London: The Kent State University Press, 2002

González de la Llana, Natalia. "Usos literarios de la religión: cuatro cuentos de Borges." *Tonos Digital. Revista de Estudios Filológicos* 22 (January 2012): http://www.tonosdigital.es/ojs/index.php/tonos/article/view/743/519 [19.12.2017]

Hammond, J. Samuel & Marie K. Hammond. "Creation and Sub-creation in *Leaf by Niggle*." *Inklings Forever* 7 (2010): http://library.taylor.edu/dotAsset/afcf88aa-52b7-4dda-8e6b-d5ef-d2e6b1f6.pdf [19.12.2017]

Manlove, Colin N. *The Impulse of Fantasy Literature*. Kent, Ohio: Kent State University Press, 1983

Martín Ruiz, Pablo. "De Almotásim a Abenjacán: dinámicas entre composición y lectura en la ficción de Borges." *Cuadernos LIRICO* [Online 23.01.2015]: http://lirico.revues.org/1961 [19.12.2017]

Roas, David. *Teorías de lo fantástico*. Madrid: Arco Libros, 2001

Rodríguez Monegal, Emir. "Borges: una teoría de la literatura fantástica." *Revista Iberoamericana* 95, vol. XLII, (April-June, 1976): https://revista-iberoamericana.pitt.edu/ojs/index.php/Iberoamericana/article/view/3101 [19.12.2017]

Sarlo, Beatriz. *Borges, un escritor en las orillas*. Buenos Aires: Ariel, 1995

St. Clair, Gloriana. *Tolkien's Cauldron: Northern Literature and* The Lord of the Rings. University Library Scholarships, January 2000: http://repository.cmu.edu/cgi/viewcontent.cgi?article=1067&context=lib_science [19.12.2017]

Svensson, Anna. "Borges en Gotemburgo: sobre su conferencia 'La literatura fantástica' y sus contactos con el Instituto Iberoamericano." *Anales Nueva Época* 11 (2008): 25-47: https://gupea.ub.gu.se/bitstream/2077/10436/1/gupea_2077_10436_1.pdf [19.12.2017]

Tolkien, J.R.R. "Leaf by Niggle." *Tree and Leaf.* London: Unwin Paperbacks, 1979

---. "Mythopoeia." *Tree and Leaf.* London: HarperCollins Publishers, 2001

---. *The Letters of J.R.R. Tolkien.* Ed.: Humphrey Carpenter, with the assistance of Christopher Tolkien. London/Boston/Sydney: George Allen & Unwin, 1981

---. *Tolkien On Fairy-stories.* Expanded edition, with Commentary and Notes. Eds.: Verlyn Flieger, Douglas A. Anderson. London: HarperCollins Publishers, 2014

Wolf, Mark J.P. *Building Imaginary Worlds. The Theory and History of Subcreation.* New York/London: Routledge, 2012

"The board is set, the pieces are moving"

Horrifying Armies of Darkness and their Function as Embodiments of Evil and Catalysts of Change within Subcreated Worlds

Franz Klug (Jena)

1. Introduction

"The board is set, the pieces are moving"—these words by Gandalf the wizard refer to the great war against the dark lord Sauron. As on a chess board the forces of light do battle against the armies of darkness. "Army of darkness" is a term used in the fantasy genre to refer to a force lead by a malevolent agency that consists of different monsters, demons, undead creatures and corrupted humans. Gandalf's words could be said to refer to and reflect the effect armies of darkness have on fantasy worlds. They act as catalysts of change within subcreated worlds and their moves subsequently affect the infrastructures of secondary worlds. Most importantly, they embody views on the nature of Evil and allow for a closer examination of Evil in theological and ethical terms. Thus, the analysis of how armies of darkness represent Evil as a concept forms a central part of my paper. First of all, I am going to analyse how J.R.R. Tolkien's armies of darkness are constructed and which existing concepts from the primary world might have inspired them. It shall also be demonstrated how, in turn, Tolkien along with other sources of inspiration, affected the armies of darkness in the *Warhammer* Universe and George R.R. Martin's Known World of Westeros.

2. Tolkien's Armies of Darkness

We know monstrous armies from mythology and folklore. The Wild Hunt is a ghostly cavalcade of undead riders haunting the winter skies between Christmas and Twelfth Night. Loki led an army of giants at Ragnarök. The Celtic god Bran reanimated fallen warriors as mute half-dead. Tolkien re-invented such monstrous armies as armies of darkness for the Fantasy genre. Having taken formerly individual monsters and banding them together into diverse armies, Tolkien unknowingly became a trendsetter for future fantasy. The author wrote in his famous essay *On Fairy-stories* that "in such 'fantasy'... new form is made... Man becomes subcreator (41f.)." Or, as J.P. Wolf puts it in analogy to Tolkien: "Subcreation, then, involves new combinations of existing concepts, which, in the building of a secondary world, become the inventions that replace and reset Primary World defaults…" (24). In this sense, Tolkien was a subcreator who invented new forms and "newly combined existing concepts" (ibid.).

Tolkien's invention and terming of beings display different degrees of subcreation. New labels were used for existing concepts that sometimes underwent minor changes. Urulóki, for instance, was a new term from Tolkien's Quenya language which was used to defamiliarise the concept of a fire-breathing dragon. Wolf notes that "[i]nvented languages… can introduce new concepts, objects, or beings, which have otherwise no words for them, or rename existing things so that the audience will consider them anew" (184). Tolkien took the dragon from Norse and Christian mythology and gave it a new creation myth, depicting them as abominations bred out of several creatures by Morgoth (Schneidewind, *Drache* 168). Furthermore, he classified the dragons, differentiating between fire drakes and cold drakes, as well as non-flying versus air-borne creatures.

At other times, existing terms were utilised by Tolkien to label entirely novel concoctions made from existing concepts. Orc and goblin are used as terms for a new race of monsters that Tolkien describes as malicious, fanged creatures with sallow skin that rejoice in torture and murder. Tolkien commented on his choice: "The word is as far as I am concerned actually derived from Old English orc, demon, but only because of its phonetic suitability (L 144)." The existing concept of the goblin was adapted from George Macdonald's *The Princess and the Goblin* and folklore but significantly changed. Tolkien's goblins are nearly man-high creatures that live in a war-like society and exceeded Macdonald's goblins' wickedness and cruelty by far.

Then again, some creatures could be viewed as Tolkien's very own creations. In these cases, the connection to existing concepts is barely noticeable and the analysis of these lineages is aggravated by the fact that many of Tolkien's creatures stem from etymological deliberations. The balrog (Sindarin: Demon of Might), for instance, is an awe-inspiring demon which bears a faint resemblance to Norse figures such as the fire god Logi or the fire giant[1] Surtr but has been altered nearly beyond recognition. The balrog's almost ethereal body of shadow and flame sets itself apart from the image of a giant, corporal man riddled in flames. Tolkien's Nazgûl (Black Speech: ringwraiths), on the other hand, cannot be traced back to any tangible mythological source. As a concept they are inarguably unique. Tom Shippey approaches the concept by thoroughly examining the etymology of 'wraith'[2] (*Author* 121-128). The etymological con-

---

1   See Tom Shippey's discussion of Tolkien's essay "Sigelhearwan" (*Road* 39).
2   Shippey draws attention to the OE verb wriðan and its connection to the nouns 'wreath' (something that is twisted) and 'wraith' (ghost). Shippey uses this consideration as the starting point of analysing the ringwraiths as twisted creatures.

sideration of the word gûl might also shed some light on the concept's possible origins. On closer inspection, the word, which means 'phantom, shadow of dark magic, necromancer' (Tolkien, *Parma* 11, 79) in Black Speech and 'evil or perverted knowledge, necromancy, sorcery' (MR 350), reminds one of the Arabic word ghoul which literally translates into 'he seized'. The ghoul[3] from The Arabian Nights is an evil phantom which seizes and feasts on corpses. The word seize comes from Old French seisir 'to take possession of' but might also be etymologically related to the Old English secan 'to seek'. The Nazgûl are humans which had been seized by the Dark Power of the Ring. The Dark Power is something that takes possession of its victim and turns it into a shadowy phantom.[4] In that way, the Nazgûl's mortal coils are devoured by that black sorcery and through them others may be physically devoured, when they are hurt by the Nazgûl's Morgul knives. Moreover, the Nazgûl are also the ones who 'seek' the One Ring for their master. The Dark Power itself seeks out and afflicts its victims.

In some ways, Tolkien's armies of darkness also bear resemblance to the build-up of primary world armies from antiquity and the early middle ages. The orcs constitute the infantry, cavalry, siege units, mechanics and scouts. The corrupted men are auxiliary and mercenary troops which aid Sauron's armies with their pirate fleets, war elephants, chariots and cavalry. These are the familiar traits and patterns of behaviour exhibited by an army that make us relate to the secondary world creations. It is the fantastical creatures who constitute the biggest difference. The dragons as giant war monsters which act as flame throwers, siege beasts or air force, are examples of such monsters. In an early draft by Tolkien there were even inanimate, mechanical dragons[5] reminiscent of modern war machines. Furthermore, troops[6] like the balrogs and barrow-wights spread supernatural horror to dishearten their foes.

---

3   David Day lists the word ghoul as a possible etymological source of the name Gollum (H 20f.). Gollum was likewise afflicted by the power of the Ring and his shape dwindled. The carnivorous qualities of the ghoul are retained in that the evil magic and its phantoms, which are both denoted by the word gûl, cause the victim's physical form to be devoured. The Lord of the Nazgûl threatens Éowyn that her "flesh shall be devoured..." until only her "naked spirit" remained (Tolkien, LotR III 116)." Éowyn calls him the "lord of carrion"(ibid.) which further links the Nazgûl to a ghoulish creature and desecrator of corpses.

4   This consideration also relates to the "wraithing process" as described by Shippey and what he terms as a state of being 'eaten up inside' (Author 125f.).

5   Cf. LT 2 169, 176, 213. John Garth suggests that these war machines could be viewed as an allegory of the tanks used in the Battle of the Somme (220f.).

6   The barrow-wights could be viewed as shock troops since several of them were sent to Cardolan by the Witch-king to expel Dúnedain settlers (see LOTR Appendix A 'Eriador, Arnor, and the Heirs of Isildur'). Tolkien's earlier drafts would generally justify applying the term troops to balrogs because he numbered them in "the hundreds" (LT 2 170) but one could still view the remaining seven balrogs (MR Section 2 note 50) from later drafts as unique commanding units.

3. Armies of Darkness in the *Warhammer* World

The tabletop game *Warhammer* puts forward highly diverse and elaborate armies of darkness, satiating the subcreators' urge for completeness and their "encyclopaedic impulse" (Wolf 30), as Wolf terms it. *Warhammer* is a so-called open world and as such is developed by multiple authors and is subject to transmedial growth. I will concentrate on the armies of Chaos, Greenskins and the Undead of Sylvania[7] since these armies exhibit the closest similarities to Tolkien's armies of darkness. The humanoid rat-men of the Skaven, the savage Beast Men and the Dark Elves, for instance, are more indebted to other fantasy paragons.

To start with the vilest faction, Chaos is basically a vast assembly of several armies paying homage to the Dark Gods. These twisted deities are called Tzeentch, Slaanesh, Nurgle and Khorne. Their names are among the most original ones in the *Warhammer* Universe. It is hard to reconstruct the names' original sources, safe for the foul god Nurgle's, whose name and characteristics have been inspired by the Old Hebrew god of death and decay, Nergal. Consisting of gigantic demonic monstrosities, Daemonette-warrior witches, fell sorcerers and mortal auxiliary forces, the sinister armies harassing and harrowing the *Warhammer* universe are reminiscent of the forces the Eastern Roman emperor Lucius deploys against Arthur in the *Alliterative Morte Arthure*[8]. Next to Persians, Saracens and Tartars among other regular human troops this assemblage of armies also boosts sixty giants together with fiends, with witches and warlocks (*Robbins* 612f.). Similar army constellations are already to be encountered in Tolkien's work of fantasy and the professor's etymological creation of names is far superior to the admittedly rather modest attempts made by the *Warhammer* developers. Although the developers have come up with new creative concepts for their world, most of these are just nominal compounds. For example, the label Chaos Warrior combines the Greek khaos: 'abyss, that which gapes wide open, is vast and empty' and the Old Northern French werreier: 'a warrior, soldier, combatant, one who wages war.' This label denotes a soulless, superhuman warrior in heavy plate armour who serves the powers of the abyss. Chaos is used as a noun modifier to imply that something is tainted and warped by the energies of Chaos. In that way, *Warhammer* features Chaos dragons, Chaos trolls and also Chaos giants, for instance. Next to these concepts unique to *Warhammer*, there are also new concepts which owe much to Tolkien's ideas. For instance, Archaon the Everchosen as a man who gave up his humanity

---

7   The histories of these armies are related in full in the respective army books by Games Workshop.

8   I would like to thank Professor Thomas Honegger for pointing out the similarity between the Chaos hordes and the monstrous elements in the emperor Lucius' Eastern armies as depicted in *The Alliterative Morte Arthure*.

and became a mighty sorcerer king (cf. *Warhammer Wiki*, 'Archaon') matches Tolkien's concept of the Witch-king, the Captain of Despair.

Warhammer's orcs are not a near-perfect match to one of Tolkien's creatures as Archaon is, they are, however, an excellent example of the application of a Tolkienesque term to a new, strongly modified concept. *Warhammer's* orcs are green, bulky, taller than men, gorilla-like and fiercely independent. They understand themselves as a proud warrior society thirsting for plunder and conquest like the Vikings. In the *Warhammer* successor *The Age of Sigmar* the creatures were even further defamiliarised by calling them Orruks, a term derived from Tolkien's Black Speech Uruk and the Primitive Quendian roots Ruku: 'dreadful shapes' and Órok: 'Goblin'. They have been disambiguated from the goblins again and both races are termed Greenskins. The goblins are the smaller, more cunning, humanoid cousins of the orcs. Together with the trolls, they are the typical allies of the orcs.

Concerning the structure of their armies, *Warhammer's* orcs and goblins form tribal and racial coalitions. These are aligned with different Troll species, green Dragons called wyverns, giant spiders and giants. The Greenskins put forward surprisingly sophisticated armies. Orc boar riders, goblin wolf riders and spider riders as well as charioteers form the cavalry. Since they are an independent people and not part of some wizard's army as they are in Tolkien's work, they lack human auxiliary forces. In fact, a *Warhammer* Greenskin would regard it as shameful and a slight to his status as a warrior to fight alongside a human. Instead, the Greenskins have their own specified units, partly drawn from the ranks of their equally monstrous allies. In that way, the Arachnarok spiders function like siege elephants and the Black Orcs supply highly disciplined elite warriors in superior iron harnesses.

While there are comparatively strong links between Tolkien's fell troops, the forces of Chaos and the Greenskins, the zombified corpses of *Warhammer's* undead armies of Sylvania are only remotely connected to Tolkien. In this context, the term undead is used to express the creatures' state as hovering between life and lifelessness. Some of them have died and were brought back to the living world while others never died, becoming demons who feed on the life force of mortals. Seductive vampires lead shambling masses of zombies, skeletal warriors and ghouls into battle. There are giant war monsters like the Varghulf and many air force units like the Fell Bats and the Zombie dragons. The term Varghulf literally means 'Outlaw devil-wolf' and is composed from Old Norse vargr "outlaw", and ulf, a wolf, wolfish person, devil. The Varghulf is a giant monstrous vampire outcast who looks like a cross between a bat and a wolf. The zombie dragon is a newly coined noun compound referring to an Undead Dragon, the term zombie acting as a noun modifier. The idea of the dragon as the ultimate obstacle is paired with the terrifying concept of Undeath. Tolkien's Undead were rather more classical in nature. However, there are also similarities to be found. For example, the Grave Guards or Wights are nearly identical to Tolkien's barrow-wights in that these warriors likewise still wear their former armour and, similarly to Tolkien's spectres, a pale light flickers in their eye sockets.

4. G.R.R. Martin's Army of the Dead

George R.R. Martin and the producers of the HBO series *A Game of Thrones* [GOT], David Benioff and D.B. Weiss, developed a horrifying army of undead consisting of White Walkers and Wights. White Walker is a term coined by Martin to denote the concept of a supernatural, ice-skinned sorcerer harnessing the element of ice and re-animating the dead as servants in the manner of a Necromancer. The concept of the Sluagh, a Celtic embodiment of the Wild Hunt[9], could have served as an inspiration. According to to folklorist Katherine Briggs, these spirits had "unerring venomous darts" and "commanded men to follow them... who slew and maimed at the bidding of their spirit masters" (374). The White Walkers also seem to owe much to the concepts of folkloric Undead with magical abilities and Tolkien's Barrow-Wights. Tolkien's Barrow-Wights have eyes glowing in an icy light, spread cold and harness fog, like Martin's White Walkers.

The wights are basically corpses crudely reanimated by the White Walkers. These dead beings return as feeble-minded, jerking puppets, which are remote-controlled by their masters' fell magic. Martin's wights seem to share their state of Undeath and their blue eyes with Tolkien's undead. Interestingly enough, in this case we could talk about the adaption of an adaption[10], since Tolkien's barrow-wights are like the Old Norse draugr. Draugr denotes a revenant and Old Saxon wiht means 'thing, demon'. Martin's Wights are revenants, demon-like and beings since death robbed them of their subjectivity. Martin seems to have taken the zombie from contemporary horror movies and changed it by endowing his undead with draugr traits and characteristics of other folkloric undead. Historian Carolyne Larrington elaborates that the draugr, like Martin's wights, assault "cattle, sheep and humans[,] ...tearing them limb from limb" (85f.). Wight is also used as a noun modifier to refer to any creature resurrected by the White Walkers. The army is boosted by giant war monsters

---

9   The German folklorist Jacob Grimm was the first to document the concept of the Wild Hunt in his book *Deutsche Mythologie* (1835).

10 In their book *A Theory of Adaption* (2013), Linda Hutcheons and Siobhan O'Flynn, among other things, describe an adaption as a "creative and interpretative act of appropriation/ salvaging" (9). Tolkien committed that "creative and interpretative act", when he took the existing concept of the draugr as the basis for his barrow-wights; and Martin, in turn, seems to have appropriated both the draugr-concept and Tolkien's idea of the barrow-wight when he created his White Walkers and Wights.

like wight giants and bigger animals like wight bears. The wight of the dragon Viserion is the sole air force and most valuable asset of the army. He is clearly based on the concept of *Warhammer's* zombie dragon.

5. Armies of Darkness as Catalysts of Change within Subcreated Worlds

Tolkien's armies of Evil as well as their follow-ups influenced the secondary world infrastructures of their respective imaginary worlds as catalysts of change. Timelines, mythology, geography and nature constitute such infrastructures. Wolf states that "timelines and narratives have to contend with… changes and often include migrations, the establishment of countries, and the catastrophic events that decimate them" (165). Such events are often triggered by the forces of evil. According to Wolf, by piecing together infrastructures the narrative evolves, evoking a sense of historicity (189). Within a world history "[w]ar… is often a continuation of conflicts begun long before the main characters were born" (Wolf 192). Events of war such as harrowing sieges, battles, the despoiling of nature and forced migration, for instance, act as important narrative threads ("chains of events") which greatly contribute to narrative braids ("interwoven individual narrative threads") and lead to causal braiding "in which the events of one thread have outcomes in other threads" (Wolf 199).

The scope of Tolkien's creation is so vast that the impact of his armies of darkness can only be regarded at a cursory glance in this essay. These armies' modes of action could be summarised the following way. First of all, the destruction or perversion of nature at the hands of the dark lords and their minions is a recurring topic in Tolkien's work. In that way, Morgoth has the Lamps and the Trees of Light destroyed and ravages the earth by building his underground fortresses of Angband and Utumno, as well as by erecting the artificial mountains of Thangorodrim. Secondly, Tolkien relates the destruction of kingdoms and cities through the armies of darkness, such as the Sacking of Gondolin and the destruction of Arnor. Thirdly, the expulsion and or annihilation of peoples often feature in Tolkien's work. The Dúnedain are greatly diminished and expelled from Arnor, the dwarves nearly perish in the Goblin Wars and the wars in Rohan and Ithilien trigger refugee movements.

Later fantasy worlds were guided by Tolkien's example. *Warhammer's* Chaos-hordes taint nature with their Warp-energies, ravage the human Empires and drive their populations before them. GOT's White Walkers bring about a threatening climate change, destroy the Wildling settlement Hardhome and cause the Wildling-nations to take flight. In doing so, both *Warhammer* and GOT feature armies of darkness which affect their worlds on the level of eschatological scenarios like the Christian Apocalypse and the heathen Ragnarök. Tolkien's work also exhibits eschatological leanings in that it features the apocalyptic battle Dagor Dagorath and, as Michaël Devaux[11] puts it, "the apocalypse… is diluted in the history of Middle-earth" (114). To consider Tolkien's work and its relation to the Christian Apocalypse and Ragnarök at this point would go beyond the scope of this paper. That is why I am going to limit the discussion of eschatological themes to *Warhammer* and GOT.

According to St. John's Book of Revelations[12], which relates the happenings of the Apocalypse, seven seals are opened. Death, who emerges from the fourth seal on a pale horse (John 6:7-8), could be likened to the Night King from GOT. Warhammer's Archaon resembles the second rider, War, in that he rides on a hellish war horse and that he is "granted a 'great sword' [the Slayer of Kings] to take peace from the earth" (John 6:3–4). Archaon leads the war[13] as a representative of the Chaos Gods who are four in number, like the Apocalyptic Riders[14]. Moreover, Archaon became a follower of Chaos after he had renounced the true gods Sigmar and Ulric. Thus, he could be viewed as an embodiment of the 'Anti-Christ' such as John describes him in the *First Epistle*: "Who is the liar but the one who denies that Jesus is the Christ? This is the antichrist, the one who denies the Father and the Son" (2:22). Moreover, Archaon's sword seems to be ablaze with dark energies and also makes him appear like an antithesis to Christ and his Flaming Sword[15]. Both fantasies also echo a theme from Judgement Day, the resurrection of the dead. GOT's Army of the Dead could be viewed as a macabre version of the dead's resurrection before Judgement Day, a Zombie Apocalypse in a medieval setting. *Warhammer's* sorcerer Nagash[16], likewise, raises the dead to fight the forces of Chaos during the End Times.

Warhammer's End Times and the White Walker invasion also exhibit strong parallels to the concept of Ragnarök. The end of a century long summer and the beckoning of a harsh winter in GOT seemingly reverberates the Fimbulvetr preceding Ragnarök. As on the eve of Ragnarök, wars devastate Westeros and brothers turn against brothers. For example, Renley Baratheon is fighting his sibling, Stannis. In *Warhammer*, the wars of the Chaos Invasion precede and bridge the End Times. The undead wight giants following the Night King's army resemble the Jötnar marching towards Ragnarök from icy Jötunheimr. In the same way, the Chaos hordes advance from their icy homeland, the Chaos Wastes,

---

11   See Devaux's discussion of Tolkien and eschatology in his essay Devaux, Dagor.

12   See, for example, The Revelation of John in *The Cambridge Bible Commentary* (1965)

13   For a full account of the End Times, consult the Black Library's The End Times Series (2015-16), a summary of these happenings is to be found under 'The End Times': http://warhammerfantasy.wikia.com/wiki/The_End_Times

14   Beginning at John 6:1-8.

15   See John 14:6.

16   Perhaps the undead mage Nagash is etymologically related to Nachash, the Snake, (cf. Num.21:6-9) who tempted Eve. This would be corroborated by Nagash's possible symbolic interpretation as an embodiment of vanitas and human sin.

and they bring both Chaos giants and hulking human warriors with them. There has not been an actual Ragnarök-like scenario in GOT yet. However, the Army of the Dead bears similarities to the Helkerle, an army from the Underworld, brought by Loki. We also encounter the motif of the world tree Yggdrasil in GOT in form of the Three-eyed Raven's tree which is burned by the undead.

Warhammer's link to Ragnarök proves to be much stronger, though. The hordes of the Blood God Khorne devastate the Empire with fire, like the Norse fire giants from Muspellsheim. The Incarnates, a group of demigods, ride down the Steilstraße of the holy capital Middenheim and are aided by Nagash's undead troops. Together they mirror the Æsir riding down the rainbow-bridge Bifröst accompanied by the reanimated Einherjer. Ulric, the god of battle, wolves and winter, could be said to resemble both Odin and Thor during Ragnarök, in that he half smashes Archaon's skull with his hammer but is killed by the Chaos demigod. Sigmar tries to avenge his father-figure Ulric, as Víðarr avenged his father on the wolf Fenrir. As the radiant Sigmar in his golden armour fights Archaon, who yields his flaming blade, the two of them bear a strong resemblance to the opponents Freyr and Surtr. It is said that both Sigmar and Archaon disappear into the shadows as the Old World is consumed by fire and the vile, mutating Warp-energies of Chaos. The *End Times* Epilogue[17] relates that the world tree, the "Oak of Ages was swallowed last of all". The skies burn and the stars dwindle in "a cold maelstrom". These happenings mirror the destruction of Yggdrasil and Fenrir consuming the luminaries. An act of 'uncreation' takes place and only a burnt-out husk of a world remains, leaving behind an anti-cosmic void like Ginnungagap. *Warhammer's* earth stays destroyed but life newly appears in other spheres in analogy to the events described in Snorri Sturluson's *Prose Edda* book "Gylfaginning". This renewed world is the setting for The Age of Sigmar. Like Odin, Ulric stays dead but Sigmar is reincarnated in likeness of Baldr in the *Poetic Edda* poem "Völuspá". While the monsters and evil gods are destroyed for good during Ragnarök, the gods of Chaos triumph at the End Times, consume the world and raise their fallen champions[18].

All these examples have demonstrated how armies of darkness affect the infrastructures of their secondary worlds, and it has also been proven that the Armies of Evil play a crucial role in advancing the narrative.

17　Cf. 'Archaon.' (http://warhammerfantasy.wikia.com/wiki/Warhammer_Wiki/)
18　While the End Times Epilogue leaves this in doubt, *Warhammer's* sequel *Age of Sigmar* indicates that many champions of Chaos were indeed raised as demons after the eschatological climax of *Warhammer.*

6. Armies of Darkness as Theological and Ethical Embodiments of Evil

According to Wolf, an author may embed his worldview into his subcreated world which in turn may implicitly represent that view (192). Wolf elaborates the following:

> The way actions and consequences are connected also imply a worldview, …how events lead one to the next, where characters' actions take them in the end—all of these things, when combined, indicate a particular view of how the world operates, or should operate.   (32)

Compliant with Tolkien's worldview, Evil cannot create anything of its own accord, no entity capable of emotions can be utterly evil and those that strife for power, become evil. T.A. Shippey identifies the evil powers of Tolkien's cosmos as partly Boethian by nature. Shippey sums up the Boethian view the following way: "[T]here is no such thing as evil. What people identify as evil is only the absence of good… [and Evil is] 'a parasite, not an original thing'" (130). Shippey corroborates his view by referring to Frodo and Sam's conversation in 'The Tower of Cirith Ungol' and by closer examining the orcs.

In his essay *Tolkien and the Nature of Evil*, Scott A. Davison draws attention to Tolkien's letter 183 in which the author wrote: "In my story I do not deal with Absolute Evil. I do not think that there is such a thing, since that is Zero" (*Letters* 243 qtd. in Davison 102). Davison summarises that "St. Augustine and Tolkien agree that nothing is completely and utterly evil, since existence itself is good" (ibid. 103). Evil is deviate in that it disrupts existence, despoiling and exploiting both landscapes and the beings that people them. The orcs and the Nazgûl are nothing but corruptions. The orcs, however, are not mere machines and know emotions like fear, greed and hatred, negative as these might be. Shippey profoundly discusses the orcs and and comes to the conclusion that they have a moral consciousness and even a sense of camaraderie[19]. Yet, they still commit hideous crimes which they do out of exercising their free will, which Boethius and the general Christian faith view as the origin of Evil. Tolkien's orcs are not utterly evil; they are just as much sinners as they were sinned upon, for they were created by evil acts. Based on Tolkien's statement, Davison deducts that "the more evil something is, the more nearly it approaches nothingness" (102). The Nazgûl are perpetrators of evil acts but at the same time their victims. They desired to live forever, thereby rebelling against the nature of mortal life

---

19 Shippey unrolls the orcs' moral dimension and draws attention to their notion of comradeship in his essay Shippey, *Orcs*.

and fell victim to the powers promising that eternal life. They ended as mere shrouds which gradually approached nothingness.

The Nazgûl bear witness to the corruptive influence of the Ring's absolute power. In that context, Shippey refers to the adage stated by Lord Acton in 1887: "'All power corrupts, and absolute power corrupts absolutely'" (*Author* 115). Shippey establishes that all "seizures of power, no matter how 'strong or well meaning' the seizers, will go the same way" (ibid. 116). Even wise beings like Gandalf, so Shippey, "would begin with the best of intentions[, if they owned the Ring], but would come to enjoy, having their intentions achieved, the use of power itself, and would end as dictators over others…" (ibid. 119). Saruman had the good intention of saving himself and the other Istari by treading the path of power and took the view that the end justified the means. *Warhammer's* Archaon was once a holy knight, who was foretold that one day he would become the Everchosen champion of Chaos. By pretending to align himself with Chaos, Archaon thought he could, once he was powerful enough, destroy his hateful masters but he succumbed to Chaos' offer of power.

However, *Warhammer,* for the most part, lacks a Boethian perspective on Evil. The Chaos Gods do taint their servants but they also craft their very own, perverse creations. Thus, there is something like 'evil existence' in *Warhammer.* In that, the game's story partly seems to be indebted to Manicheaism which Davison sums up the following way, "Good and Evil are locked in a struggle for world domination, and since they are equally balanced in power, it is not clear which, if either, will win in the end" (Davison 100). In *Warhammer* the 'positive' forces of Order (like the High Elves or the human Empire) are aligned against the 'negative' forces of Chaos, Destruction (as, for instance, the Greenskins) and Death (like the Undead of Sylvania). Shippey notes that, in his opinion, Tolkien's work also showed a Manichean tendency which, in turn, contradicted the Boethian view the author held. As Shippey points out, evil seems to be depicted both as an absence but also, according to Manicheaism, as an independent force, the Dark Power. Shippey connects Manicheaism to Dualism, remarking that both share "the belief that the world is a battlefield between the powers of Good and Evil, equal and opposite—so that one might say there is no real difference between them and it is a matter of chance which side one happens to choose" (*Author* 134). *Warhammer* is about eternal battles, thought out between contending forces which could be viewed as both equal and opposite. Indeed, on closer inspection, there seems to be not one people in *Warhammer* which is fully moral and decent. The human Empire is filled with religious zealots who conduct witch-hunts and the High Elves view most other peoples as 'lesser' races. Especially during the End Times, the lines between Good and Evil become blurred when the forces of Order forge an alliance of convenience with the undead and the Greenskins[20]. They do not fight for a greater good but for the preservation of their own power and for their very survival. The Chaos hordes, then, could only be termed as evil insofar that they surpass the other peoples' wickedness. In their blind fanaticism they even hazard the catastrophic end of the world itself.

To some extent, *Warhammer* seems to be beyond Good and Evil. In his treatise of the same name (1885-6), Friedrich Nietzsche states his most famous aphorism: "There are no moral phenomena at all, only a moral interpretation of phenomena..." (*Good* 108). This gives way for an anarchistic perspective, namely, that in the absence of moral law, everything was permitted. The Gods of Chaos, for instance, promise their followers such an age of anarchy and the Greenskins also appear to follow that philosophy. In that sense, *Warhammer's* philosophy appears to be related to moral nihilism.

To the question of 'what is good?' Nietzsche answers: "All that heightens the feeling of power, the will to power, power itself in man" (*Anti-Christ* 231). Power is considered desirable by all the *Warhammer* peoples, fair and foul alike. They seem to embrace that part of Nietzsche's philosophy. Evil in *Warhammer* is a potent and prosperous force and wars are a legitimate way of gaining power. While we witness a 'twilight of the other gods' during the End Times, the Chaos God's power is revealed and reasserted. Their followers seem to gain a questionable state of 'martyrdom' and are raised as powerful demons after their deaths. In that way, the End Times can also be viewed as juxtaposed to the Christian Apocalypse which ends with the remuneration of the righteous and the punishment of the wicked. In contrast, Tolkien's Dagor Dagorath, which was also to some extent modelled on the Apocalypse and Ragnarök, is won by the forces of Good and Morgoth is enchained. That Evil triumphs at such a crucial point of *Warhammer's* narrative either suggests that Evil might also finally triumph or that it will at least eternally prevail as an opposing force. Evil's triumph is the triumph of power, that which is normally viewed as 'good' by the other peoples as long as they themselves are the ones holding the power. *Warhammer's* forces of Evil bear stigmata but their immoral deeds more often than not go unpunished; on the contrary, they are rewarded. *Warhammer's* Sylvanian vampire counts, for instance, thoroughly enjoy life's

---

20 The Greenskins live in a repressive society of authoritarian orc-bosses, value cruelty and cunning above all else and delight in killing. They view themselves as the good side and as the physical ideal, in contrast to their 'repulsive' enemies (compare the usual notion of Evil and ugliness as related in Honegger, *Phänomenologie*). One of their redeeming qualities is their humour. The Night-Goblin boss Skarsnik, for example, offers this comic account of his alleged encounter with one of the orcish gods, "I was all drunk one night, and da stars swam and went all green. And this big orc made of stars, he said, 'You!' – 'e shouts lots. 'You! Little greeny! ...Go home and be da biggest and bestest gobbo since Grom da Paunch flattened da pansies [sic]!'" This is a quality they inherited from Tolkien's orcs, see Shippey's discussion of orcish humour in Shippey, *Orcs*.

pleasures and their youthful state of 'undeath'. Tolkien's Nazgûl, in contrast, appear like an inversion of *Warhammer's* vampires. Vampires are visible to mortals but invisible in mirrors while it takes the Ring as a 'mirror' to see the Nazgûl. Vampires enjoy their prolonged lives and increasingly gain health by consuming blood while the Nazgûl increasingly dwindle. They commit their wicked deeds with impunity and do not have to suffer the dire consequences which the Nazgûl[21] have to contend with.

Martin views his world's moral dimensions as different "shades of grey[22]" and this ambivalence aggravates the definition of what an army of 'darkness' is in Martin's terms. The forces of Daenerys Targaryen or Cersei Lannister could conversely be viewed as either as good or evil, depending on the viewer's perspective. As Martin put it, everyone is the "hero of [their] own story[23]" and "a villain is a hero of the other side[24]". The White Walkers might very well think that they are the heroes and view the humans as the villains who ought to be purged. They appear to partly embody a Boethian perspective on Evil, in that they are corruptions of existence, which is benevolent by nature. To my mind, they are definitely not a Manichean force of Evil because they are not opposed by any discernible power of Good. In fact, the White Walkers and their servants appear less evil than many living humans from the series. The White Walkers lack the humans' marked sadism. They do not skin their victims alive like Ramsay Bolton, nor do they turn someone into life food for ravenous dogs, as the 'heroine' Sansa Stark does. Yes, they do not discriminate, killing women, children, the young and the old, but many human armies do exactly the same. In contrast to these humans, the White Walkers are apparently not driven by the lust for power and riches.

Since we neither know their ethics nor their motives, they appear as unmotivated as a natural force or a pandemic. The series GOT explains that the Children of the Forest created the White Walkers from humans to fight humans who laid waste to their natural habitat. Thus, the White Walkers and their shambling servants could be viewed as nature striking back[25] against its defilers, the humans who destroyed nature and the Children who broke nature's laws of life and death. Like a natural catastrophe, the White Walkers are a man-made disaster which quickly developed a life of its own and started going on an unstoppable rampage that threatens to destroy the world. Carolyne Larrington draws attention to commentator Sean T. Collins who views the Army of the Dead as "'the series' vision of war itself: death breeding death

---

21   Amy Amendt-Raduege elaborates on the Nazgûl's tragic situation in Amendt-Raduege, *Better*.
22   See Jessica Salter's interview with Martin.
23   See Christina Radish's interview with Martin.
24   See Abbie Bernstein's interview with Martin.
25   This has also been the topic of several eco-horror movies. See Penner/Schneider, "Die Rache der Natur" in Penner/Schneider, *Horror*.

until there is nothing left'" ('Game of Thrones Recap: Dawn of the Dead', qtd. in *Winter* 87). War is another man-made disaster which can easily escalate into a global crisis and threaten the world's existence. For all of the reasons named above, the eschatological leanings of GOT seem to make sense. On the one hand, the White Walkers and their Army of the Dead could be viewed as the executioners of an icy Ragnarök. On the other hand, they could be viewed as passing judgement on the warring humans by bringing about an apocalypse. The Army of the Dead serves as a projection of man-made evils like natural catastrophes and wars but it is, strictly speaking, not a force of Evil in itself. In that way the Army of the Dead could be viewed as part of a cautionary tale about the very real threats of climate change and fatal wars.

7. Conclusion

Now that the smoke of battle has lifted, we behold quite a revealing examination concerning all of these exemplary armies of darkness. Tolkien's formative influence on armies of darkness has been proven by demonstrating how *Warhammer* and GOT picked up on the author's astounding creations and employed similar strategies for worldbuilding. It has been substantiated that these armies of darkness, like chess pieces on a board, act as catalysts of change which affect secondary world infrastructures and narrative. Last but not least, it has been established that the concept of Evil manifests itself differently in the various armies of darkness which constituted the subjects of this paper's investigation. Tolkien's armies of darkness, for the most part, represent a Boethian embodiment of Evil as an absence of good but also depict Evil as the incarnate thirst for power. Tolkien's renunciation of the thirst for power is contrasted by *Warhammer's* affirmation of power and war. *Warhammer* could be called Manichean or dualistic but, most notably, seems to foreground Nietzsche's ethos of power. The Army of the Dead in GOT does not appear to be a manifestation but rather a projection of Evil in form of the man-made evils of ecocide and war. As more and more new, fell armies are raised and unleashed by their authors, it remains to be seen how Tolkien's work along with that of other present subcreators will influence the future evolution of these dark armies in terms of worldbuilding.

Bibliography

Printed Sources

Amendt-Raduege, Amy. "Better Off Dead: The Lesson of the Ringwraiths". *Fastitocalon. Volume 1 — Immortals and Undead*. Eds.: Thomas Honegger, Fanfan Chen. Trier: Wissenschaftlicher Verlag Trier, 2010, 70-82

Briggs, Katherine. 'Sluagh.' *A Dictionary of Fairies* [1976]. London: Routledge, 2011, 373-374

Davison, Scott A. "Tolkien and the nature of Evil". In: *The Lord of the Rings and Philosophy*. Eds.: Gregory Bassham, Eric Bronson. Chicago: Open Court, 2003, 99-109

Day, David. *The Hobbit Companion* [1997]. London: Pavilion Books, 2012

Devaux, Michaël. "Dagor Dagorath and Ragnarök: Tolkien and the Apocalypse". *Hither Shore* 6 (2009): 102-115

Garth, John. *Tolkien and the Great War*. London: Harper Collins, 2003

Honegger, Thomas. "Zur Phänomenologie von Gut und Böse". In: *Eine Grammatik der Ethik*. Eds.: Thomas Honegger, Frank Weinreich. Saarbrücken: Verlag der Villa Fledermaus, 2005

Hutcheonson, Linda & Siobhan O' Flynn. *A Theory of Adaption* [2006]. 2nd ed. London: Routledge, 2013

Larrington, Carolyne. *Winter is Coming*. London: Tauris, 2016

Nietzsche, Friedrich. "Beyond Good and Evil" and "The Anti-Christ". In: *A Nietzsche Reader*. Transl.: R.J. Hollingdale. New York: Penguin, 1977, 230-231

Penner, Jonathan & Steven Jay Schneider. *Horror Cinema*. Hamburg: Taschen, 2012

Schneidewind, Friedhelm. 'Drache, Drachen.' *Das große Tolkien-Lexikon*. Berlin: Lexikon Imprint Verlag, 2001, 166-170

Shippey, Tom. *The Road to Middle-earth*. London: Harper Collins, 1992

---. *J.R.R. Tolkien - Author of the Century* [2000]. London: Harper Collins, 2001

---. "Orcs, Wraiths, Wights: Tolkien's Images of Evil". In: *Roots and Branches: Selected Papers on Tolkien by Tom Shippey*. Eds.: Thomas Honegger et al. Zurich/Bern: Walking Tree Publishers, 2007, 243-266

Tolkien, J.R.R. *Tolkien on Fairy-stories* [1947]. Eds.: Verlyn Flieger, Douglas A. Anderson. London: HarperCollins, 2014

---. *The Lord of the Rings: The Return of the King* [1955]. Boston: Houghton Mifflin Company, 1997

---. *The Letters of J.R.R. Tolkien* [1981]. Ed. Humprey Carpenter. London: HarperCollins, 1995

---. *The Book of Lost Tales Volume 2*. London: HarperCollins, 1992

---. *Morgoth's Ring*. London: HarperCollins, 2002

---. "Parma Eldalamberon XVII". Ed.: Christopher Tolkien. Altadena: The Mythopoeic Society, 1995

Wolf, Mark J.P. *Building Imaginary Worlds* [2012]. London: Routledge, 2016

Internet Sources

'Archaon.' 9 Aug. 2017. <http://warhammerfantasy.wikia.com/wiki/Warhammer_Wiki/>

Benson, Larry D. (Ed.). 'Alliterative Morte Arthure, Part I.' 12 Jan. 2018. <http://d.lib.rochester.edu/teams/text/benson-and-foster-king-arthurs-death-alliterative-morte-arthur-part-i/>

Bernstein, Abbie. "Interview: GAME OF THRONES creator George R.R. Martin on the future of the franchise – Part 2". 2 Feb. 2018. < http://www.assignmentx.com/2011/interview-game-of-thrones-creator-george-r-r-martin-on-the-future-of-the-franchise-part-2/>

Collins, Sean T. 'Game of Thrones Recap: Dawn of the Dead.' 10 Sept. 2017. <https://www.rollingstone.com/tv/recaps/game-of-thrones-recap-dawn-of-the-dead-20150531/>

"End Times, the". 10 Feb. 2018. < http://warhammerfantasy.wikia.com/wiki/The_End_Times>

Radish, Christina. "George R.R. Martin Interview GAME OF THRONES". 13 Feb. 2018. < http://collider.com/george-r-r-martin-interview-game-of-thrones/>

Salter, Jessica. "Game of Thrones's George RR Martin: 'I'm a feminist at heart'". 12 Feb. 2018. <https://www.telegraph.co.uk/women/womens-life/9959063/Game-of-Throness-George-RR-Martin-Im-a-feminist.html>

One Pair of Eyes:
Focalisation and Worldbuilding

Allan Turner (Gateshead)

This article is about literary worldbuilding, with the emphasis on the adjective "literary". Of course, anybody can make up an imaginary world in private, but then they are under no obligation to consider how they will present their world to others within a clear and cogent narrative framework expressed through language. The present study will investigate one technique used in a literary genre, typically a novel, although it might also be a narrative poem, to open up a world unfamiliar to the reader: focalisation, through which the world may be explored through the eyes of a participant in the narrative. I propose to compare the use of focalisation in the worldbuilding of Tolkien with that of Sir Walter Scott's historical novels *Waverley* and *Rob Roy*.

From the point of view of conventional literary criticism, it might seem unusual to make a direct comparison across genres in this way, since the historical novel, which represents past events in the real world, and the fantasy novel, which involves beings or powers not observable in our known world, were routinely considered to have a completely different ontological status. However, with more research being devoted to the phenomenon of imaginary worlds, the opinion has been growing that within the sphere of fiction the distinction between the realistic and the imaginary may be scalar rather than absolute. Mark J.P. Wolf has proposed that there are "degrees of subcreation", since there can be wide variations in secondary worlds (that is, any fictional world that is not entirely congruent with the Primary World as we know it), in terms of their relationship and accessibility to the Primary World in time, space and human experience (25-29). He cites the example of Tolstoy's *War and Peace*, which, although it is built around historical events, nevertheless features invented characters and their equally invented estates.

The categories proposed by Wolf seem to offer a powerful tool for understanding what exactly imaginary worlds are and how they can be created. However, they remain on a very general level, particularly since they cover a number of different media including film and video games, so that their usefulness for the investigation of purely literary worldbuilding needs to be established through case studies based on concrete examples. One such study is that by Dimitra Fimi which compares three examples of medievalism, by Tolkien, Thomas Chatterton and Umberto Eco. Each of these texts involves a representation or reimagining of aspects of the Middle Ages which in spite of, or rather because of, the manifest attempts to create a sense of historical reality, for example by "forged" documents, actually distances the action from the Primary World so that in each case an imaginary world is brought into being with a greater or lesser degree of inner consistency and separateness from the reader's own experience. Her conclusion, as reflected in the title of her article, is that medievalism in itself can be considered a kind of subcreation.

The two novels by Scott that will be considered here can certainly not be classified as medievalism unless that term is to be extended to cover the representation of *any* pre-modern culture. Indeed, many of the events and characters had been experienced by some elderly people, such as Alexander Stewart of Invernahyle, who recounted them to Scott in his youth, and the historical documents that he introduced in the Magnum edition to underline the historicity of his narratives were unquestionably real. However, Scottish society had changed so much since 1745, both in the Highlands and in the Lowlands, that he was necessarily striving to recreate a culture with which his contemporaries had lost direct contact, so there is a parallel at least to that extent to Chatterton and Eco. The following comparison with Tolkien on the micro-level of focalisation will examine the phenomenon from a different direction.

In addition to this, I will attempt to link the macro-level arguments of Wolf with a more detailed linguistics-based theory to give them a grounding which at present may be largely implicit. Linguists tend to wonder: how does language work? And in particular: what makes communication through language possible? Similarly, we may ask ourselves how it can make sense to talk about the "character" even of such a fascinating invention in the realistic novel tradition as Jane Austen's Emma Woodhouse, given that Emma does not exist and never has existed; she consists only of black marks on white paper.[1]

There have been a number of theoretical approaches that have attempted to explain the link between word and idea in terms of human cognitive experience. One that is particularly useful for the present purpose is *Text World Theory* by Joanna Gavins, which takes into account not only everyday registers but also literary texts, and indeed has the advantage of linking well with literary theories like the narratology of Gérard Genette. Gavins explains that for the cognitive linguist, worldbuilding is not restricted to imaginative literature, but rather it is what we do every time we communicate through language. Making or receiving utterances involves creating mental representations of human experience in a number of different ways. Each time we conceptualise a situation, we build something like a small world embodying that time, that place, those participants, and so on.

An example of a short text making a simple text world is: "Can we come in?" The request presupposes an enclosure of some kind with an entrance, with at

---

1   Film adaptations of novels are of course a totally different phenomenon, which anyway could not exist without a reading of the written text.

least two people outside ("we") and at least one inside, who has the authority to give or withhold permission. Note that the meaning is derived not just from the words themselves, which individually have little definable semantic content, but from the interaction of this form of words with our knowledge of the world and the situations that may arise in it.

This assumed knowledge of the world suggests that we do not have to build up our world from scratch every time. Instead we acquire a repertoire of frequent situations that have their own "scripts", that is to say standard patterns of discourse where similar kinds of utterance regularly occur. A typical script of this kind is the restaurant, where we have internalised a standard sequence of events (requesting a table, looking at the menu, ordering, paying the bill, etc.) and the forms of words used to facilitate it. Whether or not the responses come in the expected form can tell us something about the internal text worlds of the other participant(s) in the discourse, or what we perceive as their "character".

These limited text worlds, that is to say the mental representations that we create for ourselves, can be extended by negotiation with other participants in the discourse. Gavins gives an example from her own experience of such a successful negotiation of an unexpected turn in a familiar script, where she goes into a sandwich shop in Madison, Wisconsin, and tries to order a sandwich from the list displayed (her comments after the first and second turns are omitted here):

> S1: I'll have a chicken sandwich please.
> S2: Sure. What kind of cheese?
> S1: No, a chicken sandwich.
> S2: Sure. What kind of cheese?
> S1: I don't want cheese.
> S2: It's included.
> S1: You mean I have to have cheese?
> S2: No, you don't have to have it, but you're paying for it.
> S1: But I can have a sandwich without cheese?
> S2: I guess.
> S1: OK, I'll just have chicken on its own, then.
> S2: No cheese?
> S1: No cheese.

(19-20)

The different cultural backgrounds of the British participant (S1) and the American one (S2) means that they start off with slightly varying mental representations of the situation. In particular, S1 does not realise that, since Wisconsin is the dairy state of America, a large amount of cheese is eaten there, so that it is a standard ingredient in sandwiches; therefore S2's initial response makes her feel that something has gone wrong with the script. S2 on the other hand does not realise that cheese is not a usual ingredient of chicken sandwiches in some other places, and also finds it strange that someone should not want something that they are paying for. However, both speakers apply the Gricean cooperative principle and negotiate their way to an understanding, through the achievement of which they both slightly expand their own text world. This outlines one important function of dialogue in narratives which present an unfamiliar world to the reader.[2]

Another important feature of our mental representational ability is seen in the first example, "Can we come in?" The verb *come* normally expresses motion towards the speaker, e.g. "Come here", and is contrasted with *go*, which would suggest movement away from the present position. However, "Can we go in" would signify something different and can only be imagined as addressed to the speaker's companion(s) outside the enclosure. What has happened is that the speaker has cooperatively expressed the situation from the point of view of the other participant. This human ability to see through someone else's eyes, known as projection, is the means by which we can become absorbed in stories. Projection also allows us to react to the responses in fictional scripts just as we would do in the real world, creating an empathy with characters like Emma Woodhouse, who do not exist outside the minds of readers. It explains the importance of focalisation (sometimes known in English as "point of view") as a novelistic technique which enables us to explore the text world through the eyes of one or more of its characters. We are, as it were, inside the story.

Note that focalisation is not to be confused with narrative voice. In *The Hobbit* there is a sometimes intrusive narrative voice that presents and comments on the plot from outside as it unfolds, but all the events as they happen are seen as through the eyes of Bilbo, and we follow the feelings aroused in him by them—he is the focaliser. Nothing is directly experienced where he is not present, so that other events have to be told to him afterwards for our benefit, such as the dwarves' escape from the goblins in the Misty Mountains.

Focalisation in *The Lord of the Rings* is more complex, where the intrusive narrative voice has been largely eliminated. At first, we perceive events almost entirely through Frodo, just like a second Bilbo, but from Book IV on the fo-

---

2   The misunderstandings and explanations in this dialogue also underpin a point made by Wolf in Chapter 1, implicitly in his frequent use of the word default in relation to the known facts of the Primary World, and explicitly in his citation of Marie-Laure Ryan's "principle of minimal departure" (55): we assume that the world depicted in a work of fiction functions in a way that conforms to our own experience until something is presented to the contrary. Gavins makes it clear that this is not a purely literary phenomenon; in fact, the whole of human discourse is a "dynamic cognitive process" dependent upon the exploitation and expansion of experiential knowledge (24).

calisation shifts increasingly to Sam as Frodo becomes more and more fixated on his struggle with the Ring and Sam has to take the initiative. However, there are many chapters in which the Fellowship is scattered and neither of these main focalisers is present. In some situations, the focalisation is passed to the other hobbits, in particular to Pippin in Minas Tirith or Merry with the Rohirrim, including the striking passage in V/3 as the Rohirrim ride down from the mountains to Dunharrow and Merry feels "borne down by the insupportable weight of Middle-earth" (791). Otherwise the focalisation is much weaker, as in the chase of Aragorn, Legolas and Gimli through Rohan after the Orcs, much of which is not seen from the particular point of view of any of the characters involved, but only in a generalised way through the eyes of all three, if at all. Thus, the impression that the narrative is hobbit-centred, as implied by the conceit of the Red Book of Westmarch, is strengthened by the literary (and cognitive) technique of focalisation.

Tom Shippey in *The Road to Middle-earth* (81) points out that Bilbo (and by extension Frodo and the other hobbits) helps to mediate the archaic, heroic world to a modern reader who is uneasy with the idea of heroism. That is a very important point, but it is only one of the more refined aspects of the mediating function of hobbits. On a more general level, the hobbit focalisers take the role of inexperienced strangers in a big wide, unknown world. To put it in cognitive terms, their repertoire of scripts within the fictional text world is very restricted, and it is only as they expand their mental representations that readers have the opportunity to expand their own conceptions of Middle-earth.

A similar narrative technique can be seen in Scott's historical novels. *Waverley,* commonly regarded as the first successful historical novel in English, was published 1814 but begun several years earlier. *Rob Roy,* which is vaguely similar in subject matter but set in an earlier period of Scottish history, followed in 1817. Both novels take place against the background of two armed rebellions by Scottish Highlanders against the Hanoverian government of Britain in favour of the Catholic House of Stuart, the former kings of Scotland, the last of whom, James II of England and VII of Scotland, had been deposed in 1688 to guarantee a Protestant succession. The uprisings led by his son in 1715 and his grandson, Bonnie Prince Charlie, in 1745 could be seen as the last flare-up of the conflict between Catholics and Protestants like that which had dominated Germany in the 17th century. The suppression of the second of these rebellions led to the systematic eradication by the British government of the archaic clan structure that had survived in the Highlands and was unique in western Europe.

In his youth, Scott had talked to survivors of the 1745 uprising and drew on these first-hand experiences to present what was probably an idealised view of a past age. According to Shippey he was like William Morris and Tolkien in feeling "the perilous charm of the archaic world of the North" (80). The historical events of *Waverley* took place only 60 years before he began writing it (hence its subtitle, *'Tis Sixty Years Since*, which the narrator repeats on several occasions to remind readers of the time difference), but the huge change in social structures had made the old Highland culture seem like a lost world, a fantasy which just happened to be real. In this novel, though, the past as a foreign country applies in more than one sense, since although Scott was writing for his fellow-Scots who were becoming unfamiliar with parts of their national past, he also felt an ambition to mediate Scottish history and culture to his substantial English readership, for many of whom Scotland was still strange and remote, even after a century of political union.[3]

Edward Waverley is a young Englishman who has grown up with little parental supervision and has spent a lot of his time reading romances, so that he has hardly any direct experience of the world. When his uncle, who is a Stuart sympathiser, decides that he should join the army as a career, he is sent to join his regiment in Scotland, with a recommendation to visit a friend of his uncle not far away from the army headquarters. On this visit he first experiences the culture of the Lowland Scots, with its significant linguistic and social differences, but also with a political difference, since it is here that he first becomes aware of the Scottish resentment of Hanoverian rule from England. Not only that, but through a chance event—his host's cattle are stolen by raiders from the Highlands—he comes into contact with a Highland chieftain, Fergus Mac-Ivor, through whom he not only experiences Highland culture but also finds himself becoming involved in the rebellion on the side of Charles Stuart.

The novel is focalised strongly through the character of Edward Waverley, similar to Bilbo Baggins in *The Hobbit*. It also has a similarly intrusive narrator, much more in the style of earlier authors like Fielding. Just as we have seen that Tolkien avoided that fault in *The Lord of the Rings*, so Scott had learnt to avoid it in *Rob Roy* by making that novel a first person, homodiegetic narrative, so that nothing intrudes between the focalisation of the hero Francis Osbaldistone, also a young, inexperienced Englishman caught up in Scottish affairs, and the reader. Both of these characters actually experience *two* new cultures: that of the Lowland Scots, in their way of life much closer to the English, and the more exotic, traditional and feudal society of the Highlanders. Georg Lukács claims that Scott's heroes are deliberately made ordinary and neutral because their main function is not to enact their own passions but "to bring the extremes whose struggle fills the novel, whose clash expresses artistically a great crisis in society, into contact with one another" (36). It might also be argued that

---

3   In the General Preface of 1829 he states: "I felt that something might be attempted for my own country, of the same kind with that which Miss Edgeworth so fortunately achieved for Ireland – something which might introduce her natives to those of the sister kingdom, in a more favourable light than they had been placed hitherto, and tend to procure sympathy for their virtues and indulgence for their foibles" (Waverley, 352f.).

this same neutrality enables them to act all the more effectively as focalisers, as conduits to convey the discovery of place and custom to the reader.

Scott uses the inexperienced Waverley as a focaliser in just the same way as Tolkien uses Bilbo, as the representative of the normality of the reader who has to negotiate his way through new places and situations, thus revealing them to the reader at the same time. In cognitive terms, Waverley starts off with his familiar presuppositions but finds he has to change and expand his mental representations on the pattern of Gavins's cheese sandwich example, as in the following passage in which he slowly works out in conversation with his host's daughter who exactly Fergus Mac-Ivor is and how he can help to restore the Baron's stolen cattle:

> The Baron having also retired to give some necessary directions, Waverley seized the opportunity to ask, whether this Fergus, with the unpronounceable name, were the chief thief-taker of the district? "Thief-taker!" answered Rose, laughing; "he is a gentleman of great honour and consequence; the chieftain of an independent branch of a powerful Highland clan, and is much respected, both for his own power, and that of his *kith*, *kin*, and *allies*."
> "And what has he to do with the thieves then? Is he a magistrate, or in the commission of peace?"
> "The commission of war rather, if there be such a thing," said Rose; "for he is a very unquiet neighbour to his *un-friends*, and keeps a greater *following* on foot than many that have thrice his estate. As to his connection with the thieves, that I cannot well explain; but the boldest of them will never steal a hoof from any one that pays *black-mail* to Vich Ian Vohr."   (70)

Waverley's first guess is that Mac-Ivor must be a man who earns a living by catching thieves, a concept that must have been familiar to him from his background in the English countryside. When Rose points out his error, he then makes a second assumption, an officer of the law, again taken from completely the wrong cultural context. It will not fit in with his pre-existing conceptual categories that someone can be a gentleman and at the same time collect "blackmail", or to use the modern term, protection money. It is not surprising that Rose laughs, since false cultural assumptions of this kind often appear comical, at least to an outsider. This laughter is important also because it allows the reader, who is experiencing this through Waverley's eyes and is probably also still struggling to understand, to laugh off his or her own incomprehension too. It is worth noting that Scott helpfully italicises some words as a visual clue that they belong to a culture different from that of the reader and might therefore be misunderstood, even as Rose offers further potential for confusion by referring to Mac-Ivor by his Gaelic title, Vich Ian Vohr.

One equivalent of such a misunderstanding in *The Hobbit* is deliberately played for comedy:

> "If you must know more, his name is Beorn. He is very strong, and he is a skin-changer."
> "What! a furrier, a man that calls rabbits conies, when he doesn't turn their skins into squirrels?" asked Bilbo.
> "Good gracious heavens, no, no, NO, NO!" said Gandalf. "Don't be a fool Mr Baggins if you can help it [...] He is a skin-changer. He changes his skin: sometimes he is a huge black bear, sometimes he is a great strong black-haired man with huge arms and a great beard."   (146-147)

Bilbo's supposition might have been reasonable in the Shire, or even more so in the reader's 1937 England, but he needs to build a new mental representation that will be valid in Wilderland.

Literary worldbuilding also makes implicit use of the scripts that were mentioned above as patterns for verbal interactions. Although there are no restaurants in an archaic world, nevertheless there are banquets, which also create the expectation of a certain sequence of events—food, entertainment, social interaction—but also allow for novel situations which may have to be negotiated, like a more complex version of buying a chicken sandwich without the cheese.[4]

The most significant banquet in *The Lord of the Rings* is the one that takes place in the house of Elrond at the beginning of Book II, where Frodo acts as the focaliser. Through the "many meetings" he (together with the reader) extends his text world by seeing familiar persons in a new context, and therefore gains a first glimpse of their importance in a wider history than has been evident so far. The courteous behaviour of his neighbour in picking up his scattered cushions leads to an extended conversation with Glóin, which opens up new perspectives of prosperity, but also disquiet, at Erebor, as well as connecting at a deeper narrative level with the history of Bilbo and his acquisition of the Ring. The banquet is completed by an entertainment with poetry and music, where Frodo is reunited with Bilbo, through which he comes to understand something of the power of elvish art, but also gains further evidence of the evil of the Ring through its momentary effect both on Bilbo and on himself.

---

4   I am grateful to Thomas Honegger for suggesting to me the significance of different treatments of the banquet script by different authors, and to Dimitra Fimi for reminding me of the Henneth Annûn episode.

er

A further example of negotiating a meal script appears when Frodo and Sam are entertained by Faramir at Henneth Annûn. There is a comic exchange when the hobbit servant Sam misunderstands the purpose of the bowl of water offered to him to rinse his hands, and solves the problem by using it to wash his head. The Gondorian waiting on him tentatively misinterprets this as a Shire custom, and is partially corrected by Sam, who has not understood the full significance of the question. Shortly afterwards, Frodo is made to think critically about the manners of the Shire when he is introduced to the Gondorian custom of facing west before the meal.

Scott makes use of a similar script, since Waverley as focaliser experiences not one banquet but two. The first takes place in the Lowlands, and is used by the author to recreate a sense of Lowland customs from a recent but nevertheless vanished past cut off from the English reader both in time and space. It is at this small dinner that he is first introduced to Balmawhapple, who will turn out to be his antagonist. His (and our) understanding of the banquet script is extended as he finds himself faced with a degree of ceremony that he is not used to, involving the ritualised drinking of large amounts of alcohol, and we follow his thoughts as he tries to negotiate this without causing offence. However, his efforts fail because the others have drunk more than he has, and an incident occurs which will cause difficulties for him in the future.

The second banquet takes place as a vivid introduction for both the hero and the reader to the completely different culture of the Highlands. Through Waverley's eyes we experience a much more extensive account of a feudal feast in the communal hall of a great chieftain who relies on such lavish entertainment to guarantee the loyalty of his followers. As a ritual preparation a surly old woman comes to wash his feet, which is not a part of the script that is familiar to him, so he has to decide how to respond appropriately. Fortunately, he reaches the correct decision by giving her a generous tip. There follows a detailed description of the proceedings seen from the point of view of his position near the head of the table, where in a hall full of retainers of all social classes, the behaviour lower down is depicted in a way that the reader, through Waverley's eyes (and ears), is likely to find excessive and even primitive:

> Lower down stood immense clumsy joints of mutton and beef, which, but for the absence of pork, resembled the rude festivity of the banquet of Penelope's suitors. But the central dish was a yearling lamb, called "a hog in harst", roasted whole. It was set upon its legs, with a bunch of parsley in its mouth, and was probably exhibited in that form to gratify the pride of the cook, who piqued himself more on the plenty than the elegance of his master's table. The sides of this poor animal were fiercely attacked

> by the clans-men, some with dirks, others with the knives which
> were usually in the same sheath with the dagger, so that it was
> soon rendered a mangled and rueful spectacle.   (96)

However, in spite of the emphasis on its unfamiliarity, the meal is seen to follow
a set of conventions that prevent it from deteriorating as disastrously as the
convivial evening in the Lowlands.

The focalisation makes use of a kind of indirect free speech which subtly
underlines the extent to which the feast is alien to Waverley's experience and
sense of decorum:

> The bagpipers, three in number, screamed during the whole time
> of dinner, a tremendous war-tune; and the echoing of the vaulted
> roof, and clang of the Celtic tongue, produced such a Babel of noises,
> that Waverley dreaded his ears would never recover it.   (96f.)

The horror that English people claim to feel towards bagpipes is well known,
so clearly this is presented as Waverley's subjective impressions; a Scot would
be highly unlikely to think of the sound of bagpipes as "screaming" or of the
Gaelic language as a "clang". The focaliser here mediates the scene not so much
to the experience as to the prejudices of the English readers.

It is hoped that these few examples will have gone at least a part of the way to
demonstrating that focalisation is an important literary technique in the creation
of a credible world that is unfamiliar, but can nevertheless be mediated for the
reader by using the viewpoint of a character whose nucleus of experience is not
so different from the reader's own. In doing this, the author chooses situations
which correspond to the archetypal ones in which human beings negotiate an
extended mental representation of the world around them. Because of the dis-
tancing effect of time and change, the historical novel depends to some extent
on worldbuilding, just as in fantasy and science fiction, with which it is more
commonly associated. If there were not a considerable overlap between the
historical novel and the Tolkienian immersion fantasy, it would not have been
so easy for Tolkien to indulge in the joke of presenting *The Hobbit* and *The
Lord of the Rings* as histories, complete with the tongue-in-cheek paratextual
commentaries which were pioneered more than 200 years earlier by Scott.[5]

---

5   Fimi comments that, because it is patently fictitious, the paratextual framing of both
    Tolkien and Eco ironically undermines the sense of historical veracity at the same time
    as it appears to strengthen it on the surface level. Note that Scott's paratexts are ironi-
    cal only when they are concerned with the putative author, since the Waverley novels
    were originally published anonymously. Any historical documentation is meant to be
    taken at its face value.

Bibliography

Fimi, Dimitra. "The Past as an Imaginary World: The Case of Medievalism." In: *Revisiting Imaginary Worlds: A Subcreation Studies Anthology*. Ed.: Mark J.P. Wolf. New York/ Abingdon: Routledge, 2017. 46-65

Gavins, Joanna. *Text World Theory: An Introduction*. Edinburgh: Edinburgh University Press, 2007

Lukács, Georg. *The Historical Novel*. Harmondsworth: Penguin, 1981

Scott, Walter. *Waverley*. Ed.: Claire Lamont. Oxford: Oxford University Press, 1986

Shippey, Tom. *The Road to Middle-earth*. 3rd edition. London: HarperCollins, 2005

Tolkien, J.R.R. *The Hobbit*. London: HarperCollins, 1998

---. *The Lord of the Rings*. 50th anniversary edition. London: HarperCollins, 2005

Wolf, Mark J.P. *Building Imaginary Worlds: The Theory and History of Subcreation*. New York, 2012

Then Smaug Spoke:

On Constructing the Fantastic via Dialogue in Tolkien's Story Cosmos[1]

Timo Lothmann, Arndt Heilmann, Sven Hintzen (Aachen)

> *the story has to be told, and the dialogue conducted*
> *in a language*   (L 144)

Introduction and Scope

In this study, we intend to have a closer look at dialogue in a representative set of texts from the Middle-earth legendarium in order to inspect the functional potential of dialogue in general, and its worldbuilding capacity in particular. The analysis of selected examples of dialogic interaction (e.g. the Smaug–Bilbo colloquy from *The Hobbit*) points to salient differences in the setup and the function of the dialogues under concern. In this respect, the detected patterns lend themselves to be fed into a model of dynamic dialogue types which we will offer as an intermediate summary of this research project.

In the course of the quantitative and qualitative inspection of dialogue patterns, we combine corpus-analytical tools from linguistics with a cognitive approach. For instance, we include an exemplary discussion of metaphors in dialogue and their eventual significance in the worldbuilding process at hand. Ultimately, it is our aim to contribute to a coming closer to an understanding of the fabric of Tolkien's worlds, and of the fantastic in secondary worlds in general.

Approaching Dialogue

With respect to the wide functionality of dialogue, Mildorf and Thomas (2) state:

> [Dialogues] play a formative role by creating characters and presenting them in interaction, by puncturing as well as building narrative structures, by affording positions for interactions between characters or narrators and their audiences...

---

1   This study is also published in a slightly extended version in Fimi/Honegger, *Worldbuilding*.

Being aware of the diversified, dynamic and overlapping functions such as the sociocultural negotiation of power hierarchies, commonness, tradition, emotion, or viewpoints, we assume that authors or narrators present crucial, representative bits of intersubjective language behaviour so readers can use these instances to mentally build and modify fictional characters and the social fabric they act in. Consequentially, we see dialogue as a building block of the conceptualisation of the secondary world (cf. FS; Wolf), hence as a fundamental element of fictional worldbuilding. In this context, Ekman and Taylor rightfully remind us that the term worldbuilding has been employed widely and for different purposes, thus blurring its explanatory potential. We want to refer to worldbuilding as the joint, yet individual enterprise in the author's and the readers' minds to the end that an imaginary, non-primary story world becomes real on the basis of the 'laws' of that world combined with the author's and the readers' diversified experience. Seen in this way, the argument comes full circle: worldbuilding is a concerted *dialogic* activity in itself.[2] It involves both a subcreating text author and engaged text readers.[3]

Ideally, the author offers worldbuilding blocks that are stable enough to be identified as reliable and consistent secondary world elements by readers who may then become agents in the dynamic process by picking these blocks up, filling possible gaps (e.g. typical traits of a certain story character) during immersion[4] and potentially re-using them in new subcreational contexts. Rebounds into the primary, 'real life' world are possible as well, where meanings may be constructed and negotiated on the basis of primary and secondary world experience combined.[5] The analysis of concrete language use, or *verbalisation* (Hasan, *Verbal Art* 96f.), is our key to come to terms with the elusive building processes. Character-to-character dialogue with all its performative pragmatics constitute, as hinted at above, environment-transforming events per se, which are mediated within a narrative framework. Along these lines, we want to look into dialogue as a meaningful formative tool.

---

2   Cf. Bakhtin's notion of dialogism as a structuring force that generates discourse via literary art. Applied to the Tolkien context, Saxton (170) states in this regard that "Middle-earth is, indeed, a remarkably dialogic space."

3   *Subcreation* is used in the Tolkienian sense here of reinstantiating the divine act of creation by means of text (cf. L 153; FS 52); cf. also Wolf.

4   In the context of immersion, Lothmann and Scholz have offered a fruitful approach to the building of stable secondary worlds based on Blending Theory (according to Fauconnier and Turner). On gaps as potential story loci and the incompleteness of imaginary (secondary) worlds, cf. Doležel.

5   Pervasive effects of fiction on readers' primary world lives are described as a consequence of immersion by e.g. Green and Dill. The far-reaching effects may offer new perspectives and even include personality changes; cf. Caracciolo (*Virtual Body*); Djikic and Oatley.

Text Basis and Method

For the present study, we consider the texts *The Silmarillion* (S), *The Hobbit* (H), and *The Lord of the Rings* (LotR) a representative cross section of Tolkien's oeuvre related to Arda, and Middle-earth settings in particular. A fully machine-readable corpus was thus compiled to serve the purpose of investigation at hand. The corpus is constituted of 712,930 words in total and comprises OCRed versions of the full S, H, and LotR according to Tolkien without prefaces, appendices and commentaries.[6] Notably, spoken parts constitute 37.6% of the entire corpus (Fig. 1), varying between 11.6% in S and 46.8% in LotR.

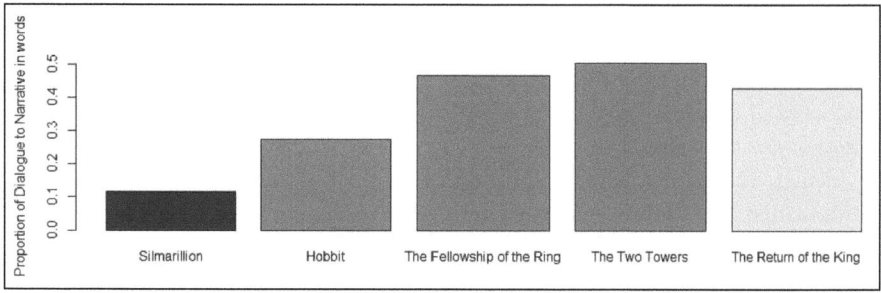

Fig. 1: Ratio of spoken parts in the corpus[7]

For our investigation, we operationalised 'dialogue' as every string of characters within quotation marks and assigned the remainder to a category 'narrative'. Using *Python* (v3.6) and its package *re* (v62) we identified such 'dialogue' and 'narrative' by means of regular expressions.[8] The extracted stretches of text were automatically tokenised and tagged for part-of-speech (PoS) with *TreeTagger* (v3.2.1; cf. Schmid). This allowed us to count the number of words and calculate the ratio of dialogue in the corpus.

For the additional comparison of the conditions 'spoken' and 'narrative' on a word level, we used linear mixed regression modelling.[9] The variables under

---

6   Though S, H, and LotR are stylistically diverse, we do not go so far here to treat the texts as registerially diverse. While S, for instance, is rather a compilation in terms of narrative organisation and leaves considerable gaps for the reader to fill in terms of worldbuilding, we assume a wide-ranging cohesion of sub-creation across all these texts that cover millennia of secondary world history; cf. the concept of 'inner consistency of reality' in Tolkien (FS 59).

7   Fictional literature for the younger often features a higher proportion of external representation via direct speech (cf. Joy); within our corpus, LotR would fall more into this logic than H.

8   Cf. Python Software Foundation. 'Regular expressions' are (abstract) character strings that can be used to generate search patterns for searching an input text.

9   The statistical analyses were performed in *R* (R Core Team) using generalised linear mixed models with the package *lme4* (cf. Bates et al.). The mixed model allows to factor in idiosyncrasies of the different corpus texts with respect to the investigated feature.

investigation were *relative number of pronouns*, *lexical density*, and *type-token ratio*. We assumed that these variables capture aspects of worldbuilding on an abstract level. We added a random effect to capture different baselines of each measure per corpus part (S, H, LotR I, LotR II, LotR III), and we added fixed effect to control for the progression within the parts. This progression measure was based on chapters and was normalised so that, for instance, the last chapters and the middle chapters of each corpus part corresponded to one another.[10] One result was that pronoun use is significantly higher in the spoken parts of the corpus (of all words) than in the narrative (11.9% vs. 7.9% of all words; χ^2=372.12, p<0.001). Further, spoken parts are lexically denser[11] than the narrative ones (63.3% vs. 61.1%; χ^2=98.5, p<0.001); cf. Fig. 2.

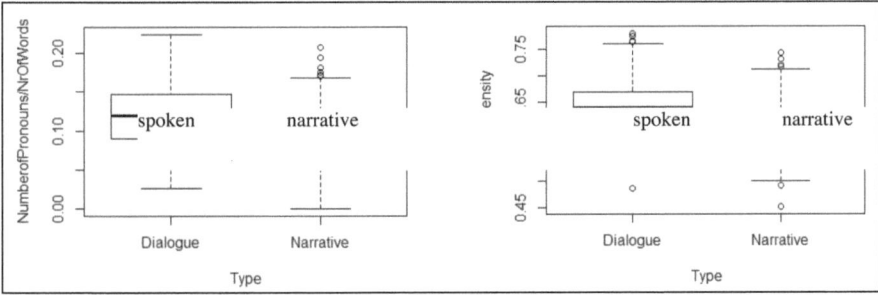

Fig. 2: Ratio of pronouns and lexical density in 'spoken' vs. 'narrative'[12]

Additionally, the type-token ratio revealed the spoken parts to be slightly yet significantly more diverse[13] than the narrative parts (66.6% to 64%; χ^2=46.44, p<0.001) in our corpus. The data illustrate how spoken and narrative parts differ notably in Tolkien's work under concern. In total, with further investigation required, the results point to a decisive role of speech (and thus dialogue) in worldbuilding, thus complementing and specifying the function of the narrative parts in the process.

Clearly, the category 'spoken' as identified above includes all 'true' dialogue instances which are seen here as purposeful spoken conversation with at least two participants and at least two conversational turns, i.e. the participants add an active spoken contribution to a particular conversational exchange con-

---

10   Normalisation was done by converting the chapter to z-scores, i.e. standard deviations above and below the mean.

11   Lexical density measures the proportion of lexical words in a text. It is an indicator of how many concepts are introduced and upheld in the discourse.

12   Here, only 'spoken' or 'narrative' text stretches of more than 100 words inform the analysis.

13   As the type-token ratio is a ratio between unique words to total amount of words, it is a measure of diversity. The higher the ratio, the more lexical diverse the respective text is. Here, the type-token analysis considers text stretches of more than 100 and less than 200 words.

text. Basing on this working definition, we extracted instances for exemplary analysis. We did so under the premise that "crucial structural and functional principles and patterns are at work in fictional dialogue as they are in natural conversation" (Toolan 193). Further, as dialogue is reported to function as a "gear-shifting" technique (Page in Thomas, *Dialogue* 84) that is employed at "seminal moments" in Tolkien's work in particular (cf. Joy 76), it deserves to be in the focus in what follows in chapter 4.

Via the grammatical tagging for PoS,[14] the corpus data were analysable for word class distribution. The data could then be processed with the help of the corpus tool *AntConc* (cf. Lawrence). We selected the four main lexical word classes, i.e. nouns, verbs, adjectives and adverbs, plus pronouns as we expect all of these to serve key roles in dialogue. We intend to highlight these roles by inspecting dialogue examples from across the corpus of S, H, and LotR.

Dialogue: Examples and Patterns

Example: S 39-42 (dialogue only, 661 words)

The participants of the dialogue are the Valar Yavanna, Aulë, and Manwë discussing aspects of creation. In this passage from S, there is one particularly dominating word class (Tab. 1). Nearly 26% of all words in this dialogue are nouns, which is more than 5% higher than the highest percentage of nouns in the other dialogue examples (cf. Tab. 2-4).

	nouns	verbs	adjectives	adverbs	pronouns
S 39-42	25.94%	15.58%	4.40%	6.72%	11.31%

Tab. 1: Part-of-speech ratio of S dialogue

Contentwise, the passage is concerned with mythological topics and puts historical events into the perspective of the story world cosmos. In this context, the finding above is in line with the fact that concepts and (fictional) states of affairs including mythical or mythological actors, places and conceptualisations are ideas that usually find their expression in texts via nouns.[15] In terms of the function of the nominal word class as representing material or non-material entities in the world, we can state that the worldbuilding potential of this

---

14 The annotation tool TreeTagger (cf. Schmid) was chosen for its low error rate (3%). After the automated annotation, the data were post-corrected manually to exclude errors.

15 Here, 'text' denotes all linguistic forms of a communicative act, i.e. spoken and written.

word class finds emphasis in this dialogue example. Simply put, Tolkien relied particularly on nouns here in order to construct relevant features of his legendarium such as creation myth as a constitutive and cohesive cultural element.

Example: LotR I 261-264 (dialogue only, 1,419 words)

Elrond's Council at Rivendell in LotR I is a milestone of the LotR story development due to the influential resolutions resulting from a joint interaction of multiple parties. In this passage, the involved locutors, all members of different cultures with assumedly dissimilar discussion traditions yet overlapping interests, engage in "intertraditional dialogue" (Simonson 175) out of political necessity. The dialogue (or polylogue, to be specific) features the exchange of cultural customs and stereotypes via the speech of their representatives.

The quantitative analysis of the passage shows the relative weightiness of one-word class, here verbs, compared to the other investigated examples (Tab. 2; cf. Tab. 1, 3-4). The verbal class is usually exploited to express processes or actions. Coinciding with a relatively high amount of verb-specifying adverbs, the verb ratio in this example hints at a rather action-driven motivation of the dialogue function, thus having the potential of pushing the story forward. This function is skilfully embedded by Tolkien in the multicultural dialogue.

	nouns	verbs	adjectives	adverbs	pronouns
LotR 261-264	20.31%	18.99%	5.15%	8.39%	13.9%

Tab. 2: Part-of-speech ratio of LotR dialogue

Example: H 222-227 (dialogue only, 933 words)

The Smaug–Bilbo interaction takes up considerable space in H. This hints at its decisive importance in the text (cf. also Jakobsson), also in view of the fact that H predominantly consists of non-spoken (narrative) parts (cf. Fig. 1). The significance of this dialogue relates to character development in particular. The dialogue qualifies as a case of subcreation within subcreation as the dragon becomes a narrative agent by constructing *himself* as a complex character. Drawing on Lakoff and Johnson's Conceptual Metaphor Theory, a recent study (cf. Lothmann) has shown that this self-construction is effected by metaphorical conceptualisations in particular that underlie Smaug's verbose language use in the dialogue passage. Foregrounded examples such as DRAGON is HUMAN

WARRIOR (H 226) and DRAGON is KING (later in H 233) do not only underscore the awareness of his individuality, but render Smaug's elusive Faërie nature (cf. FS 55) and motivations for action more conceptualisable within the logic of the secondary world for both his collocutor Bilbo and the reader. The Smaug–Bilbo dialogue is thus functional in character-constituting terms. It further serves as a natural frame of a challenge between interlocutors on intellectual par in lieu of a physical fight. This function is supported by the PoS data (Tab. 3).

	nouns	verbs	adjectives	adverbs	pronouns
H 222-227	19.39%	18.58%	6.73%	9.07%	16.7%

Tab. 3: Part-of-speech ratio of H dialogue (1)

Among the selected examples, this dialogue features the highest ratio of three-word classes, namely adjectives, adverbs, and pronouns. The findings match the focus on character, as especially adjectives (and their potential adverb specifiers) are used to attribute features to entities including story characters. The high pronoun ratio, i.e. here the usage of first-person pronouns by Smaug in particular, supports his self-construction within the conceptual confines of the story world, hence guiding the reader to build the story world accordingly.[16]

Example: H 4-12 (dialogue only, 1,006 words)

This dialogue example consists of the first Gandalf–Bilbo exchange and the first conversational turns of Bilbo and members of the dwarves visiting his house. Interestingly, the PoS analysis of these introductory dialogues from H revealed no domination of a particular word class (Tab. 4) in view of the other examples under concern (cf. Tab. 1-3).

	nouns	verbs	adjectives	adverbs	pronouns
H 4-12	20.7%	17.71%	6.12%	6.83%	16.07%

Tab. 4: Part-of-speech ratio of H dialogue (2)

---

16   43 of the 157 personal pronouns (and 9 of the 29 possessive pronouns) in this dialogue refer to the first person singular, i.e. the speaker Smaug.

All percentages were neither the highest nor the lowest across all categories, seemingly making it the most 'ordinary' example dialogue. However, nouns, adjectives and pronouns in this dialogue have the second-highest ratios among the examples. We may claim that the relatively high percentage of adjectives and pronouns hint at a function of additionally supporting the description of entities including story characters.

In the following chapter, we will attempt to resume the threads offered by the data and their analysis. The incipient interpretations provided here will feed a systematic framework.

Towards a Model of Dialogue and Dialogue Functions

Realities, primary or secondary, exist because of conceptualisations and their rendering by means of words. As well, all creation within the Middle-earth legendarium proceeds via language (cf. FS; Keene; Zimmer). Dialogue has a considerable role in this creation, given that there is the willingness to mentally perform it on the one hand, and that it follows an explicable, consistent logic on the other. On the basis of the depicted linguistic patterns (cf. Ch. 4) and PoS analysis in particular, we want to set forth a classification of dialogue according to four types that all inform the construction of meaning within the fictional world settings (Fig. 3). We are confident in claiming that the identified types have a broad applicability to analyses of all types of fantastic story worlds, let alone fictional literature in general.

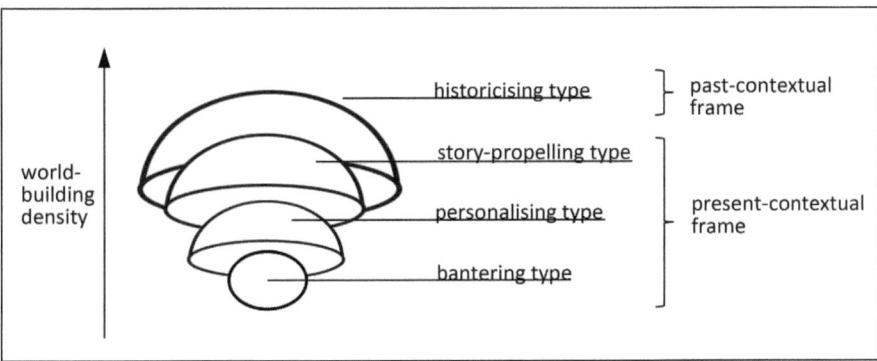

Fig. 3: Model of dialogue classification according to examples from S, H, and LotR

The types are modelled along their main functional purpose within the story fabric, which corresponds to their impact on worldbuilding, or worldbuilding density. Clearly, the types may dynamically overlap and occur in degrees within dialogue situations and contexts. The confines of the respective types, however, root in our quantitative data.

The *bantering* type

More than dialogues of other types, *bantering* dialogues are used to bring an 'everyday touch' to the conversational behaviour of the story world characters. We as readers may take up *bantering* dialogues as a tool to construct the socio-pragmatic conventions of the speakers including phatic expressions such as politeness formulae to foster social bonds, humour, casualness, playfulness, and swearing. As in primary world contexts, dialogue appears to be a natural locus of such functions in secondary worlds.[17]

The initial Gandalf–Bilbo exchange in H is an example of this type. It is particularly this example which, however undirected and marginal it may seem for the larger framework and the development of the story plot, lends itself well as an entry gate to the secondary world which the interlocutors are part of, and of which first readers still know little at this point. Readers may initiate and supplement their construction of fictional characters on the basis of the characters' behaviour in *bantering* dialogues.[18] In terms of PoS, this is supported by their featuring high percentages of pronouns and character-descriptive adjectives. In this respect, the *bantering* type overlaps with the following one.

The *personalising* type

Via this dialogue type, the fictional self can be transactionally constructed (cf. Magnusson in Thomas, *Fictional* 60). Here, the self vis-à-vis the other is stressed in the light of characters being pivotal anchors within secondary world settings.[19] The reader may thus obtain insight into the characters' nature and motivations. The quantitative PoS analysis showed a connection between such

---

17 Note that the bantering dialogues in the Tolkienian context are, as are other dialogue types mentioned in this chapter, characterised by an edited quasi-mimesis that is likely to be influenced by novel writing conventions of the time (cf. Mepham 412). Specifically put, the dialogues do not involve an imitation of everyday primary world speech as readers would employ it in their speech behaviour. Thus, the corpus dialogues miss out on vernacular, hesitation phenomena, tags, or other features of spoken grammar that readers are used to. Cf. also Oatley.

18 In this context and with particular respect to the Gandalf–Bilbo exchange in H, cf. Wegener and Lothmann. Dialogue per se is helpful in the event of coming to terms with the secondary world as dialogue is a tool that connects the readers' daily habits and communicative experiences with the story characters' life spheres.

19 Cf. similarly Caracciolo (*Narrative Space* 425).

a *personalising*, i.e. character-building, function and dialogues with the highest percentage of adjectives, adverbs, and pronouns.

The Smaug–Bilbo exchange in H is an example of the *personalising* dialogue type. There, Smaug conceptualises himself as a deep and dynamic individual character, even as a cultural representative and moral authority. Worldbuilding (including an understanding of the Faërie logic of the secondary world) thus gains density on a micro-level.[20] Still, this is to be separated from dialogue types in which processes or historical contextualisations are in functional focus; cf. c) and d) below.

The *story-propelling* type

Story-propelling dialogues are used in order to push the story forward and to highlight decisions and actions made in the present context. As actions may be described, planned and executed by more than one individual and may refer to a historical chain of events, this dialogue category is in between the micro- and macro-levels of building the secondary world. The PoS analysis supports the separate *story-propelling* type, which features a significantly high ratio of verbs and thus a clear focus on processes.

The Council of Elrond dialogue may serve as an example of this type. In this example, intercultural negotiation leads to collaboration. Importantly, the main course of story actions is set via dialogue, which itself adds coherence to both story and the story world (cf. Simonson 178). Sharing opinions and stories is intrinsic to *story-propelling* dialogues as a process itself that leads to further meaning-making processes (i.e. action) within the secondary world context. This includes intra- and intercultural aspects as well as the techniques of poetry and song.

The *historicising* type

Our model includes a *historicising* category that comprises the dialogues with a macro-level and high-density worldbuilding function. In the Tolkien context, matters of myth and cosmology are discussed here to be taken up as a basic

---

20 The *personalising* function includes the display of ideolectal, ethnolectal or multilingual competence; cf. the use of lexical and grammatical archaisms by Theoden in LotR II (507) or the pronunciation particularities of the Rohirrim in general (cf. LotR II 496-497) which are intended to be added to character (or group) conceptualisation by the reader. On the link-ups of language and landscape, cf. Smith (74). On different stylistic features of the speech of LotR protagonists, cf. Shippey.

temporal and moral framework that the concerned (fantastic) story characters are subject to. An example of this is the Yavanna–Aulë–Manwë dialogue in S.

Nouns prevail as the by far most significant PoS in dialogues of this type, which suits the function of conveying concepts, actors, places, and states of affairs from story times past, including previously unknown and Faërie ones. Nonetheless, they help provide a past-contextual frame for the story present and are decisive in terms of story world coherence, or Überbau. In the context of Tolkien in particular, *historicising* dialogues add depth to the subcreational construct in terms of a diachronic story dimension, as well as its deeper moral significance throughout.[21] This dialogue type and function is in line with Hasan's *theme* within her linguistics-based framework of verbal art (cf. Hasan, *Verbal Art*; *Private Pleasure*). In this vein, the *historicising* type is used to act, as a high-order meaning-organisational instrument and via a systematic patterning of linguistic choices, towards an informed engaging with a story-encompassing *theme* by the reader.[22] The framework implies that a systematic patterning within a text, or foregrounding (cf. Hasan, *Verbal Art* 96, 101), fosters the perception of that very text as a coherent unit. Dialogue of the types described in this chapter, i.e. types b), c), and d) in particular, feature such patterning on the basis of PoS. It is stated in general here that dialogues contribute to a consistent foregrounding that promotes, if not eases, effective secondary worldbuilding. Overlapping of types is assumed to be frequent and boundaries are fuzzy, for instance at the Council of Elrond when Elrond 'historicises' by creating context in space and time across a longer text passage (LotR I 237-239) to ratify the intercultural connections of the dialogue participants. Clearly, he does so for the reader as well.

Conclusion and Outlook

A statistical analysis of prominent linguistic features, i.e. part-of-speech in particular, has led to a function-based classification into four main dialogue types in the Tolkien corpus under investigation. These *bantering*, *personalising*, *story-propelling*, and *historicising* types have been modelled to cover the range of styles (from colloquial to solemn) and topic dimensions (phatic communi-

---

21 In Tolkien's *historicising* dialogues, the temporal dimension is stressed by the occasional use of antiquated verb and pronoun forms, which further adds a certain exaltedness to the conversational context; cf. e.g. "If thou hadst thy will" (S 40).

22 According to Hasan (cf. *Verbal Art* 100), the theme or deeper meaning relates to an issue that is of relevance for the author's and the readers' (shared) cultural community as a whole, including norms of social (co-) existence, and ontological worldviews in general. Tolkienian themes deal, among other things, with hope and loss, mortality, ethical imperatives, enchantment, or the evil within. On linguistic choice, cf. Halliday; Hasan (*Choice*).

cation, character, plot development, or mythohistorical contextualisation) from a micro- to a macro-level of systematic foregrounding, thus representing their complementary impact on worldbuilding density and coherence. In this regard, dialogue shows to be more than a technique, i.e. more than a mere alternative container of story material. Dialogue as identified here is used as a frequent, versatile and strategic device that has a decisive share next to non-dialogue in the building of a secondary world setting. Our presented model is meant to offer opportunities for the study of fictional literature beyond Tolkien's Middle-earth story cosmos.

Spoken words in dialogue add relevant meaning-making potential to the reader's individual worldbuilding approaches. Dialogue, and this means not only instances in pivotal story scenes, may be seen in this respect as a catalyst that adds 'architecture' in terms of depth, detail, and consistency on the basis of conceptual and according linguistic choices by the author. With respect to Tolkien's fictional fantasy where "all magic is linguistic in inspiration" (Zimmer 65), dialogue is a major skeleton key to unlock the workings of Faërie, for instance to learn about Smaug's complex personality directly from his own utterances, and to bring that character construction into line with the secondary world reality that surrounds him. Tolkien's agents within the secondary world across several texts (here: S, H, LotR) act within "a world for the languages" (L 165), thus also within a world for dialogue. Dialogue represents an offer to the reader to engage in the worldbuilding process.

For a better understanding of the nature of dialogue and its functional breadth in fictional texts, it is as advisable as it is promising to continue this project. We intend to validate and strengthen the corpus findings with experimental methods. For instance, we expect different sets of reading behaviour for the four dialogue types presented here. By using eye-tracking as a next step, we want to contribute to making worldbuilding, and the elusive conceptualisations involved therein, visible and thus render it a more quantifiable object of research. Further, via eye-tracking means, we can move away from an idealised, modelled reader to the actual readers in the flesh, as it were. Additionally, with more insights from interdisciplinary approaches and by enhancing the corpus beyond Tolkien and beyond fictional fantasy genre restrictions, it will be interesting to see the particular impact of dialogue on readers' immersion.

After all, worldbuilding is part of our "craft[ing] shared stories" (Saxton 165). We can safely assume that this co-architecturing of the fantastic by author and readers relies to a significant extent on systematic cognitive and linguistic patterning. In the event of crafting, we have the opportunity to appreciate the art-ness of texts (cf. Hasan, *Verbal Art*) and, even more so, secondary worlds as cultural artefacts.

Bibliography

Bakhtin, Mikhail. *The Dialogic Imagination: Four Essays*. Austin: University of Texas Press, 1982

Bates, Douglas et al. "Fitting Linear Mixed-effects Models Using {lme4}." In: *Journal of Statistical Software* 67 (2015): 1-48

Caracciolo, Marco. "The Reader's Virtual Body: Narrative Space and Its Reconstruction." In: *Storyworlds* 3 (2011): 117-138

---. "Narrative Space and Readers' Responses to Stories: A Phenomenological Account." In: *Style* 47 (2013): 425-444

Doležel, Lubomir. *Heterocosmica: Fiction and Possible Worlds*. Baltimore: Johns Hopkins University Press, 1998

Djikic, Maja & Keith Oatley. "The Art in Fiction: From Indirect Communication to Changes of the Self." In: *Psychology of Aesthetics, Creativity, and the Arts* 8 (2014): 498-505

Ekman, Stefan & Audrey I. Taylor. "Notes towards a Critical Approach to Worlds and World-building." In: *Fafnir: Nordic Journal of Science Fiction and Fantasy Research* 3, 3 (2016): 7-18

Fauconnier, Gilles & Mark Turner. *The Way We Think: Conceptual Blending and the Mind's Hidden Complexities*. New York: Basic Books, 2003

Fimi, Dimitra & Thomas Honegger (Eds.). *Tolkien and Literary Worldbuilding*. Zurich et al.: Walking Tree Publishers, 2018

Green, Melanie C. & Karen E. Dill. "Engaging with Stories and Characters: Learning, Persuasion, and Transportation into Narrative Worlds." In: *The Oxford Handbook of Media Psychology*. Ed.: Karen E. Dill. Oxford: Oxford University Press, 2013. 449-461

Halliday, M.A.K. *An Introduction to Functional Grammar*. London: Arnold, 1989

Hasan, Ruqaiya. *Linguistics, Language, and Verbal Art*. 2nd ed. Oxford: Oxford University Press, 1989

---. "Private Pleasure, Public Discourse: Reflections on Engaging with Literature." In: *Language and Verbal Art Revisited: Linguistic Approaches to the Study of Literature*. Eds.: Donna R. Miller, Monica Turci. London: Equinox, 2007. 13-40

---. "Choice, System, Realization: Describing Language as Meaning Potential." In: *Systemic Functional Linguistics: Exploring Choice*. Eds.: Lise Fontaine et al. Cambridge: Cambridge Univ. Pr., 2013. 269-299

Jakobsson, Ármann. "Talk to the Dragon: Tolkien as Translator." In: *Tolkien Studies* 6 (2009): 27-39

Joy, Louise. "Tolkien's Language." In: *J.R.R. Tolkien: 'The Hobbit' and 'The Lord of the Rings'*. Ed.: Peter Hunt. Basingstoke: Palgrave Macmillan, 2006. 74-87

Keene, Louise E. "Restoration of Language in Middle-earth." In: *Mythlore* 20, 4 (1995): 6-13

Lakoff, George & Mark Johnson. *Metaphors We Live by*. Repr. Chicago et al.: University of Chicago Press, 2003

Lawrence, Anthony. *AntConc*. Version 3.4.4. Software. 2017. http://www.laurenceanthony.net/software/antconc (2017-10-23)

Lothmann, Timo. "The Ravaging and Hoard-guarding Antagonist: A Cognitive Approach to 'Dragon' Conceptualisations in 'Beowulf' and Selected Writings of Tolkien." In: *Fastitocalon* 6 (2016): 169-184

Lothmann, Timo & Janek Scholz. "Derived from and Flowing into Reality: Faërie as a Conceptual Framework for the Blending of Story Rooms." In: *Hither Shore* 12 (2015): 8-20

Mepham, John. "Novelistic Dialogue: Some Recent Developments." In: *New Developments in English and American Studies: Continuity and Change. Proceedings of the Seventh International Conference on English and American Literature and Language*, Kraków, March 27-29, 1996. Ed.: Zygmunt Mazur. Kraków: Universitas, 1997. 411-431

Mildorf, Jarmila & Bronwen Thomas. "Introduction: Dialogue across Media."
In: *Dialogue across Media*. Eds.: Jarmila Mildorf, Bronwen Thomas. Amsterdam et al.:
Benjamins, 2017. 1-15

Oatley, Keith. "A Taxonomy of the Emotions of Literary Response and a Theory of Identification in Fictional Narrative." In: *Poetics* 23 (1994): 53-74

Python Software Foundation. *Python*. Software. 2017. https://www. python.org (2017-10-23)

R Core Team. "R: A Language and Environment for Statistical Computing. R Foundation for
Statistical Computing." 2017. 23 Oct. 2017: http://www.R-project.org/

Saxton, Benjamin. "Tolkien and Bakhtin on Authorship, Literary Freedom, and Alterity."
In: *Tolkien Studies* 10 (2013): 165-181

Schmid, Helmut. "Improvements in Part-of-Speech Tagging with an Application to German."
In: *Proceedings of the ACL SIGDAT-Workshop*. Dublin, 1995

Shippey, Tom. *J.R.R. Tolkien: Author of the Century*. London: HarperCollins, 2001

Simonson, Martin. *'The Lord of the Rings' and the Western Narrative Tradition*. Zurich et al.:
Walking Tree Publishers, 2008

Smith, Ross. *Inside Language: Linguistic and Aesthetic Theory in Tolkien*. Zurich et al.: Walking
Tree Publishers, 2007

Thomas, Bronwen. "Dialogue." In: *The Cambridge Companion to Narrative*. Ed.: David
Herman. Cambridge: Cambridge University Press, 2007. 80-93

---. *Fictional Dialogue: Speech and Conversation in the Modern and Postmodern Novel*. Lincoln
et al.: University of Nebraska Press, 2012

Tolkien, J.R.R. *The Letters of J.R.R. Tolkien*. Ed.: Humphrey Carpenter. London:
Allen and Unwin, 1981

---. *The Hobbit or There and Back Again*. Rev. ed. New York: Ballantine Books, 1982

---. *The Lord of the Rings*. London: HarperCollins, 1995

---. *The Silmarillion*. Ed.: Christopher Tolkien. London: HarperCollins, 2008

---. *Tolkien on Fairy-stories*. Eds.: Verlyn Flieger, Douglas A. Anderson. London:
HarperCollins, 2014

Toolan, Michael. "Analysing Fictional Dialogue." *Language and Communication* 5 (1985):
193-206

Wegener, Rebekah & Timo Lothmann. "'That's not Normal Rabbit Behaviour': On the Track of
the Grammar of Fictional Worlds." In: *On Verbal Art: Essays in Honour of Ruqaiya Hasan*.
Eds.: Rebekah Wegener et al. Sheffield et al.: Equinox, 2018. 252-278

Wolf, Mark J.P. *Building Imaginary Worlds: The Theory and History of Subcreation*. New York
et al.: Routledge, 2012

Zimmer, Mary. "Creating and Recreating Worlds with Words: The Religion and the
Magic of Language in 'The Lord of the Rings'." In: *VII: An Anglo-American Literary
Review* 12 (1995): 65-78

Forms of Racism as a Facet of World-building in Fantasy Literature

Nilüfer Ulusoy-Schmitz (Alsdorf)

There is no denying the fact that forms of racism are still an omnipresent and current issue of our communities. Recent years have shown that right-wing populist positions are on the rise again, recklessly toying with public opinion in the face of migration, ethnic riots and their alleged consequences. Taking the course of the 20th century into consideration, it is obvious that racism could be regarded as one of the most defining problems of modern history. Thus, authors of fantasy literature as Tolkien or Lewis were confronted with a wide range of results of racist ideologies. They experienced the aftermath of xenophobic positions either at first-hand or observed them in the media (cf. Saler 177). Fittingly, Pavel points out that "[the] real world … cannot be kept out of fictional texts" (Pavel 28), which suggests that various forms of racism are integrated into works of fantasy literature either in a critical or undiscerning way. In this context, Fimi remarks that "a fantasy world … reproduces some of the concepts and prejudices of the 'primary' world" (Fimi 159). Maybe due to this circumstance, Tolkien's works—as it is well-known—are occasionally facing criticism regarding seemingly racist tendencies to be found within his Secondary World (cf. e.g. Ibata). What is more, Tolkien's œuvre has every now and then been used to support racist policies, as Saler points out (cf. Saler 162).

The paper at hand is, in a first step, intended to present fundamental concepts of racism, thus elaborating on different subtypes of this issue based on the groundwork of Albert Memmi and other scholars of different fields. This theoretical background is further applied to Tolkien's *Lord of the Rings*, Rowling's *Harry Potter* Series and Patrick Rothfuss's *Kingkiller Chronicle*—works that have attracted the attention of a huge amount of readers in the course of the last decades. In doing so, questions referring to the function of racism in fantasy literature and its contribution to the structure of imaginary worlds are going to be examined.

In the early 16th century, the term "race" was first used for describing traits of human beings (cf. Nothwehr 6). This was a fatal step towards deterministic interpretations of differences among humans. The distinction of races was based on aspects such as skin colour, eye colour, language, customs and more. Especially the period of colonial history with its societal and cultural aftermath has further deepened this position (cf. Miles 81). However, there is no "scientific support for the belief that the world's population is divided into a number of discrete biological types or 'races'" (Miles 82), although, at the time of Tolkien's peak of work, the term 'race' was still referring to a valid scientific category (cf. Fimi 158). As a societal phenomenon, racism influenced works of art, since racial themes are as old as literature itself. When we think of the numerous examples in literature, in which one can observe racist tendencies, as for example in William Shakespeare's plays *Othello* or the *Merchant of Venice* or in children's classics like Mark Twain's *Huckleberry Finn*, this is made obvious. Literary characters are discriminated against on the basis of features as skin colour or origin, hence reflecting racist attitudes within societies. The definition of racism and its sub-forms, as "[there] is no single, unitary racism that is everywhere the same" (Miles 85), remains a topic open for debate (cf. Miles 79; Rana 28).

A widely accepted and frequently cited definition of racism (cf. Rana 29) has been given by the French writer and sociologist Albert Memmi in his seminal work titled *Le Racisme: Description, Définition, Traitement* from 1982. Memmi states that racism means to falsely connect different features of a human being and creating one complex, thus forming groups (races) that are different from each other in a biological sense (cf. Memmi 97). In a next step, these (far-fetched) differences are used as a basis for subjugating another group of individuals, while securing economic, political and psychological advantages and privileges for one's own seemingly pure and admirable group (cf. Memmi 97). In this context, Memmi differentiates between several basic characteristics of the notion of racism. First, the recognition of a difference between individuals or groups and secondly, the attribution of a negative value to these persons (cf. Nothwehr 6f.). After that, the difference and its negative quality is imposed on a whole group and ultimately, within a fourth phase, these negative prejudices are used in order to justify actions against the subjugated group (cf. Nothwehr 6f.). While this biological racism is—according to Memmi—a newer phenomenon, he stresses that racism as such means to be afraid of biological differences and feeling 'threatened' by their effect on one's individual or collective integrity (cf. Memmi 100). So, racism stands for the generalised and absolute value attributed to alleged or real differences that are used by an *accusateur* at the expense of the *victime* (cf. Memmi 103). In addition to that, the accusations are generally directed to all members of one particular group and are not limited in a temporal manner, making it almost impossible to alter this hierarchy among these groups without effort from both sides (cf. Memmi 114). A system of domination and subordination is maintained (cf. Miles 84). Thus, racism is a collective judgement, a social construct, that both offender and victim are confronted with from their earliest experiences onward (cf. Memmi 115). It "attacks along many fronts and in many forms, deploying whatever is at hand and even what is not, inventing when the need arises" (Memmi 78).

While Memmi mainly concentrates on the definition, forms and consequences of biological racism[1], Rommelspacher further distinguishes between forms of racism that are supported by the entire system of a society itself, i.e. structural or institutional racism emanating from institutions and institutional policies within a society, and those forms of racism merely upheld by individuals and their beliefs and actions, i.e. individual racism (cf. Rommelspacher 30).

In addition to racism, the two notions of ethnocentrism and xenophobia require greater attention and have to be differentiated from this main concept in different respects. Ethnocentrism is the belief in the "inherent superiority of one's own ethnic group and a tendency to view and judge alien groups from the perspective of one's own" (Sutherland 275). Even more than racism as such, ethnocentrism explicitly adds the feature of ethnicity to the concept and, in highlighting distinctiveness, language and culture (cf. Weiss 26f.), one's own race is provided with a superior value without always going so far as to violently subjugating another community (cf. Weiss 17), but rather considering these other groups as secondary and inferior to one's own (cf. Geiss 31). Admittedly, almost every society has considered itself as the very centre of the world and its history, with its members seeing their own development and experiences mainly from their individual or societal perspectives (cf. Geiss 33).

Xenophobia as the stronger form of ethnocentrism in turn is the fear or hatred of strangers or of people who are culturally different from oneself (cf. Geiss 28). In comparison to racism, it is a vague psychological concept and does not necessarily entail an ideology of domination and subordination. It can however be seen as an elementary precondition of racism (cf. Geiss 28) being a plain resort to hatred and enmity towards strangers, not solely because they are different, but because they are not part of one's own social group. What remains to be said about these different phenomena elucidated above is that all of them are—to a certain degree—a consequence of a certain lack of familiarity with 'the Other' (Miles 85), as it is (cf. Liebhart et al. 7; Rana 26). At the same time this very attitude of creating 'the Other' entails a strengthening of group identification and cohesiveness (cf. Kidder & Stewart 51) on the part of the *accusateur*, because "[in] order to define my own self, I have to compare it with an Other" (Rana 16). Owing to this, our reality is simplified by forming categories of 'us' and 'them' and assigning particular features to whole communities, not individuals, without putting too much effort into testing these or getting to know each other (cf. Rana 26).

---

1   Weiss adds a second form to this biological one, which she calls **cultural racism**, resting on a cultural superiority of one group over another (cf. Weiss 27) on the basis of cultural traditions (cf. Rana 29). In this respect, Miles adds that traits as diet, cloths or religious belief may be used in terms of this form of racism (cf. Miles 89).

With these fundamental ideas kept in mind, a closer look at racism and its sub-forms in fantasy literature needs to be cast. First, Tolkien's *Fellowship of the Ring* is to be examined. As it is documented in his letters, Tolkien challenged the use of the term 'race' and argued that language users belong to different peoples rather than races (cf. Fimi 139). Hence, his distinction followed the romantic identification of a nation with its language and culture (cf. Fimi 139). He was moreover strongly against the Nazi Regime and famously "refused to declare an Aryan origin but he constructed a mythical world where racial purity is the norm and where there exists a strict racial hierarchy with mongoloid orcs at the bottom" (Fimi 157). In addition to that, Tolkien also stated that "the treatment of colour nearly always horrifies anyone going out from Britain, not only in South Africa" (L61, 73). He also noted that there is "nothing about British or American imperialism in the Far East that does not fill me with regret and disgust" (L100, 115). In the course of his work, the readership is yet confronted with many different humanoid races that reveal different levels of racism in their attitude and behaviour towards each other. This determines the way alliances and enmities are represented. The supremacy of the Elves over the other Middle-earth beings for instance seems only natural as they are introduced and represented as biologically and spiritually superior to mankind (cf. Fimi 143). Furthermore, there is a strong dichotomy of light and dark, good and evil, east and west. Those men of the Third Age, who were allied to the good side were fair and modelled after Europeans, very much created after Tolkien's own likings (cf. Fimi 140), whereas the evil men and Orcs were dark-skinned and of Mongoloid appearance (cf. Fimi 150).

Hobbits, in turn, take up a predominant role within the plot, as they are the first major characters to be encountered in Tolkien's Secondary World, the mediators (cf. Salo 25) and shall therefore be analysed with regard to the underlying question introduced above. Tolkien constructs the Shire as a self-dependent, secluded (cf. Honegger 65) society modelled after 19th century rural England (cf. Walker 52). This seclusion can also be observed in the attitude of its inhabitants. The Hobbits seem divided and ethnocentric, consisting of groups that object and meet each other with a natural mistrust, which can be seen by means of several quotations. Thus, many statements refer to those Hobbits that live outside Hobbiton, the starting point of the journey. Daddy Twofoot remarks about the Buckland folk "no wonder they're queer ... if they live on the wrong side of the Brandywine River" (LotR I 22) and Lobelia Sackville-Baggins rejects Meriadoc by saying "You don't belong here; you're no Baggins" (LotR I 39). Even admirable and heroic Samwise reveals that he "had a natural mistrust of the inhabitants of other parts of the Shire" (LotR I 93) and Farmer Maggot tells Frodo the following: "[you] should never have gone mixing yourself up with Hobbiton folk ... folk are queer up there" (LotR I 94). The latter is even more absurd as Tom Bombadil utters utmost respect for him (cf. LotR I 132).

Furthermore, Tolkien uses the terms colony and colonists when talking of the Shire. Buckland is seen as "a sort of colony from the Shire" (LotR I 98) and the people of the Shire are referred to as colonists from the perspective of the Hobbits inhabiting the city of Bree as "they claim... to have done everything before the people of the Shire, whom they refer to as 'colonists'" (LotR I 8). This use of words is especially significant as it may simultaneously remind the readership of the history of colonisation and its associations with the development of racial categories. The Hobbits generally reject many forms of outer strangeness, which is again conveyed by Farmer Maggot, using the words "this fellow was the most outlandish I have ever set eyes on. He won't cross my land without leave a second time, not if I can stop it" (LotR I 92). The Hobbits are obviously afraid of strangers and rather want to remain secluded than getting mixed up with outlanders and their business (cf. Shippey 116) as the subsequent lines stress: "as the days of the Shire lengthened, they spoke less and less with the Elves, and grew afraid of them, and distrustful of those that had dealings with them" (LotR I 7). This fear is so strong that Farmer Maggot is always on the watch: "I was just going to set my dogs on any strangers" (LotR I 92). He even has several well-meant pieces of advice at his disposal: "and don't get mixed up with these outlandish folk" (LotR I 95). Hobbits are mostly presented as ethnocentric and slightly xenophobic at the very beginning of the novel. This attitude underlines their backwardness and seclusion, while at the same time pushing away the strangeness lurking at the borders. They fear strangers and prefer to think about races such as Elves in an abstract manner and people like Ted Sandyman grow very sceptical whenever something strange is happening, as the conversation in the Green Dragon Inn reveals (cf. LotR I 44). Likewise, well-respected persons as Gandalf are considered "disturber[s] of the peace" (LotR I 41) and the Gaffer tells his son not to mix with Elves and dragons, but rather to deal with cabbages and potatoes (cf. LotR I 24). Hobbits do not tend to travel, and those who get out of the Shire are looked upon suspiciously. Due to this, Bilbo and Frodo are ultimately considered awkward and strange (cf. LotR I 95). While "uncommon" Hobbits learn to overcome their attitudes, many Hobbits remain secluded and afraid of outsiders (cf. LotR I 1). The first is convincingly emphasised by the tender bonds that Frodo, Sam, Merry and Pippin develop during their journey through Middle-earth and the fact that they only reach their goals owing to their cooperation with and support of companions of other races. The latter aspect strongly stresses the necessity of crossing borders and overcoming fears and prejudices by establishing ties with 'the Other'.

The second example to be presented in this essay is the one of Patrick Rothfuss's *Kingkiller Chronicle*. Before working with the novels themselves, it should be mentioned that Rothfuss has clearly positioned himself against racism in social networks. For instance, he writes on Twitter that "Racism is like cancer.

When you see it, you have to root it out fast, or it spreads and metasticizes" (@ Patrick Rothfuss).

The protagonist Kvothe of his *Kingkiller Chronicle* is brought up as part of an ethnic minority, the so-called Edema Ruh. They live and work in troupes of traveling players and musicians sometimes very similar to the stereotypical presentations of Sinti and Roma as they are shown in other media. This ethnic group is repeatedly discriminated against by various members of society. Edema Ruh suffer from structural and institutional racism. For instance, the mayor of the town in one of the stories that Kvothe's father, Arliden, tells him, wants the troupe to "camp outside town and no one will bother you so long as you don't start any fights or wander off with anything that isn't yours" (Rothfuss, *Name* 64) to make sure that they will not cause any trouble. This treatment underlines that Ruh are treated differently because of preconceived beliefs and attitudes towards their race and culture. Edema Ruh are obviously considered and despised as natural thieves and troublemakers. Fittingly, one of the learned masters of the university, Kvothe attends after his troupe is killed by the mysterious group of the Chandrian in order to become an arcanist, reveals similar prejudices against his people and origin. This master Elodin explains that "Edema Ruh make exceptionally poor students ... fine for rote learning, but the study of naming requires a level of dedication that ravel such as yourself rarely possess" (Rothfuss, *Name* 335). In this context, the degradation of his community, the protagonist Kvothe even talks about the systematic and extensive slaughter of his people in the past, which could be considered a genocide, as the following lines may suggest: "I spoke in anger. 'Ravel' is a term my people find particularly offensive. Its use makes light of the systematic slaughter of thousands of Ruh" (Rothfuss, *Wise* 95). This treatment is further characterised by racial slurs and Edema Ruh seem to commonly suffer from political persecution and violence. Kvothe adds that their persecutors "hunted us like foxes. For a hundred years Ruh-hunt was a favourite pastime among the Aturan upper cruts" (Rothfuss, *Wise* 317). The Edema Ruh also face individual racism because of the internalised rejection and hatred of Ruh that can be observed within every social class. Not only the members of aristocracy or higher levels of society, but also members of lower social groups seem to despise and openly reject them. The utterances of Schiem, whose social status is further underlined by the particular register, support this impression: "Oi'm not some lying Ruh, spinning stories to scare yeh out o'pennies, boy," he said, plainly irritated" (Rothfuss, *Name* 582). This is additionally supported by the attribution of over-generalised biological traits to Kvothe and the Edema Ruh conveyed in the words spoken by Seth: "I think you look kinda like one of them Ruh. You got them eyes. The men around him craned to get a better look at my face" (Rothfuss, *Wise* 976). An especially significant example of individual racism is depicted by the extreme hatred of Lady Meluan Lackless, which she expresses towards Kvothe's origin during their meeting within the palace of Maer Alveron. Not knowing that it was Kvothe's artistic talents that brought her and her fiancé closer together, the wealthy and noble Lady remarks that the "roads are always thick with Ruh bandits this time of year … She said the word with such a weight of cold loathing … She hated the Ruh. Not the simple distaste most people feel for us, but a true, sharp hate with teeth in it" (Rothfuss, *Wise* 504). Not only the fact that she seems to suspect every Ruh of assaulting and robbing innocent wanderers seems appalling, but also protagonist's casual statement about the widespread distaste for the Edema Ruh is eye-catching. Thus, hatred and harsh prejudices against the protagonist's community and very person prevail within Rothfuss's Secondary World, both reminding his readership of comparable contexts in their own reality as well as influencing his characters' actions and attitudes. Kvothe himself is often dismayed by these tendencies, casually hiding his own origin, and attempts to change the common perception of his kin e.g. by purposely slaughtering fake, criminal Edema Ruh and saving kidnapped girls from them.

The last example is the *Harry Potter* Series by J.K. Rowling. Rowling worked in the research department of Amnesty International's Headquarters in London. In her commencement address at Harvard University from 2008 *The Fringe Benefits of Failure, and the Importance of Imagination*, she explained that her time there influenced her as a writer and that her books are intended to teach how to confront, eradicate and ameliorate racism: "[every] day, I saw more evidence about the evils' humankind will inflict on their fellow humans, to gain or maintain power. I began to have nightmares, literal nightmares, about some of the things I saw, heard and read. And yet I also learned more about human goodness at Amnesty International than I had ever known before" (*Fringe*). In her novels, various races are ranked and classified within a social hierarchy with regard to the way they interact with the wizarding community. The first group is made up of those races connected to the Dark Arts and the practice of Dark Magic, as for example giants or the basilisks. Especially the latter were bred by dark magicians and only Parselmouths could control these fantastic beasts for their dubious purposes (cf. Rowling, *Phantastische* 4f.). Giants on the other hand sided with Lord Voldemort in the First Wizarding War and were therefore nearly hunted down to the point of extinction by wizards (cf. Rowling, *Goblet* 470). Seemingly "good" wizards and witches interact with the aforementioned mostly by considering them as foes (cf. Horne 80). The next group consists of other beings which are either deemed dangerous or used due to their capacity for work. The negative role of the troll in *Harry Potter and the Philosopher's Stone*, who attacks the school (cf. Rowling, *Philosopher* 188), has to be contrasted with the function of the security trolls in *Harry Potter and the Prisoner of Azkaban*, as these are used to protect the portrait of the fat lady guarding the entrance to the Gryffindor Tower after she has been attacked by

Sirius Black (cf. Rowling, *Prisoner* 292). Another significant example is that of dragons, who are used within the Triwizard Tournament, and guard Gringotts, while at the same time being hunted for their flesh and other materials to be used as ingredients in potions (cf. Rowling, *Phantastische* 11f.). This conveys that the standing of some magical beings and creatures is directly connected to their usefulness for the wizarding community (cf. Horne 80). Another group is made up of members of those races, which have decided to isolate themselves from wizards (cf. Horne 80), as for example the centaurs living in the Forbidden Forest at the borders of Hogwarts or the Merpeople living in the Black Lake (cf. Rowling, *Phantastische* 57f.). The groups that deserve most of the attention are indeed those that act closely with wizards, viz. that of house-elves and goblins. House-elves "willingly serve the wizards as servants or slaves, accepting their subservient role in a racial hierarchy" (Horne 80). As opposed to this, members of the race of goblins relate to the wizarding community mostly as equal partners in business (cf. Horne 80) as several scenes in Gringotts show. However, they are still discriminated against and considered dangerous because of past rebellions. They are not even allowed to carry a wand (cf. Rowling, *Deathly* 395). In *Harry Potter and the Order of the Phoenix*, Harry learns about the statue of magical brethren in the Ministry of Magic. It is a group of statues presenting an admirable wizard and a gracious witch, who are encircled by bowing members of the races of house-elves, centaurs and goblins. The wizards are in the centre of the fountain and seem—in contrast to the rest of the other magical creatures—much bigger and more powerful. The fountain again underlines the hierarchical relations between wizards and racial others with the first enthroned at the very top (cf. Rowling, *Order* 127). Last but not least, the relationship between wizards and house-elves requires greater attention. House-elves suffer from various forms of racism. Their oppression goes back centuries and has long been supported by institutional policies and thus became natural, a sort of tradition. Many wizarding families and institutions readily maintain the slave status of the elves, except for Hermione Granger, the 'Mudblood'. She starts the institutional S.P.E.W. campaign—the Society for the Promotion of Elvish Welfare—to fight against the abuse of elves (cf. Rowling, *Goblet* 246). However, her campaign is not supported by other wizards (cf. Horne 86). Therefore, she starts to support the elves on a more personal level: "she starts knitting hats and leaving them around for house-elves to pick up by accident, trying to trick them into setting themselves free" (Horne 86). The elves, however, have internalised their status in society so much that they cannot or do not want to make a change. This further underlines the irony of the lack of elvish rights, a sort of self-incurred tutelage. House-elves are not capable of freeing themselves, keeping all the power in the "hands of the oppressor" (Mendelsohn 181). Only a master can grant freedom by providing a piece of clothing. Even if set free, many house-elves still decide to follow and serve their new masters as the following case shows: "Dobby is a free house-elf and he can obey anyone he likes and Dobby will do whatever Harry Potter wants him to do!" (Rowling, *Half-Blood* 421). Rowling's house-elves moreover speak in a dialect that can be compared to those of African American slaves (cf. Horne 80f.).

The wizarding society in Rowling's Secondary World is—in turn—subdivided into four distinct groups. The first comprises the pure-bloods, witches or wizards with only magical relatives like the Malfoys, also known as the 'Sacred Twenty-Eight' (Rowling, *Order* 113). The second group are the half-bloods, i.e. persons with magical and non-magical relatives (Harry Potter, Tom Riddle). The next group are the Squibs, who are persons born to magical parents who cannot perform magic themselves, like Argus Filch, and the final group are the Mudbloods consisting of witches or wizards born to non-magical parents. The term 'Mudblood' is also used as a severe insult within the wizarding realm, as it is "about the most insulting thing he could think of... There are some wizards ... who think they're better than everyone else because they're what people call pure-blood" (Rowling, *Chamber* 127). There is a strong hierarchy based on biological predetermination that is based on blood and ancestry. Concerning the relation between wizards and muggles, there seems to be a more or less strong segregation which is for example shown in Hogwarts Curriculum which only enables their students to plan a future in the wizarding society, lacking basic subjects as maths or geography perhaps needed to find a job in the muggle world. Also, there is a bilateral antagonism between Muggles and wizards, as the latter "constantly worry about the threat of Muggles discovering and invading the magical realm; the antagonism against Muggle-borns stems, in part, from a distrust of their motives after years of persecution at the hands of the nonmagical" (Anatol 170). The latter alluding to different persecutions having been conducted in our Primary World. During Voldemort's campaign against Mudbloods, Muggle studies are taught at Hogwarts based on the inherent belief of the superiority of wizards: "Muggle Studies ... is compulsory for everyone. We've all got to listen how Muggles are like animals, stupid and dirty, and how they drive wizards into hiding by being vicious toward them, and how the natural order is being re-established." (Rowling, *Deathly* 462). Fitting to the basic characteristics of racism presented above, a whole group of individuals is attributed with the same negative features, thus stressing the superiority of the wizarding community. Most absurdly, Voldemort envisioned a society consisting of pureblood wizards and witches despite being a half-muggle himself, which reminds us of the ungrounded superiority of the Aryan race postulated in the Third Reich especially by those that did not fit their own ideals. The statue 'Magic is Might' adequately underlines Voldemort's ideology in a transparent way. It can be found in the Ministry of Magic, after this has been taken over by darker powers, and depicts a wizard and a witch sitting at the top of a pile of Muggle slaves twining around their feet (cf. Rowling, *Deathly* 198f.).

To conclude, these works feature different facets and consequences of racism and its subtypes with changing emphasis.

Regarding worldbuilding, these forms support the readership in grouping or ranking the inhabitants of a Secondary World as well as conceptualising its social structure. In this context, the existence of different humanoid races, as elves, goblins and hobbits naturally, provides further grounds for interracial conflicts in comparison to our own reality. In taking up these conflicts, e.g. between house-elves and wizards, authors of fantasy literature may allude to issues of ethnic minorities to be found in our Primary World. Generally, readers can easily identify with (racial or social) outsiders such as Kvothe, Bilbo, Hermione and Harry, who are mostly successful in fulfilling their respective quests, most often also by overcoming or questioning social or racial hierarchies. However, it proves difficult to apply today's views on racism especially on the—at times—unreflected presentation of forms of racism due to zeitgeist. Thus, it e.g. "should be self-evident that it is very problematic to pursue such questions in Tolkien's work, since they could only be treated within the framework of modern perspectives on racism and racial discrimination" (Fimi 158). However, while a condemnation of racism in Tolkien's works might be futile, a description of underlying social and racial structures helps to understand Middle-earth in a better way.

Apart from that, the Primary World also features critical issues and through this connection fantasy literature is one way to challenge and question forms of racism in terms of an active anti-racist pedagogy. For example, contemporary fantasy as Rothfuss often contains characters actively fighting against racist positions. Rowling in turn makes her protagonists fight Voldemort's eugenics, while at the same time the oppression of some humanoid races is absurdly maintained by institutions such as the Ministry of Magic or Hogwarts and many individuals. After the final battle, even Harry "wonders whether Kreacher might bring him a sandwich "(Horne 97), leaving it to the reader to regain a clear view on societal problems. Especially for adult characters, it seems difficult "to engage in a discussion that might point out the ways in which their own culture is supported by the oppression of other races, especially that of the elves" (Horne 87). Thus, in some cases one might say that authors reveal certain racist structures, but leave it to the reader to identify and discuss them in order to overcome tendencies within their own Primary World societies.

Bibliography

Anatol, Giselle Liza. "The Fallen Empire: Exploring Ethnic Otherness in the World of Harry Potter." In: *Reading Harry Potter – Critical Essays*. Ed.: Giselle Liza Anatol. Westport: Praeger, 2003. 163-178

Fimi, Dimitra. *Tolkien, Race and Cultural History – From Fairies to Hobbits*. Basingstoke: Palgrave Macmillan, 2010

Geiss, Imanuel. *Geschichte des Rassismus*. Frankfurt a. M.: Suhrkamp, 1988

Honegger, Thomas. "From Bag End to Lórien: The Creation of a Literary World". In: *News from the Shire and Beyond – Studies on Tolkien*. Eds.: Peter Buchs, Thomas Honegger. Zurich: Walking Tree Publishers, 2004

Horne, Jackie C. "Harry and the Other: Answering the Race Question in J.K. Rowling's Harry Potter." In: *The Lion and the Unicorn* 34:1 (2010): 76-104

Ibata, David. "'Lord' of Racism. Critics view Trilogy as discriminatory". In: *Chicago Tribune online*, 2003. www.chicagotribune.com/lifestyles/chi-030112epringsrace-story.html (accessed 20 Sept. 2017)

Kidder, Louise H. & V. Mary Stewart. *Vorurteile – Zur Sozialpsychologie von Gruppenbeziehungen*. Weinheim/Basel: Beltz Verlag, 1976

Liebhart, Karin et al. "Fremdbilder – Feindbilder – Zerrbilder – Zur Wahrnehmung und diskursiven Konstruktion des Fremden." In: *Fremdbilder – Feindbilder – Zerrbilder – Zur Wahrnehmung und diskursiven Konstruktion des Fremden*. Eds.: Karin Liebhart et al. Klagenfurt: Drava, 2002. 7-17

Memmi, Albert. *Rassismus*. Frankfurt a. M.: Anton Hain, 1992

Mendelsohn, Farah. "Crowning the King: Harry Potter and the Construction of Authority." In: *The Ivory Tower and Harry Potter: Perspectives on a Literary Phenomenon*. Ed.: Lana A. Whited. Columbia/London: University of Missouri Press, 2002. 159-181

Miles, Robert. "The Concept of Racism – Development, Trends and Perspectives." In: *Fremdbilder – Feindbilder – Zerrbilder – Zur Wahrnehmung und diskursiven Konstruktion des Fremden*. Eds.: Karin Liebhart et al. Klagenfurt: Drava, 2002. 79-94

Nothwehr, Dawn. Defining "Racisms" in a Globalized, Terrorized, Ecologically Threatened World. In: *New Theology Review* 21.1 (2008): 5-17

Pavel, Thomas G. *Fictional Worlds*. Cambridge: Harvard University Press, 1986

Rana, Marion. *Creating Magical Worlds – Otherness and Othering in Harry Potter*. Frankfurt a.M. [u.a.]: Peter Lang, 2009

Rommelspacher, Birgit. "Was ist eigentlich Rasissmus?" In: *Rassismuskritik: Rassismustheorie und -forschung*. Eds.: Claus Melter, Paul Mecheril. Schwalbach: Wochenschau-Verlag, 2009. 25-38

Rothfuss, Patrick. *The Name of the Wind*. New York: DAW Books, 2008

---. *The Wise Man's Fear*. New York: DAW Books, 2013

@PatrickRothfuss.Twitter, 28 May 2017, 10:39 am, twitter.com/PatrickRothfuss/status /868884378142814209 (accessed 20 Sept. 2017)

Rowling, J.K. "The Fringe Benefits of Failure, and the Importance of Imagination." Commencement Speech, Harvard University, 5 June 2008. http://harvardmagazine.com/go/ jkrowling.html (accessed 20 Sept. 2017)

Rowling, J.K. *Phantastische Tierwesen und wo sie zu finden sind*. Hamburg: Carlsen-Verlag, 2010

---. *Harry Potter and the Chamber of Secrets*. London: Bloomsbury, 2000

---. *Harry Potter and the Deathly Hallows*. London: Bloomsbury, 2007

---. *Harry Potter and the Goblet of Fire*. London: Bloomsbury, 2001

---. *Harry Potter and the Half-Blood Prince*. New York: Scholastic, 2005

---. *Harry Potter and the Order of the Phoenix*. New York: Bloomsbury, 2003

---. *Harry Potter and the Prisoner of Azkaban*. London: Bloomsbury, 1999

---. *Harry Potter and the Philosopher's Stone*. London: Bloomsbury, 2000

Saler, Michael. *As If – Modern Enchantment and Literary Prehistory of Virtual Reality*. New York [et al.]: OUP, 2012

Salo, David. "Heroism and Alienation through Language in *The Lord of the Rings*." In: *The Medieval Hero on Screen: Representations from Beowulf to Buffy*. Eds.: Martha W. Driver, Sid Ray. Jefferson: McFarland, 2004, 23-37

Shippey, Tom. *The Road to Middle-earth*. London: Harper Collins, 2005

Sutherland, Leonie L. "Ethnocentrism in a Pluralist Society: A Concept Analysis". In: *Journal of Transcultural Nursing*. 13.4 (2002): 274-281

Tolkien, John Ronald Reuel. *The Letters of J.R.R. Tolkien*. Ed.: Humphrey Carpenter. London: HarperCollins, 2006

---. *The Fellowship of the Ring*. London: HarperCollins, 2005

Walker, Steve. *The Power of Tolkien's Prose – Middle-Earth's Magical Style*. New York: Palgrave Macmillan, 2009

Weiss, Hilde. "Ethnische Stereotypen und Ausländerklischees – Formen und Ursachen der Fremdwahrnehmung." In: *Fremdbilder – Feindbilder – Zerrbilder – Zur Wahrnehmung und diskursiven Konstruktion des Fremden*. Eds.: Karin Liebhart et al. Klagenfurt: Drava, 2002. 17-38

Sub-creating a World:
From Artifice to Artefact

Marguerite Mouton (Amiens)

S peaking of 'worldbuilding' seems to imply an artificial construction of worlds by writers. And analysing Tolkien's worldbuilding seems a bit risky. Indeed, the first risk is to yield to the Sarumanian temptation of breaking the white light 'to find out what it is', which, as Gandalf puts it, would be 'lea[ving] the path of wisdom'[1], or else it may lead to 'push the tower over' in order to study 'the building material' and thus waste the possibility of beholding the sea from its top[2]. Here are strong cautions against such a tendency to look for the recipe of Tolkien's work and world, for the formula of its success, to analyse his books into a collection of characters, places, narrative patterns, that can be combined indefinitely into other stories and games.

In this study of Tolkien's worldbuilding, I can see another risk, the risk, while examining this world in itself, of disconnecting it from the real world. This is precisely upon such dichotomy, such gap between the man-made world and the real one that lies the traditional charge against the work as being an escape literature[3]. Is Tolkien's world such an artificial construction, offering a refuge far from the real world?

It is interesting to look more closely at the images Tolkien offers to prompt us to be careful in this study of his art of worldbuilding. Indeed, the white light is no arbitrary construction but exists out there in nature; on the contrary, the tower is a building, an artefact made by human hands, but the sea that the tower allows to see is not, and the fable seems to imply a longing for this natural immensity, that the works of man may sometimes enable him to see.

It is in the relationship with the real world that the question arises whether the literary world is an artifice, which I will take here as being an arbitrary construction unrelated to the real world, or rather an artefact, man-made out of real-world material.

To approach the nature of this relationship between the real world and the world created (or sub-created), which shall eventually appear to be less an artifice than an artefact, this paper will focus on a letter from Tolkien to his son Christopher Tolkien dated 7-8 November 1944. It is a strange, 'very

---

1   "'... the white light can be broken.' 'In which case it is no longer white,' said I. 'And he that breaks a thing to find out what it is has left the path of wisdom.'" (LotR 259)
2   'So, they pushed over the tower, with not little labour, and in order to look for hidden carvings... But from the top of that tower the man had been able to look out upon the sea.' (MC 7-8)
3   See FS. This question has been abundantly discussed in *Hither Shore* 12.

peculiar' letter, which can 'seem all very incomprehensible' according to the author himself (L #89). Yet it is a very interesting testimony of how Tolkien sees the link between the world of his work and the real world and we will see how it transcends this problematic dichotomy and provides another pattern to understand their relationship.

Of course, we know the caution with which we must apprehend letters that were selected and truncated, and in which the author often matches his words his talk to his recipient. However, although only excerpts of the whole letter have been selected by the editor, who is no other than the aimed recipient and heir of the author, this testimony contains guarantees of credibility: Tolkien addressed it during the Second World War to his son who had been sent to South Africa by the Royal Air Force. The beginning we have of the letter shows that Tolkien is aware of a danger for his son[4]: in these conditions, we can give the letter and the emotions expressed in it some credit of authenticity. Moreover, the author mentions the fact that since it is an air letter, he had to write it without draft or proofreading, which makes this text as little 'built' as possible.

This letter, I will argue, reveals another pattern for the relationship between the world of his works and the real world, which no longer opposes two terms, but consists in a relationship between three terms linked not only by analogy but even by a continuity of being: the built world of the work, the real world, and the world of the Gospel.

The letter particularly draws attention to the common course or structure shared by the stories related to these three worlds. We will therefore focus here on the continuity between Tolkien's fairy stories, real-life stories but also sacred history (the Gospel).

It is hard to bring order into this letter and account for a unified thought where the author keeps seeking his words and expressing his own difficulty in stating clearly what he means. Indeed, Tolkien offers here a succession of narratives telling of experiences he has had. I will first study the structure of these experiences and then the conditions necessary for such experiences, experiences which can enlighten us on how Tolkien sees the real world, how he writes about it, and not, for once, about a man-made world. Therefore, they can give an element of comparison in order to estimate to what extent and in what sense his world is a built one.

---

4   "Your reference to the care of your guardian angel makes me fear that 'he' is being specially needed. I dare say it is so." (L #89)

I. The Deep Structure of Life Experience

Tolkien proposes in this letter a succession of stories, apparently gathered at random into what he labels a 'diary'. But these stories have in common to highlight a deep structure of lived experience, a structure (the deep structure of experience itself) which is similar to that of the literary device he calls eucatastrophe. Indeed, the letter tells the story of three of Tolkien's experiences: first, looking at a mole in a ray of sunshine while he is before the Blessed Sacrament; second, his impressions upon hearing the story of the little boy healed in Lourdes; and finally, what he felt during his bike ride near the Radcliffe Infirmary. We can add to these experiences the reading of his own book, the *Hobbit*, where he found again the same experience.

Thus, Tolkien multiplies the stories that share the same structure regardless of the scale, giving the impression that his worldview works like a fractal, this mathematical object whose structure does not vary when the scale is changed. The 'structure' at stake consists both in a particular succession of stages and in a reception-pattern, that is: the reactions (emotional and intellectual) it provokes in the recipient.

Indeed, looking closer at the components of these experiences, we observe that in each narrative of this letter Tolkien mixes up comments about emotions he felt ('deeply moved', 'peculiar emotion', 'sensation') and about a new awareness ('realise', 'clarities'). And he systematically emphasises the 'suddenness' of both. He describes moments of particular intensity, of intimate relationship with what *is*, with the being, of spiritual experiences which are simultaneously sensitive and intellectual experiences. Indeed, in them springs some kind of knowledge or at least of awareness, though with no reasoning involved, but in a 'straight', intuitive input.

Telling these experiences, Tolkien insists that their structure parallels that of the literary technique of eucatastrophe as he described it in his essay *On Fairy-stories*. For him then, a literary tale can reproduce the structure of spiritual experience as he has experienced it: a very powerful emotion contrasting negative and then positive feelings within a very short time. Thus, it appears that he considers the events of the real world as a story, on the model of the great history that is the Gospel, of which literary stories carry a reflection, some kind of 'glimmer', to take up Tolkien's word in the letter.

In the Gospel as in ordinary life, and also as in literary tales, the extraordinary makes 'intrusion' in the ordinary and the stories follow the same successive stages. Tolkien insists on one of these stages, which is shared by the three stories: indeed, when the daughter of Jairus has recovered from death in the Gospel, she's hungry; similarly, when the sick child is cured on the train returning from Lourdes, he wants to eat; and finally, when, for example, Frodo has just escaped the watcher-monster lurking in the lake at the entrance to the mines of Moria, he immediately feels the need for food (LotR 310). Tolkien mentions in his letter this example of how the extraordinary intrudes into the ordinary and causes consequences.

Such a conception entails a change of framework while considering the question of the relationship between real and fictional worlds: we are now confronted with three stories rather than two: two are on the primary level (the Gospel, quintessential fairy tale, and the minor Christian miracles that make intrusion into ordinary lives) and one on the secondary level (literary, sub-created works). They do not have the same status, either: coming first, there is the 'Primary Miracle' (the Resurrection), which is said to be 'the greatest' among stories and which is not 'only' a tale and thus surpasses other stories; second comes 'the lesser Christian miracles'—Tolkien here takes the example of Christian miracles that are intrusions into ordinary life and reveal what is this ordinary life in the same way as creative writing does; and finally, the literary work, true on a 'second plane'. While the status of the three stories is not the same, the difference remains unclear enough not to be too radical but to allow still a common structure.

Primary level	Secondary level	
the Gospel, quintessential fairy tale	the minor Christian miracles that make intrusion in ordinary lives	literary, sub-created works

The fairy tale, then, is no longer an artificial creation and a place to escape out of the real, but it is the structure which informs the real, the very structure of the most intimate experience of the real, and which allows access to the 'truth', understood as a place:

> … Christian joy which produces tears because it is qualitatively so like sorrow, because it comes from those places where Joy and Sorrow are at one, reconciled, as selfishness and altruism are lost in Love.

And the author goes on about the structure thus described:

> For it I coined the word 'eucatastrophe': the sudden happy turn in a story which pierces you with a joy that brings tears (which I argued it is the highest function of fairy-stories to produce).   (L #89)

We note that the author speaks of a 'function' of the fairy tale, and not of any intention of his own to make his tales parallel the structure of real life or of the Gospel. Rather, he invokes his own observation of a similar structure and emotional working between his stories and the Gospel, of which he presents himself as a common reader and experimenter. Of course, we know about Tolkien's slightly romantic tendency when he talks about how his works were written, his habit of dwelling on the idea of an uncontrolled inspiration, of a text which, as he puts it in another letter, 'flows now along, and getting quite out of hand' (L #33), and where characters appear of their own accord on the roads of his world, for example Faramir[5]. We could therefore doubt that he is here merely describing the functioning of his work and presume or suspect that it is actually a construction, or even that there is a 'missionary' intent, an intention to evangelise on the author's part[6]. What is interesting in this letter is that he does not take his books as the starting point for his reflection, but his experiences of ordinary life (for example his watching the dust playing in the sunshine) and all those, all the circumstances of his life, seem to be unified by this same experience of the sudden emotions and 'clarities' contained in eucatastrophe.

Even assuming that Tolkien is as descriptive as possible, without ideological intention, when he gives an account of his experience, yet one can wonder about the conditions of these experiences, or the inner disposition of those who go through these experiences. What are the conditions necessary for such an experience of eucatastrophe? Tolkien tells us that it is universal, that it is (to take up his own words) a 'peculiar emotion we all have—though not often'[7]. But under what conditions can we experience it?

II. The Conditions for these Life Experiences: the Attitude Implied by the Eucatastrophe

Tolkien may give us a clue to answer this question, when he invites the recipient of his letter to read a chapter of the *Lord of the Rings* in a certain way and to observe the behaviour of a character, Sam Gamgee, in the last chapter of Book 4. Here is the quote from Tolkien's letter:

> And in the last chapter of The Ring that I have yet written I hope you'll note, when you receive it (it'll soon be on its way) that

---

5   See for instance Tolkien's letter to Christopher: 'A new character has come on the scene (I am sure I did not invent him, I did not even want him, though I like him, but there he came walking into the woods of Ithilien): Faramir, the brother of Boromir'. (L #66, 1944)
6   On this question, see the discussion in Caldecott/Solari/Rance.
7   'But at the story of the little boy (which is a fully attested *fact* of course) with its apparent sad ending and then its sudden unhoped-for happy ending, I was deeply moved and had that peculiar emotion we all have—though not often.' (L #89)

Frodo's face goes livid and convinces Sam that he's dead, just
when Sam gives up *hope*.

The link between this passage of the letter and the foregoing one is not immediately obvious: while Tolkien has just explained that he had felt an eucatastrophic emotion while reading the *Hobbit*, he suddenly refers his reader to a chapter which does not at all provoke such feeling, but rather quite the contrary. Here is the passage of the *Lord of the Rings* to which he refers:

> 'He's dead!' he said. 'Not asleep, dead!' And as he said it, as if the words had set the venom to its work again, it seemed to him that the hue of the face grew livid green.
> And then black despair came down on him, and Sam bowed to the ground, and drew his grey hood over his head, and night came into his heart, and he knew no more.   (LotR 731)

Referring to this passage in his letter, Tolkien draws Christopher's attention not only to Sam's emotions and intuitions, which happen to be false, but also to the attitude of Sam on the occasion of this experience. The reader is then left to infer that such an inner disposition, namely his lack of hope, is the reason why his intuition goes wrong, i.e., why the character mistakenly believes that Frodo is dead. The anti-climax is reached because Sam has lost hope. Darkness falls because of the internal state of the character. It is the inner disposition which seems to command the external facts.

   In the same paragraph of his letter, Tolkien has just reported a comment about the miracle of Jairus' daughter, and about that of the bleeding woman of the Gospel: thus, these two passages find themselves associated with the one where Sam loses all hope. And in these passages, healing, or the return to life of the people Christ meets is explicitly linked to an act of faith on their part:

> [47] Seeing herself discovered, the woman came forward trembling, and falling at his feet explained in front of all the people why she had touched him and how she had been cured at that very moment. [48] 'My daughter,' he said, 'your faith has saved you; go in peace.' [49] While he was still speaking, someone arrived from the house of the president of the synagogue to say, 'Your daughter has died. Do not trouble the Master any further.' [50] But Jesus heard this, and he spoke to the man, 'Do not be afraid, only have faith and she will be saved.'   (Lc 8,47-50, *New Jerusalem Bible*)

We know how the virtues of faith (here called for by Christ) and hope (which Sam lacks) are closely related in Catholic Theology[8]. Moreover, this textual proximity between the comment of this biblical passage and the reference to the last chapter of Book 4 puts a special relief emphasis, *a contrario*, on Sam's lack of hope: everything happens as if this loss of hope was an obstacle to the healing of Frodo and was even a factor hastening his death by reactivating the venom.

Yet, Sam is such a positive character. How can we then understand this passage? It cannot be a definite refusal of hope, contrary to what happens for example with Saruman, who is overcome by despair and thus allows evil to triumph. But Sam is a positive character, we said, and much will rely on his capacity to hope against hope in the end, when he eventually must carry Frodo and the ring altogether[9]. So, how to understand this loss of hope at the end of Book 4, which, as Tolkien highlights, defeats or rather delays for a time the joyous-turn of the story?

A French author, Tolkien's contemporary, Georges Bernanos (1888-1948), who has written extensively on hope, both in his novels and essays[10], may help us interpret what happens to Sam in this chapter. Bernanos thus distinguishes between several forms of hope, discriminating it from optimism. He insists that 'optimism is an ersatz of hope... Nine times out of ten optimism is a form of selfishness' (Bernanos 1262, my transl.).

According to Bernanos, the optimist puts his trust in his own strength. He may mean well but he makes a mistake in the source of his hope, which in this case is self-centered and frail. And that may well be what Sam does at some stage. Accompanying Frodo throughout his quest, Sam intends to be of help, as he repeatedly argues, even perhaps to protect his master and in any case never to be separated from him. But here Sam finds himself powerless to help and even to follow Frodo. The despair he feels is a kind of death. But Bernanos goes on explaining what hope really is:

> ...optimism is a false hope for the use of the cowards and fools. Hope is a virtue, *virtus*, a heroic determination of the soul. The highest form of hope is the despair that has been overcome... You believe that it is easy to hope. But those who really hope are only those who have the courage to despair of the illusions and lies where they found a security, which they had falsely taken to

---

8   Cf. *Catechism of the Catholic Church*, § 1812-1821.
9   On Sam's relationship with hope and role within the destiny of the Ring, see for instance Fernandez.
10 Georges Bernanos is a French writer and journalist. He is the author of novels like *Sous le soleil de Satan* (1926) and *Journal d'un curé de campagne* (1936). He also wrote some essays, some of which were published after his death in *La Liberté, pour quoi faire?* [Freedom, to do what?]

be hope… To hope is to take a risk. It is even the risk of risk. To
hope is not to be complacent towards oneself. It is the greatest and
most difficult victory that a man can win over his soul… Hope
must be conquered. We can reach hope only through truth, and
at the price of great efforts and long patience. If you want to meet
hope, you must go through despair. When you go to the end of
the night, you meet another aurora.   (Ibid.)

'Hope must be conquered', says Bernanos. Hope lies beyond despair and can
only be reached through a purification of hope itself. That may be what Sam
experiences at the end of Book 4: he is obliged to let go of Frodo, to go through
loss, powerlessness, dire solitude, which sounds like a kind of death. If there
is a joyous-turn, a resurrection, there must be first death. Many of Tolkien's
characters experience this stage of purification and emerge from it fortified,
grown up, sometimes literally: this is the case of Gandalf, who falls into the
mines of Moria even though the whole quest seemed to rest on his strengths
and he comes back as a white wizard, more powerful and better prepared for
the great war at hand (LotR 495). This is also the case of Merry and Pippin,
who are abducted by the orcs and go through dark times before becoming
essential actors of the story and drinking the water of the Ents which makes
them literally grow up (LotR 471).

I believe that this passage of Book 4, to which Tolkien strangely draws
attention in his letter, invites a more nuanced and deeper understanding of
eucatastrophe. Indeed, the joyous-turn of eucatastrophe is not a happy ending
as we can find it for instance in Voltaire's *Candide*, to whom 'all is for the best
in the best of worlds'. The eucatastrophe expresses instead something of the
drama of humanity, its participation through hope and faith to Salvation but
also the need for such virtues to be purified, to go through despair to get rid
of selfishness and of an altruism relying on one's own strength, which both
disappear into love as Tolkien puts it in his letter[11]. Hope[12], like eucatastrophe,
arises in a situation that seems to have no human way out: it is the emergence of
the unexpected, of the unheard of, in this case the intuitive certitude, for Sam,
that he must go on. But this passage tells only of one of the many purifications
he must still undergo. Indeed, during the inner debate that follows, he ponders
the reason why he should go on, thinking first of taking revenge upon Gollum,
before thinking of taking up the quest. And when he finally decides to go on
with the quest, it is remarkable that he does not rely on his own strengths any

---

11 'it comes from those places where Joy and Sorrow are at one, reconciled, as selfishness
     and altruism are lost in Love.' (L #89)
12 On hope in Tolkien's Legendarium, also see Devaux.

more, nor does he choose what he wishes, but he obeys and pursues a superior interest: the purification has worked.

> 'But you haven't put yourself forward; you've been put forward. And as for not being the right and proper person, why, Mr. Frodo wasn't as you might say, nor Mr. Bilbo. They didn't choose themselves.'   (LotR 732)

In these conditions, the final happy-ending of the quest appears first as fully 'received', as a pure gift. And there have been comments on that score highlighting the arbitrary dimension of the Eagles who make an intrusion at the end of the *Lord of the Rings*, like a kind of *deus ex machina*. But at the same time the eucatastrophe also presents itself as an experience requiring an inner attitude of hope, and of genuine, purified hope, without which the disaster extends and even worsens until it ends in nothingness. In Tolkien's letter, we may have the indication that some special disposition, even by the reader, is needed if the eucatastrophe is to work, to produce its emotion and even to exist at all: such an attitude seems to be wanted for the resurrection-turn to take place. Again, the disposition implied, like the structure of the eucatastrophe, like the emotion it raises, is shared in the Gospel, in plain life events and in fairy stories.

The fundamental principle of Tolkien's world, I believe, is the eucatastrophic turn, it is what gives dynamism and meaning to his world, conferring on it a story structure, directing its elements and organising them. But this principle is not artificial, a simple literary process, it is for Tolkien what organises all experiences: be it riding his bike, looking at the dust dancing in the sunlight or listening to stories, the most profound life experience he makes is always eucatastrophic.

Therefore, the relationship between the real world and the sub-created one is no longer one of dependence or independence. Indeed, both share the same pattern, because both share it with the Gospel, which reveals the dynamism and the deepest meaning of any human story.

But such dynamism and meaning are not all roses. They do not boil down to saying that all is well in the best of worlds. With this pervasive eucatastrophic structure goes a pedagogy, demanding the participation of one's free will and maybe even its surrender, progressively eased by a course of purification and of growth.

Bibliography

Bernanos, George. *Essais et* Écrits *de combat.* Vol. II. Paris: Gallimard, 1995

Caldecott, Stratford, Grégory Solari & Didier Rance. *Tolkien, faërie et christianisme.* Genève: Ad Solem, 2002

Devaux, Michaël. *J.R.R. Tolkien, l'effigie des Elfes.* Paris: Bragelonne, 2014

Fernandez, Irène. *Et si on parlait du* Seigneur des anneaux. Paris: Presses de la Renaissance, 2002

Tolkien, J.R.R. *The Letters of J.R.R. Tolkien.* Ed.: Humphrey Carpenter with the assistance of Christopher Tolkien. Boston: Houghton Mifflin, 1981

---. *The Lord of the Rings* [1954-1955]. London: HarperCollins, 2002

---. *The Monsters and the Critics and Other Essays* [1983]. Ed.: Christopher Tolkien. London: HarperCollins, 2006

Catechism of the Catholic Church. Vatican: Libreria Editrice Vaticana, 1993

Eucatastrophe and Tolkien's Worldbuilding: *"a ray of light through the very chinks of the universe about us"*

A Theological Reading

Guglielmo Spirito (Assisi)

Meaning of *Eucatastrophe*

We need to start by focusing on what J.R.R. Tolkien himself meant with his wonderful neologism *eucatastrophe,* found in his essay *On Fairy-stories*:

> And there is the oldest and deepest desire, the Great Escape: the Escape from Death...
> But the "consolation" of fairy-tales has another aspect than the imaginative satisfaction of ancient desires. Far more important is the Consolation of the Happy Ending. Almost I would venture to assert that all complete fairy-stories must have it. At least I would say that Tragedy is the true form of Drama, its highest function; but the opposite is true of Fairy-story. Since we do not appear to possess a word that expresses this opposite—**I will call it** Euca-tastrophe. The *eucatastrophic* tale is the true form of fairy-tale, and its highest function.
> The consolation of fairy-stories, the joy of the happy ending: or more correctly of the good catastrophe, the sudden joyous "turn" (for there is no true end to any fairy-tale): this joy, which is one of the things which fairy-stories can produce supremely well, is not essentially "escapist," nor "fugitive." In its fairy-tale—or otherworld—setting, **it is a sudden and miraculous grace: never to be counted on to recur. It does not deny the existence of** dyscatastrophe, **of sorrow and failure: the possibility of these is necessary to the joy of deliverance; it denies (in the face of much evidence, if you will) universal final defeat and in so far is** evangelium, **giving a fleeting glimpse of Joy, Joy beyond the walls of the world, poignant as grief.**
>
> (FS 97-99[1], emphasis added)

---

1   The numbering of *On Fairy-stories* is by paragraphs.

But in the "eucatastrophe" we see in a brief vision that the answer may be greater—it may be a far-off gleam or echo of evangelium **in the real world.** The use of this word gives a hint of my epilogue. It is a serious and dangerous matter. It is presumptuous of me to touch upon such a theme; but if by grace what I say has in any respect any validity, it is, of course, only one facet of a truth incalculably rich: finite only because the capacity of Man for whom this was done is finite.

I would venture to say that approaching the Christian Story from this direction, it has long been my feeling (a joyous feeling) that God redeemed the corrupt making-creatures, men, in a way fitting to this aspect, as to others, of their strange nature. The Gospels contain a fairy-story, or a story of a larger kind which embraces all the essence of fairy-stories. They contain many marvels—peculiarly artistic, beautiful, and moving: "mythical" in their perfect, self-contained significance; **and among the marvels is the greatest and most complete conceivable eucatastrophe.** But this story has entered History and the primary world; the desire and aspiration of sub-creation has been raised to the fulfilment of Creation. **The Birth of Christ is the eucatastrophe of Man's history. The Resurrection is the eucatastrophe of the story of the Incarnation. This story begins and ends in joy.** It has pre-eminently the "inner consistency of reality." There is no tale ever told that men would rather find was true, and none so many sceptical men have accepted as true on its own merits. For the Art of it has the supremely convincing tone of Primary Art, that is, of Creation. To reject it leads either to sadness or to wrath.

(FS 103f., emphasis added)

Eucatastrophe. Built on *catastrophe* (Greek *kata* "down" and *strephein* "to turn"). Though in a general sense *catastrophe* can mean any kind of cataclysmic disaster, in its narrower definition it marks the downturn of fortune in Greek tragedy that leads to the protagonist's fall. By adding greek *eu* "good" as a prefix, Tolkien has reversed the meaning (and the direction) so that the "turn" leads upward to the happy ending (cf. Anderson & Flieger in FS 119).

C.S. Lewis mentions "eucatastrophe" explicitly in *Surprised by Joy*, while telling how:

> …then reading the Odyssey entire, till the music of the thing and the clear, bitter brightness that lives in almost every formula had become part of me. The wanderings mean as much as ever they

did; the great moment of "eucatastrophe" (as Professor Tolkien would call it) when Odysseus strips off his rags and bends the bow, means more.   (*Joy* 168)

In the next passages I will cite, there is also an allusion to the fleeting glimpse of Joy; no accident, I think, that he mentions the "empty Sepulchre", and "the Sun's reflection in a dewdrop": does it not sound like Tolkien's, in the 'eucatastrophe' we see in a brief vision that the answer may be greater—it may be a far-off gleam or echo of *evangelium* in the real world?

> That walk I now remembered. It seemed to me that I had tasted heaven then. True, it was desire, not possession. But then what I had felt on the walk had also been desire, and only possession in so far as that kind of desire is itself desirable, is the fullest possession we can know on earth...
>
> In my scheme of thought it is not blasphemous to compare the error which I was making with that error which the angel at the Sepulchre rebuked when he said to the women, '*Why seek ye the living among the dead? He is not here, He is risen*' [Lk 24,5]. The comparison is of course between something of infinite moment and something very small; like comparison between the Sun und the Sun's reflection in a dewdrop. Indeed, in my view, very like it, for I do not think the resemblance between the Christian and then merely imaginative experience is accidental. I think that all things, in their way, reflect heavenly truth, the imagination not least. 'Reflect' is the important word.   (*Joy* 192-194)

> So that in the Primary Miracle (the Resurrection) and the lesser Christian miracles too though less, you have not only that sudden glimpse of the truth behind the apparent Anankê of our world, but **a glimpse that is actually a ray of light through the very chinks of the universe about us**.   (L 101, emphasis added)

Indeed, I would like to argue that precisely the *chinks* are some of the most powerful elements in Tolkien's worldbuilding. A chink is a narrow opening or crack, typically one that admits light. As in Moria:

> A dim light was falling on his face. High up above the eastern archway through a shaft near the roof came a long pale gleam; and across the hall through the northern arch light also glimmered faint and distantly.

"If we could find a window it would help, but **I fear that the light comes only down deep shafts.**"
The chamber was lit by a wide shaft high in the further eastern wall; it slanted upwards and, far above, a small square patch of blue sky could be seen. The light of the shaft fell directly on a table in the middle of the room.   (LotR 337, emphasis added)

So, I daresay that perhaps the **most evocative element is precisely** what is not there: the absence of the opacity and solidity of the wall, the vacuum of an opening, which allows another dimension to enter, and to anticipate something luminous, ethereal, joyous, powerful, which is only tasted, softly, non-intrusive, like an echo or anticipation that has undoubted good flavour, and that gives a sort of proper perspective to everything else.

A long letter by J.R.R. Tolkien on *eucatastrophe*:

89 To Christopher Tolkien
7-8 November 1944
And all of a sudden, I realized what it was: the very thing that I have been trying to write about and explain—in that fairy-story essay that I so much wish you had read that I think I shall send it to you. **For it I coined the word** 'eucatastrophe': **the sudden happy turn in a story which pierces you with a joy that brings tears (which I argued it is the highest function of fairy-stories to produce)** ... **And I concluded by saying that the Resurrection was the greatest 'eucatastrophe' possible in the greatest Fairy Story**—and produces that essential emotion: Christian joy which produces tears because it is qualitatively so like sorrow, because it comes from those places where Joy and Sorrow are at one, reconciled, as selfishness and altruism are lost in Love.
... **So that in the Primary Miracle (the Resurrection) and the lesser Christian miracles too though less, you have not only that sudden glimpse of the truth behind the apparent Anankê of our world, but a glimpse that is actually a ray of light through the very chinks of the universe about us.**
I was riding along on a bicycle one day, not so long ago, past the Radcliffe Infirmary, when I had one of those sudden clarities which sometimes come in dreams (even anaesthetic-produced ones). I remember saying aloud with absolute conviction: 'But of course! Of course, that's how things really do work'. But I could not reproduce any argument that had led to this, though the sensation was the same as having been convinced by reason

(if without reasoning). And I have since thought that one of the reasons why one can't recapture the wonderful argument or secret when one wakes up is simply because there was not one: but there was (often maybe) a direct appreciation by the mind (sc. reason) but without the chain of argument we know in our time-serial life. However, that's as may be.

To descend to lesser things: I knew I had written a story of worth in *The Hobbit* when reading it (after it was old enough to be detached from me) I had suddenly in a fairly strong measure the 'eucatastrophic' emotion at Bilbo's exclamation: "The Eagles! The Eagles are coming!"... And in the last chapter of The Ring that I have yet written I hope you'll note, when you receive it (it'll soon be on its way) that Frodo's face goes livid and convinces Sam that he's dead, just when Sam gives up *hope*.   (L 99-101)

The light comes only down deep shafts...

Gimli started and then stood still as stone, staring, while the old man sprang up the rough steps as nimbly as a goat. All weariness seemed to have left him. As he stepped up on to the shelf there was a gleam, too brief for certainty, a quick glint of white, as if some garment shrouded by the grey rags had been for an instant revealed.   (LotR 514)

So, we may say that the world built by Tolkien is powerful precisely because of what it lacks, more even than because of what it has: the fissures allowed us to taste the sense of eucatastrophe, *a ray of light through the very chinks of the universe about us.*

His capacity in worldbuilding is without doubt great, the "walls" of its buildings and palaces, the solidity of his landscapes; but his "chinks", his "loopholes" are the most suggestive signs of his art, because through them, an undying Light (which is Life, resurrected Life) offers us a glimpse of the final Defeat of death, and the rescue of the whole Universe.

Theological Vision of *Dyscatastrophe* and *Eucatastrophe*

We should use a little theology here to try to grasp the meaning of the Resurrection as *"eucatastrophe"*. We need it as a hermeneutical tool to understand the depth of the Tolkienian neologism: it is a serious and dangerous matter, and it is presumptuous of me to touch upon such a theme (cf. FS 103), although I may have a little excuse because, unlike J.R.R. Tolkien, I daresay I'm a professional theologian.

By the way, Flieger and Anderson have drawn attention to the fact that newspaper reports on the *On Fairy-stories* lecture suggest that the actual lecture did not include the theological material on *eucatastrophe* that appeared in the published essay (cf. FS 130; 135). We don't know why it was so, perhaps because of his modesty and shyness to speak in public about theological matters, unlike his friend C.S. Lewis?

True restoration is inaugurated on Easter morning, the first day of the new creation. In the light of the Resurrection, history can be seen as God's great paschal design, the design that calls for the progressive personalisation and divinisation of all beings created in the likeness of God-love, all 'recapitulated' in the Son. "He who has been initiated into the hidden power of the resurrection knows for what purposes God predisposed the beginning of all things" (Maximus the Confessor, cf. Corbon 231).

"To know Christ and the power of His resurrection" (Phil 3:10-11) means, therefore, to get back into the original stream of life in which we can bring to their proper fulfilment all the incoherent, halting movements of our deepest being which is still so lost in its own complexity. Without rhetorical exaggeration, Paul can call the risen Christ the "first-born of all creation" (Col 1:15) as though His existence in the Resurrection were anterior to all being. He, in person, is the second and eternal creation which brings the first fugitive creation to a *new birth* from within. In the first creation man was the climax; in the second creation the Risen Christ becomes the root and a source of a new departure (cf. Corbon 233).

> It does not deny the existence of *dyscatastrophe*, of sorrow and failure: the possibility of these is necessary to the joy of deliverance; it denies (in the face of much evidence, if you will) universal final defeat and in so far is *evangelium*, giving a fleeting glimpse of Joy, Joy beyond the walls of the world, poignant as grief.　　(FS 99)

In this world suffering and disease are indeed "normal", but their very "normalcy" is abnormal. They revealed the ultimate and permanent defeat of man and of life, a defeat which no partial victories of medicine, however wonderful, can ultimately overcome. But in the Risen One suffering is not "removed"; it is transformed into victory. The defeat *itself* becomes victory, a way, an entrance into the Kingdom, and this is the only true *healing* (cf. Schmemann 103).

We're living in the unfolding of an *epiphany*, an *apocalypse* in which everything is already present, growing toward the final perfect manifestation. Once the living seed is present, the fruit is already present, even if it is *not yet* apparent. The paradox lies in the coexistence of the 'already' and the 'not yet' (Col 1:22). The times we live since this springtime of the Resurrection are times of a slow and patient growth (Lk 8:15; 2 Pt 3:8-9).

Paradox Resolved: the Undimming Light of the Firstborn of the New Creation

Finally, all the paradoxes of our dual condition are resolved in harmony around the pole of the liturgical drama. We are risen from death with Christ, but we also have the experience of living 'not yet' in the Kingdom. In the end, only Love will remain (1 Cor 13), for God is Love (1 Jn 4:8). Everything has a meaning and comes to fruition in the victory of love. Life and death, pain and joy, fleeting time and the eternity that already dwells in us.

And thus, Easter is not the commemoration of some event but the fulfilment of time itself, of our *real* time. For we still live in the same three dimensions of time: the world of nature, the world of history, the world of expectation. And, in each one, man is in a secret search for joy, that is, for an ultimate meaning and perfection, for an ultimate fulfilment which he does not find. On Easter night the meaning is given. And it is not given by means of "explanation" or even "commemoration", but as a gift of Joy itself, the Joy of participation in the *new time of the Kingdom*.

To experience this, one has to go to an Orthodox Church on Easter night, after the procession has gone around the church and has stopped in darkness at the closed door. Then the doors are opened with the announcement: *"Christ is risen!"* The only reality is joy and this joy is *given*.

The Orthodox called Easter the "sacrament of time". Indeed, the *joy* given on that night, the light that transforms the night into night 'brighter than day' is to become this secret joy and the ultimate meaning of all time. Time itself is now measured by the rhythm of the end and the beginning, of the end transformed into beginning, of the *"eucatastrophic"* beginning announcing the *"eucatastrophic"* fulfilment (cf. Schmemann 58).

The *Trampling down* of *death by death*, the entrance of man into the life of the Kingdom, into the immense peace of the Holy Spirit, is *given*.

The sense of gratitude, of delighted surprise because of receiving an undeserved and unexpected gift, baffles by its suddenness and its over-abundance. This is indeed the Easter experience to which *On Fairy-stories* refers, but it is also the same that is experienced in every occasion where there is a glimpse of a mysterious unexpected joy. Tolkien demonstrates his narrative ability when he makes similar moments appear in the plot of the stories of his sub-created world. This can be seen in a few examples:

> "Mithrandir!" he cried. "Mithrandir!"
> "Well met, I say to you again. Legolas!" said the old man.
> They all gazed at him. His hair was white as snow in the sunshine; and gleaming white was his robe; the eyes under his deep brows were bright, piercing as the rays of the sun; power was in his hand. Between wonder, joy, and fear they stood and found no words to say. At last Aragorn stirred. "Gandalf!" he said. "Beyond all hope you return to us in our need! What veil was over my sight? Gandalf!"   (LotR 516)

We may remember the wonder and joy that took Éomer at the arrival of Aragorn (LotR 881), or Pippin hearing "The Eagles are coming" (LotR 927), or Gandalf saying in a clear voice: "The realm of Sauron is ended" (LotR 985).

And thus, the most glorious occasions require both laughter and tears, as Sam discovers when he awakes from Mount Doom's nightmare to the bliss of beholding Gandalf in the land of Ithilien:

> Sam lay back, and stared with open mouth, and for a moment, between bewilderment and great joy, he could not answer. At last he gasped: "Gandalf! I thought you were dead! But then I thought I was dead myself. Is everything sad going to come untrue? What's happened to the world?"
> "A great Shadow has departed," said Gandalf, and then he laughed and the sound was like music, or like water in a parched land; and as he listened the thought came to Sam that he had not heard laughter, the pure sound of merriment, for days upon days without count. It fell upon his ears like the echo of all the joys he had ever known. But he himself burst into tears. Then, as a sweet rain will pass down a wind of spring and the sun will shine out the clearer, his tears ceased, and his laughter welled up, and laughing he sprang from his bed.
> "How do I feel?" he cried. "Well, I don't know how to say it. I feel, I feel"—he waved his arms in the air—"I feel like spring after winter, and sun on the leaves; and like trumpets and harps and all the songs I have ever heard!"   (LotR 987f.)

And when Sam heard that he laughed aloud for sheer delight, and he stood up and cried: "O great glory and splendour! And all my wishes have come true!" And then he wept.
And all the host laughed and wept, and in the midst of their merriment and tears the clear voice of the minstrel rose like silver and gold, and all men were hushed. And he sang to them, now in the Elven-tongue, now in the speech of the West, until their hearts, wounded with sweet words, overflowed, and their joy was like swords, and they passed in thought out to regions where pain and delight flow together and tears are the very wine of blessedness.   (LotR 990)

Here is a taste of heaven; here is laughter's resurrection, poignant as grief, the glory of the great consolation. We may recognise it in the dialogue between Faramir and Éowyn:

"Then you think that the Darkness is coming?" said Éowyn. "Darkness Unescapable?" And suddenly she drew close to him.
"No," said Faramir, looking into her face. "It was but a picture in the mind. I do not know what is happening. **The reason of my waking mind tells me that great evil has befallen and we stand at the end of days. But my heart says nay; and all my limbs are light, and a hope and joy are come to me that no reason can deny.** Éowyn, Éowyn, White Lady of Rohan, **in this hour I do not believe that any darkness will endure!**" And he stooped and kissed her brow.
And the Shadow departed, and the Sun was unveiled, and light leaped forth; and the waters of Anduin shone like silver, and in all the houses of the City **men sang for the joy that welled up in their hearts from what source they could not tell.**
                                  (LotR 998f., emphasis added)

In the dialogue between Faramir and Éowyn we therefore have a shining example of how Tolkien manages to suggest a sort of 'otherness' that reaches through an inner illumination the laborious life of the characters, opening them to hope. The world built by Tolkien shows to have different depths, it is a fabric rich in intertwined fibers, with the inner consistency of reality.

This narrative ability that weaves the sub-created world made by the Professor, is based on the reality of the Primary World. Toward the beginning of *On Fairy-stories*, Tolkien observes that "the incarnate mind, the tongue and the tale are in our world coeval" (21f.). What goes on in the author's head is precisely the reimagination of the world he already knows, and that active work becomes incarnate in the world he builds.

Only after recovering a right view and appreciation of the Primary World the author can sub-create from that world his secondary one. In this sense, sub-creation is derivative. But also, on a deeper level is this derivation true, for in building a Secondary World, the artist must imbue his people and places with life and story, and that life and story is derived from his own life, not in the sense of the content of his biography, but in the essence of the life he has been given.

Sub-creation, a true feat of worldbuilding, creates a work that is alive, alive enough to inspire a secondary belief (derived from primary belief) that is so powerful it sustains both author and reader in that world as they participate in meaning together (cf. Raimundo 13).

Resurrection, an event takes place, in which the sorrow is not simply replaced by joy, but is itself transformed into joy. Great Saturday is precisely this day of transformation, the day when victory grows from inside the defeat, when before the Resurrection, we are given to contemplate the death of death itself…

> The good novelist not only finds a symbol for feelings, he finds a symbol and a way of lodging it which tells the intelligent reader whether this feeling is adequate or inadequate, whether it is moral or immoral, whether it is good or evil. And his theology, even in its most remote reaches, will have a direct bearing on this.   (O'Connor 156)

> All tales may come true; and yet, at the last, redeemed, they may be as like and as unlike the forms that we give them as Man, finally redeemed, will be like and unlike the fallen that we know. (My 73)

There lives the dearest freshness deep down things. A river of life, rising and flowing crystal-clear. *A small square patch of blue sky could be seen.*

Conclusion: Resurrection as *the* Eucatastrophic Event

The proclamation of the Resurrection remains foolishness to this world, and it is no wonder that even Christians themselves manage to "explain it away" by virtually reducing it to the old pre-Christian doctrines of immortality and survival. And indeed, if the adoption of Resurrection is just some "doctrine", if it is something to be believed in as a mere glimpse of the "future", a mystery of the "other world", then it is not substantially different from other doctrines concerning the "other world" and can be easily confused with them. Whether it is the immortality of the soul or the resurrection of the body—we know nothing of them and all discussion here is mere "speculation". Death remains the same mysterious passage into a mysterious future.

Resurrection is the greatest "eucatastrophe" because it redeems everything that is human, everything that belongs to human life and to human love, and even the power of death is undone: everything is recovered, restored, free from the emptiness of death, made *new*.

The *great joy* that the disciples felt when they saw the risen Lord, that "burning of hearts" that they the experienced on the way to Emmaus (cf. Lk 24) was not because the mysteries of an "other world" were revealed to them, but because they saw the risen Lord with the mark of the nails in His hands and His side (cf. Jn 19, 25-29): they recognised Him because of His mortal wounds still present in His glorified body. They announced that *the new life has already begun, that He is life eternal, the Fulfilment, the Resurrection, and the Joy of the world.*

Not of some other world, but the fulfilment of all things and all lives *in Christ.* And if I make mine this *new life*, this hunger and thirst for the Kingdom, this expectation of Christ, the certitude that *Christ is Life and Light* (cf. Jn 1: 4).

What happens with all the paradoxes of our dual condition is as with the great woman of Revelation (Rev 12: 1-5), who is clothed with the sun in her heavenly glory and yet is in the pains of childbirth; she has already entered heaven and yet is still on the painful journey here below; she is at once the gracious queen and the sorrowful mother. Herein also lies the symbol of the deepest meaning of our own lives, which are ever both journeying and at journey's end, both sorrow and joy, *already* and *not yet*: "we are now the sons of God and it has not yet appeared what we shall be" (1 Jn 3:2). As long as it is still night let us look to the woman with the moon under her feet, clothed with the sun, crowned with stars, for in her all that which for us is yet to come is already accomplished. In the meantime, as the Byzantine Liturgy says, we live in hope, in "a painful joy, a radiant sadness" (cf. Rahner 112-122).

We know nothing about 'when' and 'how'. But we know that in Christ this great Passage, the *Pascha* of the world, has begun, that the light of the world comes to us in the *"eucatastrophic"* joy and peace of the Holy Spirit, for *Christ is risen and Life reigneth,* for "eyes to see that can" (LotR 239):

> a fleeting glimpse of Joy, Joy beyond the walls of the world,
> poignant as grief   (FS 99)

the great moment of "eucatastrophe" (as Professor Tolkien would
call it)   (Lewis, *Joy* 168)

Their hearts, wounded with sweet words, overflowed, and their
joy was like swords, and they passed in thought out to regions
where pain and delight flow together and tears are the very wine
of blessedness.   (LotR 990)

*The light of the shaft fell directly on a table in the middle of the room. "It looks
like a tomb…"* Unlike Balin's tomb in Moria, the source of the light comes
from the tomb itself, which is an empty tomb, according to *On Fairy-stories*.

We have not only that sudden glimpse of the truth behind the apparent
Ananké of our world, but a glimpse that is actually a ray of light through the
very chinks of the universe about us.

As in *Leaf by Niggle*, the grandeur of perspective and the depth of vision
come from the edges, from what remains beyond the boundaries of the painting (or more generally, beyond the edges—or walls—of the world built in the
work of sub-creation).

This is a powerful insight and characteristic of Tolkien's work: the world
built by him takes consistency, density, thickness and transparency precisely
from the "holes", or rather the loopholes, which allow the passage of a light
that does not set and it does not disappoint. A Light that is Life and life-giving,
which overcomes death and despair in the sub-created world as much as in the
Primary World.

The world built by the Professor is a solid world, crossed by hope and
positivity: he has been able to draw, create, describe and make us enter an
"eucatastrophic" world. This alone would already make him one of the great
builders of worlds in the history of human creativity, a sub-creator who knew
how to make wonderfully fruitful the great talent received.

Bibliography

Corbon, Jean. *Path to Freedom. Christian Experiences and the Bible.* Cincinnati (OH): St Anthony Messenger Press, 2004

Lewis, Clive Staples. *Surprised by Joy.* London: HarperCollins, 2012

O'Connor, Flannery. *Mystery and Manners. Occasional Prose.* New York: Farrar, Strauss and Giroux, 1997

Rahner, Hugo. *Our Lady and the Church.* Bethesda: Zaccheus Press, 2004

Raimundo, Jennifer. "World Building and Sub-creators. An Artist's Approach to Resurrection". In: *Mythmoot III: Ever On. Proceedings of the 3rd Mythgard Institute Mythmoot.* Maryland: Linthicum, 2015. 1-16

Tolkien, J.R.R., *The Lord of the Rings.* London: HarperCollins, 1992

---. *Tolkien On Fairy-stories.* Eds.: Verlyn Flieger & Douglas A. Anderson. London: HarperCollins, 2008

---. *The Letters of J.R.R Tolkien.* Ed.: Humphrey Carpenter. Boston/New York: Houghton Mifflin Company, 2000

Schmemann, Alexander. *For the Life of the World.* Crestwood (NY): St Vladimir's Seminary Press, 1982

"Somewhere in those long years":

Deconstructing the "Historical" Background in Tolkien's Foreword to *Farmer Giles of Ham*

Łukasz Neubauer (Koszalin)

Despite its evident conciseness of the narrative material[1] and somewhat child-oriented treatment of the hair-rising deeds of Ægidius Ahenobarbus Julius Agricola de Hammo, *Farmer Giles of Ham* constitutes one of the most intriguing literary publications ever penned by the author of *The Lord of the Rings*. Quite well known and oft-mentioned in the academic discussions are, for instance, the oral origins of what was initially but a "local family game" (L 36)[2], Tolkien's subsequent revisions of the tale (Scull & Hammond iii-xiii), inclusion of those components of his philological humour that, in the first place, amused his fellow scholars (L 31, 37, 47) and, in consequence, the layer-cake-like structure of the book which first saw print in 1949[3]. The ultimate effect of the almost-twenty-year-long process, on and off, of Tolkien's telling and retelling, writing and rewriting, typing and retyping of his work (as well as its being illustrated by Pauline Baynes) is a rather peculiar publication which seemingly could appeal to well-nigh everyone, in particular those aged 5-105, with at least a passing familiarity with certain medieval literary traditions and, most importantly, a good sense of humour.

With some of the most apparent humorous elements of the book already discussed elsewhere[4], we can first turn our attention to some of the narrative pillars of Tolkien's tale. Not surprisingly, this requires taking a quick glance at those works of the medieval canon which seem to have had the most profound effect upon *Farmer Giles of Ham*, particularly the ones that provided the book

---

1   The 50th anniversary edition, edited by Christina Scull and Wayne G. Hammond (1999), consists of 73 pages of large-print text, interspersed with 44 in-text illustrations (7-79). In addition to that, the book comprises: the editors' introduction (iii-xiii) and notes (105-127), the "First (Manuscript) Version of the story (81-100) and Tolkien's attempt at a sequel (101-103). The subsequent editions of *Farmer Giles* (2009, 2014) differ with regard to the number of pages, but the proportions between the actual narrative and the addenda are, of course, more or less the same.

2   An attempt to reconstruct the very first stages of the composition of *Farmer Giles of Ham* (and *Roverandom*) may be found in my article published in *Quaestiones Oralitatis* II 2/2016 (65-86).

3   Its very first edition, from George Allen & Unwin, came out on 20 Oct. 1949 (Scull and Hammond 373). Since then, it has been republished several times, both as an independent book and as part of omnibus editions: *The Tolkien Reader* (1966) and *Tales from the Perilous Realm* (1997).

4   See, for instance, Schneidewind, *Farmer Giles*, Kocher, *Master* 178-186 and my own contribution Neubauer, *Ignorance*.

with evident templates, spatial as well as temporal. And so, it appears that in addition to the most obvious ones that fuelled the author's imagination with regard to the specific themes, motifs and characters (*Beowulf, Vǫlsunga saga,* Chaucer's "The Reeve's Tale", Shakespeare's *King Lear,* etc.), the most significant sources of his inspiration were the various works—poems, chronicles and other prose narratives—which happen to lie within the broadly understood Arthurian tradition, where the accuracy of time, space and circumstances has always been of lesser importance than the elements of chivalric fantasy. Accordingly, the titles which regularly come up in the academic discourse are, in particular, Geoffrey of Monmouth's fictitious *Historia regum Britanniae* (completed by 1139) or the anonymous late-14th-century poem *Sir Gawain and the Green Knight,* and so the works in which the "historical" foundations are always treated with a great amount of deference, provided, of course, that they should remain applicable to the main arguments of their respective authors. In both of them, for instance, the establishment of the ancient Kingdom of Britain, the cornerstone of many a "historical" account in the Middle Ages, is attributed to Brutus, the renowned, if utterly legendary, grandson of the Trojan hero Aeneas, the same Brutus who, as was once held, gave Britain its very name (*Historia* bk. I; *Sir Gawain and the Green Knight* l. 1-19)[5].

Such, it appears, was also the general approach taken by Tolkien himself, who likewise refers to Brutus as the eponymous founder and first king of the insular realm—"since Brutus came to Britain many kings and realms have come and gone" (FG 7)—although in this case it was evidently triggered by the writer's jest-provoked wish to emulate the texts he enjoyed as a reader and worked with as a scholar, especially the latter story, relating Sir Gawain's perilous quest in the *wyldrenesse of Wyrale* (*Sir Gawain and the Green Knight* l. 701) "wilderness of Wirral"[6], where the protagonist strives to fulfil the pledge

---

5   According to Geoffrey, *Denique Brutus de nomine suo insulam Britanniam appellat sociosque suos Britones* (bk. I, ch. 21) "Brutus named the island Britain after himself and, likewise, his followers Britons". Some two and a half centuries later, the *Gawain* poet chose not to delve into such onomastic particulars, but, much as the Welsh cleric, declared that *Felix Brutus / On mony bonkes ful brode Bretayn... settes* (ll. 13-14) "Fortunate Brutus sets [i.e. establishes] high Britain on many broad hills". Geoffrey of Monmouth and, consequently, the *Gawain* poet almost certainly drew upon the earlier tradition, perhaps the early-9th-century Latin *Historia Brittonum* traditionally attributed to the Welsh monk Nennius.

6   Tolkien obviously knew the 14th-century poem inside out. In 1925, he co-edited it with E.V. Gordon and his own translation of it into alliterative verse was dramatised for the BBC to be broadcast in 1953. The latter text would then be published posthumously in 1975 (along with the translations of two other Middle English poems, *Pearl* and *Sir Orfeo*). Finally, the W.P. Ker Memorial Lecture that Tolkien delivered on 15 Apr. 1953 at the University of Glasgow came out in print in 1983 as part of the collection titled *The Monsters and the Critics and Other Essays.*

he made to his green-clad opponent on New Year's Day[7]. On the other hand, though, perfectly well known to the readers of *The Lord of the Rings* and, in particular, *The Silmarillion* should also be his scrupulous attention to detail and tendency to operate within a somewhat restricted range of narrative styles, almost invariably oscillating within the rich and colourful world of the Middle Ages, Early, High and Late. His little book is therefore a fascinating amalgamation of various medieval traditions from *Beowulf* to the late Arthurian romances, with frequent nods and winks towards Tolkien's fellow scholars or even outright buffooneries, the victims of which could be, for instance, the "Four Wise Clerks of Oxenford" (FG 15), or, rather, the editors of the *Oxford English Dictionary*: James A.H. Murray, Henry Bradley, W.A. Craigie and C.T. Onions (Hammond & Scull 111)[8].

As befits a "mock-heroic tale" (Kocher 178), *Farmer Giles of Ham* begins with a brief but almost indispensable mock "foreword" (FG 7-8), which, Christina Scull informs us, gradually "developed through several drafts" (viii), the earliest of which must have been written in the second half of 1946. It is certainly a late addition which may have its far-reaching roots in the fact that Tolkien read it on a number of occasions to other academics[9], whose favourable reactions evidently made him realise that, at long last, in its successive versions, this particular fragment of the "history of the Little Kingdom" (7) gradually turned into a book whose sole target group was no longer that of young children and adolescents, although this, he admits in a letter to Allen & Unwin, should "not necessarily prevent them from being amused by it" (L 119). It might also be that the foreword was intended, perhaps "unconsciously at first, but (more) consciously in the revision" to provide a "satirical extension" to Tolkien's lecture and, subsequently, essay, *Beowulf: The Monsters and the Critics*, in which he famously disapproves of reading the Old English poem predominantly for its often dubious, historical values and, in this way, disregarding the actual literary merits of *Beowulf*. Finally, it cannot be ruled out that by adding the foreword, Tolkien simply tried to expand his fragment of "the history of the

---

7   In the poem, Gawain agrees to play a beheading game with the mysterious green-clad knight. Its rules are deceptively simple, with the participants taking it in turns to chop off the opponent's head with an axe. What initially appears to be a thoroughly undemanding task (Gawain is to strike first), soon turns into a nightmare, as the Green Knight picks up his severed head and, upon leaving King Arthur's court, reminds the now stupefied protagonist to keep his side of the bargain in a year and a day.

8   In 1919-1920, Tolkien was employed by the *Oxford Dictionary of English* to research the etymological roots of several words beginning with the letter *w* (Carpenter 140).

9   One such reference may be found in his letter to C.A. Furth of Allen & Unwin (7-24-1938). Having read it to the members if the Lovelace Society, Tolkien reflects that, much to his surprise, "the audience was apparently not bored—indeed they were generally convulsed with mirth" (L 39). Christina Scull and Wayne G. Hammond date the reading to 14 Febr. 1938 (227).

Little Kingdom" (FG 7), so that it would finally meet the requirements of his publisher, anxious to see a new book from the author of *The Hobbit*[10].

On the other side of the coin, it was almost certainly not an attempt to draw upon the colloquial, dialogue-like manner of narration, found in all the earlier drafts of the book. This had practically become a thing of the past by the time Tolkien submitted the final version of *Farmer Giles of Ham* to George Allen & Unwin[11]. Whatever the case may be, one should bear in mind the fact that it was, in all likelihood, "an afterthought, not written until the story proper had been in existence for many years" (Scull ix), and so its point of view, significance of time and space as well as the overall tone are quite noticeably, though never dramatically, different from the proper story of Ægidius Ahenobarbus.

At this point it ought perhaps to be reminded that, unlike a preface or intro- duction, a foreword is usually a short composition at the beginning of a book which is typically written by another person, i.e. other than the primary author of the publication (Cuddon 350). Its purpose may be, for instance, to praise the author or shed some light upon the origins and development of the text, its subsequent editions, heretofore criticism, etc. To illustrate, the 2014 edition of Tolkien's *The Lord of the Rings* begins with a five-part prologue written by the author himself (1-16), preceded by a note on the text by Douglas A. Anderson (2005; ix-xv), another one on the revised text by Christina Scull and Wayne G. Hammond (2014; xvi-xix) and a foreword to the second edition of the book, also written by the librarians from Massachusetts (xx-xxiii).

This, however, is not the case with *Farmer Giles of Ham*. Here, the foreword was obviously written by Tolkien himself, although on the first two pages of his little book he does assume an altogether different persona, namely that of a modern "editor" who, in a tongue-in-cheek manner, explains the benefits of translating "this curious tale, out of its very insular Latin into the modern tongue of the United Kingdom" (7)[12]. While this metafictional practice of introducing

---

10   In his correspondence, Tolkien frequently alludes to its brevity and informs the then prospective publishers how the short narrative may be expanded into a book-length format. On 24 July 1938, i.e. more than eleven years before its ultimate publication, he tells C.A. Furth of Allen & Unwin that he has rewritten it to "about 50% longer" (L 39). A few months later, on 2 Febr. 1939, Tolkien ponders on the possibility of writing "more light-hearted stories of the Little Kingdom to go with *Farmer Giles*" (42). Much of the same intent is his later letter to Stanley Unwin, dated 7 Dec. 1942, in which he suggests adding "one or two similar tales, and include[ing] some verse on similar topics" (58).

11   The only tangible remnant of that is the famous reference to a blunderbuss (FG 15), which in its earlier form would take the form of a verbal interaction between an inquisitive child and the knowledgeable narrator (82), an interaction doubtlessly echoing a genuine question once asked by one of Tolkien's sons. The so-called "First (Manuscript) Version" (81-100) preserves a few more such instances.

12   These benefits, the narrator maintains, are, above all, "the glimpse that it [i.e. the book] affords of life in a dark period of the history of Britain" and "the light that it throws on the origin of some difficult place-names" (FG 7).

alleged translators, compilers, etc. is not in the least new—apart from Geoffrey of Monmouth's *Historia*, there are notable examples of it in, for instance, Miguel de Cervantes's *Don Quixote* (1605) or James Macpherson's *Songs of Ossian* (1760)—Tolkien's rationale behind the employment of this technique is markedly different from those of his literary predecessors. Cervantes, Macpherson and other literary "forgers" evidently wished to provide their respective works with more credibility, boldly claiming that theirs were in fact genuine narratives. In the case of the former, it was the events that, the Spanish writer claimed, had taken place a few decades earlier in La Mancha; in the latter, it was the ancient songs that the Scottish poet alleged to have collected in the Highlands of Scotland and carefully translated from the Gaelic language[13]. It is naturally hard to estimate the number of people who, back in the 17th or 18th centuries, actually accepted the authors' assertions as true. Some may have indeed swallowed the bait, but there is little chance that many readers would have done the same in the mid-20th century, although the story of Orson Welles's famous radio adaptation of H.G. Wells's *The War of the Worlds* (1938) demonstrates that successful mass "deceptions" were not necessarily unthinkable in more or less the same time frame[14].

It appears, however, that what Tolkien wished to achieve by introducing the voice of a knowledgeable "translator" and "editor" was an almost complete reversal of meanings. Indeed, the more serious and bookish he tries to sound by alluding to certain timeworn and clichéd elements of medieval British culture (such as the aforementioned eponym Brutus or the semi-legendary King Coel), the more ludicrous he actually sounds, although, at least on the surface, the said allusions never seem to be completely outside the realm of literary possibility. A good illustration of that might be the opening passage of the foreword, where Tolkien, as a knowledgeable "translator" and "editor" of the book, makes an attempt to reconstruct the literary background of the "real author" of *Farmer Giles of Ham*. Despite the fact that his opinion of the "author's" evident limitations with regard to his knowledge of geography gives the impression of being academically sensible[15]—and, in fact, bears some resemblance to the genuine efforts of modern scholars to unmask, for instance, the *Gawain* poet on the basis of his dialect—there could be no doubt that Tolkien is pulling the reader's leg. There was never any realm, lying within the physical

---

13 In the case of Cervantes, it was, in all likelihood, just a clever "marketing trick". When it comes to Macpherson, the reasons for his forgery appear to have been more patriotic than commercial.

14 Aired on 31 Oct. 1938, in the form of dramatised news reports, *The War of the Worlds* is believed, perhaps exaggeratedly, to have caused a small-scale panic in various parts of the USA.

15 According to Tolkien, the "author" of the tale almost certainly "lived... in the lands of the Little Kingdom" (FG 7). His assertion, based solely upon the fact that the "geographical knowledge as he shows... is of that country, while of regions outside it, north or west, he is plainly ignorant" (7) gives, of course, the appearance of a sound philological argument.

boundaries of the British Isles, known to its inhabitants, both then and now, as the "Little Kingdom" (or *Parvum regnum*). Sure enough, the Middle Kingdom from which King Giles's miniscule dominion eventually secedes could, and perhaps should, be identified (if only upon the geographical grounds) with the Anglo-Saxon kingdom of Mercia (Shippey 59). However, the realm over which the once reluctant hero comes to preside has absolutely no territorial, political or other correspondence in the history of early medieval Britain, even in the "dark period" that the "editor" enigmatically refers to when he expounds upon the historical merits of his Modern English "translation" (FG 7). In effect, with this evident lack of any territorial foundation, the "ancient" tale of Ægidius Ahenobarbus loses much of its "historical" veracity, at least in the eyes of the older, more historically-informed readers.

It soon becomes even less reliable, following the subsequent assertion of the "editor" that the book he converted "into the modern tongue of the United Kingdom" (FG 7) was originally written in Latin. Or, in point of fact, "very insular Latin" (7), which seems to imply that, at least potentially, its reading could have been affected by the grammatical and/or lexical inconsistencies of the language employed by the British "author"[16]. To make the matters worse, we are told that, regardless of its (in)correctness, even the Latin text should not be perceived as a primary source for the tale, since "it is evidently a late compilation, full of marvels, derived not from sober annals, but from the popular lays to which its author frequently refers" (7). By saying this, Tolkien appears to have made the book's veracity even more doubtful than Geoffrey of Monmouth, who, in the opening chapter of his *Historia regum Britanniae* maintains that it was based upon some *Britannici sermonis liber vetustissimus* (ch. 1), the "ancient book in the British tongue" which he claimed to have received from *Walterus Oxinefordensis archidiaconus*, a genuine historical figure known to have served as the archdeacon of Oxford during much of the first half of the 12th century (c. 1112-1151)[17].

If, therefore, the account of Ægidius Ahenobarbus is already not-quite-reliable at the level of its earliest known "source materials", the aforesaid "popular lays" (FG 7), then each of the subsequent "layers" of the narrative inevitably acquire the appearance of being more and more fictional. So much so that its ultimate version, Tolkien's *Farmer Giles of Ham*, being, of course, a double "translation" from, we may assume, the ancient British tongue, via Latin, is now but a distant echo of the "historical truth". Quite deliberately, it seems, the book thus comes

---

16 The sense of Tolkien's remark is that the language of "this curious tale" is corrupted, and thus somehow removed from the classical Latin of Cicero, just as the "Frensh" that Chaucer's Prioress speaks "ful faire and fetisly" is certainly not the high-status variety heard in Paris, but a much less prestigious one, one that she learnt at the Benedictine abbey of "Stratford atte Bowe" (*The Canterbury Tales*, "General Prologue" 124-125).

17 Few scholars today, however, believe Geoffrey's claim to have any historical foundations.

to reflect the same multi-layered tradition that gave us, for instance, the legendary King Arthur; the Arthur who, in his genuinely historical, early-6th-century, context was not necessarily the crowned monarch he is regularly depicted as in the much later medieval romances. Or, better still, if we take into consideration the actual extent of Tolkien's literary interests and sources of inspiration for his own works of fiction, *Farmer Giles of Ham* is, at least in some degree, like the curious allegorical tower built from "an accumulation of old stone, part of an older hall" (BMC 7), which the Oxford scholar famously envisions in *Beowulf: The Monsters and the Critics*. It may be "nonsensical", it may have "no sense of proportion", but from the top of it one may be "able to look out upon the sea" (8). That is to say, a given tale (be that of Beowulf, Arthur or Giles) could be criticised for its numerous historical inconsistencies or compositional flaws, yet the fundamental merit of it should always lie in the story itself, its narrative unfolding, character development, dramatic potential, adventurous plot twists and, in some cases, humorous punches. Without at least some of them, no matter how dexterous it should be on the purely compositional level, the story would lose much of its literary appeal and value.

There is, of course, no verifiable proof that, in the years that followed its original publication, *Farmer Giles of Ham* enjoyed a particularly high degree of success amongst the medieval scholars in Britain[18]. In fact, it seems far more likely that, with the exception of some of Tolkien's fellow scholars, C.S. Lewis, Owen Barfield, Hugo Dyson and other Inklings, the lavishly illustrated book was mainly purchased by the parents (many of whom, perhaps, still remembered the enormous success of *The Hobbit* in the late 1930s and early 1940s) of primary school-aged or early adolescent children. Nevertheless, it is not improbable that at least a fraction of the 5,000 copies of its first printing was read by the academics who, much as the aforementioned members of the Lovelace Society, ended up being "generally convulsed with mirth" (L 39). If the modified—or, it should perhaps be said, medievalised[19]—rendering of Tolkien's tale had been so favourably received in 1938, it seems quite reasonable that, more than a decade later, its expanded print version (including the mock-historical foreword) would have raised a smile (or two) on the faces of those for whom philological research into early medieval literature constituted daily bread. It is not difficult, for instance, to picture them perceptibly amused by the author's not infrequent references to the numerous difficulties commonly encountered by all sorts of

---

18 It is known, however, that within the first two months or so more than "2,000 copies of the first printing of 5,000 of *Farmer Giles of Ham*" (Scull & Hammond 379) were sold. Nevertheless, we are informed that it did not sell as well as had been hoped by the publisher (379).

19 In the earliest phases of its existence, it was, Tolkien says, but a light-hearted tale "of a 'no time'" (L 133), with little, if any, direct references to the Arthurian matter.

medieval scholars: problems with the dating of a text,[20] ambiguities stemming from the not quite reliable origins of some toponym,[21] or even certain lexical cruces that, every now and then, turn out be a genuine nuisance for the readers of early medieval literature[22]. Convulsed with mirth or merely chuckling, it is at least plausible that some of Tolkien's fellow scholars (or those of them who cared to buy the book[23]) found his medieval additions (including the foreword) genuinely amusing or even well-aimed as academic self-mockery.

To all the rest of the readers of *Farmer Giles*, young in body or at heart, the medieval elements almost certainly did not seem to be in any way unbefitting. After all, an overwhelming majority of European folk and fairy tales, stories of magic and wonder, as well as all sorts of abridgements and retellings of various heroic poems, sagas and chivalric romances (so popular in, particularly, the 19th and early 20th centuries) are, almost as a rule, set against a medieval backdrop, both real and imagined. It seems reasonable, then, to infer that to those people whose educational background was not strictly speaking academic, readers whose everyday interests did not necessarily revolve around the early Middle Ages and its historical writings, the narrator's assertion that the events outlined in his translation are believed to have taken place "somewhere in those long years…" (FG 8) looked much more like the conventional "Once upon a time", "A long time ago" or "There was once" than the Old English *in gear-dagum* or Latin *olim erat*. Likewise, unfamiliar to them would also be the interpretational, editorial, translational or other philological impediments that medieval scholars recurrently come across in their work. In consequence, unless some apparently inexplicable oddity should catch the eye of a more observant reader (such as the plainly anachronistic blunderbuss or the "Four Wise Clerks of Oxenford"), the actual character of most of Tolkien's medieval-inspired buffooneries and absurdities in *Farmer Giles of Ham* would most likely come unacknowledged, unrecognised or unappreciated, quite seamlessly integrated within the folk-tale-like narrative of sapient beasts, witless giants, magical swords and fabulous dragon hoards.

---

20 "Somewhere in those long years, after the days of King Coel maybe, but before Arthur or the Seven Kingdoms of the English, we must place the events here related" (FG 8).

21 "An excuse for presenting a translation of this curious tale… may be found in the glimpse that it affords of life in a dark period of the history of Britain, not to mention the light that it throws on the origin of some difficult place-names" (FG 7).

22 "Some may well ask what a blunderbuss was. Indeed, this very question, it is said, was put to the Four Wise Clerks of Oxenford" (FG 15). For Tolkien's analyses of individual words in early medieval literature, see, for instance, his examination of Old English terms *lof*, *dom*, *hell* and *heofon* in *Beowulf: The Monsters and the Critics* (36-42) and, in particular, the troublesome noun *ofermod* in *The Homecoming of Beorhtnoth Beorhthelm's Son* (13-18).

23 According to Tolkien, not many of his colleagues could openly "admit knowledge of [his] 'fantasy'… without loss of academic dignity" (L 25).

Finally, constituting the original (one could even add pre-scriptural) audience of the tale, there are the writer's own children: John (b. 1917), Michael (1920), Christopher (1924) and Priscilla (1929) who, over the course of nearly two decades, saw the story progress from some indefinable "local family game played in the country" (L 43)[24] to the scrupulously medievalised (though still thoroughly light-hearted) book that was ultimately published in the autumn of 1949. For them, its gradual evolution must have been particularly interesting, even if their responses to the final version of the tale were somewhat different from how they perceived the adventures of Farmer Giles in the late 1920s and early 1930s, when it was almost certainly a major story in their father's bedtime repertoire[25]. It may be assumed that, in some way, the narrative grew with them, the medieval elements perhaps gradually turning up, as, bit by bit, they came to first recognise, then appreciate and finally, particularly in the case of Christopher, share some of their father's academic interests.

In effect, the temporal framework which the little book ultimately acquires[26] and the sense of antiquarian grandeur that the fictional "translator" and "editor" discloses in its foreword are some of the most significant (and, not surprisingly, observable) factors which make the published version of *Farmer Giles of Ham* so markedly different from the earlier versions of the narrative; a narrative known to have been hitherto related by the not-quite-medieval "Daddy" (81ff.). Hence, the question which naturally arises in the reader, in particular one whose critical reflections are in some way stimulated by his or her awareness of Tolkien's medieval interests, is: what age group was the book actually written for? Interestingly, it appears that the author himself was often (and at various stages of its development) at a loss as to who should actually find it entertaining. It surprises him when the members of the Lovelace Society are "convulsed with mirth" (L 39), which, in his opinion, means that the narrative "has taken on a rather more adult and satiric flavour" (39). More than ten years later, once it has been published, he is worried by the fact that the book has, in the end, turned into "a donnish little squib" (138), and, in consequence, does not quite sell as well as it could (provided, of course, it had been better targeted). Nearly seven decades after its publication (and two more that seem to have elapsed since the "local family game" began to take the form of a tale), it appears that

---

24 It seems quite probable, given the character and extent of Tolkien's philological interests and the hint he seems to be giving in the foreword (FG 7), that the purpose of this game was to make up some truly absurd theories explaining the origins of certain place names in and around Oxfordshire.

25 In 1949, John and Michael, who in all likelihood took part in the original "family game", were 32 and 29 respectively. Christopher, who would have doubtlessly heard some of its earliest versions, was 25 and Priscilla had just turned 20.

26 There are no allusions whatsoever to any historical (or even quasi-historical) context in the First (Manuscript) Version of *Farmer Giles of Ham*, the only "temporal" marker being Tolkien's folk-take-like "Once there was..." (81).

his concerns were fortunately premature. The young readers simply like it for its lively and entertaining plot, finding, as was hoped by the writer, "the character and adventures of its hero attractive in themselves" (FG 7). Those who are more advanced in age—Tolkien fans and scholars alike—take more pleasure in its sophisticated philological humour. Lacking the mock-historical foreword (as well as the overall medieval flavour that came in the subsequent versions of *Farmer Giles of Ham*), the book would certainly not become what it is today—a "fabulous tale of the days when giants and dragons walked the kingdom, full of scholar's wit [and] with graceful drawings entirely suited to the text" (*The Sunday Times*[27]).

Bibliography

Burrow, J.A. (ed.). *Sir Gawain and the Green Knight*. Harmondsworth: Penguin Books, 1972

Carpenter, Humphrey. *J.R.R. Tolkien. A Biography*. London: HarperCollins, 2002

Chaucer, Geoffrey. *The Canterbury Tales*. London: Penguin Books, 2013

Cuddon, J.A. *The Penguin Dictionary of Literary Terms and Literary Theory*. London: Penguin Books, 1992

Geoffrey of Monmouth. *Historia Regum Britanniae. A Variant Version*. Ed.: Jacob Hammer. Cambridge, MA: Medieval Academy of America, 2013

Kocher, Paul H. *Master of Middle-earth: The Achievement of J.R.R. Tolkien*. London: Thames and Hudson, 1973

Neubauer, Łukasz. "Plain Ignorance in the Vulgar Form: Tolkien's Onomastic Humour in *Farmer Giles of Ham*". In: *Laughter in Middle-earth: Humour in and around the Works of J.R.R. Tolkien*. Eds.: Thomas Honegger and Maureen F. Mann. Zurich/Jena: Walking Tree Publishers, 2016, 89-104

---. "'Wówczas tatuś rozpoczął opowieść': Próba rekonstrukcji oralnych początków wybranych utworów dziecięcych J.R.R. Tolkiena". In: *Quaestiones Oralitatis* II 2/2016. Wrocław: Instytut Studiów Klasycznych, Śródziemnomorskich i Orientalnych, 65-86

Schneidewind, Friedhelm. "*Farmer Giles of Ham*: The Prototype of a Humorous Dragon Story". *Tolkien's Shorter Works*. In: *Essays of the Jena Conference 2007*. Eds.: Margaret Hiley & Frank Weinreich. Zurich/Jena: Walking Tree Publishers, 2008, 77-100

Scull, Christina & Wayne G. Hammond. *The J.R.R. Tolkien Companion and Guide. Chronology*. London: HarperCollins, 2017

Tolkien, J.R.R. "Beowulf: The Monsters and the Critics". *The Monsters and the Critics and Other Essays*. London: HarperCollins, 2006

---. *Farmer Giles of Ham*. 50th Anniversary Edition. Eds.: Christina Scull & Wayne G. Hammond. Boston/New York: Houghton Mifflin Company, 1999

---. "The Homecoming of Beorhtnoth Beorhthelm's Son". *Essays and Studies by Members of the English Association* 6 (1953): 1-18

---. *The Letters of J.R.R. Tolkien*. Edited by Humphrey Carpenter with the assistance of Christopher Tolkien. London: George Allen & Unwin, 1981

https://tolkieniano.blogspot.com/2011/10/farmer-giles-di-ham-edizione.html

---

27   https://tolkieniano.blogspot.com/2011/10/farmer-giles-di-ham-edizione.html

'In the Perilous Realm or in its Shadowy Marches':

Standing between Spaces and Inhabiting Multiple Worlds with the Eld Green and Kyn Folk

Christine Vogt-William (Bayreuth)

> The *wyr* is the spirit language of kinship,
> a part of you, of all the Folk and our land,
> and that means we have to respect it and give it care,
> to honour its strengths and also its weaknesses.
> Words give shape to the world and our relationships,
> but they can poison as readily as they can heal.
> We must listen to what those voices tell us,
> not drown them out with our own wants.
>
> Justice, *Kynship* 133

The world of Middle-earth is very much invested in relations that cross the boundaries between human contexts and what Tolkien referred to as the Perilous Realm—the world of Faerie:

> *Faerie* contains many things besides elves and fays, and besides dwarfs, witches, trolls, giants or dragons; it holds seas, the sun, the moon, the sky; and the earth, and all things that are in it; tree and bird, water and stone, wine and bread, and ourselves, mortal men, when we are enchanted…
> Most good 'fairy-stories' are about the *aventures* of men in the Perilous Realm or upon its shadowy marches… The definition of a 'fairy-story—what it is, or what it should be—does not then, depend on any definition or historical account of elf or fairy, but upon the nature of *Faerie*; the Perilous Realm itself, and the air that blows in that country… *Faerie* cannot be caught in a net of words, for it is one of its qualities to be indescribable; though not imperceptible.   (FS 9-10)

It is these 'shadowy marches' of, and liminal relations with the Perilous Realm that are conducive for explorations of the infrastructures deployed in fantasy literary world-making, using Tolkien's concept of Primary and Secondary Worlds (FS 47-49). Notably, Tolkien's descriptions of Faerie and the Perilous Realm bear a distinctly European cultural stamp, informing most forms of fantasy writing available today. Seen in this light, I would venture to ask how non-European (writers' and readers') cultural contexts relate to Tolkien's fantasy works in particular.[1] Against this canvas, I address a Secondary World which evinces connections with Tolkien's understandings of worldbuilding, while foregrounding a particular non-European cultural context.

Cherokee writer Daniel Heath Justice's fantasy trilogy *The Way of Thorn and Thunder: The Kynship Chronicles*[2] brings Indigenous North American (US and Canadian) perspectives, worldviews, mythologies and histories of the Indigenous Primary World into cultural conversations with Tolkien's *The Lord of The Rings*. The trilogy evokes the Primary World's historical periods of the 1700s and 1800s, when European colonising agents moved into Indigenous North American territories, displacing indigenous peoples from their geophysical and cultural spaces.

A key device deployed by Justice in his literary worldbuilding of the Eld Green is the *wyr*—an ethereal force imbued with materiality through a species of tree sacred to the Everland Folk. The wyrwood tree provides resources for *wyr*-wielding practices and for everyday life needs and consumption; it is described in detail in the glossaries to all three volumes:

> WYRWOOD
> A type of tree that grows only in 'Holds, the wyrwood is a vital resource to the Folk. Its leaves and naturally shed outer bark... can be used for durable wyrweave fabric, clothing and armour; its red roots and fallen branches can be shaped by Wielders into both armour and weapons, as can its rarely accessed heartwood

---

1   '... indeed, one might ask if Tolkien had envisioned non-white and non-Christian readers as consumers of his texts, and how such readers might receive his shaping of characters like the Haradrim, the Drúedain, and Orcs, using medieval racial stereotypes and the connotations they carry.' (Vogt-William 311)

2   Since the *Kynship Chronicles* are not necessarily known among the greater fantasy reading public, a brief synopsis of the narrative follows:
Central to the trilogy is the concept of a primeval natural realm, known as the Eld Green, peopled by seven nations of Aboriginal Folk known as the Kyn, and sundry other races of beings, who exist alongside the Human world. At one point in their Folk history, the boundary between the Eld Green and the Human world is breached by an ambitious Human who desired the powers of the Kyn Folk. This historical catastrophe leads to the Melded World, juxtaposing the industrialised Human world against the rest of the Eld Green which functions through a natural force known as the 'wyr'. The heroine of the story is the young she-Kyn warrior Tarsa de'Shae who comes of age as a *wyr* force Wielder. The narrative charts her progress as a Wielder and a spokesperson of the Eld Folk, when Humans attempt to penetrate the hidden lands of the Eld Green, in order to acquire the riches these contain, while colonising the region and its peoples. As the Everland is torn apart by internal divisions amongst its Folk and the ever-encroaching threat of colonisation and slavery spearheaded by the Human Dreydmaster Lojar Vald of Eromar, Tarsa and her companions take on adversaries from the real and the spirit worlds in order to restore the balance in both.

and its golden sap is both nourishing and medicinal. The tree roots of living wyrwood draw poisons out of the surrounding soil, thus purifying both earth and water. Its lofty canopy provides housing for many Folk, as do the massive trunks of the more ancient trees. In many ways, the wyrwood tree provides the daily link between the Folk and the *wyr* currents of their homeland.

(Justice, *Wyrwood* 222)

The name of this tree notably serves as the title of the second volume of the *Chronicles*—thus rooting the concept of the *wyr* in the material world of the Eld Green. *Wyrwood* (2006) structurally marks this section of the narrative with a hinge function, where the impending sense of cataclysmic change contains a second upheaval in Folk history that is a consequence of colonising violence and power abuse. This narrative frame is congruent with Tolkien's plot of two historical upheavals in Middle-earth caused by Morgoth and Sauron consecutively. While Morgoth and Sauron (a Vala and a Maia) can be considered border transgressive agents between the 'Spirit World' (Ea?) and Middle-earth, the two agents of upheaval in the Eld Green are Human men (Kaantor and Vald), who also transgress the boundaries between the Spirit World and the Eld Green.

At the same time, *Wyrwood* explores the development of agency and self-knowledge in the key characters, contingent on Secondary World genealogical principles derived from Primary World Indigenous concepts of history and kinship, significant to Indigenous political frameworks of decolonisation and claims to sovereignty. The wyrwood tree and the *Wyrwood* text then instantiate literary negotiations between histories of colonial violence in the Indigenous Primary World and fictional imaginations of political agency in the Secondary World using the mythologies that have cultural cachet in both worlds.

In considering how cultural mythologies are allocated hierarchical positions in knowledge frameworks, Justice observes the necessity of acknowledging that fantasy literature is burdened with its own problems concerning its position vis á vis realistic fiction, which for the most part is

… framed by social presumptions that naturalize colonialism and its effects and presume the inevitability of Indigenous deficit is as much a compromised perspective as that of imaginative fiction, if not more so, as it reinforces oppressive presumptions through its assumptions of benign, authorized authenticity.

(Justice, *Wonderworks*)

In this light, 'real' representations of Indigenous positions and productions can be extraordinarily problematic, since realistic fiction and criticism can perpetuate disempowering narratives about Indigenous positions that furnish minoritised readers with limited, limiting and often abject, pessimistic images, based on constructed stereotypes which do not allow for more complex narratives. From this perspective, readers should then ideally question whether such representations of marginalised identities by hegemonic perspectives can be accepted as 'realistic'.

In asking whether marginalised perspectives have been able to articulate their own stories, knowledges, truths and shape their own literary worlds, readers could function as tricksters in the sense that Minnesota Anishinabe novelist and philosopher Gerald Vizenor describes: "The native trickster teases the ownership of ideas and history, that long history of territorial dominance, and the reduction of imagination to serve the causes of cultural discovery and possession" (Vizenor/Lee 127). Such reading and writing practices then constitute the decolonising imperative that many Indigenous writers and scholars invest in their works, which entails challenging hegemonic positions of certain kinds of cultural knowledges.

Justice sees the genre as offering much potential in articulating decolonisation and self-determination agendas, thus underscoring his contention that fantasy literature allows readers to imagine otherwise, "to believe in possibilities beyond the... often oppressive realities to which our differences, whatever they may be, are subject" (*Wonderworks*). That fantasy and fairy story can encourage readers to question the currency of the Primary World's codes and credos is a function that Tolkien himself has addressed in *On Fairy-stories*, where he posits a need to recover clarity of vision (FS 57-58). Thus, the acts of reading and writing fantasy literature allow for platforms where readers of all cultural backgrounds can recognise, question and challenge asymmetrical power operations and oppressions that are in place in the Primary World.

Clarity from the Perilous Realm: Recovery and Relationality in Indigenous Literary Worldbuilding

Against the backdrop of such a decolonial imperative, the epigraph to this essay bears some reflection. This teaching from a she-Kyn Elder (Unahi) defines the *wyr* as the principle of kinship shaping the Eld Green. Thus, an important aspect of literary world-making in Justice's *Kynship Chronicles* is that of kinship congruent with Mark Wolf's concept of relationship systems in world-making, more particularly the infrastructure of genealogies:

> Genealogies function as extensions of characters, which in turn
> provide continuity across a world's eras. Many worlds begin as the
> background to the story of a character's entire life... Ancestors and
> descendants are the most common way of temporally extending a

character. Names and characteristics are often passed along from parent to child as well as titles, property and proprietary knowledge... sometimes objects and their history provide a throughline linking the works of a world together... Genealogies give characters context through structures of kinship and friendship, as characters understood by the influence of ancestry, upbringing and companionship. The deeds and failings of ancestors often provide a foreshadowing that colors their descendants' self-images and expectations... Finally, genealogies can link stories together as each character's life history becomes another narrative thread in a world's narrative fabric.   (Wolf 171)

Wolf defines the function of genealogies in worldbuilding as extending characters and providing them with complex physical and philosophical contexts that build upon each other to constitute the Secondary World. Such contexts include the relational principle of kinship; this is rendered incarnate through the *wyr*, which is derived from the memories, myths, teachings and languages of the Folk within their territory, connecting concepts of blood family, tribal affiliations and indigenous nationhood.

That kinship is foregrounded in the trilogy is obvious in the title *The Kynship Chronicles*, whereby the spelling of the word 'Kyn' differs minimally from the word 'kin'. It references actual biological kinship systems, but extends it to different races and species, as well as to the physical and spiritual worlds of the Eld Green which itself plays a prominent role in the story. The concept of relations through Kynship/kinship thus plays out on individual and community levels, the past and the present, between the living and the dead. The Folk, Humans, animals, werebeasts or ferals, and plantlife contribute to conceptions of Eld Green society as rooted in multiple histories and epistemologies—thus echoing at certain levels Tolkien's own investment in cultural and ontological diversity in Middle-earth. The Folk are collectively known as 'Unhuman', as opposed to Humans, who are depicted as one among many species of being. This particular characterisation, as I see it, is an ironic philosophical commentary on Enlightenment[3] humanist traditions in the Primary World. Here,

---

3 Despite laudable attempts to address the allegedly universal 'rights of man' embraced during this period in European history (said to have originated in the scientific revolutions of the 16th and 17th centuries and lasting through the 18th century's political—French and American—revolutions), critical race and gender scholars have pointed how far from 'Enlightenment' the celebrated thinkers of the era were (e.g. Kant, Blumenbach, Gobineau) in practice and worldview. It is significant that this era is congruent with European colonial activity in the rest of the world, where the rights of women and non-white, non-European, racialised peoples were overlooked, indeed violated in the context of the colonial enterprise:

the category of the 'human' is constructed as a universalist trope applicable to certain hegemonic groups, and is set in opposition to those who are declared to be 'subhuman', savage and uncivilised.[4]

Such investment in genealogies and kinship is contingent on Justice's own scholarly work in Indigenous North American literatures and cultures:

> Indigenous nationhood is… also an understanding of a common social interdependence within the community, the tribal web of kinship rights and responsibilities that link the People, the land, and the cosmos together in an ongoing and dynamic system of mutually affecting relationships. It isn't predicated on essentialist notions of unchangeability; indeed, such notions are rooted in primitivist Eurowestern discourses that locate indigenous peoples outside the flow and influences of time… Agents of change exist in relationship to one another and demonstrate by those interactions their ability to both influence others and to be self-determining; … the representations of Indians as absolute Others relegates us to the role of museum artifacts of ever-diminishing authenticity. The recognition of some sort of relationship between and among peoples—the ever-contextual contours of kinship—returns us to the physical realm of the participatory.   (Justice, *Criticism* 151)

Particularly, the concept of kinship then informs Indigenous concepts and contexts of peoplehood and citizenship as relations among diverse cultural groups within Indigenous contexts and the physical environment in which they make homes, as well as between Indigenous and non-Indigenous worldviews. These questions point out how cultural Othering practices built on essentialist and reductive representations evident in the common colonial anthropological

---

When Enlightenment thinkers do turn their attention to the social standing of women or of non-white people, they tend to spout unreasoned prejudice. Moreover, while the philosophies of the Enlightenment generally aspire to or pretend to universal truth, unattached to particular time, place or culture, Enlightenment writings are rife with rank ethno- and Eurocentrism, often explicit. (see *Stanford Encyclopedia of Philosophy*, online, accessed 02-24-2018)

4   Ramon Grosfoguel provides a succinct description of the human/subhuman binary:
The people classified above the line of the human are recognized socially in their humanity as human beings and, thus, enjoy access to rights (human rights, civil rights, women rights and/or labor rights), material resources, and social recognition to their subjectivities, identities, epistemologies and spiritualities. The people below the line of the human are considered subhuman or non-human; that is, their humanity is questioned and, as such, negated (Fanon 1967). In the latter case, the extension of rights, material resources and the recognition of their subjectivities, identities, spiritualities and episte-mologies are denied. (10)

trope of the savagism/civilisation binary should be challenged through fantasy literature as a vehicle for critical thinking.

Justice's literary motivations stem from his own critical engagement with hegemonic methods of literary worldbuilding in the fantasy genre; he inquires into the possibility of fantasy narratives where Indigenous perspectives form the main focalising points:

> How might the world look different if we didn't start with the corrosive and simplistic binary of "savagism vs. civilization"? What would fantasy fiction look like with women, Indigenous people, queer folks, and other stereotyped or marginalized communities at the centre rather than the margins? Do our imagined secondary worlds have to look to Europe and its patriarchal and colonial legacies for inspiration, or can we look to the deep roots of this land and the cultures, perspectives, lineages, genders, and histories embedded here?   (Justice, *Overview*)

Such perspectives on colonial histories of Indigenous peoples in the Primary World from an Indigenous fantasy writer and literary scholar provide productive points of departure for readers and writers of fantasy literary works to consider other cultural contexts in the shaping of Secondary Worlds. Mindful of the necessity of imagining otherwise in his world-making project, Justice also accesses resources from his own Indigenous cultural background:

> I've always been influenced by strong women, mountain folks and down to earth figures and people who kind of stand between the spaces and inhabit multiple worlds. So, these are the characters that I write about... I think of *The Lord of the Rings* and *The Lord of the Rings* movies, ...I am much more interested in the weird homosociality of the hobbits, the fey beauty and elegance of the elves.   (McKenegeny 72)

These forms of liminality ("people who... stand between the spaces and inhabit multiple worlds") resonate with Tolkien's own subcreative stance, where "good 'fairy-stories' are about the *aventures* of men in the Perilous Realm or upon its shadowy marches" (FS 10). Proving to be just as much of a Perilous Realm as Middle-earth, the Eld Green is an imaginary textual space where marginalised Indigenous positions (reminiscent of Primary World North American contexts) are represented through multifaceted and complex characters who claim agency and citizenship. These characters are notably not congruent with numerous mainstream representations of Indigenous North Americans, which insist on the abjection of Indigenous positions. Tolkien's Perilous Realm can thus be re-imagined and given substance in Justice's narrative as follows:

1) The Everland and its Folk constitute the Perilous Realm for Humans in this Secondary World
2) The Human world outside the Everland is the Perilous Realm for the rest of the Folk
3) The *wyr*-Wielders are representative of the Perilous Realm for the rest of the Folk as well as for Humans
4) The Spirit World represents a Perilous Realm for the Folk and for Humans

These readings of the trope of the Perilous Realm apply and work coevally in Justice's Eld Green. Tolkien defines the Perilous Realm as a space of uncertain marvels, wonder, enchantment, strangeness, unpredictability and danger that cannot be explained with realistic and scientific frameworks. The principle of Faerie marks the Otherness of the Perilous Realm; this Otherness can be read as a recasting of the constructions of Otherness imposed on Indigenous positions by colonising powers. Hence a fluid understanding of Tolkien's Perilous Realm would be productive in engagements with Justice's Eld Green, which is predominantly marked by relations, belief systems and histories congruent with Indigenous spirituality and decolonial politics.

My understanding of the Perilous Realm as a possible decolonial space of discomfort and displacement then will be brought to bear on my readings of excerpts from Chapter 11 in *Wyrwood*, entitled 'New Worlds and Old', demonstrating how representatives of the Folk and the Humans 'stand between spaces and move between worlds' in the Eld Green. The spirit realm is embedded as a Perilous Realm in the narrative logics of the Eld Green, much in the manner that Eldamar and Valinor are present in *The Lord of the Rings*. However, while the spirit world is often presented as a space of action and relationality in the Eld Green, Valinor and Eldamar are often evoked through legend from human perspectives, and memory from Elven perspectives respectively—with occasional material interventions by Manwe's eagles and Sauron's Balrog.

The following excerpts present the diverse Folk on different trajectories to save the Everland from the impending colonisation by the Human Dreydmaster Lojar Vald, who intends to subjugate the Folk by forcibly relocating them away from their homeland, and then draining their *wyr* in order to enhance his own Dreyd powers (*Wyrwood* 172-175). The different narrative strands evoke the sense of impending change that will reorder the world:

> We are about to leave the Everland." … "We are coming to the human lands now…"

...the entire world seemed to collapse into thunderous madness...
Quill sobbed, and above everything the piercing shriek of the
spirits on the Threshold of the Everland, torn and twisted in the
Melding-made barrier between the worlds. The chaos seemed to
last for an agonizing age, but it eventually passed... "How many
times have you gone through that?" ...
Denarra shrugged wearily... "I've crossed the boundary more
times than I can count, but I have never felt anything as awful
as this. Something terrible is happening..."   (137-138)

They were an odd pair—the hulking Gvaerg-matron... and the
bent she-Kyn... but they understood each other well... The world
had changed much in the years since the bloodsong called them
to be Wielders, and not for the better... And often lately they
shared the visions of Unahi's dream-world travels, where she
caught glimpses of Tarsa's difficult journey...
"Do you think they're ready?" the she-Kyn stared off into the water.
"...There's no stopping this storm now. We just have to pray that
the seeds we planted will have roots deep enough to endure."
                                                          (141-143)

Men were everywhere in the Everland, even this far into the inter-
ior. Things had accelerated far beyond anything they'd expected...
They'd come so far in such a short time, and they were still so
far... from the Tree that called to her..., pulling her forward with
increasing insistence. Tarsa didn't know what was coming in the
days ahead, but the ice-cold knot in her stomach gave her more
hesitation than hope.   (143-144)

In the first excerpt, the half-Human, half-Kyn Strangeling Denarra Syrene and
the female Tetawi Dolltender Quill Meadowgood are in the process of crossing
the enchanted border[5] of the Everland into Human territory (137-138). This
boundary—generated by the *wyr* between the natural world and the spirit

---

5   The tropes of the border and the borderland have specific value in Indigenous North
    American creative work and critical scholarship, when taking into account how indigenous
    living spaces and resources have been annexed by colonial powers, thus contributing to
    displacements and disenfranchisements of Indigenous peoples. Political perspectives
    around the recasting of colonised space have been theorised by Mexican indigenous
    gender scholar Gloria Anzaldua in *Borderlands / La Frontera* (1987). Defined as a space
    of violent cultural encounters informed and influenced by power asymmetries, Anzal-
    dua observes that borderlands can also work as spaces of resistance, deconstruction and
    reconstruction in processes of individual and collective self-definition (20-23). Borders
    are significant in processes of inclusion and exclusion, while breaching boundaries can

world—had been rent asunder by an ambitious Human man (in the mythical and historical time of the Everland). With its integrity damaged, this liminal space is a highly sensitive and fraught transcultural contact zone due to the abuses perpetrated by Humans on the Folk, the Beastfolk and plantlife of the Everland. Nevertheless, interactions and relations between the living and the spirit denizens do take place across this Perilous Realm between the worlds. The current crossing experienced by Quill and Denarra is more tortuous than usual due to the upheavals in the spirit world caused by Vald's machinations.

In the second excerpt Unahi and Biggiaba, a she-Kyn and a she-Gvaerg, both *wyr*-Wielders, have witnessed historical upheavals due to onslaughts from enemies both outside and within the Everland. Both these matriarchal Elders are not only repositories of the Folk's living history—they are also teachers and warriors in their own right. They are living connections with the spirit world, manifest in their ability to dream-travel as well as commune with ancestor spirits, thus involving that realm directly in the lives of the Everland Folk.

The third excerpt tells of Tarsa's return to the Everland with her quest companions after their near-fatal meeting with the Dreydmaster Vald in Eromar. On reaching the Everland's capital city Sheynadwiin, they intend to report to their council of elders about Vald's treachery (and another Folk Nation's betrayal of the Everland). At the same time, Tarsa is conscious of her growing connection to the Eternity Tree at the heart of the Everland as a young *wyr*-Wielder. Due to her insufficient training and the impending threat, Tarsa experiences a form of fragmentation requiring her to explore her relationships to the *wyr* of the natural and spirit worlds, while preparing to battle Vald on the physical plane.

The sense of doom evident in all three excerpts resonates with Frodo's and Aragorn's stories (including their doubts, sense of inadequacy and courage against the odds) in the Hobbit and Human contexts during the War of the Ring. Notably the majority of the key protagonists are in line with Justice's agenda of 'imagining otherwise', where erstwhile marginalized Indigenous women and queer folk are the main agents of change in these stories.

Another central example denoting how Wolf's world-making infrastructure of genealogy and Justice's kinship concept work together, is the sacred Eternity Tree, Zhaia—herself a character in the narrative that addresses the principles of genealogy and kinship in the indigenous understandings of the Folk:

> This is a story of the First Days, and the beginning of the Kyn...
> In a birthing storm that made the Three Worlds tremble, the se-
> ven Branches emerged from the loins of their deep-green mother,
> Zhaia, the True Tree: Oak, Pine, Willow, Thorn, Cedar, Apple,

---

herald changes in world orders and worldviews as depicted in these particular excerpts from Justice's trilogy, where specifically female agency is foregrounded.

and Ash. Born of leafy-haired Zhaia and her green-skinned lover, Drohodu, Grandfather of the Mosses, the first Kyn danced to life in their new world, and they gave joy to their Mother and Father and to their world. Their roots drank deeply from the endless Eld Green...

The Kyn grew strong and flourished, and each family Branch brought different gifts to all the People... When all was in balance, ...the People flourished.

But there came a time when some of the restless ones—those who watched the stars and turned from the green world—lingered too long in the heavens and forgot about their deep roots... Some of the People dug deeply in the earth and turned away from the sky, thinking to return to the balance, but they forgot the sunshine... Those treading firmly on the Celestial Path called themselves Shields, for they saw themselves as guardians of a new way of being in the world, ... Those holding fast to the Way of the Deep Green were the Greenwalking Wielders, and they drew on the lifeblood language of the Eld Green, the wyr, and ignored the gathering storm...

This is a teaching. It is a reminder, and a remembrance.

(Kynship 14-16)

This particular 'cycle' inserts the creation myth of the Kyn into the main narrative flow, as "a teaching and a remembrance", embedding Kyn cosmogonic history as cultural memory imparted as knowledge and as acknowledgment of ancestral and environmental kinship. Thus, the Eternity Tree's story is integral in its role of anchoring Tarsa on her journey of self-discovery, while its history is a paratextual insert (set in italic font) into the main narrative evoking both the historicity and the mythic knowledge of the Kyn Folk. Additionally, the family trees of two groups of Kyn Folk are addressed as Branches of the Eternity Tree, showing the diversity, dissension and the two main worldviews within Kyn society. Graphic illustrations of the genealogies of two Kyn warriors are provided—the Greenwalker Wielder Tarsa de'Shae and the Shield politician Neranda Ak'Shaar, seduced by Vald (*Wyrwood* 8, 206)—demonstrating their particular kinships through generations and through the texts, underscoring their key antagonistic roles in the interlacing narratives of the *Chronicles*.

These paratextual and ancillary insertions fulfil Wolf's concept of genealogies as world-making devices (170) by evoking kinship with the natural environment, the spirit world, Kyn histories as well as with the Human world outside the boundaries of the Everland. Both, the Folk and the Eternity Tree recall Tolkien's Middle-earth, its Free Peoples and the Two Trees of Valinor (Laurelin and Telperion) in *The Silmarillion* as well as Yggdrasil, the World Ash of Norse mythology. These trees literally root genealogies in their respective texts, serving to mark spaces, histories and politics shaping these worlds; they also signify the beauty and the mystery of the Perilous Realm—and its potential dangers.

The Perilous Realm as Conceptual Space of Decolonial Disruption: Interrogating the Savagism vs. Civilisation Binary

A salient parallel strand of inquiry in my endeavour here, is to explore how Tolkien's deployment of the figure of the 'savage' in his magnum opus stands in dialogue with Justice's representation of Indigenous kinship and peoplehood as the pivot of the fantasy world of the Eld Green. My point of departure is Tolkien's portrayal of the Indigenous folk of the Drúedain in *The Lord of the Rings* (LotR III 813-815). The depiction of Ghan-buri-ghan makes much of the Wild Man's bodily Otherness, alongside his speech and the forms of knowledge that the Drúedain possess, clearly placing this ethnic group on the margins of normative European understandings of civilisation and humanity. Elsewhere, I have argued that the Drúedain's hesitant will to cooperate with the Rohirrim in the War of the Ring is a decolonial gesture, whereby Walter Mignolo's definition of decolonial gestures is pertinent in the context of indigenous colonised positions demanding justice "that would contribute to… re-surgence, and re-existence of people whose values, ways of being, thoughts and stories were degraded in order to be dominated" (Mignolo). Justice's world-making strategies demonstrate similar decolonial gestures, allowing women, queer folk, Indigenous and other marginalised communities to take centre-stage in his narrative universe, while evoking Primary World histories of colonial activity causing indigenous disenfranchisement as the temporal framing for the narrative. This decolonisation imperative is invested in forms of relationality where "the storied expression of continuity that encompasses resistance" moves "beyond it to an active expression between the People and the world" (Justice, *Criticism* 150). This resonates with Wolf's concept of genealogies as implemented in fantasy world-making processes (170-183).

Justice's trilogy advocates the need for decolonisation imperatives in fantasy literature, where conventionally "[t]he savagism vs. civilization binary that has so deformed colonial understandings of Indigeneity is very much the worldbuilding template in fantasy fiction" (*Wonderworks*). In this light, while Tolkien's sources for his representation of the Drúedain are grounded in the medieval tropes of the Wild Man rooted in the savage/civilised binary, he does not seem to have accessed other sources pertaining to actual Indigenous folk in the Primary World.[6] He does, however, state at one point: "Red Indians were better: there were bows and arrows... and strange languages and glimpses of an archaic mode of life, and above all forests in such stories" (FS 55).[7] Using the term 'Red Indians' (alongside 'strange' and 'archaic') at the beginning of

---

6   Richard Echo Hawk, however, posits that besides Finnish, Norse and Germanic myths Tolkien had read about Pawnee creation myths in a volume entitled *Traditions of the Skidi Pawnee*, which was available in Oxford University Library. These stories were translated into English and written down between 1899 and 1903, as told by a prominent Skidi cleric named Roaming Scout, and published in 1904 by George Dorsey and James R. Murie with Houghton Mifflin and Co. in Boston, and with D. Nutt in London (see www.worldcat. org/title/traditions-of-the-skidi-pawnee/oclc/2321966). Echo Hawk traces connections between Skidi Pawnee myths and Tolkien's *The Silmarillion* and *The Hobbit*, observing that Tolkien did not reveal his accessing the *Traditions of the Skidi Pawnee* (1904) for his own mythology for England:
     Textual evidence reveals that Tolkien studied the Skidi legendarium carefully for prac- tical ideas about how to craft the appropriate tone for his mythology. It had to be "more coherent" but still "primitive" mythology. Traces of color borrowed from obscure Pawnee would lend a desirable air of "primitive growth". But in order for Tolkien's English mytho- logy to be seen as "English", these borrowings could never be recognized as indigenous to any realm other than the realm of his own English imagination. For this reason, he could never reveal his use of *Traditions of the Skidi Pawnee*... Tolkien seemed to always feel that his mission as a writer had to do with serious matters pertaining to the cultural soul of his homeland and its European cultural environs. America was not in his mission statement. (Echo Hawk 152f.)
7   In current contexts, from the 1960s and 1970s onwards, the term 'Red Indians' and others like 'redskins' have been criticised for their offensive racialised connotations in designations of Indigenous Americans and Canadians by European colonising powers. Today, many indigenous peoples of the United States choose to designate themselves as 'American Indians', while another acceptable self-designation is 'Native American'. It is imperative to note that these designations are not homogenously used by all Indigenous North American peoples. For discussions of acceptable cultural designations, see the Native American Journalists' Association website (http://www.naja.com/sites/naja/ uploads/images/2017/NAJA_Reporting_and_Indigenous_Terminology_Guide.pdf). Powhatan-Renape Native American Studies scholar Jack Forbes observes: 'A problem arises,... when North American and British whites want to call Native Americans 'Red- skins' or 'Red Indians' or 'Red People'... These differentiations can have important political and social implications...' (1993: 99). Referencing racialised colour schemes, Forbes also notes Carl Linnaeus' *System of Nature* (1735, 1ˢᵗ ed.) as describing Indigenous peoples as "Americans (copper-colored)"—where 'copper-colored' might be taken to signify an allusion to 'redskins' (103).
     Anthropologist Nina Jabslonski, too, notes the ordering of races in Carl Linnaeus' hier- archies of human beings, where North American Indigenous peoples are defined thus: "*homo americanus*: red, choleric, erect, hair black, straight, thick; nostrils wide, face harsh, beard scanty, obstinate, content, free; paints himself with find red lines; regulated by customs" (128). Jablonski adds: "To light-skinned Europeans, people such as American Indians... were savages and heathens..." (142).
     These designations demonstrate how the Indigenous peoples of North America have been described and perceived using biological terms that construct these groups as racialised, along with colonial notions of savagery ascribed to their features and difference from European understandings of civilisation. At the same time, the cultural heterogeneities among Indigenous North American groups are ignored.

the 20th century from his own cultural perspective as an Englishman, Tolkien demonstrates the Othering evident in this description.[8] His reading of Indigenous languages, living spaces and weaponry, situates them in a pre-modern context "predicated on essentialist notions of unchangeability" (Justice, *Criticism* 151), where, however very often "[d]eficit remains the defining trope for Indigenous people in the settler-colonial binary" (*Wonderworks*; Criticism 159). And yet, the evocation of this perspective pertained to a certain characteristic that Tolkien thought indispensable—the trope of 'primitiveness' was necessary for his mythology for England (see Scull/Hammond 441). Tolkien's reference to Indigenous American contexts as redolent with stories is a recognition of their rich mythologies – which might then be read as an endorsement by a canonical fantasy writer for the cultural epistemologies of a marginalised group.[9]

Despite such endorsements on Tolkien's part, Justice is critical of how mainstream fantasy literature has hitherto dealt with the trope of the cultural Other:

> Indeed, if any literature can be said to be the safe haven of this intellectually and morally bankrupt concept, it is that nebulous textual archive known variously as genre, adventurer, or heroic fantasy, wherein largely white heroes possessed of courage and sometimes strange talents struggle to challenge evil and reaffirm the values of social conservation and right order—namely might is right. Civilization is bad or good, savages are noble or brutish, yet in either case, the conflict between simple primitivism rooted/trapped in the past and a contemporary progressivism of technological complexity is the superstructure undergirding the narrative content of most genre fantasy.   (*Wonderworks*)

Justice's critique of how civilisation and savagism are presented in the fantasy genre thus underscores how 'largely white heroes' have crystallised as the norm which wields power within the text in the shaping of fantasy literary worlds. At the same time this hegemonic position functions as a marker of the genre itself that in turn exerts a certain power of recognition and acceptance on readers.

---

8   Richard Echo Hawk observes that Tolkien's comment on 'Red Indians' is not present in "Manuscript A" or "Manuscript B" of *On Fairy-stories*. Echo Hawk posits that the comment most likely was inserted in the preparation of "Manuscript C" in 1943 (see Echo Hawk 218 endnote 349, Chapter 22 'Tolkien's Tree of Tales"). The rationale for this decision on Tolkien's part would bear some exploration.

9   Amy Sturgis and David Oberhelman's seminal 2009 edited essay collection *The Intersection of Fantasy and Native America* considers how canonical fantasy literary texts (e.g. by Tolkien, Lewis, Le Guin, McCaffrey, Rowling) could productively dialogue with Native American literatures, which mobilise Indigenous mythologies in literary world-making (Introduction, v).

In a similar vein, Pawnee historian Roger Echo Hawk takes up Tolkien's 'Red Indians' remark in his discussion of how comparative mythologists and anthropologists of Tolkien's time treated the cultural productions from those considered 'primitive' by hegemonic European positions, whereby the prevalent stance was one of social evolution:

> Seeing "primitive" people as enduring childlike representatives of an early evolutionary stage in human history, mainstream academicians decided "that only primitives maintain a working mythopoeic ability"—the ability to invent mythic master narratives and believe in myth…
>
> Racial Indians, no matter how elaborate their cultural circumstances, always fell under this race-based rubric. It isn't clear the level of familiarity Tolkien would have had with the ethnographic discourse surrounding racial Indians, but even a passing acquaintance would have affirmed this cultural prejudice…
>
> For Tolkien the qualities of "primitive" helped imbue his storytelling with a sense of historical depth—his folk of a vanished past could be differentiated in cultural terms from contemporary people who saw themselves as Christian and civilized.
>
> (Echo Hawk, 140-142)

Examining the terms 'primitive' and savage' in comparative mythological discourses at the end of the 19th and the beginning of the 20th centuries, Echo Hawk points out distinctly colonial forms of language in descriptions of peoples who do not correspond to Eurowestern ideals of humanity, progress, knowledge and civilisation.[10] Echo Hawk's and Justice's decolonial reading frameworks recognise "that colonial discourse typically rationalizes itself through rigid oppositions such as maturity/immaturity, civilization/barbarism, developed/developing, progressive/primitive" (Gandhi 32). Hence the 'savage' is constructed as an unknowable, undisciplined, even monstrous cultural Other from a hegemonic colonising stance, demonstrating forms of power and privilege in the generation of and dissemination of knowledges about marginalised groups. And yet, Tolkien required figures designated as 'primitive' according to the anthropological discourse of the day, in order to confer 'historical depth' to Middle-earth, while linking it to other manifestations of the Perilous Realm. What are we to make of this as readers?

---

10 Echo Hawk cites the works by Edward Burnett Tylor (*Primitive Culture*, 1871) and George Bird Grinnell (*The Indians of Today*, 1911) as well as the studies of these ethnographic and anthropological scholars by comparative mythology scholars Christopher Vecsey (*Imagine Ourselves Richly*, 1988) and Alan Dundes (*Sacred Narrative: Readings in the Theory of Myth*, 1984).

Echo Hawk also charts a cultural and literary influence (attributed to Andrew Lang) on Tolkien's generic identification and analysis of the main tropes and devices of fairy stories, redolent with distinct European cultural epistemes (FS 36-40).[11] Similar forms of relationality between writers resonate in Justice's idea of genealogical connections with Tolkien's works, persona and social interactions: "I wanted to live in the England I read about... I wanted to go to Oxford and wear tweed with patches and smoke a pipe and sit in oak-panelled drawing rooms and talk about big ideas with other sophisticated, cultured, civilised people" (McKenegeny 70). His admiration for Tolkien notwithstanding, Justice notes the colonial tropes and discourses in the Professor's works (which often serve as models for recent generations of writers), albeit he recognises Tolkien's critical stance on power and hubris:

> The textual archive that has grown up, mushroom-like, around J.R.R. Tolkien's great shadow, is for better or for worse, informed by the same ideological apparatus that shaped his legendarium, his great myth-building project. Tolkien's epic story of pastoral goodness besieged by swarthy techno-fascist hordes added a moral certitude, literary cachet, and coherent secondary world mythology to heroic fantasy... a cosmos where heroic/tragic acts of righteous conquest affirm the right of chosen men to lay claim to lands, resources, and peoples, a world where mainly virtue is ordained, and for a time at least, rewarded (although in Tolkien's legendarium power accompanied by hubris always collapses upon itself, with other power occasionally surviving). (*Wonderworks*)

Despite his own critical perspective on these features of modern fantasy literary worlds, Justice recasts superhuman Tolkienian figures like Elves in Indigenous terms for his Eld Green, whose impending disappearance heralds new world orders aligned with the rule of Men as set out in Tolkien's Secondary World. This resonates with romanticised anthropological representations of Indigenous folk as a vanishing race of 'noble savages', making way for modern man.[12] At the same time the trilogy destabilises these recognisable tropes in rather unexpected ways, begging clearer definitions as to how 'civilisation and culturedness' are

---

11 Echo Hawk notes the influence of Andrew Lang's work (*Custom and Myth*, 1884) on Tolkien's own *On Fairy-stories*, where "it is probably not coincidence that Lang and Tolkien both subscribed to the general tone of European and American orderings of humankind, categorized both in racial and cultural terms..." (141)

12 Notably, Tolkien's Elves cannot be read as marginalised, considering their hegemonic importance in world-making genealogies as the First Children of Ilúvatar in Middle-earth. However, the sense of their impending disappearance from Middle-earth as a cultural group fading away into mythic time is used by Justice in reading elves and Fair Folk as a variation on the trope of the 'noble savage'.

understood. Indeed, one might say that Ghân-buri-Ghân and his people have been given more substance, anchoring them firmly in the soil of the Eld Green.

One method of doing this was by conferring gender, racial and other forms of bodily diversity on the Folk. Bisexual and transgender sexual orientations are embedded as 'normal' in descriptions of these communities, while femininity is set into a more egalitarian frame is evidenced in the gendered identity of the Eternity Tree, the "deep-green mother, Zhaia, the True Tree" (*Kynship* 14). Notably, the 'deep green' of nature and diverse other skin hues as well as a range of bodily features are set up as normative referential frames that privilege physical and cultural differences not aligned with whiteness.

Unahi is a Gandalf-like guide and teacher to Tarsa de'Shae, who embarks on two parallel quests—much like Frodo in the *Lord of the Rings*, who sets out to destroy the One Ring and, in the process, attains self-knowledge in his quest to save his Hobbit community. While Gandalf's relationship to Frodo can be read as that of a surrogate father's (an affective attachment based on homosocial bonds), Unahi is biologically related to Tarsa—she is her maternal aunt and herself a *wyr* wielder, who functions as a surrogate mother to the young warrior. This also resonates with the uncle-nephew bond between Bilbo and Frodo Baggins—and Bilbo's bequeathing of the Ring Quest to Frodo (unbeknownst to both at first). One notes however that Justice has reconceived of the traditional male wizard guide and teacher as a female elder, who wields power openly and is respected, feared and in some cases rejected, in her community because of this.

Two other prominent female characters also "stand between spaces and inhabit multiple worlds": Denarra Syrene and Quill Meadowgood. While biological kinship and Kyn genealogies are prioritised in the stories of Unahi and Tarsa, Quill and Denarra's stories come together in a moment of crisis, to form affective kinships based on principles of sisterhood and female friendship. Both figures step out of the backcloth of the Eld Green, from seemingly marginalised communities among the Folk, to take up different trajectories to the main quest narrative. Although they are not Greenwalkers or Shields like the hegemonic Kyn (a position resonating with that of the Eldar in Middle-earth), Denarra and Quill demonstrate other methods of accessing and working with the *wyr*.

As a mixed race Kyn-Human Strangeling, who has elected not to declare her allegiance to either race, Denarra embraces the advantages that belonging to both races affords. She lives according to her own rules and conceals her *wyr*-wielding capabilities, in order not to excite hostility:

> It had been years since she'd been home; …her father's people had no great love for a Strangeling who seemed bent on following the wild ways of her Human mother far more than the grounded Kyn teachings of her father… Denarra would always be tied to her birth-home through blood and history. She could keep running

> for the rest of her life, but she'd never be free of the Everland; it
> would always inhabit her, twisted deep within spirit and memory,
> no matter how far the road might stretch. And the closer she came
> to the often unseen barrier between the Reach of Men and the
> lands of the Folk, the clearer that link became. *(Wyrwood* 92-93)

Denarra might be considered generically kin to Tolkien's Half-Elven dynasties of Elrond and Elros. Indeed, she might be even read as a more active Arwen Undómiel, who, despite her father Elrond's choice to align himself with the Eldar, still bears the history of the Half-Elven in her genealogy, as does Aragorn, descendant of Elros, who chose to be of Men. Denarra does not follow traditional feminine roles and expectations (based on rather Victorian gender ideals) imposed on Arwen in Tolkien's narrative, as the Elven princess whose hand is given in marriage to the victorious returning King, Aragorn named Elessar. Notably Denarra is not invested in the heterosexual contract that informs Tolkien's narrative; rather she is bisexual in her romantic involvements with both Unhumans and Humans, and does not entertain the option of loyalty or subservience to a single partner. While Arwen waits in her paternal home of Rivendell, Denarra chooses to travel, making home where she chooses with her ragtag performance troupe and indulging in a form of sexual promiscuity that readers would not associate with the chaste Elven woman. Denarra, however, does claim and use her powers as a Wielder in aid of her chosen family (described as a "motley company of actors, acrobats, musicians and minor miscreants"; *Wyrwood* 92), untrammelled by the traditions and expectations of the Green-walker Kyn of Everland. She moves freely between Chalimor, "the greatest city of Men in the Reach" (*Wyrwood* 92) and the Everland. Thus, Denarra Syrene can be read as a border figure, both for the Everland Folk and for Humans—a liminal citizen of the Perilous Realm.

Quill is a Dolltender, a Tetawi *wyr* worker who is able to tap into the *wyr* in dolls made from dried fruit and vegetables. While developing intimate familial relationships with these dolls in their anthropomorphic shapes, Quill receives spiritual guidance and is able to work with the *wyr* for the good of her own people. Having lived a sedentary life in the Tetawa community, a diminutive Hobbit-like people, Quill is apprehensive about leaving her familiar home space of Spindletop to venture out into the world, in the way her Tetawa partner Tobhi Burrows does:

> Quill remained beside the hearth until late in the night. Her
> thoughts spun wildly, and they kept coming back to Tobhi's story
> the night before when he'd recounted his adventure. She felt so
> helpless. She couldn't go with Tobhi; his path was dark to her.

But there was another option, a path that grew clearer even as her heart grew heavier from the thought of it.

She turned to look at the dolls on their shelves, their puckered faces pinched into looks of disapproval. Her own lips tightened defiantly... She was tired of feeling scared and helpless. Tobhi was willing to sacrifice so much to save their people. He needed her now more than ever. May she could do something to help, even if she wasn't by his side at Sheynadwiin.

"Yes," she whispered. "Somebody's got to tell the Reachwarden about Vald's treachery. He's the leader of the Reach, more powerful than Vald even. I know that good people will not let this happen. They've got to be told the truth." She stood up. "And I guess I'll just have to go to Chalimor to do it."   (*Wyrwood* 111-112)

Thus Tobhi, who accompanies Tarsa on her mission to stop Vald, might be read as an Indigenous Sam Gamgee.[13] Quill then would be the equivalent of Rosie Cotton, Sam's great love. Unlike Rosie, who remains in the Shire waiting for Sam (the reader does not know much about her perspective on the War of the Ring), Quill decides to join the fight against the Dreyd. She sets out to inform and mobilise law makers in Chalimor, who are invested in justice. Together with Denarra, Quill does great things and pays a great price in the final battle (she becomes barren).

In these characterisations, I see Unahi, Tarsa, Denarra and Quill acting as 'agents of change' who challenge and destabilise the savage/civilised binary, as well as received gender perceptions.

Concluding Remarks

While I have taken the liberty of mapping certain similarities between Tolkien's narrative universe and Justice's Secondary World, I would note that *The Kynship Chronicles* are very much capable of holding their own as fantasy works. I see these stories, in Gerald Vizenor's words, as "shamanic, more visionary

---

13 Notably, Justice has produced a series of drawings of both Tarsa and Tobhi, beginning in the 1990s and finalised in 2009. Tarsa was modelled at first on his imagination of Tolkien's Galadriel and a female figure from the Masters of the Universe secondary world ('She was Tarsa Le'Shae, then a neutral good elven druid (inspired in part by Teela from Masters of the Universe and Galadriel, Tolkien's own lady of the trees'). His initial designs of Tobhi are reminiscent of the hobbits in Ralph Bakshi's 1978 film adaptation of *The Lord of the Rings* ('...he was then Toby Burrows, a chaotic good halfling ranger—a somewhat more backwoods version of Frodo and Bilbo Baggins, I suppose.'). These drawings were published on an older version of Justice's *imagineotherwise.ca* website, which has however been since overhauled and redesigned; these drawings are no longer available for view.

than victimry" (Vizenor/Lee 134), and thus contingent on Justice's decolonial vision for fantasy literature. As a Secondary World, the Eld Green offers new approaches to fantasy genres through the concept of kinship on several levels: within the Secondary World, read against the Primary World of Indigenous North American contexts, and read against Tolkien's Middle-earth.[14]

Justice's worldbuilding is an example of Wolf's contention on how philo-sophical outlooks can be embodied in narratives to fulfil specific purposes: "The many default assumptions that are reset can be used to introduce new ways of thinking, just as encountering a new culture can force one to see the world in a new way" (193). *The Kynship Chronicles* contest simplistic colonial categories in order to expand the reach of contemporary Indigenous literatures but also to expand the remit of fantasy literatures in general, to include non-European cultural contexts as well as non-European reading and writing publics. To this end, Amy Sturgis states:

> These works must not only be read, however, they must also be analysed on their own merits as stories, and brought alive in dialogue about the fantasy genre. To do otherwise is to suggest that the ethnic/geographical/historical background of the tales and their authors somehow disqualifies these stories from being taken seriously or counted among other representatives of world fantasy. If we as scholars, as teachers, and as consumers continue to allow Native American fantasy, both historical and contem-porary, to be the sole domain of those who look at the texts as artifacts rather than art—as simply reactions to the experience of colonialism, for example—we are complicit in marginalizing and historicizing Native American literature, ...to be analysed through anthropological and ethnohistorical lenses without regard for what

---

14 My trajectory of enquiry in this project has been limited to tracing genealogical connections between Justice's and Tolkien's works, while exploring how Mark Wolf's infrastructure of genealogies can be fruitful in reading this particular Indigenous North American fantasy trilogy. This is within the purview of the 2017 Tolkien Conference on Literary Worldbuilding in Augsburg, Germany. More productive readings can however be un-dertaken with regard to examining further connections to Indigenous North American mythologies, histories, cultural resources and critical scholarship in ways pointed out by David Oberhelman and Kathleen Washburn in their 2013 reviews of *The Kinship Chronicles* in *Studies in American Indian Literatures* and in *The American Indian Quar-terly* respectively. In the introduction collection *The Intersection of Fantasy and Native America*, Oberhelman invites readers to engage with how the fantasy genre can offer new theoretical and literary insights in order to access works by Indigenous writers Louise Erdrich, Gerald Vizenor, and Leslie Marmon Silko, among others (v). At the same time, I would advocate engaging with the works of these writers in order to acquire insights to how fantasy works as a genre in Native American literary texts alongside more realistic tropes, so as to recover new ways of clarifying vision in Tolkien's sense.

messages—beautiful, challenging and true—they might offer for a common humanity. The challenge is to take Native America out of the museum of our minds as something past, primitive, and finished, and instead view it as part of our global today, vibrant, evolving, and immediately relevant.   (15)

Sturgis's observation that considering Indigenous North American fantasy texts as mere reactions to colonial experiences would be to do them a disservice, does bear reflection. However, I remark that the colonial contexts contributing to the political self-perceptions of Indigenous North Americans cannot be discounted, in the ways that these worldviews have historically shaped Indigenous cultural productions. An insertion and assertion of Indigenous perspectives and cultural productions in the genre of fantasy literature demonstrates how Justice's concept of "the interpretive significance of the relationship between kinship, people and decolonization" (*Criticism* 148) functions in *The Kynship Chronicles* as a world making device in the sense of Wolf's infrastructure of genealogies. Here I see Justice's trilogy as instantiating a move from Mignolo's decolonial gesture to a decolonisation imperative:

> Literary expression—in its broadest and most inclusive definition—is a profoundly powerful exercise of the ways in which that relationship is made manifest… The decolonization imperative in our literature both reflects indigenous continuity of the past and present and projects that continuity into the future. Stories, like kinship, like fire, are what we do, what we create, as much as what we are. Stories expand or narrow our imaginative possibilities— physical freedom won't matter if we can't imagine ourselves free as well. To assert our self-determination, to assert our presence in the face of erasure, is to free ourselves from the ghost-making rhetorics of colonization. Stories define relationships, between nations as well as individuals, and these relationships imply presence—you can't have a mutual relationship between something and nothingness. Indigenous nationhood is predicated on this understanding of relationship.   (Justice, *Criticism* 150)

Justice's epic fantasy actively generates kinship with other fantasy literature texts, among them, Tolkien's own *Lord of the Rings*. *The Kynship Chronicles* implement complex Indigenous contexts and histories that expand on what Tolkien himself has imagined for his Drúedain, whose rather singular perspective may be regarded as a form of mythical 'primitive undergrowth' for his stories of Elves, Men and Hobbits. Justice's Indigenous Unhuman Folk demonstrate that they are more than just undergrowth to give substance to European mythologies of

Tolkien's ilk. The literary world-making device of kinship thus extends imagining forms of citizenship and agency, and is conducive to doing the cultural work of claiming dignified forms of self-defined subjecthood.

Bibliography

Anzaldua, Gloria. *Borderlands / La Frontera: The New Mestiza*. San Francisco: Aunt Lute Books. 1987

Echo Hawk, Roger. *Tolkien in Pawneeland: The Secret Sources of Middle-earth*. CreateSpace Independent Publishing Platform, 2013

"Enlightenment". https://plato.stanford.edu/entries/enlightenment/#SciManSubEnl (No pagination). Accessed 02-24-2018

Forbes, Jack. *Africans and Native Americans: The Language of Race and the Evolution of the Red-Black Peoples*. University of Illinois Press. 1993

Gandhi, Leela. *Postcolonial Theory: A Critical Introduction*. New York/Chichester: Edinburgh University Press. 1998

Grosfoguel, Ramon. "What is Racism?" *Journal of World Systems Research* 22 (2016): 9-15

Jablonski, Nina. *Living Color: The Biological and Social Meaning of Skin Color*. Berkeley/Los Angeles: University of California Press. 2012

Justice, Daniel Heath. *The Way of Thorn and Thunder: The Kynship Chronicles*. Ontario: Kegedonce Press. 2005, 2006, 2007

---. *Kynship*. Vol.1. 2005

---. *Wyrwood*. Vol. 2. 2006

---. "'Go Away, Water!' Kinship Criticism and the Decolonization Imperative." In: *Learn, Teach, Challenge: Approaching Indigenous Literatures*. Eds.: Deanna Reder, Linda Morra. Waterloo, ON: Wilfried Laurier University Press. 2016. 147-167

---. "Overview". http://imagineotherwise.ca/ 2018 (No pagination). Accessed 02-25-2018

---. "Indigenous Wonderworks and Settler-Colonial Imaginary." *APEX Magazine*. 08-10-2017 (No pagination). https://www.apex-magazine.com/indigenous-wonderworks-and-the-settler-colonial-imaginary/ Accessed 01-26-2018

McKenegeny, Sam. "'To Fight Against Shame Through Love': A Conversation on Life, Literature and Indigenous Masculinities with Daniel Heath Justice". *Studies in American Indian Literatures* 26 (2014): 62-80

Mignolo, Walter. "Looking for the Meaning of Decolonial Gesture." *E-misferica Gesto Decolonial* 11.1 (2014). No pagination. http://hemisphericinstitute.org/hemi/pt/e-misferica-111-gesto-decolonial/mignolo

Oberhelman, David. "'Coming to America': Fantasy and Native America Explored, an Introduction." In: *The Intersection of Fantasy and Native America: From H.P. Lovecraft to Leslie Marmon Silko*. Eds.: Amy Sturgis, David Oberhelman. Altadena, CA: The Mythopoeic Press. 2009. iii-vii

---. 'The Way of Thorn and Thunder: The Kynship Chronicles by Daniel Heath Justice (review).' *Studies in American Indian Literatures* 25 (2013): 118-120

Sturgis, Amy. "Meeting at the Intersection: The Challenges Before Us." In: *The Intersection of Fantasy and Native America: From H.P. Lovecraft to Leslie Marmon Silko*. Eds.: Amy Sturgis, David Oberhelman. Altadena, CA: The Mythopoeic Press. 2009. 11-22

Tolkien, J.R.R. *The Lord of The Rings*. Boston: Houghton Mifflin. 1994

---. *Tree and Leaf*. London: HarperCollins. 2001

Vizenor, Gerald, & A. Robert Lee. *Postindian Conversations*. Lincoln/London: University of Nebraska. 1999

Vogt-William, Christine. "Tolkien's Green Man: The Racialised Cultural Other Within and Green Spaces in *The Lord of The Rings*." In: *There and Back Again: Interdisciplinary Perspectives on Tolkien and His Works*. Eds.: Monika Ludwig-Kirner et al. Zurich/Jena: Walking Tree Publishers, 2017. 305-339

Washburn, Kathleen. "*The Way of Thorn and Thunder: The Kynship Chronicles* by Daniel Heath Justice (review)." *The American Indian Quarterly* 37 (2013): 400-403

Wolf, Mark J.P. *Building Imaginary Worlds: The Theory and History of Subcreation*. New York/London: Routledge. 2012

Satirical Worldbuilding:
from Brobdingnag to Tralfamadore

Ross Smith (Madrid)

It is a curious irony that the greatest of satirical worldbuilders, Jonathan Swift, should be popularly remembered as a writer of children's stories. Nothing could be further from the truth. Swift never wrote anything for a juvenile audience and there is certainly nothing childlike, for instance, in his suggestion that the British government should alleviate the poverty of the Irish by allowing them to sell their children as food to rich English landowners, as was the case in his satirical essay *A Modest Proposal For preventing the Children of Poor People From being a Burthen to Their Parents or Country, and For making them Beneficial to the Publick*, published in 1729. Yet it is interesting to note that such misinterpretations—suffered by Tolkien as well, thanks to the overriding popularity of Bilbo Baggins—actually reflect their great characters' universal appeal. A child can appreciate that much of *Gulliver's Travels* is funny, even if not for the right reasons.

When discussing the subject of worldbuilding for satirical purposes, Jonathan Swift looms as large on the horizon as Tolkien does with respect to worldbuilding in general. The term "satire" (i.e. a literary or dramatic work that uses exaggeration, irony, parody, caricature and ridicule to criticise human frailties) entered the English language in the 16th century, via French from Latin. The golden age of English satire came in the early 18th century, the principle figures being Swift himself and his friends Alexander Pope and John Gay. Their targets, in addition to feeble and vice-prone humanity in general, included government, royalty, religion and the law, as well as their fellow writers and poets.

Gulliver's Travels, titled *Travels into Several Remote Nations of the World* when first published in 1726, was initially devised by Swift as a parody of the "travellers' tales" subgenre which had reached a pinnacle of popularity seven years earlier with the publication of Defoe's *Robinson Crusoe*. Over the course of its composition, however, it became much broader in scope. Swift was an admirer of the great English statesman and philosopher Thomas More. He would have been familiar with More's *Utopia* (1516) and may well have decided to borrow More's narrative devices—an invented country and a decent but gullible visitor who reports on his travels—to provide the framework for his own, considerably more aggressive commentary on the prevailing social and moral conditions of England. As his work progressed, however, Swift began to create something quite novel, a story containing not just one but numerous invented lands, including a flying island and a bizarre range of inhabitants. By the time

Gulliver's Travels was complete, a new literary subgenre had come into being: worldbuilding for satirical purposes.

The story itself is for the most part ingenious and highly inventive, though the tone darkens considerably towards the end. Swift was a clever and innovative worldbuilder. *Gulliver's Travels* is divided into four parts, in each of which its hero, Lemuel Gulliver, visits a new country. These tend to be islands lost in vast oceans which no-one has yet discovered. In Part I Gulliver is employed as a ship's surgeon and his vessel is wrecked in a storm. In the following parts, he is successively marooned, attacked by pirates and finally, having ascended to the position of ship's captain, abandoned in a small boat by his crew following a mutiny. In each case he ends up ashore in a strange land where he meets the inhabitants, learns the language well enough to discuss politics with the local dignitaries, then somehow manages to get back to England. Logically, since the work is a large-scale parody, Swift is not too concerned about verisimilitude.

The first two countries visited by Gulliver broadly correspond to western Europe with regard to their inhabitants, flora, fauna, etc., the sole exception being that, in relation to Gulliver's own stature, in the first (Lilliput) everything is tiny while in the second (Brobdingnag) everything is gigantic. The Lilliputians' diminutive status is used by Swift to criticise the analogous small-mindedness and petty concerns of Lilliput's politicians, nobles and generals—for instance, whether heels should be high or low, or whether eggs should be cracked at the big or small end—and to satirise what he regarded as the pointless political and religious controversies prevalent in his own country. At the same time, situations are generated that enhance the book as a comical adventure story, such as the episode in which Gulliver is roused from his sleep by the inhabitants of the capital to help put out a fire at the queen's palace; Gulliver obliges via the expedient of urinating from his enormous height onto the burning building.

In Brobdingnag, in contrast, the massive scale of the local inhabitants is reflected in their broad-mindedness and equanimity with regard to war, politics and religion, and they are shocked by Gulliver's description of the corruption and greed that he (i.e. Swift) deems to exist in England's public affairs. After hearing an account from Gulliver of the situation in his homeland in relation to these matters, the king of Brobdingnag is moved to remark: "I cannot but conclude the bulk of your natives to be the most pernicious race of little odious vermin that nature ever suffered to crawl upon the surface of the earth" (Swift 121). Gulliver is inclined to agree and his diminishing appreciation of his fellow creatures is hastened by the fact that the massive size of the Brobdingnagians allows him to observe them at very close quarters, an experience he finds disgusting as he cannot fail to notice their physical imperfections on an enormously magnified scale. These misanthropic asides are a foretaste of the scathing assault on humanity in general to be found in the final part of the book.

Swift's inventiveness really takes flight in the third of Gulliver's voyages, in which the traveller ends up on a deserted shore and is rescued by a ladder dropped from a huge circular flying machine. It turns out that this flying island, called Laputa ("the whore" in Spanish, as Swift was doubtless aware), is inhabited by the king of Balnibarbi and contains his entire court. The king takes advantage of this enormous vehicle to move around his domains, spying on his subjects and, if necessary, meting out punishment from his highly advantageous position. In his habitually candid and rather pedantic tone, Gulliver provides us with a detailed scientific description of how the flying island works, which would not have been out of place in the nascent science fiction stories written by Jules Verne 150 years later: "The flying or floating island is exactly circular, its diameter 7873 yards, or about four miles and a half, and consequently contains ten thousand acres. It is three hundred yards thick" (183). At its centre is a great chasm with a cave beneath which contains the ingenious magnetic system that drives the island. "The place is stored with great variety of sextants, quadrants, telescopes, astrolabes and other astronomical instruments. But the greatest curiosity, upon which the fate of the island depends, is a loadstone of a prodigious size, in shape resembling a weaver's shuttle. It is in length six yards, and in the thickest part a least three yards over" (184). Swift's creation of a gigantic airborne vehicle driven by a complex and scientifically plausible mechanism is a very early instance of science fiction and a landmark in worldbuilding literature. The use of science by those in power to keep their subjects under surveillance also foreshadows the omnipresent control exercised by the State in the great anti-totalitarian satires of the 20th century, Zamyatin's *We* and Orwell's *Nineteen Eighty-Four*.

Gulliver eventually descends from Laputa to Balnibarbi and visits the Grand Academy of Lagado, where the king's mathematicians and scientists, treated by Swift as half-mad pedants, are engaged in a number of bizarre projects aimed at improving life in the kingdom. Gulliver tells us: "The first man I saw was of a meagre aspect, with sooty hands and face… He has been eight years upon a project for extracting sunbeams out of cucumbers, which were to be put in phials hermetically sealed, and let out to warm the air in raw inclement summers" (199). Gulliver also meets "… a most ingenious architect, who had contrived a new method for building houses, by beginning at the roof, and working downward to the foundation; which he justified to me, by the like practice of those two prudent insects, the bee and the spider" (200). He eventually enters the school of languages, where three professors sit in consultation upon improving the language of their own country. "The first project was, to shorten discourse, by cutting polysyllables into one, and leaving out verbs and participles, because, in reality, all things imaginable are but norms. The other project was, a scheme for entirely abolishing all words whatsoever; and this was urged as a great advantage in point of health, as well as brevity." (206). It is quite feasible that these satirical projects for simplifying language provided George Orwell with a starting point for the creation of "newspeak", which together with "doublethink" was to be an essential component of the internal coherence achieved in *Nineteen Eighty-Four*.

Gulliver continued from Balnibarbi to the kingdom of Luggnagg, a land of unhappy immortals, where he stayed for three months, after which he returned once more to England, via Japan (the only real country mentioned in the *Travels* other than England itself).

Gulliver's Travels is intended as fierce social critique but can be read simply as an adventure story. It is also an outstanding exercise in misanthropy. Few works of fiction express such a degree of contempt for humanity as Part IV of *Gulliver's Travels*, where the unwilling tourist winds up in the land of the Houyhnhnms. Here lives a race of completely rational, gracious, peace-loving creatures called the Houyhnhnms, along with a breed of brutish, degenerate, dirty and violent beings known as the Yahoos. The former resemble horses, while the latter look like primitive humans. Gulliver does his best to distance himself to the greatest extent possible from the Yahoos, whom he despises for their uncouthness, despite their physical resemblance to him. Conversely, he adores his equine hosts. He is given a hut to live in, where he does his best to emulate the Houyhnhnms in his habits, and considers himself very fortunate to be so far removed from the rest of humanity. Gulliver expresses his contentment in the following terms:

> I enjoyed perfect health of body, and tranquillity of mind; I did not feel the treachery or inconstancy of a friend, nor the injuries of a secret or open enemy. I had no occasion of bribing, flattering, or pimping, to procure the favour of any great man, or of his minion; I wanted no fence against fraud or oppression: here was neither physician to destroy my body, nor lawyer to ruin my fortune; ... no stupid, proud pedants; no importunate, overbearing, quarrelsome, noisy, roaring, empty, conceited, swearing companions; no scoundrels raised from the dust upon the merit of their vices, or nobility thrown into it on account of their virtues; no lords, fiddlers, judges, or dancing-masters.   (312)

The true extent of Swift's apparent hatred of the human race is debatable. In a letter to Alexander Pope dated 29 September 1725 and written during the composition of *Gulliver's Travels*, Swift said that his loathing concerned the human species as a whole, but that he was capable of liking specific individuals. In the same letter he mentioned that "the chief end I propose to myself in all my labours is to vex the world rather than divert it"[1]. This could be taken to imply that, by means of grotesque exaggeration, Swift sought to shake people out of their complacency with regard to their own status and importance in the scheme of things, warning us that if we are not always on our guard against vice and do not strive to be morally decent, we can easily sink to the level of the repugnant Yahoos. This interpretation would suggest that Swift is more a Christian firebrand than an absolute misanthrope, bearing in mind that he was a clergyman and a renowned preacher as well as a writer. He certainly thought that he had plenty to rage about: his memorial tablet in Saint Patrick's Cathedral in Dublin contains an epitaph, written by Swift himself, which says that he lies "where savage indignation can no longer tear his heart".

Future Imperfect: Wells, Huxley, Orwell, Zamyatin

As we can deduce from certain episodes of *Gulliver's Travels*, one of Swift's aims was to break a lance in favour of traditional learning. He regarded the progress made in mathematics and astronomy by such thinkers as his contemporary, Sir Isaac Newton, with alarm and he reflected this by repeatedly trying to ridicule scientists in his fiction, particularly London's Royal Society in Part III of *Gulliver's Travels*. Between the Ancients and Moderns, Swift clearly preferred the former.

This mistrust of the increasing power of science and technology was to become a major theme in satirical worldbuilding. By the second half of the 19th century Britain was in the grip of rampant industrialisation, with the enormous social turmoil it implied. This was the backdrop against which the English author and science fiction pioneer, Herbert George Wells, wrote his classic story *The Time Machine*.

The Time Machine, published in 1895, was H.G. Wells' first novel and it brought him fame and success virtually overnight. It concerns a Victorian scientist, referred to throughout simply as "the Time Traveller", who constructs a vehicle that travels through time. In his first journey on the machine, the Time Traveller is transported to the year 802,701, which is sufficiently far ahead to allow virtually anything to have happened on earth in the meantime (compare this with Orwell's *Nineteen Eighty-Four*, which is set a mere 36 years after the year it was written). In this distant future, Wells envisages a paradisiacal world of exuberant vegetation, constant sunny weather and no bothersome insects. Rising up here and there from among the trees and trailing plants that cover the gentle countryside where the time machine has landed are enormous build-

---

1   The full letter can be read at: https://en.wikisource.org/wiki/Author:Jonathan_Swift/Letters

ings, or palaces, many of which are in ruins, apparent witnesses to a powerful civilisation now long gone.

The Time Traveller soon comes into contact with the inhabitants of this benign country: the Eloi, ethereal, childish creatures that are human in form but smaller and weaker than the people of the Time Traveller's epoch. They seem to suffer no illnesses or old age and do not work or farm, apparently living off the fruit by which they are surrounded. After remaining among the Eloi for some days, the Time Traveller comes to the conclusion that he has arrived at a decadent phase of mankind's development.

> It seemed to me that I had happened upon humanity upon the wane… For the first time I began to realise an odd consequence of the social effort in which we are at present engaged. And yet, come to think, it is a logical consequence enough. Strength is the outcome of need; security sets a premium on feebleness. The work of ameliorating the conditions of life—the true civilising process that makes life more and more secure—had gone steadily on to a climax. (Wells 34)

However, he alters this view when he encounters the other humanoid inhabitants of this apparent Eden, known as the Morlocks, mysterious underground dwellers that only come to the surface at night. The Time Traveller pursues the Morlocks through their tunnels because they have stolen his time machine, and discovers a realm of huge underground vaults and ancient machinery. It is here that he learns the unpleasant truth: the Morlocks are cannibals. The feeble and simple Eloi depend on the savage but intelligent Morlocks for shelter and clothing, and in return the Morlocks prey on them.

Following this discovery, the Time Traveller comes up with a new theory for these two poles of human evolution, which provides the author with the opportunity to express his concerns about the possibly disastrous consequences for humanity of progressive industrialisation and mechanisation. Originally, the Eloi would have been the dominant upper class, living a life of ease, while the Morlocks were the poor proletariat, working at the machines and eventually driven completely underground along with their industrial resources. Wells theorises that intelligence is the result of and response to danger; in the absence of any challenges to their physical security, the Eloi have gradually lost the spirit, intelligence, and strength habitually enjoyed by homo sapiens. For their part, the subterranean Morlocks retained their intelligence as they needed their wits to survive, and eventually assumed a dominant position in relation to the enfeebled former upper class residing on the surface.

By imagining these hyperbolic scenarios Wells issued a warning on the potential harm of man's excessive dependence on machines. He also wished to challenge the scientific assumption that mankind's evolution would be eternally positive. Wells envisages a process of natural selection lasting almost a million years, but which does not end in a utopia in which disease, old age and inequality have been overcome, but rather in a degenerate nightmare. This idea would be taken up again a century later by the great satirist Kurt Vonnegut Jr. in his novel *Galapagos* (1985), in which, following an epidemic that kills almost all mankind, a tiny group of survivors marooned on a Pacific island gradually evolve backwards.

These misgivings concerning the virtues of technology and the benevolent future development of mankind were vindicated with shattering force during Wells' own lifetime. The occurrence of two global wars in less than half a century and the appalling events these conflicts unleashed destroyed the optimistic vision of a science-driven utopian future and ushered in an age of pessimism and uncertainty. As is comprehensible, this provided fertile ground for anti-utopian fantasists. Between 1932 and 1953, three novels were published which are of key importance in the development of satirical worldbuilding, these being Huxley's *Brave New World*, Orwell's *Nineteen Eighty-Four* and Bradbury's *Fahrenheit 451*. All are set in future versions of planet earth in which democracy has been eradicated and apparently never-ending dictatorships have been installed. Of the three, the most enduringly relevant is Orwell's classic satire.

George Orwell's influence on 20th century thinking was immense. Other writers doubtless had a greater literary impact but no-one played a bigger role in shaping public opinion, thanks in particular to the power of satire combined with imagination. It is interesting to note in this respect that in the famous (or infamous) "Books of the Century" survey conducted by the UK bookstore Waterstones and the BBC's Channel 4 in the late 1990s, Orwell's *Nineteen Eighty-Four* was ranked second and *Animal Farm* came third.[2] This is a remarkable performance in view of the fact that these books had been published more than half a century earlier, yet over the decades Orwell's most powerful literary creations have acquired iconic status. Doublethink, newspeak, thoughtcrime, Big Brother, the Thought Police, Room 101, the slogans of the omnipotent Party—*Freedom is Slavery, War is Peace, Ignorance is Strength*—have become part of mainstream western culture and still emerge frequently in the media, particularly in political debate. In early 2017, *Nineteen Eighty-Four* even became a best-seller again due to the number of references made to it in the news media in the light of the dubious treatment of the truth evidenced by Donald Trump's press team. It is no exaggeration to say that, if one were forced to name the iconic 20th century British novel, the choice would almost certainly be between Orwell and Tolkien.

---

2   I hardly need to mention that the number one spot was occupied by *The Lord of the Rings*.

Orwell creates a decadent, run-down vision of London following a nuclear conflict, in which war-damaged buildings remain unrepaired and where the only constructions reflecting technological progress are the imposing Ministries. The world is divided into three great blocks (a satirical reference to the real blocks that had emerged after World War II), Oceania, Eurasia and Eastasia, totalitarian super-states continuously at war with each other. Britain, a part of Oceania, is called Airstrip One. The action takes place in and around London and little is said about the rest of the planet except with reference to the ongoing war. The city is dotted with monolithic government buildings and there are posters of the dictator (known simply as Big Brother) on every corner, appropriately for what is a satire on Soviet-style authoritarian rule.

In *Nineteen Eighty-Four,* art has been removed from daily life. A simple glass paperweight with a piece of coral trapped inside is revered by the dissident protagonist, Winston Smith, as an object of absolute beauty; he has been surrounded by ugliness his entire life. Drabness, uniformity and the absence of free aesthetic expression throttle individualism. Winston's mere possession of the paperweight is highly suspect; his purchase of a blank book in order to write a diary is absolute heresy.

Like in most novels set in a dystopian future, what Orwell actually wished to criticise was the present (the title was obtained by inverting the last two digits of 1948, the year in which Orwell finished the novel). One overriding message in *Nineteen Eighty-Four* was that if totalitarianism—whether Communist or Fascist—were allowed to become truly entrenched in Europe, getting rid of it would be almost impossible. This had to be prevented by the continued exercising of free choice, i.e. the freedom to decide on how and by whom we are to be governed. In the world of Big Brother, the individual will can only be exercised in small, daring gestures: keeping a diary, buying an art object, etc. Happiness is not an issue; the ruling Party tells the population that they must be happy because they are fortunate enough to be governed by a wise and benevolent ruler. Of course, the opposite is true: the inhabitants of Orwell's dystopian society suffer a dull and predictable existence, living in constant fear of being denounced to the Thought Police by their workmates, neighbours, or even their own children. The iron grip of the Party is so tight that Orwell, pessimistically, sees no way of escape.

Moving from *Nineteen Eighty-Four* to *Brave New World* is like stepping out of a gloomy cellar into the full light of day. The London portrayed in Huxley's work is sparklingly clean and ultramodern. Central London, separated by broad parkland from the rings of outlying suburbs, is packed with gleaming skyscrapers. The high-rise tone is set by the opening words of the novel: "A squat grey building of only 34 stories" (Huxley 1). This "squat" building turns out to be the Central London Hatchery and Conditioning Centre, where human babies of varying intellectual and physical capacities are produced (pregnancy is regarded as a disgusting anachronism). Most other government buildings are considerably higher: "The various Bureaux of Propaganda and the College of Emotional Engineering were housed in a single sixty-story building in Fleet Street" (56). As can be seen, the essence of Huxley's story is conveyed simply and efficiently via the names of buildings. All citizens, from high-caste Alphas to the lowly Epsilons, are looked after by a global government called the World State. Within the domains of the World State infrastructures are advanced and efficient. However, certain wild regions still exist and one of these (in New Mexico) contains a Savage Reservation where humans still live and reproduce in the ancient mode. They are treated as a tourist attraction.

Brave New World examines the dangers of behavioural manipulation on a social scale, while in conceptual terms it is a discussion about freedom versus happiness. Echoing Plato and Nietzsche, Huxley asks: is it better to allow the masses to choose how they are to be governed, and due to their ignorance risk disaster, or would people be happier if they were ruled by a wise and magnanimous despot? When Huxley wrote his book, these were the issues of the day. The Great Depression in America had generated economic turmoil around the world, causing uncertainty as to the essential feasibility of democracy. A generalised uprising of the poorer classes was regarded as a real possibility. Huxley's own position was ambiguous, to say the least. As David Bradshaw tells us in his introduction to the 2007 edition of *Brave New World*, shortly before the publication of his novel Huxley publicly supported social measures of this kind: in a BBC radio interview, he even mentioned the need to protect the "Western European stock" (Huxley xxii). His correspondence from this period contains references to the potential dangers posed by the uneducated masses for the intelligentsia. Therefore, although he himself later referred to *Brave New World* as a satire, he does not clearly position himself against the kind of society he depicts. After all, most of its inhabitants are happy, even if they have never had any alternative. The Alphas, in accordance with their prenatal programming, enjoy their intellectual work and abhor anything resembling manual labour, while the lower cast Deltas are happy with their menial tasks and pity the intellectually burdened Alphas. Mustapha Mond, Resident World Controller of Western Europe and one of the chiefs of the World State, is by far the happiest and most balanced character in the book. In contrast, his rival in a memorable Socratic confrontation over the benefits of learning and literature, John the Savage, ends up hanging himself. Even the two most rebellious Alphas, Bernard Marx and Helmholtz Watson, who perhaps due to some minor prenatal failure at the Hatchery are incapable of accepting the status quo, are not entirely horrified at the prospect of being exiled to remote locations such as Iceland and the Falkland Islands, since they will be able to meet other like-minded dissidents. And of course, if anyone starts to feel a bit depressed, they can always take a good dose of "soma" and drift away into narcotic bliss.

For Huxley, the use of drugs as an artificial means to calm depression and pain and thereby enhance social harmony was not a satirical conceit, as the modern reader might suspect. Quite the opposite: he was an enthusiastic proponent of such options, and in his 1962 novel *Island* a similar drug is used as a way of obtaining enlightenment.

Following the horrors of the Nazi regime the entire concept of eugenics became taboo in Western intellectual debate and any notions that Huxley's satire might have favoured such solutions were hastily swept under the carpet. In an objective reading of the novel from a modern perspective, however, the ambivalence remains.

In the future societies these authors describe, novels, plays and poetry, except those written or adapted by government specialists for mass consumption, are regarded as subversive since they might encourage individual expression and creative thinking. Most literature is therefore banned. It is interesting to note that in these great satirical works, William Shakespeare is taken as the universal representative of the human creative spirit. Shakespeare's verses are used in *Brave New World* as a counterweight to the soulless uniformity imposed by the ruling regime. In *Nineteen Eighty-Four*, the simple mention of the playwright's name is hugely symbolic. Orwell's main character has a dream of freedom and rebellion against Big Brother, the Party and the Thought Police: "Winston woke up with the word 'Shakespeare' on his lips" (Orwell, *1984* 28).

In Ray Bradbury's *Fahrenheit 451* (1953) the ownership of Shakespearian works is seen as the epitome of subversion. The prohibition of literature is of course the core of Bradbury's book, which is set following two atomic wars at an unknown time in an unspecified city. The description corresponds to a standard township in America's Midwest. Families have their own separate houses, although we are told that these dwellings have had their porches removed in order to discourage neighbours from coming together and talking. As in *Nineteen Eighty-Four*, war is a constant presence and bombers drone overhead.

In Bradbury's dystopia keeping even a single volume is prohibited and is punishable by death. In an unexpected semantic twist, firemen no longer put fires out, but cause them in order to destroy books. The novel's main character, Guy Montag, is a fireman, but he harbours doubts over his professional activity. Like Winston Smith, his yearning for freedom is expressed in terms of paper. Smith keeps a diary; Montag secretly stores books. The society painted by Bradbury leans more towards Orwell than Huxley. Repression is the norm and the population's happiness is not of much interest to the regime (to illustrate this, the book commences with a suicide attempt by Montag's wife). However, *Fahrenheit 451* does end on a more hopeful note than *Nineteen Eighty-Four*, as Montag, who torches his boss to save his books, manages to escape and joins a roving band of secret book lovers who keep literature alive by memorising the classics.

The symbolic weight of burning books reflected Bradbury's own fears about the right-wing censorship he observed in American society at the time. It is significant that *Fahrenheit 451* coincided with McCarthyism. Ironically, the novel itself, so critical of attempts to suppress individuals' freedom of expression, was subjected to an expurgation process by Bradbury's own publisher in America, with such words as "hell", "damn" and "abortion" being deleted. Several attempts were also made to ban its use for teaching purposes in schools due to obscene language, the fact that a bible is burned and the unfortunate portrayal of firemen.

The use of technology for purposes of repression and control is a common theme in Orwell and Bradbury. They both foresaw the enormous manipulative power of television. One of the most potent symbols of *Nineteen Eighty-Four* is the "telescreen", which serves not only to disseminate propaganda but also to spy on the population, both outdoors and in their own homes. Television screens are also used to impose control in *Fahrenheit 451,* though in a different fashion that will be familiar to the modern reader. The living room in the home of the book's protagonist, Guy Montag, has walls that consist almost entirely of TV screens. This is where his wife, Mildred, and the other housewives pass their free time, taking part in banal interactive television shows designed to keep the populace entertained and intellectually anaesthetised. When Montag produces a book and starts reading, his wife and neighbours, busy entertaining themselves with the "parlour walls", are utterly scandalised. It hardly needs to be added that ultramodern weaponry is available to the police in these dystopic societies whenever they need it.

Fahrenheit 451, Brave New World and *Nineteen Eighty-Four* have acquired such status that they are virtually synonymous with their celebrated authors. In Orwell's case, indeed, the publication of *Nineteen Eighty-Four* elevated him to the rank of Cold-War icon and stellar 20th century novelist. It is therefore somewhat ironic to consider that, if it were not for a relatively unknown book written in Russian two decades earlier by a mostly forgotten author who died in poverty, Orwell's most famous work would never have come into existence. That book (in its English translation) is called *We* and was written by the Russian author Yevgeny Zamyatin.

The publication history of *We* is complex and entirely worthy of the epoch it seeks to satirise. Zamyatin's book was the first novel to be banned from publication as ideologically unsuitable by the Soviet censors, in the early 1920s. It was therefore necessary to smuggle a manuscript of the book abroad and the first published edition was actually in English, not Russian, appearing in New York in 1924. New translations of *We* were then published in Czech in 1927 and in French in 1929. A Russian language version did not appear until 1952 (again in New York), 15 years after Zamyatin's death. *We* was finally published in the author's home country during Gorbachev's Glasnost in 1988.

Although Zamyatin's futuristic novel is far less famous than Orwell's, much has been written in academic forums about the influence of *We* on *Nineteen Eighty-Four*. Orwell could hardly deny this, since his awareness of the existence of *We* was no secret. Orwell wrote a review of Zamyatin's book which appeared in the edition of *Tribune* magazine of 4 January 1946, three years before the publication of *Nineteen Eighty-Four*. His article was actually based on the French translation. In his review, Orwell refers to *We* as "one of the literary curiosities of this book-burning[3] age" (Orwell, *Collected Essays* 72). He expresses his admiration for the book, though not in particularly effusive terms: "So far as I can judge it is not a book of the first order, but it is certainly an unusual one, and it is astonishing that no English publisher has been enterprising enough to reissue it" (72). Orwell's admirably succinct description of *We* is as follows:

> In the twenty-sixth century, in Zamyatin's vision of it, the inhabitants of Utopia have so completely lost their individuality as to be known only by numbers. They live in glass houses (this was written before television was invented), which enables the political police, known as the "Guardians", to supervise them more easily. They all wear identical uniforms, and a human being is commonly referred to either as "a number" or "a unif" (uniform). They live on synthetic food, and their usual recreation is to march in fours while the anthem of the Single State is played through loudspeakers. At stated intervals they are allowed for one hour (known as "the sex hour") to lower the curtains round their glass apartments… The Single State is ruled over by a personage known as The Benefactor, who is annually re-elected by the entire population, the vote being always unanimous. The guiding principle of the State is that happiness and freedom are incompatible. In the Garden of Eden man was happy, but in his folly he demanded freedom and was driven out into the wilderness. Now the Single State has restored his happiness by removing his freedom.
>
> (Orwell, *Collected Essays* 73)

It is interesting to note Orwell's comment in the sense that people lived in glass houses because television had still not been invented; it seems that he was looking ahead to his own book in which, thanks to the telescreen, such glass buildings are no longer required in order to spy on the populace. In fact, the number of intersections between *We* and *Nineteen Eighty-Four* are so numerous that it would be pointless to question its influence on Orwell's creation,

---

3 As he is writing in 1946 we must imagine that Orwell is referring to Nazi Germany, but the echo of *Fahrenheit 451* is disquieting.

as Orwell himself was aware. What is amusing is the enthusiasm with which Orwell claims in his *Tribune* review that Zamyatin's novel must have been an influence on Huxley's *Brave New World*. Orwell repeatedly questioned *Brave New World*'s literary merit and in his review of *We* he did not forgo the opportunity to pour scorn on Huxley's work, pointedly questioning the book's originality: "The first thing anyone would notice about *We* is the fact—never pointed out, I believe—that Aldous Huxley's *Brave New World* must be partly derived from it. Both books deal with the rebellion of the primitive human spirit against a rationalised, mechanised, painless world, and both stories are supposed to take place about six hundred years hence" (Orwell, *Collected Essays* 72). In fact, Huxley denied any such influence and stated this in a letter to Christopher Collins from 1962 in which he claims that he wrote *Brave New World* long before he had heard of *We* (Russell 13). In the absence of any direct evidence one way or the other we will have to take Huxley's word for it, despite the rather self-interested suspicions of Orwell and others, including the American writer Kurt Vonnegut Jr., whose first novel *Player Piano* (1952) borrowed heavily from Huxley, and Natasha Randall, author of the 2007 translation of *We* used in this essay.[4]

We is commonly regarded as a satire on Soviet Russia but Orwell disagrees, saying: "What Zamyatin seems to be aiming at is not any particular country but the implied aims of industrial civilisation" (Orwell, *Collected Essays* 75). If this is the case, then *We* should be seen as a link in the chain that commenced with *Gulliver's Travels* and *The Time Machine*, as discussed above, and continued through Jack London's Socialist apology *Iron Heel* (1908). The target of these critical works is not just repressive government but the broader issue of social disruption caused by industrialisation. In any case, considering its remarkable life story and its huge influence, Zamyatin's novel must be regarded as one of the most important dystopian satires in European literature.

Scholarly Skirmishes

The novels studied so far in this essay may be uncontroversially classed as science fiction (with the exception of the unclassifiable *Gulliver*). However, not all satirical worldbuilding falls into the sci-fi domain, and we should now turn our attention to works whose authors, also writing in the pre- and post-World War II period, belong more to the genre of fantasy literature.

In 1949, J.R.R. Tolkien, known at the time as a children's author and distinguished academic, published *Farmer Giles of Ham*, a minor gem of satirical worldbuilding. Tolkien was never one for aggressive satire—mild irony was

---

4   For Vonnegut and Randall references see: https://en.wikipedia.org/wiki/Brave_New_World

more his style—and accordingly the tone of *Farmer Giles* is considerably gentler than that of the other books discussed above. In its superficial structure and overall theme, Tolkien's short tale is a parody of knightly romance in which a fearless warrior takes on, and vanquishes, a pitiless dragon. In *Farmer Giles of Ham*, the fearless warrior is in fact a very reluctant farmer, mounted not on a war steed but on his farm horse and accompanied only by his faithful dog. For its part, the dragon, absurdly named Chrysophylax Dives[5], seems dreadful enough at first but as soon as it sees itself in danger (menaced by a magic sword) it collapses and begs for mercy. As with *The Time Machine, Brave New World* and *Nineteen Eighty-Four*, the action takes place in the south-east of England. The relevant territory is called the "Little Kingdom", the period being some fictitious phase of the Middle Ages when knights, dragons and giants were still common. As already noted with respect to the hero and the dragon, Tolkien employs the typical satirical device of making things their opposites. The king of the Little Kingdom, far from being wealthy and wise, is ignorant and broke. When Farmer Giles succeeds in frightening off a giant that is threatening the land, the king has to reward him with a fancy but seemingly useless old sword since he has no gold or silver left. This is a fortunate error, as the sword turns out to be magical and particularly useful for fighting dragons. As for knightly valour, when the opportunity arises to attack the dragon in its lair and seize its treasure, the knights sent by the king for this purpose turn out to be cowardly, foppish theorists and it is Giles himself who has to save the day.

Farmer Giles functions on various levels. The first layer is the universally recognisable tale of a basically honest, everyday bloke who makes it to the top thanks to his quick wits and a bit of luck. The second layer is the dragon story satire that may be appreciated by the lay reader. However, there is another level which is more difficult to capture. It turns out that *Farmer Giles of Ham* is loaded with philological in-jokes which only a trained etymologist would be capable of identifying[6]. This provides Tolkien, *inter alia*, with the opportunity to poke fun at his former employers at the *Oxford English Dictionary* and also, by means of carefully described but completely false etymological deductions concerning place names, to lampoon his fellow philologists, particularly those who get too carried away in their speculation.

One gets the feeling that Tolkien, when constructing the Little Kingdom, decided to have a quiet chuckle at the expense of his fellow lexicographers and philologists. Of course, Tolkien was not the first to make fun of his peers by means of satirical worldbuilding. Quite the opposite: although the great authors discussed here may have held lofty principles and pursued noble aims in their

---

5   *Chrysophylax* (Χρυσοφύλαξ) is Greek for "gold-guard" and *dīves* is Latin for "rich".
     Source: www.tolkiengateway.net
6   See Shippey 111-113.

criticism of human vice and vanity, they were certainly not above taking a dig at their colleagues. We have seen the example of Jonathan Swift, whose greatest satire started life as a parody of travel story writers. For his part, Wells wrote *The Time Machine* partly as a response to what he saw as excessively rosy depictions of man's future, particularly as painted by William Morris. Huxley reported similar motives for writing *Brave New World*, while in *Nineteen Eighty-Four*, Orwell, a journalist himself, launches a ferocious criticism of the news media. This is clearly a field which serves for both generic broadsides and private vendettas.

Although it was not published until 1949, *Farmer Giles* was most probably conceived in the 1930s at the time Tolkien was working on *The Hobbit* (Shippey 111). It was also during this period that Tolkien's friend and fellow philologist Clive Staples Lewis published his first work of fiction, *The Pilgrim's Regress* (1931). Cast in the mould of Bunyan's *The Pilgrim's Progress,* Lewis' book is an allegory of the author's private pilgrimage towards the Christian faith. Placing *The Pilgrim's Regress* next to *Farmer Giles of Ham* is rather unfair to Lewis. *Farmer Giles* is a marvel of economy while *The Pilgrim's Regress* is tediously long-winded, and where *Farmer Giles* is light-handedly erudite *The Pilgrim's Regress* is oppressively learned. Lewis actually published an apology in the second edition of his novel for the excessive number of intellectual allusions it contains. In his *mea culpa*, Lewis explained that this overdose of scholarship was due to the fact that he reckoned only he himself and a few other ardent intellectuals would ever read the book. In any event, setting aside these caveats, *The Pilgrim's Regress* is of interest because it is the work in which Lewis most decidedly combines worldbuilding (a map is included) with satirical intent. Barbed allusions are plentiful. Among others, Lewis attacks D.H. Lawrence, Sigmund Freud, Gertrude Stein and James Joyce, the first two for their sensuality, the latter two for their incomprehensibility. As well as reflecting the author's metaphysical preoccupations *The Pilgrim's Regress* is a mirror of the intellectual and political concerns of its time and it is interesting to note that, in line with Wells and Huxley, and among many other topics, it discusses the rise of machinery in combination with the threat of working-class revolution. This occurs when the Guide (names are entirely transparent in *The Pilgrim's Regress*) mentions a slave revolt in which the masters have been obliged to build machinery in order to reduce manual work: "And this seems to them so important that they are suppressing every kind of knowledge except mechanical knowledge" (Lewis 191). It is illustrative that Lewis headed the page from which this quote is taken as follows: "*The change from classical to scientific education strengthens our ignorance.*" Swift would have approved. But he does not think we need to worry: "There will be no radical change. And as for permanence—consider how quickly all machines are broken and obliterated" (192).

This wishful thinking reflected a contempt for the apparently unstoppable advance of technology that C.S. Lewis shared with Tolkien and with another English fantasist that Lewis admired, the artist and writer Mervyn Peake. Peake's most complex worldbuilding venture was the widely misjudged *Titus Alone* (1959), the last of his Gormenghast novels, which shows a Swiftian virulence in its rejection of modernity. In the first two novels of his famous series—*Titus Groan* (1946) and *Gormenghast* (1950)—Peake's satirical eye is focused on ridiculing the typically English adoration of pomp, ceremony, tradition and ancient ritual. In this and most other respects, the vast, crumbling castle of Gormenghast is still in the dark ages. In *Titus Alone*, however, this gothic spell is quickly shattered by the appearance of a bizarre, noisy motor car, driven by an enigmatic new character called Muzzlehatch. This new world of automobiles, flying machines and glass skyscrapers, dominated by a sinister caste referred to simply as the "scientists", belongs more to a Kafkaesque domain of uneasy dreams than to the world of solid rock and stone. Many Peake fans are shocked and disappointed by this fracture, but to understand *Titus Alone* such regrets must be abandoned and we simply have to accept that the author's focus has shifted.

In *Titus Alone*, the scientists are malevolent. They work in a massive building referred to merely as "the factory". Titus visits the factory one morning, riding through a nearby lake on horseback (nature placed in direct confrontation with modern ugliness) until he comes within sight of the building with its high chimneys and countless portholes.

> Letting his eye dwell for a moment on a particular window, he gave a start of surprise, for in its minute centre was a face, a face that stared out across the lake. It was no larger than the head of pin. Turning his eyes on the next of the windows, he saw, as before, a minute face. A chill ran up his spine and he shut his eyes, but this did not help him, for the soft, sick, sound seemed louder in his ears and the far musty smell of death filled his nostrils. He opened his eyes again. Every window was filled with a face, and every face was staring at him, and the most dreadful of all else, every face was the same.
>
> It was then that from far away there came the faint sound of a whistle. At the sound of it the thousands of windows were suddenly emptied of their heads.   (Peake 120)

This disturbing scene is reminiscent of both *We*, with its multitude of marching, depersonalised citizens, and of the faces of prisoners, likewise stripped of their identity, peeping through the windows and fences of concentration camps. This provides us with a clue as to the author's intentions. Like so many other novelists and poets of his generation, Peake's writing is infused with the horror of his war experiences. He worked for the British army as a war artist at the end of World War II; he saw first-hand the ruins of German cities that had been flattened by allied bombing and accompanied the troops sent to liberate the Bergen-Belsen concentration camp. What he witnessed there, inevitably, had a profound impact on him and this filtered into his fiction. Along these lines, therefore, the factory in *Titus Alone* is both a manufacturing facility and a prison. It produces ray guns, but also tortures inmates. The scientist that runs it is a perverse experimenter in the mould of the devilish doctors and social scientists of the Nazi regime. It is the supreme instance of evil in *Titus Alone*, where science is treated as a source of pain and despair, rather than hope.

In addition to his horrified rejection of the Nazis' methods, Peake's condemnation of science must also stem from the treatment he received as he battled against mental illness in the later stages of his life. While attempting to complete *Titus Alone,* Peake had to suffer the brutal surgical experiments prevalent in the 1950s, which merely made his condition worse[7]. This could hardly have brightened his view of modern medicine. Indeed, it is a common observation that the satanic darkness of both *Titus Alone* and *Nineteen Eighty-Four* springs largely from the fact that both of their authors were seriously ill when the books were completed and, we may surmise, both suspected that they did not have much longer to live.

Cold-War Prophets: Vonnegut and Lem

The next two authors to be discussed in this essay, Stanislaw Lem and Kurt Vonnegut, can be seen as representing a change in the direction of worldbuilding satire, after many decades of a more or less linear progression. By the end of the 1950s, thanks to the successful reconstruction of Europe and the apparent robustness of the democratic system, concerns about a world-wide slide into tyranny had diminished and the immediacy of the horrors of World War II was beginning to fade. It also became clear that technological progress was inescapable. As a result, satirical worldbuilding underwent a certain broadening of focus, even though science and armed conflict continued to be central issues, as could hardly be otherwise in the age of the Cold War.

Kurt Vonnegut Jr. was the most significant English-language satirist of that uncertain era. He wrote about the darkest aspects of humanity in a detached, offbeat style that generated a striking contrast between the message and the form of delivery. Humour was an essential component of his creativity, and satire was an essential ingredient of his humour. To some extent, he smuggled

---

7   See Moorcock's discussion in the introduction to the revised 2011 edition of *Titus Alone.*

in the more profound aspects of his work under a superficial mantle of gently delivered, rather zany comedy, in which comic sci-fi played a central role.

It is in Vonnegut's second novel, a science-fiction spoof titled *The Sirens of Titan* (1959), that we are introduced to the inhabitants of the planet Tralfamadore. From a conceptual viewpoint, *The Sirens of Titan* is largely concerned with the question of free will versus chance. Do we control our lives, or are we fortune's fools? This theme is explored through the volatile lives of its two main characters, Malachi Constant, a millionaire who at the beginning of the novel considers himself to be the luckiest man on earth, and Winston Niles Roomford, a time traveller trapped in a cosmic spiral which Vonnegut calls the *chrono-synclastic infundibulum*, as a result of which he is only capable of materialising on earth for a few minutes at a time. Constant's changing fortunes take him to Mars, where he manages to desert from an army that will shortly invade the earth in flying saucers, then to Mercury, where he resides for time in a deep tunnel in the company of translucent, kite-shaped beings that feed on planetary vibrations, and finally to Titan, one of the moons of Saturn. It happens that Roomford also lives on Titan, as it is the only place where he can exist as a solid human being. Here, we discover that Roomford has befriended a robot space-pilot by the name of Salo, from the planet Tralfamadore. Salo eventually explains to Roomford that the history of the human race has been manipulated by the Tralfamadorians in order to create an advanced civilisation capable of producing a spare part needed for Salo's broken-down spaceship, which is marooned on Titan. Vonnegut's comical conclusion is that we should stop feeling so self-important; for all we know, we are merely pieces in the grand strategy of an alien intelligence.

The Tralfamadorians reappear sporadically through Vonnegut's novels and play an important role in his most famous work, *Slaughterhouse Five,* published in 1969. *Slaughterhouse Five* is the story of Billy Pilgrim, whose name inevitably brings to mind John Bunyan's *The Pilgrim's Progress*, not to mention C.S. Lewis's *The Pilgrim's Regress*. However, Billy is not a conventional pilgrim journeying piously from one earthly location to another; he is a pilgrim in time. Unfortunately, he is not capable of controlling his time travel, so in the course of the novel he jumps backwards and forwards randomly among the main events of his life (including his death). Vonnegut's book is largely a condemnation of war, in particular, the Vietnam War, in which his country was involved when he wrote *Slaughterhouse Five*. In contrast to the narrative tactic employed by Orwell, Vonnegut uses Billy's time travel to move backwards, rather than forwards, in time, describing his own memories as a US prisoner of war during the bombing of Dresden in World War II instead of inventing a future scenario for his satirical purpose.

In a parody of the classic "kidnapped by aliens" sci-fi tale, in *Slaughterhouse Five* Billy Pilgrim is abducted by Tralfamadorians and taken in their flying saucer to their home planet, where he is to be placed in a zoo. We are informed that the Tralfamadorians are shaped like a toilet plunger with a hand stuck at the end of the handle, containing a single eye. They live in four dimensions and experience time as a never-ending moment running from the beginning to the end of the universe. On Tralfamadore, Billy's living conditions are described thus:

> And Billy travelled in time to the zoo on Tralfamadore. He was forty-four years old, on display under a geodesic dome. He was reclining on the lounge chair which had been his cradle during his trip through space. He was naked. The Tralfamadorians were interested in his body—*all* of it. There were thousands of them outside, holding up their little hands so that their eyes could see him. Billy had been on Tralfamadore for six Earthling months now. He was used to the crowd.
> Escape was out of the question. The atmosphere outside the dome was cyanide, and Earth was 446,120,000,000,000,000 miles away. (141)

The Tralfamadorians even find him a mate, in the hope that they will reproduce. In addition to parodying science fiction, Vonnegut mocks humanity's vain sense of superiority over the rest of nature. Mankind imprisons animals in zoos for them to be observed as a form of idle entertainment: in Billy Pilgrim's case, it is the scientifically backward and physically puny human that is on display.

Another character that pops in and out of Vonnegut's novels is the science fiction author Kilgore Trout, whom Vonnegut employs as a vehicle for expressing his contempt for the sci-fi genre. In *Slaughterhouse Five* Trout is Billy Pilgrim's favourite writer. It has to be said, however, that the simple-minded Billy is not a very discerning reader. Trout shares with other science fiction writers what Vonnegut evidently regards as a very common weakness: he has great ideas, but no literary talent. This is stated in the following unequivocal terms in *Slaughterhouse Five*:

> "Jesus—if Kilgore Trout could only write!", Rosewater exclaimed.
> He had a point: Kilgore Trout's unpopularity was deserved. His prose was frightful. Only his ideas were good.   (138)

The satirising of science fiction and fantasy writers by other science fiction and fantasy writers became something of a literary niche in the latter part of the 20th century, with such novelists as Michael Moorcock, Harry Harrison, Douglas Adams and Terry Pratchett following Vonnegut's lead. But the fiercest critic of them all was the great Polish author Stanislaw Lem. In 1975, in the journal *Science Fiction Studies*, Lem actually published an article under the heading: *Philip K. Dick: A Visionary Among the Charlatans.*[8] With a title like that, there is little need to explain the theme. Lem hammered the point home in his 1968 novel *His Master's Voice*, when the narrator describes how one of the scientists trying to decode radio messages from outer space seeks to draw inspiration from science fiction books:

> One day I found him amid large packages from which spilled attractive, glossy paperbacks with mythical covers. He had tried to use, as a "generator of ideas"—for we were running out of them—those works of fantastic literature, that popular genre (especially in the States), called, by a persistent misconception, "science fiction". He had not read such books before; he was an-noyed—indignant, even—expecting variety, finding monotony. "They have everything *except* fantasy", he said. Indeed, a mistake. The authors of these pseudo-scientific fairy tales supply the public with what it wants: truisms, clichés, stereotypes, all sufficiently costumed and made "wonderful" so that the reader may sink into a safe state of surprise at the same time not be jostled out of his philosophy of life.   (Lem, HMV 106)

Lem's virulent dislike of other sci-fi writers may partly have been due to what he perceived as a lack of recognition of his own work in the United States, which at the time was the most important science fiction market. But there is more to it than that. Lem himself had a background in science—he had trained as a doctor—and he therefore had an insider's knowledge. He respected scientific rigour, but found it to be in very short supply in the real world. Accordingly, much of his satirical worldbuilding is aimed not only at the amateurs of science fiction but also at the trained and practising professionals of hospitals, laboratories and observatories, for what he saw as their unfailing tendency towards banality, obfuscation and a general lack of seriousness, not to mention chronic mutual suspicion and an incapacity to cooperate (Lagado comes to mind). One particular area of both astronomy and science fiction addressed in depth by Lem was that of potential contact with an alien intelligence. Lem derided science fiction stories in which humans and aliens communicate with each other. For Lem, the possibility of such communication was a groundless assumption: he considered that any kind of information exchange between humans and intelligent aliens would be supremely difficult, and most probably impossible. This is a recurring theme in his fiction. In the above-mentioned *His Master's Voice*, a group of eminent scientists toil for months in a secret desert location trying to understand radio communications that have been picked

---

8   The article can be read here: http://www.depauw.edu/sfs/backissues/5/lem5art.htm

up from space, probably sent by intelligent extra-terrestrials. By the end of the book, after all kinds of experiments and apparent breakthroughs, most of the scientists have fallen out, their government sponsors are exasperated and no one is any the wiser as to the actual meaning of the radio waves.

Lem also censured the US government's obsession with deadly weapons in his novel: we eventually find out in *His Master's Voice* that the administration's real interest in the deciphering project is to find out whether the alien messages can be used for military purposes (this book was also written at the height of the Cold War). At the same time, the author criticises those scientists who are willing to knowingly cooperate in such bellicose projects.

Scientists are again parodied in Lem's most famous novel, *Solaris* (1961). The action takes place far in the future on Solaris, a planet which orbits two suns. The surface of Solaris is mostly covered by an "ocean", which in fact is a single, gigantic, sentient being. Over this hovers a scientific outpost from earth. The human community has been trying to communicate with the ocean for decades, without success. In the meantime, the scientific discipline of Solaristics has developed, which due to the failure to establish any meaningful communication with it, has degenerated into the simple observation and categorisation of the phenomena that take place on the ocean's surface, accompanied by the usual interdisciplinary bickering.

> A multiplicity of schools appeared, that often fought furiously with one another. It was the time when Panmaller, Strobla, Frehouss, le Greuill, and Osipovich were active; Giese's entire legacy was subject to devastating critique.   (Lem, *Solaris* 165)

The precision of the sham erudition is worthy of Borges. This is Lem's way of satirising what, in his opinion, constitutes far too much of the day-to-day business of scientists in the real world: huge amounts of vacuous theorising, for very little real gain. Like in *His Master's Voice*, at the end of *Solaris* the characters have done a great deal on the dramatic plane, but they are no closer to entering into contact with the alien being than at the beginning. It should be added, however, that the book does end on a hopeful note.

Lem's novels often depict fairly ordinary people trying to come to grips with complex situations. His work has a powerful philosophical and moral component: he believed that humans are essentially good, but was not convinced that they could overcome their limitations. As his fiction suggests, he was particularly concerned about what the future would hold for us and much of his scientific work was devoted to this area. Lem's rather exasperated lack of faith in human intelligence, but also his holding-back of outright condemnation, distances him in this respect from Swift and Orwell, and brings him closer to Kurt Vonnegut. His characters soldier on, despite the odds, hoping things will turn out well but without any factual basis for this optimism. Rather like most of humanity, in fact.

The State of the Art

A s we have seen in this discussion, over the years the overlapping genres of science fiction, speculative fiction and fantasy have shown themselves to be an ideal medium for social satire, as they allow authors to create whatever worlds they need—earthly or alien, past or future, grotesque or exquisite—to serve as a background for their condemnation of contemporary society's most undesirable aspects. This condemnation covers a wide range of topics, from specific issues like judicial and political corruption, warmongering and the inappropriate use of technology, to more general considerations such as humankind's apparently incurable arrogance and short-sightedness.

On the journey from Brobdingnag to Tralfamadore the art of satirical worldbuilding has never ceased to evolve and it has crossed into the new millennium with more vigour than ever. The public appetite for social criticism combined with powerful imagination seems to be insatiable, and this is reflected by the enormous success of two contemporary authors, Margaret Atwood and Neil Gaiman.

Atwood's celebrated novel *The Handmaid's Tale* is a powerful totalitarian satire and a stark warning against the same right-wing Christian fundamentalists that attacked Ray Bradbury three decades earlier. The book was published to considerable acclaim in 1985 but attained even greater fame in 2017 thanks to its having been turned into a record-breaking television series and also because, in the Donald Trump era, it seems more relevant than ever. As Atwood herself has pointed out, the vile practices she describes in her book all existed in some part of the world when *The Handmaid's Tale* was originally published, and this depressing situation has not improved at all in the decades since then.

Neil Gaiman's *American Gods* (2001) also combines literary speculation with strong social criticism. The title of the novel refers to an imaginary conflict between the old deities (Scandinavian, West African, Slavic, Egyptian) carried by their believers to the New World, and the gods of modern society such as television, technology and the stock market. This confrontation underlies the dramatic action of the novel but it also functions as a satire directed against the frivolity and transitoriness of modern western society, whose "gods" seem trivial and short-lived compared with the great myths and creeds of the past. Gaiman's novel has also received what seems to be the ultimate accolade of this screen-driven era, namely, its transformation into a television series. This is rather ironic, given the novel's satirical attitude towards television, but Gaiman evidently knows a good deal when he sees one and has happily collaborated as an "executive producer" in the production of the series. Orwell or Tolkien might have turned their noses up at such a proposal, but those were other times.

Bibliography

Atwood, Margaret. *The Handmaid's Tale.* London: Jonathan Cape, 1986

Bradbury, Ray. *Fahrenheit 451.* New York: Ballantine Books, 1991

Gaiman, Neil. *American Gods.* London: Headline, 2001

Huxley, Aldous. *Brave New World.* London: Vintage, 2007

Lem, Stanislaw. *His Master's Voice* (trans. Michael Kandel). London: HBJ, 1984

---. *Solaris* (trans. Bill Johnston). Krakow: Pro Auctore Wojciech Zemek, 2014

Lewis, C.S. *The Pilgrim's Regress – Wade Annotated Edition.* Michigan: Eerdmans, 2015

Orwell, George. *Nineteen Eighty-Four.* Harmondsworth: Penguin, 1954

Orwell, Sonia Brownell (ed.). *The Collected Essays, Journalism and Letters of George Orwell. Volume IV: In Front of Your Nose, 1945-1950.* London: Secker & Warburg, 1968

Peake, Mervyn. *Titus Alone* (revised edition). New York: The Overlook Press, 2011

Russell, Robert. *Zamyatin's We (Critical Studies in Russian Literature).* Bristol: Bristol Classical Press, 2000

Shippey, Tom. *The Road to Middle-earth.* London: HarperCollins, 2005

Swift, Jonathan. *Gulliver's Travels* [1726]. San Francisco: Ignatius Press, 2010

Tolkien, J.R.R. *Farmer Giles of Ham* (in: *Tales from the Perilous Realm*). London: HarperCollins, 2002

Vonnegut, Kurt. *Slaughterhouse Five; or, the Children's Crusade.* New York: The Dial Press, 1999

---. *The Sirens of Titan.* New York: The Dial Press, 1999

Wells, H.G. *The Time Machine* [1895]. New York: Signet Classics, 1984

Zamyatin, Yevgeny. *We* (trans. Natasha Randall). London: Vintage, 2007

"[T]he sewers and the magic and the dark"—in Search of Individuality and Fundamental Reality in Neil Gaiman's *Neverwhere*

Magdalena Mączyńska (Opole)

N eil Gaiman in *Neverwhere* presents an intricate portrayal of London that is in itself an interesting conglomeration of the old and the new, of main streets crowded with tourists and places that slip out of memory—"[t]here were a hundred other little courts and mews and alleys in London just like this one, tiny spurs of old-time, unchanged for three hundred years" (*Neverwhere* [N] 79). London's uniqueness appears to be based in equal measure on monuments and landmarks as well as on the past events that have defined the city. Gaiman's use of myths and legends that creates a fully-fledged description of London reminds one of Philip Sheldrake's remark that "[p]lace depends on relationships and memories as much as on physical features" (8). Being a confusion of colours, noises, architectural styles and various people, London constantly expands, changes and develops. Yet Gaiman shows that London's complexity goes deeper than that, for there exists a subterranean city of London Below. Both Londons are like two sides of the same coin, bound together though possessing distinctive features. The cities permeate one another, what happens in London Above seems to reverberate in the Underside. And yet a simple distinction into a light and dark city is inadequate, for both are dangerous, each in its own distinct way.

The geography of London Below is complex and tangled. The Underside is literally below Britain's capital, yet it stretches also vertically, ranging in depth rather than height. Directions in the Underside seem to shift, as if someone reversed an hourglass—such notions as inside and outside are liquid. London Below may be accessed from various spots scattered throughout the capital city that are easily discernible for those who know where to look. Nevertheless, ordinary inhabitants of London Above are utterly oblivious as to the existence of an alternative world beyond their immediate and tangible surroundings. London Below mirrors the layout of Britain's capital, since even the underground has the same general outline. Tracks and tunnels sometimes seem to merge, or overlap though often they lead to utterly different and unexpected destinations; tube stations have strange doubles—somehow familiar yet much more lethal.

The boundaries of London Below appear to stretch and fluctuate during the night-time. The Underside, a world of shadows and dim lights, expands when darkness envelops also the capital. Piotr Kowalski notes that night is associated with danger, it suspends all sense of directions thus introducing the lack of certainty. It is a time of chaos when the everyday rationality is shattered and another reality dominates (351). Therefore, one is not surprised that gloom triggers the expansion of the Underside. The inhabitants of London Below know and are accustomed to the lack of light, consequently they wander freely within the confines of the upper city that temporarily gains the quality of their own world. They hold their markets and meetings in the most unusual places—for a short period of time Harrods or HMS Belfast (to name just two of the extraordinary locations) become extensions of the Underside, enclaves of magic and strangeness that for a while exist simultaneously in both Londons.

In the Underside nothing is certain and straightforward, even buildings are more than their outward structure suggests—Door's house has every room located not only somewhere else but also sometime else, it is thus scattered all over the Underside and throughout various epochs, preserving remnants of past ages. The fabric of the house consists of numerous overlooked or forgotten places and objects that have been taken from London Above where they may even no longer exist. It is a building that actually has no easily discernible location—a house with numerous portals leading to different destinations. Door's family home draws attention to the fact that London Below defies linear time (one may meet there the remnants of Roman troops and whole medieval courts squeezed into underground trains), which, paradoxically, predisposes it to become storage for London's past—"[t]here are little bubbles of old time in London, where things and places stay the same, like bubbles in amber... There's a lot of time in London, and it has to go somewhere—it doesn't all get used up at once" (N 229). Therefore, nothing is lost—even smells, impressions and memories linger on. The labyrinth situated at the very bottom of the Underside best illustrates its eclectic nature. The labyrinth itself is a jigsaw puzzle of everything that has been discarded, forgotten or is bygone in London Above—times, places, days and nights have blended together to form a structure that transcends the two cities. Cobbles, mud, or wooden boards merge into a construction that defies any laws of logic and yet tells the complex story of the capital.

Neverwhere develops the idea that the uncanny is quite near the everyday, it is "what comes out of the darkness" (Royle 108). However, it does not rush to disrupt the reality of the primary world, it invades the lives of those who seem to be sensitive to the very notion of the eerie. Richard Mayhew has not sought anything beyond his mundane and ordinary existence, and yet his own character makes him susceptible to the other dimension. Richard may be seen as an outsider due to his origin and behaviour. He has neither blended in nor attuned to London and, in fact, he does everything to leave it this way; he has not seen the sights until forced to do so, he does not relish the atmosphere of the city and does not participate in any of its numerous events. One is stricken by the superficiality of the life he leads, which appears to be devoid of any purpose—the only meaning it has is associated with Richard's girlfriend who is very much determined to achieve something grand in her life. Richard is convinced that her biggest achievement would be the day when—"they would make her Prime Minister, or Queen, or God" (N 13), yet Jessica has much more mundane goals. She does not care about Richard as such, she is interested in becoming a wife of somebody influential, or rather of someone who could become influential with the right guidance. She believes Richard to be the right candidate, even though she does not try to truly know him as a person. Jessica has created an ideal version of Richard to which he has to conform whether he likes it or not. In her determination to get what she wants, Jessica is rather terrifying, which Richard constantly tries to deny. Strangely enough the main protagonist not only continues the relationship but even (with gentle coaxing) becomes engaged to Jessica.

Richard does not appear to lack or want anything. Being neither truly happy nor completely depressed, he allows Jessica to make decisions for him. As Gaiman himself admitted: "I wanted a hero who was not a hero. I wanted somebody who was a little bit everybody, someone… who was going to get by on essentially a good heart and good intentions, which were going to get him into deep trouble, but perhaps get him out again as well" (in White). Therefore, it may not be denied that Richard is an insipid character, till the moment when he meets Door and through her the Underside. In the bustle of London, he is the only person willing to help without calculating the outcome of such a deed because he is not indifferent to other people's needs. Richard has got "a good heart… Sometimes that's enough to see you safe wherever you go… But mostly, it's not" (N 4). His empathy and compassion single him out, though, paradoxically, the features do not make survival in any of the worlds easier. Instinctively feeling that this is the right thing to do, he completely selflessly aids the girl. In this manner Richard involuntarily welcomes the eerie world of London Below and its inhabitants into his life. As a result, the city he has traversed so many times loses its comforting familiarity.

Gaiman develops the notion that individuals need to have certain predispositions in order to be able to cross the threshold of the other dimension. Practical and self-interested Jessica would not even believe in the existence of such a place as London Below. Her fiancé is initially not aware of another city or another way of life but he does not reject or denigrate the uncanny when it invades his life. The fact that Richard pays attention to Door is exceptional, the more so that the inhabitants of London Above do not notice those populating the other city. The protagonist, therefore, appears to be attuned to the eerie.

The act of helping Door singles Richard out. The other dimension changes his life surreptitiously, even though he is initially ignorant of the consequences of his actions. Every question he asks, every step he takes in the company of the Marquis de Carabas tightens Richard's ties with the other side. He becomes invisible to all his colleagues and acquaintances. People's attention slides over him as if he were wiped clean out of London Above, which (as the protagonist finally realises) is exactly what has happened. "As a child, Richard had had nightmares in which he simply wasn't there, in which, no matter how much noise he made, no matter what he did, nobody ever noticed him at all" (N 59)—to his horror the dreams become tantalisingly true. He is terrified, for everything he has taken for granted fails to make sense. Richard gradually fades from the city he knows—he loses his job, his position and everything he owns. It needs to be emphasised that his absence is not noticed. People have forgotten him or do so the minute they see him; he effectively vanishes out of memory, which shows how dispensable and insignificant Richard actually is. He begins to question the solidity of the surrounding world because the indifference of those around him suddenly deprives it of meaning.

Having lost his identity in London Above, the protagonist is denied the right to function within its structures. He is neither punished nor rewarded, he (without fully realising it) has just slipped through the fabric of the universe like many individuals populating the Underside. The inhabitants of London Below form a very specific group of beings that do not belong anywhere else—"[t]here's London Above... and then there's London Below—the Underside—inhabited by the people who fell through the cracks in the world" (N 126). They are the outcasts, for whom the vibrant nature of the Underside proves to be the only appropriate habitat.

Richard is physically present in London Above, but he has no social existence within its boundaries. His life is stripped of all its distinctions—his work, home and acquaintances have no longer any connection with him. His status is initially ambiguous, for he functions on the border of the worlds hence being part of neither of the cities. It is worth mentioning that the liminal sphere offers only stagnation and the existence that is no more than a state of suspension. Liminal beings are "in bondage, limited by their passive or catalytic role and often physically confined to a particular area... They are not capable of change or growth—indeed, their double nature may be the product of a specific act of metamorphosis interrupted at a halfway point" (Clute 581). The main protagonist quickly comprehends that only few manage to lead their existence skipping between dimensions. Having access to the sky and high open spaces that are separated from the subterranean tunnels crisscrossing the city itself, Old Bailey functions in the sewers as well as on the rooftops. Since Richard has neither the experience of Old Bailey nor the listlessness of a liminal creature, his only choice is to enter London Below—he ventures deep within the bowels of the city on a quest to regain his previous life. However, the task proves to be much more significant and complicated—Richard sets off to restore the coherence of the city he knows, but, in fact, he eventually discovers the hitherto unrealised side of his own character.

Any secondary world "is a real wilderness, and those who go there should not feel too safe" (Le Guin 79), therefore, one is not surprised that Richard's first conscious entrance to London Below resembles a descent to hell. The hall of the ratspeakers displays all the stereotypical features of a mediaeval inferno, and yet (or maybe exactly because of that) the protagonist finds it utterly terrifying. The surroundings are appalling, but it is the realisation that the Underside is not the figment of his imagination that shatters Richard's beliefs. Nicolas Royle notes that "[t]he uncanny involves feelings of uncertainty, in particular regarding the reality of who one is and what is being experienced" (1), which aptly describes Richard's initial experiences in London Below. He is engulfed by the feeling of the surreal, as he ventures into a world where all the rumours and legends are not only true but also dark and menacing—the border between the imaginary and real is not as much as blurred but completely abolished. The dimension of London Below poses no direct threat to Londoners Above, as it has no bearing on their reality. Nevertheless, Richard (having lost the right to tread above ground) eventually learns that not minding the gap in the tube has serious repercussions not connected with the travelling trains.

The Underside tests Richard's expectations, changes conventions, invalidates his knowledge. Richard is completely unprepared to face the strange and unrelenting character of London Below, though his struggle with the physical dimension of the place is only a prelude to the hero's journey to self-awareness (to use Joseph Campbell's term). Each task and obstacle (some of them gaining the significance of rites of passage) reveals something about Richard's character and moulds him into a new being.

Richard's desperate search for both Door and a way out leads him to Night's Bridge, a construction that makes him reformulate ideas concerning danger. The bridge is a structure leading straight into darkness "that is something solid and real, so much more than a simple absence of light" (N 101). It reacts to individuals who enter the bridge by taunting and probing them. The night at Night's Bridge invades Richard's mind and enters his body. It resembles a conscious being—enveloping him, almost suffocating. Richard experiences the accumulation of all the fears of mankind, as on the bridge "[a]ll the nightmares that have come out when the sun goes down, since the cave times, when we huddled together in fear for safety and for warmth, are happening" (N 102). The horrors are idiosyncratic, as those who walk across the bridge fill in the night with their own nightmares that sometimes engulf them.

Richard has to cope with the aftermath of the passage, which is the more traumatic, since he feels responsible for Anaesthesia's death—his guide and the first friend in London Below. Of the two of them only Anaesthesia was well aware of the dangers posed by the bridge, and still she was unable to survive the encounter with the night. Richard's reaction to her demise draws attention to the fact that he focuses on the people around him. He is genuinely interested in Anaesthesia's story, and therefore, he feels her loss the more acutely. What is more, he is appalled at the lack of reaction at the little girl's passing. Richard's shock reveals his initial incomprehension of the nature of London Below. He is vulnerable not because of his physical weakness, but because he does not recognise the rules governing the Underside.

London Below proves to be a physical as well as a metaphysical journey, Richard's ordeal, an opportunity to prove his qualities, since "[h]e had gone beyond the world of metaphor and simile… and it was changing him" (N 310). Interestingly enough, the pivotal moment comes when he has to face not the tangible dangers of London Below but his own fears and shortcomings. The trial at the Blackfriars involves acknowledging his susceptibility to other people's opinions that prove to be so devastating that Richard almost succumbs to the thought of committing suicide. The tube station reflects and exaggerates individuals' failures and insecurities, thus Richard starts to believe that his "life's a joyless, loveless, empty sham" (N 249). In the underground station Richard has to deal not only with his past but also with the phantasmagorical present. The notion of reality is additionally blurred by what he sees and hears. Wondering whether he has simply gone mad, he questions the existence of the Underside itself. His mind begins to disintegrate when he confronts his previously un-realised demons. It becomes evident that fears stay the same regardless of the dimension, though in London Above it was easier not to acknowledge them. Richard, therefore, faces the insignificance of his life in the capital; he is being destroyed by his own uncertainty and the fear to disappoint others. Lonely and deprived of dignity, he has to restore his own integrity. The protagonist is forced to consider his character and expectations and thus he is able to sort out his priorities. The ordeal is a moment of awakening for Richard—he acknowledges his shortcomings though at the same time he regains his independence.

Richard survives the wrecking and exhausting trial of the Blackfriars, though he has yet to find physical courage. He enters the labyrinth at the end of Down Street not fully aware of the dangerous Great Beast of London. One is reminded of Campbell's remark pertaining to the hero's ordeal that has "to pass within the labyrinth… The passage of the mythological hero may be over-ground, incidentally; fundamentally it is inward—into depths where obscure resistances are overcome, and long lost, forgotten powers are revivified, to be made available for the transfiguration of the world" (27). The labyrinth is the ultimate rite of passage that establishes Richard as an individual in the Underside. He is no longer defined by the opinions of others—he becomes the warrior, the hunter, a rightful member of London Below (even though he realises it only after his return above ground).

The transformed protagonist eventually wins his way back to London Above and manages to regain everything he possessed before meeting Door. Furthermore, he is given the opportunity to lead a relatively happy if somewhat uneventful life. And yet Richard understands that he can no longer be satisfied with such prospect. Despite the fact that the world around him is logical as well as predictable, it appears to lack significance. Richard admits that "if this is all there is, then I don't want to be sane" (N 371). Having once experienced the allure of the Underside, he is unable to ignore its existence. To his own surprise Richard realises that he belongs to the other city. He comprehends that London Below with all its grime, danger and ruthlessness is much more real than the city he inhabits. He longs for "the sewers and the magic and the dark" (N 126) and the chance to prove himself yet again; the comfort and quiet of London Above and a vision of a good life are no longer sufficient to keep him satisfied. Gary K. Wolfe observes that "[u]nderlying the belief in the fantastic world itself… is a deeper belief in the fundamental reality that this world expresses" (232), which is what Richard finally discovers. Having survived in London Below, he is not willing to accept the conformity of his regained existence. This time voluntarily he steps to the Underside in order to be true to his own heart.

Stefan Ekman remarks that heroes in fantasy stories often venture into the unknown by crossing borders that "are areas of transition that subvert and undermine the reader's first impressions. They provide the hero with a 'there' while never promising that the same hero will come back again" (72). Accordingly, Gaiman elaborates on the idea that the Underside in the most unlikely ways saves Richard Mayhew, who becomes fully aware of his own strengths as well as weaknesses only when he enters the other dimension. It constantly probes his resilience and proves that "when it came to real blood, real pain, he simply got on and did something about it" (N 32). Although London Below gives the impression of being phantasmagorical, it is, in fact, as real as the capital itself (though much more significant). It makes Richard aware of his own nature, dreams and desires, as he sheds his insipidity layer after layer.

Darkness is traditionally associated "with evil, death, ignorance, falsehood, oblivion, and despair" (Ferber 112) and yet the dark of the Underside does not indicate deception. In point of fact, it triggers the awakening of the main protagonist, his re-established sense of self-awareness and individuality. London Below uncovers genuine qualities by disrupting conventions and exposing false pretences. As Gaiman aptly comments, the Underside is "the place of the things that *are*" (N 310), for in their essence they are authentic.

Bibliography

Campbell, Joseph. *A Hero with a Thousand Faces*. Princeton: Princeton UP, 2004

Clute, John & John Grant. *The Encyclopedia of Fantasy*. London: Orbit, 1999

Ekman, Stefan. *Here be dragons. Exploring Fantasy Maps and Settings*. Middletown: Wesleyan UP, 2013

Ferber, Michael. *A Dictionary of Literary Symbols*. Cambridge: CUP, 1999

Gaiman, Neil. *Neverwhere: Author's Preferred Text*. London: Headline Review, 2005

Kowalski, Piotr. *Kultura magiczna. Omen, przesąd, znaczenie [Magical culture. Omen, superstition, meaning]*. Warszawa: Wydawnictwo Naukowe PWN, 2007

Le Guin, Ursula K. "From Elfland to Poughkeepsie". In: *The Language of the Night. Essays on Fantasy and Science Fiction*. Ed.: Susan Wood. New York: Harper Perennial, 1993. 78-92

Royle, Nicolas. *The Uncanny*. Manchester: Manchester UP, 2003

Sheldrake, Philip. *Spaces for the Sacred. Place, Memory, and Identity*. Baltimore: The Johns Hopkins University Press, 2001

White, Clare E. "A Conversation with Neil Gaiman". In: *writerswrite.com*. The Internet Writing Journal, March 1999. Access: 02-17-2018

Wolfe, Gary K. "The Encounter with Fantasy". In: *Evaporating Genres*. Middletown, Wesleyan UP, 2011. 68-82

Game of Thrones Seen through the Prism of Tolkien's Theory on Fairy Stories

Annie Birks (Angers)

Preamble

Given the genre, scope and worldwide success of the *Game of Thrones* television series, an investigation into whether it contains Tolkien's in-gredients of a good fairy story as presented in his essay *On Fairy-stories* might appear relevant and legitimate to anyone interested in fantasy.

The apparent ability of George R.R. Martin and executive producers David Benioff and DB Weiss to draw HBO viewers "into" the story does not just seem to produce a fusion of modern viewers' horizons worldwide. It also seems to emphasise to what extent these sub-creators' worldbuilding skills can offer more than an entertaining "observed artifact" (Stableford 46).

In this kind of "surrogate experience" (ibid), can the viewers find recovery, escape and consolation? Does Tolkien's concept of applicability emerge as an ingredient of the series by providing new perspectives?

In an attempt to answer these questions and to better understand this phenomenon in the light of Tolkien's theory, this paper will examine online comments from the fandom community, press articles, and more specifically the results of a survey carried out in 2015 among more than 2,000 students in the French University town of Angers[1].

Prerequisite: Inner Consistency of Reality

> To make a Secondary World inside which the green sun will be credible, commanding Secondary Belief, will probably require labour and thought, and will certainly demand a special skill, a kind of elvish craft.   (TL 51)

These few lines of Tolkien's essay *On Fairy-stories* clearly synthetise the *sine qua non* for any successful fairy story. Once your mind enters the story, you believe it "while you are, as it were, inside" because what is related "is 'true'" in the

---

1   This paper, which is part of a more comprehensive ongoing study, concerns the first seven seasons of *Game of Thrones*. To simplify matters, the series is referred to as GoT, the seasons as 'S' and the episodes as 'E'.

diegetic world, "it accords with the laws of that world". "The moment disbelief arises, the spell is broken; the magic, or rather art, has failed" (40f.). And if the art has failed there is no desire to explore, revisit and linger in the story.

To give but one example, when Daenerys Targaryen hatches three dragon eggs on her husband Khal Drogo's funeral pyre and walks naked and unscathed out of raging flames, no aficionado of the series questions the relevance of this most welcome eucatastrophe within the diegesis. Even if this "sudden joyous 'turn'" (TL 68) does not accord with the laws of our Primary World and even if her followers themselves are taken aback, Daenerys' immunity to the fire makes sense within the story[2]. So do the scenes when she rides her dragon Drogon. The actress's convincing performance, added to the special effects rendering of the scene, undoubtedly vouch for what Tolkien called "inner consistency of reality" (TL 70). So much so as when Drogon is wounded by a spear in a battle against the Lannister army, or worse even, when her other dragon Viserion is killed by a spear thrown by the Night King, leader of the White Walkers, the entire GoT fandom appears to be affected, as this comment posted online testifies:

> ...For one, we never expected to sob actual tears over a dragon. Neither, it seems, did the entire GoT fandom, because after Viserion meets his icy end in season seven, the entire internet about lost its mind. Between the overall grief of losing one of Daenerys's three children and the heartwrenching realization that Viserion will have to fight his two brothers as an undead slave of the Night King, the entire ordeal was just too much.[3]

The ancient Greek philosopher Aristotle advised the epic poet to prefer probable impossibilities to possibilities which are not convincing (126). And the French poet and critic Boileau said that "truth can sometimes not be plausible" and "the mind remains insensitive to something it does not believe" (99). Whatever opinion one might entertain on Daenarys and her dragons, it is most *un*likely that one remains insensitive.

In the above-mentioned survey (carried out during and after S4), students were asked to express their opinion on the credibility of various aspects of the series. Only 5.8% stated their lack of conviction concerning the fantastic ele-

---

2   However, in a discussion with fans, Martin said: "TARGARYENS ARE NOT IMMUNE TO FIRE! The birth of Dany's dragons was unique, magical, wonderous, a miracle. She is called The Unburnt because she walked into the flames and lived. But her brother sure as hell wasn't immune to that molten gold."
     http://web.archive.org/web/20000615222300/http:/www.eventhorizon.com/sfzine/chats/transcripts/031899.html (Sept. 2017)
3   https://www.popsugar.com/entertainment/Reactions-Viserion-Dying-Game-Thrones-43911320. (Sept. 2017)

ments; 29% were half convinced and the majority, 66.3%, found these aspects perfectly credible. Some considered that the authors had cleverly managed to make the fantastic elements credible by introducing them gradually and that they even managed to convert to fantasy spectators who were reluctant to creatures such as dragons and white walkers.

On 31 March 2013, in *The Independent*, the British journalist Sarah Hughes said the series was "so compelling", "well crafted, wittily scripted and just over the top enough to keep you tuning in each week."[4] Over the past seven years the series has won 212 awards, among which were 38 Emmys,[5] without mentioning the two records from the Guinness Book of World Records "Most pirated TV program and Largest TV drama simulcast."[6]

By making dragons and white walkers credible (without mentioning many other aspects of the series), Martin and the showrunners certainly required "labour and thought", together with "a special skill, a kind of elvish craft". Can they be counted among "the few" who "attempted such difficult tasks" and obtained "a rare achievement of Art: story-making in its primary and most potent mode"? (TL 51) The amplitude of the public reception seems to corroborate this hypothesis.[7]

Recovery

If a good fairy story first and foremost requires credibility it is nevertheless characterised by what Tolkien called "arresting strangeness" (TL 50) which can help us "clean our windows", rediscover things around us, refresh our vision and regain "a clear view" (TL 58f.). In one of his letters he once wrote:

> I would claim, if I did not think it presumptuous in one so ill-in-structed, to have as one object the elucidation of truth, and the encouragement of good morals in this real world, by the ancient device of exemplifying them in unfamiliar embodiments, that may tend to "bring them home".   (L 194f.)

Can we say that GoT has the potential to draw viewers out of their familiar perceptions and act as a sort of eye-opener? Does the series encourage the

---

4   http://www.independent.co.uk/arts-entertainment/tv/features/living-in-a-fantasy-world-with-game-of-thrones-8555623.html (Sept. 2017)
5   https://en.wikipedia.org/wiki/List_of_awards_and_nominations_received_by_Game_of_Thrones (Sept. 2017)
6   Ibid.
7   See Nielsen Media Research, https://en.wikipedia.org/wiki/Game_of_Thrones_(season_7) (Sept. 2017)

elucidation of truth and the encouragement of good morals via the examples or counter-examples of unfamiliar embodiments?

There is no doubt that these notions are relevant when it comes to the series. GoT features such a broad array of characters whose conspicuous personalities reveal many shades of human nature triggering constant readjustment of personal opinion. Such is the case of Sansa Stark for example whose characterisation in S7 is a far cry from what it was in S1. In an online post on 9 February 2017[8], someone wrote a plea in defence of the elder daughter of the Stark family, arguing that:

> Every character has haters for various reasons, and they feel completely justified for it. That's totally fine, but if you hate Sansa Stark because of her past characterization, you're wrong and I'm here to tell you exactly why.

The author explains how Sansa developed from being "a preteen girl", "soft", easily fainting and crying, "naive, lost in dreams of perfect princes, and undeniably spoiled" into becoming "a formidable lady of a great house". What is more "Sansa's greatest mentors are the very people she despises: Cersei Lannister and Petyr Baelish". However,

> it doesn't mean that she admires them or wants to be like them at all. It means that, considering the circumstances, they helped open her eyes to the truth of what being a woman in Westeros is like and led the charge that ripped away Sansa's naïveté.

Still according to the author of the post, Sansa also learns lessons

> from her mother and father. It's the fundamental reason that Sansa remains a figure of good in the world of GoT; she may have been through some of the ugliest trials, but she also knows the good in the world. She knows how important honor, loyalty, and trust are in a world so full of darkness. Combine that with her lessons at the hands of Cersei and Littlefinger, and she's grown into a formidable lady of a great house.

In *L'art des séries télé*, the novelist and semiologist Vincent Colonna observes that most television series encourage good morals more than we might think (116). Not only do they warn us about the consequences of our choices but they invite us directly to make the right choices. And it is in that sense that GoT could be regarded as an eminently moral story in spite of what might be said

---

8   https://www.popsugar.com/entertainment/Why-Sansa-Stark-Best-Character-Game-Thrones-43749811 (Sept. 2017)

about its most violent scenes (namely in terms of rape and murder). It is clear that Martin and the showrunners invite us to face up to reality and not give in to denial, a point of view echoed by Tyrion Lannister in the book *A Game of Thrones*: "Most men would rather deny a hard truth than face it." (Martin 121)

The rape of Sansa by Ramsay Bolton—which actually does not appear in the book—was "almost universally decried by fans". *Vanity Fair* published an article with the title "GoT absolutely did not need to go there with Sansa Stark"[9]. And Jill Pantozzi, Editor in chief of the media fan website *The Mary Sue*, wrote: "After the episode ended, I was gutted. I felt sick to my stomach."[10] Hard truths about human nature seem to be forced upon viewers without any compromise.

The author of the post on Sansa wrote: "She's been through Hell and back, but she's survived." She definitely "comes out stronger, smarter, and more determined than before. She is not the same little girl whom Cersei called 'little dove'."[11]

As a matter of fact, the series abounds in situations showing that reality is not at all what one might have imagined or want to imagine. As in Sansa's case, the characters are constantly brought to readjust their perception of things for if they don't, life doesn't do them any favours.

Take the example of other members of the Stark family (usually ranked first in the best GoT Houses)[12]: the Lord of Winterfell, Ned Stark, his wife, Lady Catelyn, and their eldest son Robb. These characters have to face the consequences of their own shortcomings. In S1, Ned is beheaded and in a gruesome scene known as the Red Wedding (S3), Catelyn, Robb and his pregnant wife Talisa (although not present at this scene in the book) are treacherously stabbed during the ceremony. This episode actually caused such an upset that some viewers poured their sadness, outrage and even their hatred of G.R.R. Martin.

As far as Martin is concerned, it seems that the scene was born with great difficulty as the following interview reports:

> That was the hardest scene I've ever had to write… It was like murdering two of your children. I try to make the readers feel they've lived the events of the book. Just as you grieve if a friend is killed, you should grieve if a fictional character is killed. You

9   https://www.vanityfair.com/hollywood/2015/05/game-of-thrones-rape-sansa-stark (Sept. 2017)

10 https://www.theguardian.com/books/2015/jun/04/george-rr-martin-game-of-thrones-rape-reality-of-war (Sept. 2017)

11 https://www.popsugar.com/entertainment/Why-Sansa-Stark-Best-Character-Game-Thrones-43749811
    http://www.cosmopolitan.com/entertainment/tv/a12103579/littlefinger-death-game-of-thrones-season-7/ (Sept. 2017)

12 https://www.ranker.com/crowdranked-list/best-game-of-thrones-houses

should care. If somebody dies and you just go get more popcorn, it's a superficial experience isn't it?[13]

Yet the paradigm which is usually consensual is that virtuous characters should be rewarded sooner or later, even at the cost of terrible ordeals (cf. poetic justice). In *GoT and Philosophy*, Silverman describes Ned Stark as "fiercely loyal to his family, friends and kingdom" with a "history of courage in battle", "a deep sense of duty, which causes him to abandon his personal safety and comfort for the sake of the good of the kingdom and his friends" (64). However, instead of being rewarded, he is betrayed, humiliated and sadistically beheaded by the king, in front of his own daughters. Among the frequent comments attempting to explain Ned's dreadful fate, are mentioned his naivety and lack of vigilance which are a disservice to his excessive sense of duty, honour and honesty. When he confronts Queen Cersei with his knowledge of her son Joffrey's incestuous origins, he is too gullible to assume that she will surrender to exile as he requires her to do. As could be read on the social cataloguing website *goodreads.com*[14], Ned acts with naïve honesty and honour towards people who are not trustworthy: "His mistake was assuming everyone else behaved the same way"; "He was an honourable fool and died because of it"; "He did his entire family a disservice by not opening his eyes to what's really going on"; "What he did cost him dearly. Every member of his family suffered/and still is suffering for his decision. Does that make him a bad person? No, just a short-sighted one".

His execution follows a logical chain of choices and behaviour patterns ultimately including supporting his wife's decision—out of love and concern for her—to imprison Tyrion Lannister in an attempt to seek justice for her son Bran. However tragic Ned's execution might be, it is easily explained by tracing back the cause-and-effect sequence. The Red Wedding could be decrypted on the same basis:

Catelyn Stark arrested Tyrion for the attempted murder of Bran, which was an illegitimate move. A fan wrote: "Catelyn Stark… made all the wrong decisions. She would let her emotions cloud her judgement time and again". [15]

In spite of his many proven qualities, Robb Stark broke his oath with Lord Walder Frey who had agreed to join forces with him providing Robb married one of his daughters. By listening to his heart instead of performing his duty, he married Talisa Maegyr and triggered a whole series of tragic consequences. In a forum, a fan stated:

---

13 http://ew.com/article/2013/06/02/game-of-thrones-author-george-r-r-martin-why-he-wrote-the-red-wedding/ (Sept. 2017)

14 https://www.goodreads.com/topic/show/1033139-ned-stark---a-fool-or-too-honorable-for-his-own-sake (Sept. 2017)

15 https://www.quora.com/Game-of-Thrones-Season-1-Why-does-Lady-Stark-arrest-Tyrion-Would-Ned-Stark-have-approved-of-that-decision (Sept. 2017)

> Robb should have sent his mother back to the twins [Frey's Castles] to pick the prettiest bride and brought her to Riverrun after his first victories and sealed/fulfilled his oath. Robb should have known better. He threatened to hang the Greatjon as an Oathbreaker, then he became one himself… You could see it coming…[16]

At the end of S4, the following observations were posted on *thoughtcatalog.com*[17]:

> The Season finale of GoT shocked a lot of people, myself included. As the credits were rolling, I proceeded to wipe my tears away and pick my jaw up off the floor… There is a running joke between fans of the book and show that says you should never get too attached to a character, because it most likely means that George RR Martin will kill him or her off. Although this appears to be true more times than not, it is not just senseless killing – there is a method behind the madness. Martin doesn't kill off characters just for the sake of it; there is always a reason, even if the readers and viewers don't see it yet. I like to think their deaths affect him just as they do for us… There are some very real life lessons that can be learned from many of his characters.

One of the students from the survey regarded the series as very realistic in so far as the characters reap what they sow: "It is like in real life, if one makes a mistake, one pays for it. We are not miraculously saved."

Aristotle insisted that the events of the story must follow a logical, probable or necessary, sequence of events (Colonna 93). The sequence must in no way be arbitrary. After due reflection, it appears that events in GoT confirm the impression one might have when watching the title sequence, i.e. a complicated clockwork mechanism where all the components are linked, leading us to expect that, "actions form a logical sequence according to the physical and social laws commonly accepted", "one event leads to another as it does in real life, following an accordion effect where the least action often has multiple consequences, some of which were not intentional" (Colonna 93).

---

16 http://asoiaf.westeros.org/index.php?/topic/90316-if-robb-had-married-the-frey/ (Sept. 2017)

17 https://thoughtcatalog.com/lauren-santye/2015/06/10-admirable-traits-of-our-favorite-game-of-thrones-characters/ (Sept. 2017)

Escape

T alking about recovery or "return and renewal of health" implies the acknowledgment of initial deficiencies. The paths leading to "recovery" are not always easily perceptible and the task can be arduous when one is busy coping with everyday life occupations and caught in a societal system which is not always conducive to sitting back, taking stock of one's life and seeing things from a refreshed point of view.

Tolkien considered that one of the attributes of a good fairy story was precisely to offer an opportunity to escape, to temporarily leave what we commonly call "real life" to let oneself be arrested and to return to the Primary World with a renewed outlook on things. He carefully warned us however not to confuse the escape of the prisoner with the flight of the deserter. One can assume that the former might refer to the healthy attitude of those seeking to escape what prevents them from seeing things clearly and the latter to the not so noble attitude of those wanting to run away from what life seems to be putting on their plates.

Viewers' opinions differ on the escapist potential of the series. The actress Nathalie Dormer who stars as Queen Margaery considers that "GoT is **not** for people who watch TV as a form of escapism." "All I know is that I turn on the news, and it's covering a boy drowning off the coast, or children being shown beheading videos. The horror of human nature is prevalent in our world, and I appreciate that some people want to turn on the telly for escapism—but if that's what you want, don't watch GoT", Dormer said.[18]

Ken Tucker, among others, partly explains the success of the "swords-and-sex-fantasy programme" by precisely its capacity to provide escapism[19]:

> In appealing to its audience's need for escapism, GoT revitalised a genre that few knew needed revitalising: the sword-and-sandals saga…

The soundtrack to the series is even publicised on *primephonic.com* with the catchphrase: "Dive into the world of fire, ice, dragons and battles with this escapist fantasy soundtrack!" Then comes a whole series of good reasons why one should download this "powerful maelstrom", among which:

> In fast-paced 21st century life, escapism is as relevant as ever. Audiences were initially drawn into the world of GoT for its literary

---

18   http://indianexpress.com/article/entertainment/television/game-of-thrones-isnt-escapism-natalie-dormer/ (Sept. 2017)

19   http://www.bbc.com/culture/story/20140407-why-people-love-game-of-thrones (Sept. 2017)

and cultural significance, but probably even more so for its escapist value. From the outset, *The Songs of Fire and Ice* epic fantasy series of novels has gripped the imaginations of millions, and its adaptation as a HBO series GoT has brought the other-worldliness to an even wider audience. And what is more convincing in helping us escape our world of escalating financial woes, cynical capitalist opportunism and environmental scares than attention-grabbing plots, plotting characters and characteristic music scores?

In *The Independent,* the British journalist Sarah Hughes mentions "David S. Goyer, the writer behind Da Vinci's Demons," who said that he hoped his show would "appeal to GoT fans", adding "people are loving historical fantasy and escapism right now, which tends to happen when times are hard and there's uncertainty in the world."[20]

85.9% of the students surveyed considered that the series offered an opportunity to escape from their everyday life. One of them explained that GoT provides such an imaginary and entertaining world, so credible and yet so remote from our reality that it acts as a superb window opening onto another world which helps us temporarily forget our everyday problems. With its medieval setting, its fantastic elements, its various cultures different from ours yet finding resonance in our collective cultural psyche, GoT is so different from our world that it easily provides escapism. It transports us into a world which is half realistic half fantastic which allows us to identify with some of the characters and situations. Other students said:

> "Before each episode, I never know what is going to happen
> and therefore I am completely surprised and captivated, that
> is the way I escape!"
> "I don't think of anything else"
> "I only focus on what is on the screen"
> "The series helps us to clear our head"
> "The series allows us to live extraordinary adventures"
> "We have real heroes to admire and real villains
> that we love detesting"
> "It provides 'Escapism from banality'"

To describe the series, some used terms such as "off-beat, addictive, absorbing, attractive, recreational, suspenseful ..."; they emphasised their sensitivity to the landscapes which are dream-inductive with the different filming locations (Iceland, Ireland, Croatia, Malta, Morocco ...); a student wrote:

---

20 http://www.independent.co.uk/arts-entertainment/tv/features/living-in-a-fantasy-world-with-game-of-thrones-8555623.html (Sept. 2017)

It [the series] opens the door into a world which echoes the imaginary world of our childhood: castles, kings and queens, dragons, magic… Although this childhood world is totally perverted by adult behavior, it creates a feeling of frustration which encourages us to carry on with the series hoping that things will eventually turn out to be more in line with the secure image of our childhood. These elements lead to escapism.

Consolation

Consolation is what Tolkien regarded as the highest function of a good fairy story. Yet, when it comes to GoT one could be tempted to assert that if there is one thing that it cannot do, it is precisely to bring consolation. In 2013, one could read on a blog: "Brutal cruelty, sex, and disloyalty are the hallmarks of Martin's world".[21] In 2014, on the website of Rant, Inc., someone wrote:

In truth, GoT is a sad, nihilistic commentary on humanity and humans in general. Its popularity is a glaring, insightful exposition on the state of our culture and there is nothing good to be said about it. There is an abundant, even gratuitous fascination and obsession with all things vulgar.[22]

During the summer 2017 on *reddit.com*, the "American social news aggregation, web content rating and discussion website", someone said: "I want to watch this show but I'm afraid I'll be scarred for life. I'm fine with the nudity/sex but I'm not so sure about the gory violence. How bad is it? Give me some examples…" Other people replied: "This show is not for you"; "One man crushes another man's head (by pushing into his eyeballs with his thumbs, no less) with his bare hands"; "Skinned humans, beheading, burning people alive, head crushing, stabbing through the eye, entrails ripped out, mass murder…"; "a woman eats a horse heart, a man tries to stuff his intestines back inside himself while lying on a pile of bodies…"

That same summer just after the beginning of S7, Catherine Gee and Fred Heffer in *The Telegraph* wrote[23]:

---

21 https://voxday.blogspot.fr/2013/08/the-grimy-pessimism-of-george-rr-martin.html (Sept. 2017)

22 http://www.rantnow.com/2014/06/02/game-of-thrones-and-the-nihilism-of-pop-culture/ (Sept. 2017)

23 http://www.telegraph.co.uk/tv/0/game-thrones-shocking-deaths-moments/ (Sept. 2017)

> The seventh S of GoT has begun, and the quality remains consistent; certainly, that is, in its ability to mortify viewers each week. Barely an episode of this fantasy series goes by without a moment that causes slack-jawed shock from its viewers. George RR Martin, who wrote the *Songs of Fire* novel series on which the drama is based, has a brutal, ruthless approach to storytelling – one shared by the makers of the HBO show.

And the list of anathematising criticisms on Martin and the showrunners expanded. Yet on 25 August 2017, in *Time Entertainment* one could read: "Critics Can Call Out GoT All They Want. But Viewers Don't Care.[24] This would tend to show that the majority of viewers are not "scarred for life" as the person on *reddit.com* feared (unless they are masochistic).

The student survey revealed that even if the majority answered in the negative when they were asked if GoT was a source of consolation, comfort or encouragement, a fair number of them (just under 600) thought the opposite.

As a matter of fact, it appears that the series brings several sources of consolation, comfort and encouragement. The first source stems precisely from its gory side. A number of students consider that, given the gruesome medieval background and some of the characters' trajectories, the series allows us to put our own problems into perspective.

"Life in the Middle Ages as imagined in the series is much tougher and crueler than our own life"; "I am glad I did not have to live in the Middle Ages because of women's condition in those days. I therefore consider that my life is much better, it brings me comfort"; "There are always worse situations than ours in the world"; "The series even makes our politicians appear quite reasonable". Some mention modern advantages like hygiene, security, relative tranquility, life conditions in general. In a word as a student says: "All these horrors which take place in this series, wars, murders, rapes… make me realize how lucky I am to live in our modern world in Europe."

What also brings consolation is the feeling of justice which ends up prevailing even if one has to put up with long periods of suffering. The series offers memorable eucatastrophic scenes along these lines such as:

- The death of Daenarys's abusive brother, Viserys, on whose head Khal Drogo poured molten gold as he was craving for a "Golden Crown". (S1, E6)
- Bronn's victory over Lady Arryn's champion in his trial by combat in the Eyrie to free Tyrion Lannister. (S1, E6)
- Daenerys emerging alive from her husband's funeral pyre with her baby dragons (S1, E10) as previously mentioned.

---

24 http://time.com/4913940/game-of-thrones-critics-viewer-ratings/ (Sept. 2017)

- The liberation of Slaver's Bay by Daenerys. This is how she explains to Sir Jorah the reason why she decides to lead a military campaign with the aim of "liberating the enslaved populace of Slaver's Bay":
  "The Masters tear babies from their mothers' arms. They mutilate little boys by the thousands. They train little girls in the art of pleasuring old men. They treat men like beasts…"
  Upon which Sir Jorah Mormont comments: "It's tempting to see your enemies as evil, all of them. But there's good and evil on both sides in every war ever fought."
  But she replies: "Let the priests argue over good and evil! Slavery is real. I can end it. I will end it. And I will end those behind it… They can live in my new world, or they can die in their old one."[25]
  And she proceeds to order both her army to slaughter the slavers and her dragon Drogon to unleash fire onto Kraznys the slave trader in the city of Astapor. (S3, E4)
- The death of Queen Cersei's son, Joffrey Baratheon. As Christopher Hooten wrote in *The Independent*, 04-14-2014: "GoT S4 E2 sees fans jubilant over King Joffrey's Purple Wedding. Joffrey Baratheon, very possibly the most hated man in Westeros". Someone tweeted: "For once, *GoT* has caused me happy tears instead of sad ones." Another wrote: "I just watched Joffrey die… Then watched it again, and again, and again… Best Sunday ever."[26] (S4, E2)
- Jon Snow's resurrection after "one of the greatest cliffhangers in the history of fantasy" as one could read on *rollingstone.com*[27]. (S6, E2)
- John Snow's victory over "smiling psychopath Ramsay Bolton's army" thanks to the intervention of the Knights of the Vale.[28]
- Ramsay Bolton's death, eaten by his own dogs: "Ramsay Finally Died On GoT & His Death Was Befitting Of His Actions".[29]
- And the most recent striking eucatastrophe in S7: the death of Petyr Baelish nicknamed Littlefinger. As one could read in *The Independent* on 28 August 2017: "There emerges a strong sense of justice in the decisions made by some characters".

25 http://gameofthrones.wikia.com/wiki/Liberation_of_Slaver%27s_Bay (Sept. 2017)
26 http://www.independent.co.uk/arts-entertainment/tv/news/game-of-thrones-season-4-episode-2-sees-fans-rejoice-over-king-joffreys-purple-wedding-9258397.html (Sept. 2017)
27 http://www.rollingstone.com/tv/lists/25-greatest-game-of-thrones-moments-w443332/the-hound-and-arya-team-up-w443356 (Sept. 2017)
28 Ibid.
29 https://www.bustle.com/articles/167790-ramsay-finally-died-on-game-of-thrones-his-death-was-befitting-of-his-actions (Sept. 2017)

A student commented:

> The series brings me some sort of encouragement, especially the Khaleesi [Daenerys]. She brings back hope. She has been offered by her brother to marry someone [Khal Drogo], having to undergo her brother's tantrums and mad desire to become king. She has lost a child and then her husband but she recovered. She started from nothing and began to build something big, as the proverb goes: 'still waters run deep'. She makes me understand that one can be at one's lowest ebb and then recover gradually, slowly but surely.

And that is precisely what one expects from a good fairy story, the consolation that brings us "Joy beyond the walls of the world, poignant as grief" (TL 68).

> It does not deny the existence of dyscatastrophe, of sorrow and failure: the possibility of these is necessary to the joy of deliverance; it denies (in the face of much evidence, if you will) universal final defeat.   (Ibid)

And GoT's heroes, as in *The Hobbit* and *The Lord of the Rings* are precisely those you might least expect. As Elrond points out:

> Such is of the course of deeds that move the wheels of the world: small hands do them because they must, while the eyes of the great are elsewhere.   (LotR1 352)

In this particular series, the wheels of the world are not moved by the small hands of a group of hobbits but by the small hands of characters depicted as outsiders or outcasts, physically or socially flawed. As G.R.R. Martin explained in an interview for the French magazine *Lire* in March 2015 (23):

> Like Tyrion, I have always been attracted to these kinds of "broken things". People who are not like everybody else, who are a bit marginal. Those who are rejected, for one reason or another. It is about them that we must write – not about the ones who already have everything. The best stories are born of conflict, difficulties. So, it is true that most characters in GoT are individuals who do not fit into their society. There are women who claim men's roles, like Arya. Boys like Sam, who is fat and wants to read and dance but who does not want to fight with swords. Jon Snow, a bastard. Tyrion a dwarf. Dany, who has lost everything at the beginning of the story; or others still who lose things on the way...[30]

---

30 My translation

So, all these "bastards, cripples and broken things" "outcasts, second-class citizens for whatever reason"[31] "representing all tiers of societal and class systems"[32] who seem to be doomed to a miserable fate, become the true heroes of the story. But owing to their choices and behaviour, the support and guidance they get, and owing to their sub-creators' elvish craft, they bring comfort and consolation in a world where there is hardly any hope, or as Tolkien would say "hope without guarantee" (L 237).

Bran has become a cripple. He is surprised to be still alive and holds on to his fate although his dream to become a knight has been shattered. He develops a gift which allows him to travel in time and space. By embracing his new capacities, Bran satisfies that human desire to "escape from death" and "visit, free as a fish, the deep sea; or the longing for the noiseless, gracious, economical flight of a bird …", "the desire to converse with other living things…" "visiting other realms with which Man has broken off relations, and sees now only from the outside at a distance…". "There are a few men who are privileged to travel abroad a little; others must be content with travellers' tales" (TL 66f.). Bran belongs to the first category…

Brienne of Tarth who has always dreamt of becoming a knight brings consolation as she is capable of defending herself. Yet her disparaging physicality and status as a woman in a world dominated by men could have been factors of discouragement and self-dissuasion.

And then there are Tyrion, Sam, John, Daenarys, Arya… all these 'marginal' characters who are regarded by viewers as role models in their own respective ways. In fact, some viewers say that the series resembles more and more a good fairy story in so far as, as the seasons advance, the notion of consolation is more and more relevant.

As a conclusion to these brief reflections on GoT and Tolkien's theory on fairy stories let us remember Martin's well-known comment when he was called "the American Tolkien":

> I revere *Lord of the Rings*, I reread it every few years, it had an enormous effect on me as a kid. In some sense, when I started this saga I was replying to Tolkien…[33]

Can we say that this Tolkien fan has been successful in his reply and completed the big picture by highlighting the paths to be avoided rather than the paths

---

31 https://www.theguardian.com/books/2014/aug/11/george-rr-martin-in-quotes-i-love-writing-about-bastards (Sept. 2017)

32 http://screenprism.com/insights/article/are-outsiders-the-most-powerful-characters-in-game-of-thrones (Sept. 2017)

33 https://www.theguardian.com/books/2014/aug/11/george-rr-martin-in-quotes-i-love-writing-about-bastards (Sept. 2017)

to be trodden? Besides, couldn't we regard the fans' eagerness to discover the final season as further evidence that the series is indeed a good fairy story, if we go by Tolkien's comment below?

> If they [fairy stories] awakened desire, satisfying it while often whetting it unbearably, they succeeded.   (TL 43f.)

Bibliography

Aristotle. *Poétique*. Paris: Belles Lettres, 1990

Bisson, Julien. "George R.R. Martin, le (très) grand entretien", in: *Lire, Hors série* N°20, March 2015

Boileau, Nicolas. *L'art poétique*. Paris: Garnier–Flammarion, 1969

Carpenter, Humphrey (Ed.). *The Letters of J.R.R. Tolkien*. London: George Allen & Unwin, 1981

Colonna, Vincent. *L'art des séries* télé. Paris: Payot & Rivages, 2015

Jacoby, Henry (Ed.). *Game of Thrones and Philosophy*. New Jersey: John Wiley & Sons, 2012

Martin, George R.R. *A Game of Thrones*. London: HarperCollins, 2011

Stableford, Brian. *The A to Z of Fantasy Literature*. Plymouth: Scarecrow Press, 2009

Tolkien, John Ronald Reuel. [1954]. *The Fellowship of the Ring*. London: Allen and Unwin, 1981

---. *Tree and Leaf*. London: Allen & Unwin, 1964

"I regard men and women as all human". Women's History in the World of George R.R. Martin

Isabel Busch (Bonn)

In an interview with *The Telegraph* in 2013, George R.R. Martin, author of *A Song of Ice and Fire*, explains why his female characters are three-dimensional, instead of conforming to stereotypical fantasy tropes, and his attitude can be summarised with the following statement: "I regard men and women as all human" (quoted in Salter). He deliberately creates well-rounded women in his work. Seeing that in the creation of Westeros (and Essos) he is borrowing heavily from real world history it is also true that his female characters reflect women from real world history.

The same is true for a seemingly purely fantastical type of female characters: warrior women, which can be defined as both women who do actual, armed fighting, and as women who command armies and/or defend fortresses, castles or even cities. Women's history, which aims for making the often ignored women of history visible, helps to uncover the potential real-world counterparts for several of Martin's warrior women. The author himself is aware of how realistic his warrior women are:

> I wanted to present my female characters in great diversity, even in a society as sexist and patriarchal as the Seven Kingdoms of Westeros. Women would find different roles and different personalities, so women with different talents would find ways to work with it in a society according to who they are.
>
> (quoted in Guxens)

Although Westerosi society is dominated by patriarchal and martial values, women are not expressly forbidden to carry arms and to fight, but it is rather frowned upon further south of the Neck, except for Dorne: "Westerosi women... becoming warriors... is [not] encouraged or seen as acceptable and feminine by many Westerosi" (Garcia Jr. "Warrior Women").

Similarly, in medieval and modern early times, women taking up arms were not widely accepted, and in singular cases women like Jeanne d'Arc could either gain popularity or notoriety. However, noblewomen and queens in command of armies and defending castles were, on the whole, accepted, like Æthelflæd (c. 870-918), the eldest daughter of King Alfred the Great, who was recognised as a skilled tactician. Another example is Nicola de la Haye (1150/1156-1230), castellan of Lincoln Castle and Sheriff of Lincolnshire, who defended Lincoln Castle against a French army. Martin's world of Westeros also provides women of that kind.

Agnes Blackwood

One of these army-leading women in Westerosi history, as presented in *The World of Ice and Fire*, is Agnes Blackwood. At an unknown date before Aegon's conquest, Agnes was ruling Lady of Raventree Hall in her own right (cf. Martin, García Jr., Antonsson 154). At that time, House Hoare ruled the Iron Islands and used to raid the riverlands. When Harwin Hoare invaded the riverlands, Agnes Blackwood was the last of the riverlords to defy him. She combined her armed forces with those of Tommen Tully and marched on Harwin. However, she was betrayed by Lothar Bracken, and handed over as a captive to Harwin, together with two of her sons. He strangled the boys in front of her. When Agnes was not intimidated by this act and allegedly declared "I have other sons", Harwin was impressed by her and offered to spare her life, in order to make her his 'salt wife' (ibid.). Agnes refused and, again allegedly[1], defiantly replied: "I would sooner have your sword inside me than your cock" (ibid.). She was then killed by Harwin, but her 'prophecy' that his family line would one day end "in blood and fire" would become true, when Aegon the Conqueror and his sister-wives Visenya and Rhaenys kill the last of the Hoares (ibid.).

Agnes was the ruling Lady of Raventree Hall, which was possibly due to a lack of male heirs. Centuries earlier, when House Blackwood was ruling the river-lands in general, an attempt to make Shiera Blackwood Lady of Raventree Hall had failed, because the other lords of the riverlands had refused to be ruled by a woman (ibid.). Therefore, Agnes' position as a ruling lady at the head of an army was more due to adapting to particular circumstances than to an egalitarian attitude. However, Westerosi history knows of another woman of House Blackwood who participated in a battle: In the civil war known as the Dance of Dragons, Alysanne 'Black Aly' Blackwood commanded archers in the Battle of the Kingsroad (cf. Martin, García Jr., Antonsson 228).

1　Even in the fictional historical accounts of Westeros, Martin, Garcia and Antonsson have the maesters, the chroniclers of Westeros, discuss historical accuracies.

Caterina Sforza (1463-1509)

O ne potential historical model for the Lady of Raventree Hall is Caterina Sforza, Countess of Forli and Lady of Imola. She was famous for her beauty, which she keenly tried to preserve, for her courage and fearlessness. She was also rather 'infamous' for her alleged pitilessness towards her enemies and even more for her supposed licentiousness. Although it is true that she dealt harshly with her enemies and took lovers[2], Antonia Fraser advises to treat these allegations with care.

She points out that women overstepping gender boundaries, like warrior women, and/or women who have political enemies, have often been subjected to being attacked on a personal, particularly on a sexual level: "The sexual freedom of choice which Caterina Sforza determinedly exercised gave useful ammunition to those opposed to her for quite different reasons; here was a Warrior Queen whose lustfulness could be denounced to good effect" (Fraser 197). Fraser calls this the "Voracity Syndrome" in her analyses of 'warrior queens' (Fraser 11f.). Caterina was also derided by Niccolò Machiavelli, possibly because he had not done well when he had met with her as a young diplomat for Florence (cf. Lev 3).

Although Martin has not provided a thorough backstory of Agnes Blackwood, in which she might or might not display similar characteristics, Caterina's story of a warrior woman is somewhat similar to hers.

The first time Caterina had to defend one of her castles was in 1488, when her husband Girolamo Riario was murdered as a result of a plot. Caterina and her children managed to escape from imprisonment to the Castle of Forli, in whose defence Caterina was active. When the rebels threatened to kill her children, Caterina allegedly challenged them by claiming that she could have other children. There are several versions of how exactly she might have phrased this, some are even quite vulgar. If she said something to this effect in the first place, then it would resemble Agnes Blackwood's words to Harwin Hoare. In any case, Caterina claimed to be pregnant, so that the rebels knew that harming her children was useless, thus were they saved. Agnes successfully re-established her power in Forli and Imola until 1499. Pope Alexander VI, who is also known as Rodrigo Borgia, wanted Caterina's lands for his son Cesare. When Cesare marched on Imola and Forli, Caterina first brought her children to safety, then she prepared her defence of the fortress in Ravaldino. Eventually she was taken prisoner, and she must have suffered at the hands of Cesare; according to Fraser, it was suggested that Caterina was raped by the Pope's son: "Cesare… treated her as his soldiers had treated the women of Forli" (Fraser 201). This is also reminiscent of Harwin Hoare's intention to take Agnes Blackwood back to the Iron Islands as his spoils of war. Caterina was imprisoned in the Castel

---

2   Not that taking lovers is in any way to be considered as an offence in itself.

Sant' Angelo, until she renounced her lands and titles. She retired to Florence and dedicated her remaining years to alchemical 'experiments', as well as to her children and grandchildren. She eventually died of pneumonia.[3]

Although Caterina encountered hostility, she was also admired. In the Early Modern time, when the ideas of Ancient Greece and Rome were revived, the idea of the *virago* became quite popular. According to the so-called 'one-sex model', which was based on Aristotle's ideas, men and women were basically made of the same material, but of varying 'quality' (cf. Schabert 24ff.). Men were considered to embody the 'perfect' human, women the 'imperfect' version. However, this doctrine also claims that women had the potential to attain 'perfect' humanity, meaning masculinity, by developing male attributes and characteristics (ibid.). Therefore, a woman such as Caterina Sforza might have been admired on the one hand, but be derided for a 'lack' of 'proper femininity' on the other hand.

Female Knights

The knights of Westeros, like the real-world knights, are the all-male elite warrior caste in feudal society. Even if a woman, like Brienne of Tarth in Westeros or Joan of Arc in real world history, takes up arms and displays all the ideals of chivalry, as Brienne does, knighthood is denied her. The only sort of knighthood Brienne receives, is at the hand of Renly Baratheon, when he appoints her to his Kingsguard (cf. Martin, *Clash* 344), which is usually reserved for anointed knights, meaning men. Brienne was raised in a more southern region[4], where her lack of conventional femininity has earned her the mocking nickname Brienne the Beauty, and she responds by endeavouring to be an ideal knight, renouncing conventional femininity (cf. Martin, *Clash* 344f.; 482f.). However, Brienne suffers from her internal struggle, where her desire to be a knight is in conflict with a still existing longing to be feminine as well: "All of it came pouring out of Brienne then…, the betrayals and betrothals…, Lord Renly dancing with her…, the mêlée at Bitterbridge, the rainbow cloak that she had been so proud of…" (Martin, *Feast* 672f.).

---

3   It was suggested by a fellow speaker at the conference that another historical character might fit as a model for Agnes Blackwood: Agnes Randolph, Countess of Moray, who successfully defended her husband's castle, Dunbar Castle, against the English troops under the command of the Earl of Salisbury in 1338. Like Martin's Agnes and Caterina Sforza, 'Black Agnes' boldly replied to her attacker's threats with defiance (cf. Johnson).
4   Tarth is a part of the stormlands.

Her environment is rather hostile towards fighting women, as Randyll Tarly, who embodies toxic masculinity,[5] makes clear: "The gods made men to fight, and women to bear children... A woman's war is in the birthing bed" (Martin, *Feast* 301). It can be argued that Brienne resembles Joan of Arc in this fate, seeing that one of the main charges laid against Joan in her trial was committing 'heresy' by cross-dressing (cf. Schad 111). In fact, it was this act of 'heresy' which eventually led to her condemnation (ibid.).

Even though it is hard to find women in European history who were officially recognised as knights in a fighting capacity, there is one example.[6] In 1149, when the Catalan town Tortosa was under attack by Moors, the female inhabitants played a leading role in the town's defence. In gratitude, Count Ramón Berenguer IV de Barcelona awarded these women with a knighthood and founded the all-female knightly *Orden del Hacha* (Order of the Hatchet). The women were not called upon to fight again, however. This order had for the most part a ceremonial or decorative purpose, but the women were also exempt from taxes and "took precedence over men in public assemblies" (Velde). The order existed only in the first generation.

There have been other cases in European history where women were received in certain kinds of orders and were granted knightly ranks and titles like *chevalière* or *militissa*. These women were no warriors, however (ibid.). Nevertheless, being awarded a knighthood has no connection to gender equality. It is more likely that the *Orden del Hacha* served a propaganda purpose, since women fighting for their home town or homeland were used in this way several times, either to encourage patriotism or to shame the men into fighting, with what Fraser calls the "Shame Syndrome" (Fraser 12).

In Japanese history, on the other hand, there is an equivalent to the European warrior caste of knights, which admitted women to their ranks and respected them as their equals as warriors, even as far as the 20th century: the samurai. A female samurai, called *onna-bugeisha*, would learn to defend herself, her home and her honour, mainly by using the *naginata*, a weapon similar to a halberd (cf. Hoffman). It is important to note that the defence of her home and her honour was in accordance with the Japanese gender expectations (ibid.).

---

5   'Toxic masculinity' is a term used in gender discourse, originating in psychology. Terry Kupers sums up toxic masculinity as "the constellation of socially regressive male traits that serve to foster domination, the devaluation of women, homophobia and wanton violence" (Kupers 714). Randyll Tarly exemplifies many of these traits in suppressing his son Samwell's character, which is contrary to the values of toxic (or hegemonic) masculinity (cf. Martin, *Storm* 641ff.).

6   It is to be noted that women have held the title of a knight in other respects; for example, women who have been admitted to the Order of the Garter.

However, in Japanese culture, which, according to Chris Kincaid, is mainly influenced by Confucian ideas, the woman is considered to be inferior to the man in general, and she is dependent on the man, who is seen as the head of the household (cf. Kincaid). The female samurai were generally not expected to participate in a battle, but archaeological findings support the indication that many of them did. One of the most famous female samurai, Nakano Takeko[7] (1847-1868), of the Aizu domain, initiated and led a female fighting unit, including her sister Yuko, in a battle during the Boshin War against the Imperial forces. It is said that she struck down several enemies with her *naginata* before she was shot dead (ibid.).

Warrior Women in the North of Westeros

Further north in Westeros, where conditions are harsher, it is more sensible to train women in self-defence, respectively in defending their home and children, in the men's absence. This is particularly important on Bear Island, which is often raided by the iron-born and the free folk (wildlings) alike, as Lady Maege Mormont explains to Catelyn Stark:

"We have needed to be [warriors]. In olden days the ironmen would come raiding in their longboats, or wildlings… The men would be off fishing, like as not. The wives they left behind had to defend themselves and their children, or else be carried off" (Martin, *Storm* 630). Eddard "Ned" Stark, supports his youngest daughter, Arya, in her tomboyish pursuits, by hiring a formidable Braavosi sword fighter to give her sword fighting lessons (cf. Martin, *Game* 224f.). As Arya faces peril and loss after her father's arrest and execution, she even embarks on an anti-hero character arc in her quest for vengeance, cemented in her list of people she wants to kill: "Every night Arya would say their names…, her names were the only prayer she cared to remember" (Martin *Clash* 418).

Women in early medieval Scandinavian societies faced similar situations as the women of the North of Westeros, particularly when their men were on Viking expeditions. It must have been vital for them to be able to defend their own lives, their children's lives and their homes against raiders. This theory has been corroborated by archaeologists finding individual women buried with weapons. However, archaeologists found a remarkable grave in the Swedish Viking Age town of Birka in 2017. The skeleton found in this grave has been identified as being female. This woman was buried with "a sword, an axe, a spear, armour-piercing arrows, a battle knife, two shields, and two horses, one mare and one stallion; thus, the complete equipment of a professional warrior"

---

7   The name is used here in the original Japanese style, with the family name in front of the first name.

(Hedenstierna-Jonson et al.). Moreover, included in her grave goods was "a full set of gaming pieces", suggesting "knowledge of tactics and strategy…, stressing the buried individual's role as a high-ranking officer" (ibid.). The status of Scandinavian women within society was, however, largely an inferior one (cf. Pruitt). Women were generally allocated to the domestic sphere and the duties of a housewife, but merchants' wives also participated in distributing their goods in the markets. Within the house, moreover, they were considered to be the managers in charge of everything, with a high degree of authority (ibid.). They also ran their husbands' enterprises on their own when their husbands died. 'Viking' women also accompanied their husbands to new settlements in other countries, like England, where the women were largely responsible for establishing these settlements. Furthermore, they enjoyed some legal freedoms, for example in terms of marriage. Even though their marriages were, for the most part, arranged ones, women had a vote in the choice of husband, and they had the opportunity to demand a divorce (ibid.).

Women warriors also feature in Norse mythology, like the character of Ladgertha, who has come to prominence again as a fictional figure in the popular TV series *Vikings*. The Norse/Germanic *Völsunga saga* may even provide a mythological parallel to Arya Stark with the character of Brynhildr, insofar as Brynhildr asserts her independence and takes revenge for the wrongs committed against her (cf. Schneidewind 113), as Arya does[8]. Consequently, Martin's northern women have counterparts both in Norse mythology and history.

The *Spearwives* of the Free Folk

Further north in Westeros, beyond the Wall, conditions are even harsher, and the daily struggle for existence makes it, consequently, more necessary for every woman to be able to defend herself and her home. Women also need to be able to hunt, since agriculture is not possible in the lands north of the Wall. They are not obliged to fight, but when they do, they are respected as equals (cf. Martin, *Concerning*). Women who fight not only in self-defence, but also as part of the 'army' of the free folk, are called 'spearwives', like Jon Snow's former lover Ygritte. It is telling that the one wildling who is most despised and shunned by all the other free folk, Craster, treats his 'wives' most cruelly. He keeps his 'wives', who consist of his own daughters, as his slaves, rapes them probably from a very early age on, forces them to bear his children, and makes them completely dependent on his 'protection' (cf. Martin, *Clash* 355ff.). The

---

8   It is, furthermore, possible that Brynhildr is based on an historical character as well, namely Brunichildis/Brunhilda, a West Gothic princess and queen of the Merovingians by marriage (ibid.).

other women of the free folk, however, are not only capable warriors, but claim sexual freedom for themselves. When a man wants to 'steal' a woman, as is customary, the woman is expected to put up a fight, so that the man needs to prove his strength (cf. Martin, *Storm* 208; 355; 558f.). The women of the free folk, furthermore, are completely free to use birth control (ibid. 208). This rather egalitarian society structure of the free folk sets them apart from most of the rest of Westeros, except Dorne. It is to be noted that both the most northern and the most southern region in Westeros have a more egalitarian approach to the gender question. The Dornish culture was influenced in that respect by the Rhoynish warrior princess Nymeria, who brought her subjects to Dorne. Through a political marriage with Mors Martell she gained power, and introduced Rhoynish customs to Dorne, such as a rule of primogeniture regardless of gender. This means that, as a rule, the firstborn child, male or female, is heir to the principality of Dorne. In addition to this, Dornish women enjoy a similar sexual freedom as the women of the free folk (cf. Martin, García Jr., Antonsson 240ff.) Occasionally, there are warrior women to be found as well, like Obara Sand, one of the illegitimate daughters of Oberyn Martell (cf. Martin, *Feast* 43).

The "real" Amazons: the Warrior Women of the Scythian/Sarmatian Tribes

One possible historical model for the 'spearwives' are the warrior women from the ancient nomadic tribes of Eurasian origin, particularly the Scythian tribes, which might also have served as a model for the Amazons of Greek mythology. According to Herodotus, the 'Amazons' emigrated at one point into what was known to be Scythian territory, to unite with them and form the tribe of the Sarmatians (cf. Rolle, Geschichte 102). From the time of the Persian wars onwards, the Amazons of mythology were depicted in artwork wearing Scythian clothes (cf. Krauskopf 40). Archaeologic findings in barrows, known as *kurgans*, in the steppes of the Ukraine/Southern Russia, such as the well-documented excavation by the archaeologists Jeannine Davis-Kimball and Leonid Jablonskij, have brought to light numerous women being buried with a vast variety of weapons, for instance: bows and arrows, hunting knives, short lances, javelins, battle axes, slings, and a device similar to the Argentinian *bola* (cf. Rolle, *Bewaffnung* 154f.). It would have made sense for the women in these nomadic tribes, who also lived under extremely harsh conditions, to be expected to defend not only themselves but their herds as well, on which the tribe depended. As for a general kind of equality within these tribes, like the freedom enjoyed by Martin's wildling women, there are scholars who think it is likely that the women of the Scythians and Sarmatians enjoyed a relatively high status: Sergey Makhortykh speaks of an equal position ("gleichgestellte[n]

Position", Makhortykh 145), corroborated by other researches (ibid.). Renate Rolle, in agreement with Vera Kovalevskaja, assumes that the lifestyle and economy particular to the Eurasian nomads and their dependence on cattle allowed for a different evolution of the women's position (cf. Rolle, *Bewaffnung* 159).

A Feminist Warrior Woman?

As we have seen, both Westeros and real-world history provide a variety of warrior women, and not even all of those available to us, both in G.R.R. Martin's and in our world, have been mentioned here. However, it seems that all of these warrior women claim their independence merely for themselves, apart from the free folk and the Northern women, who see the necessity to make all women strong. In the case of the free folk, women's independence goes even further, and Ygritte openly compares and favours the egalitarian status of her kind with the relatively oppressive situation of women south of the Wall: "I'd sooner be stolen by a strong man than be given t' some weakling by my father" (Martin, *Storm* 558f.). But for the most part, none of the Westerosi women strive to improve the women's situation in general, not even the few tomboyish/'mannish' girls and women, like Arya Stark and Brienne of Tarth, who see how unfair gender boundaries are. At least Daenerys Targaryen considers the sexual exploitation of girls and women by rape and selling them into prostitution to be unacceptable, even before she decides to abolish slavery in Essos in general by conquest (cf. Martin, *Game* 667ff.). It can furthermore be argued that Brienne's intention to bury three tavern prostitutes, who were hanged by Stark men, displays some sort of solidarity on Brienne's part (cf. Martin, *Storm* 27). Apart from that, there are, apparently, no open feminists in Martin's world. Feminism in a medieval setting would not be unrealistic, however. Christine de Pizan's (1364-c.1430) writings, particularly her most famous work, *The Book of the City of Ladies*, provided a major contribution to the emerging *Querelle des femmes* (the 'woman question'), making a strong case in women's favour: "Those men who have attacked women out of jealousy are those wicked ones who have seen and realized that many women have greater understanding... than they themselves, and thus they are pained and disdainful" (Pizan, translated by Richards 19).[9]

Real-world history, in fact, presents fighting women, who promoted feminism and gender equality. In European history, the women fighting in and for the French Revolution, 1789-1799, demanded equality with men in all things; they

---

9   However, it is also possible to question some of Christine de Pizan's ideas from a modern feminist perspective, for instance her claim that wives should not resent being subject to their husbands (ibid. 255).

demanded equal civic rights, and they handed in several petitions to be allowed to bear arms and to fight in the army. Women were conscious of the right to bear arms to be a male privilege, and of the nobility in general (cf. Grubitzsch 245). The more the Revolution became a war, the more women, like Pauline Léon in the name of 315 women, petitioned the *Assemblée Nationale* to allow them to defend their homes, their home country and the Revolution (cf. Grubitzsch 246). Anne-Josèphe Terwagne, known as Théroigne de Méricourt, specifically linked the right of women to bear arms with their liberation in general (ibid.).

In Chinese history, there is another warrior woman with a distinct feminist agenda: Qiu Jin[10] (1875-1907) was a poet, a revolutionary fighter and a feminist. As a girl and a young woman, she was subjected to the patriarchal practices of her country, in the shape of the mutilating custom of binding girls' feet and an oppressive marriage. Ultimately, she left her husband and her children to study in Japan. She trained in martial arts, liked to dress like Western men and joined a revolutionary group in opposition to the Qing dynasty (cf. Ashby & Gore Ohrn 181). Qiu Jin was aware of women's oppression and promoted women's rights, particularly freedom of education, freedom to marry by choice, and the abolishment of foot binding (cf. Dooling 52). She was headmistress of a girls' school, where she taught martial arts. After a failed uprising against the Qing dynasty, in which Qiu Jin was implicated by the authorities, she was executed by beheading.

As this paper has shown, the warrior women in the world G.R.R. Martin has created contribute to the question of gender in his works, and not merely represent a common fantasy archetype. The acceptance of women bearing arms and fighting are interconnected with the gender boundaries imposed on women (and men) in general. In certain regions in Westeros, the North, the lands beyond the wall, and in Dorne, fighting women are more accepted by society, and the gender roles in general are, in varying degrees, more permeable than in the other regions. Both among the free folk and the Dornish a distinct sexual liberty is to be found as well. In the rest of Westeros, women like Brienne are subjected to derision and hostility.

In real world history, there are some examples of a similar corresponding connection, as the Scythian tribes seem to suggest, at least according to some scholars, or the Scandinavian women of the Viking Age. Other examples indicate, however, that the need for women to defend themselves and their homes and families do not necessarily correspond with a general egalitarian status, as, for example, Japanese society shows. In medieval and (Early) Modern Europe, noblewomen in charge of castles and fortresses were expected to defend them, and had generally opportunities to assert their power to a certain extent, like

---

10 The name is used in the original Chinese style, with the family name, Qiu, in front of the first name.

Caterina Sforza. They were, nevertheless, walking a tightrope, because gender expectations placed them on a lower step, and assertive women like Caterina Sforza could become objects of ridicule and hostility, because they overstepped gender boundaries too much.

What Martin's stories might lack are (warrior) women with an awareness of gender inequality in general, and a subsequent endeavour to alter this situation. As the examples mentioned above have shown, there was an idea of feminism in the Middle Ages, and in later centuries women took up arms and learnt martial arts to fight for gender equality. Qiu Jin challenged misogynists in one of her poems: "Don't tell me women are not the stuff of heroes" (Qiu, translated by Chartkoff).

Bibliography

Ashby, Ruth & Deborah Gore Ohrn. *Herstory: women who changed the world.* New York: Viking Press, 1995

Dooling, Amy D. *Women's literary feminism in twentieth-century China.* New York: Palgrave Macmillan, 2005

Fraser, Antonia. *The Warrior Queens. The Legends and the Lives of the Women Who Have Led Their Nations in War.* New York: Vintage Books, 1990

García Jr., Elio M. "Warrior Women". In: *A Wiki of Ice and Fire*, 29.6.2016, http://awoiaf.westeros.org/index.php/Warrior_women (accessed 19.2.2018)

Grubitzsch, Helga. "Mit Piken, Säbeln und Pistolen… 'Amazonen' der Französischen Revolution". In: *Amazonen. Geheimnisvolle Kriegerinnen*. Ed. Historisches Museum der Pfalz. Speyer: Edition Minerva, 2010. 243-249

Guxens, Adrià. "George R.R. Martin: 'Trying to please everyone is a horrible mistake'". In: *Adria's News*, 7.12.2012, http://www.adriasnews.com/2012/10/george-r-r-martin-interview.html (accessed 19.2.2018)

Hedenstierna-Jonson, Charlotte, Anna Kjellström et al. "A female Viking warrior confirmed by genomics". In: *Wiley Online Library*, 8.9.2017, http://onlinelibrary.wiley.com/doi/10.1002/ajpa.23308/full (accessed 19.2.2018)

Hoffman, Michael. "Women Warriors of Japan". In: *Japan Times*, 9.10.2011, https://www.japantimes.co.jp/life/2011/10/09/general/women-warriors-of-japan/#.WTy8Z9gzrWc (accessed 19.2.2018)

Johnson, Ben. "Black Agnes". In: *Historic UK*, http://www.historic-uk.com/HistoryUK/HistoryofScotland/Black-Agnes (accessed 19.2.2018)

Kincaid, Chris. "Gender Roles of Women in Modern Japan". In: *Japan Powered*, 22.6.2014, https://www.japanpowered.com/japan-culture/gender-roles-women-modern-japan (accessed 19.2.2018)

Krauskopf, Ingrid. "Griechisch, skythisch, orientalisch – Das Amazonenbild in der antiken Kunst". In: *Amazonen. Geheimnisvolle Kriegerinnen*. Ed. Historisches Museum der Pfalz. Speyer: Edition Minerva, 2010. 38-47

Kupers, Terry. "Toxic masculinity as a barrier to mental health treatment in prison". In: *Journal of Clinical Psychology* 61 (2005): 713-724

Lev, Elizabeth. *The Tigress of Forli*. Boston: Houghton Mifflin Harcourt, 2011

Makhortykh, Sergey. "Die Frauen in der skythischen Gesellschaft". In: *Amazonen. Geheimnisvolle Kriegerinnen*. Ed. Historisches Museum der Pfalz. Speyer: Edition Minerva, 2010. 145-149

Martin, George R.R. *A Game of Thrones*. New York: Bantam Books, 2011

--. *A Clash of Kings*. New York: Bantam Books, 2011

---. *A Storm of Swords*. New York: Bantam Books, 2011

---. *A Feast for Crows*. New York: Bantam Books, 2011

Martin, George R.R., Elio M. García Jr., and Linda Antonsson. *The World of Ice and Fire. The Untold History of Westeros and the Game of Thrones*. London: HarperVoyager, 2014

Martin, George R.R. "So Spake Martin: Concerning Wildling women". In: *Westeros*, 3.6.2003, http://www.westeros.org/Citadel/SSM/Category/C91/P30 (accessed 19.2.2018)

de Pizan, Christine. *The Book of the City of Ladies*. Transl.: Earl Jeffery Richards. New York: Persea Books, 1982

Pruitt, Sarah. "What Was Life Like for Women in the Viking Age?". *History*, 18.11.2016, http://www.history.com/news/what-was-life-like-for-women-in-the-viking-age (accessed 19.2.2018)

Qiu, Jin. "Capping Rhymes with Sir Ishii From Sun's Root Land". Transl.: Zachary Jean Chartkoff. In: *Voices Education*, 8.12.2010, http://voiceseducation.org/content/qiu-jin (accessed 19.2.2018)

Rolle, Renate. "Zur skythischen Geschichte und Kultur". In: *Amazonen. Geheimnisvolle Kriegerinnen*. Ed. Historisches Museum der Pfalz. Speyer: Edition Minerva, 2010. 98-103

---. "Bewaffnung und mögliche Kampfweise skythischer Kriegerinnen". In: *Amazonen. Geheimnisvolle Kriegerinnen*. Ed. Historisches Museum der Pfalz. Speyer: Edition Minerva, 2010. 153-159

Salter, Jessica. "Game of Thrones's George RR Martin: 'I'm a feminist at heart'". In: *The Telegraph*, 1.4.2013, http://www.telegraph.co.uk/women/womens-life/9959063/ Game-of-Throness-George-RR-Martin-Im-a-feminist.html (accessed 19.2.2018)

Schabert, Ina. *Englische Literaturgeschichte. Eine neue Darstellung aus der Sicht der Geschlechterforschung*. Stuttgart: Kröner Verlag, 1997

Schad, Martha. *Frauen, die die Welt bewegten. Geniale Frauen, der Vergangenheit entrissen*. Augsburg: Pattloch Verlag, 1997

Schneidewind, Friedhelm. *Das neue große Tolkien-Lexikon*. St. Ingbert: Conte Verlag, 2016

Velde, François. "Women Knights in the Middle Ages". In: *Heraldica*, 21.10.2005, http://www.heraldica.org/topics/orders/wom-kn.htm (accessed 19.2.2018)

Romantische Weltgestaltung in H. P. Lovecrafts Werk

Julian T. M. Eilmann (Jülich)

Einleitung

H.P. Lovecraft (1890-1937) ist heute vor allem als Autor kosmischen Schreckens bekannt. In seinen Erzählungen wimmelt es von schrecklichen Ungeheuern und gottgleichen Wesen aus den Tiefen von Zeit und Raum, die die Welt ins Chaos stürzen (wollen). Die Protagonisten der Geschichten sind zwar zumeist Rationalisten und Wissenschaftler, aber auch sie müssen am Ende die Abgründe der Existenz erkennen und verfallen nicht selten dem Wahnsinn. Angesichts dieser destruktiv-nihilistischen Weltanschauung, wie sie in Lovecrafts Texten zum Ausdruck kommt, fällt es auf den ersten Blick schwer, hier romantische Motive zu erkennen, verbindet man mit Romantik doch Aspekte wie Sehnsucht, Märchen, Liebe sowie nicht zuletzt Ironie und Humor. Auch die Forschung sieht Lovecraft überwiegend nicht als Romantiker. Ganz im Gegenteil wird vor allem seine rationalistisch-materialistische und anti-spirituelle Denkart hervorgehoben, wie exemplarisch die folgende Charakterisierung Dirk W. Mosigs illustriert:

> Lovecraft war ein »mechanistischer Materialist« im philosophischen Sinne des Wortes, dem jeder dualistische Glaube an die Religion oder das Übernatürliche abging. Er besaß einen hellwachen wissenschaftlichen Verstand… und erfasste deutlich die abgrundtiefe Bedeutungslosigkeit und Sinnlosigkeit in dem ungeheuren mechanistischen und zwecklosen Kosmos, der von blinden, unpersönlichen (»gedankenlosen«) Kräften regiert wird.   (163)

Im Folgenden soll dennoch der Versuch unternommen werden, einige romantische Motive in Lovecrafts Werk aufzuzeigen, denn bei näherer Beschäftigung wird auffallen, dass in der Tat wesentliche Elemente der romantischen Weltanschauung Lovecrafts literarische Weltenschöpfung prägen. Für den vorliegenden Artikel habe ich romantische Elemente in zahlreichen Texten Lovecrafts untersucht, u. a. in den beiden Schlüsseltexten *Call of Cthulhu* und *At the Mountains of Madness*. Auch wenn es reizvoll wäre, die romantischen Spuren in diesen beiden Horrorerzählungen zu verfolgen, so soll stattdessen eine weniger bekannte Geschichte betrachtet werden: *The Silver Key* aus Lovecrafts Traumlande-Zyklus, da die romantischen Motive hier besonders deutlich

zutage treten. Möglichweise kann in einem zukünftigen *Hither-Shore*-Artikel
die Untersuchung der beiden anderen Texte nachgereicht werden. Angesichts
der notwendigen Kürze des vorliegenden Aufsatzes können viele Aspekte nur
in ihren Grundzügen dargestellt werden.

Lovecraft und die romantische Tradition

Wenn wir romantische Elemente in Lovecrafts Werk nachweisen wollen,
müssen wir natürlich zuerst erläutern, was wir unter »Romantik« verstehen. Angesichts eines derart schillernden Begriffs, der noch dazu in der
modernen Alltagssprache (vereinfacht und verfremdet) verwendet wird, ist
dieses Vorgehen essentiell. Hier stütze ich mich auf die Romantikdefinition
meiner Studie zu Tolkien als Romantiker (vgl. Eilmann 53-75): Wesentlich ist
die romantische Sehnsucht nach dem Übernatürlichen und Phantastischen,
was von den romantischen Autoren jeweils unterschiedlich bezeichnet wird.
Repräsentativ erscheint mir folgende Charakterisierung der romantischen Sehnsucht aus der Feder des romantischen Dichters Ludwig Uhland (1787–1862):

> Das Unendliche umgibt den Menschen, das Geheimnis der Gott-
> heit und der Welt. Was er selbst war, ist und sein wird, ist ihm
> verhüllt. Süß und fruchtbar sind diese Geheimnisse… Der Geist
> des Menschen aber, wohl fühlend, daß er nie das Unendliche in
> voller Klarheit in sich auffassen wird und müde des unbestimm-
> ten Verlangens, knüpft bald seine Sehnsucht an irdische Bilder,
> in denen ihm doch ein Blick des Überirdischen aufzudämmern
> scheint… Dies Ahnen des Unendlichen in den Anschauungen ist
> das Romantische.   (344f.)

Uhland schildert hier die typische romantische Sehnsucht. So fühlt der Romantiker, dass ihn ein Zauber umgibt, der nur darauf wartet, geweckt zu werden,
auf dass die Welt wieder in ihren magischen Urzustand versetzt werde. Eben
diese Sehnsucht nach einer Wiederverzauberung der Welt findet sich auch in
dem bekannten Gedicht *Wünschelrute* von Joseph v. Eichendorff, in dem sich der
romantische Gedankengang mit großer Klarheit und poetischer Kraft artikuliert:

> Schläft ein Lied in allen Dingen
> Die da träumen fort und fort
> Und die Welt hebt an zu singen
> Triffst du nur das Zauberwort.   (121)

Das Übernatürliche im Alltäglichen sichtbar zu machen, ist ein Verwandlungsprozess, den der romantische Dichter Novalis als Prinzip der Romantisierung bezeichnet:

> Die Welt muß romantisirt werden. So findet man den urspr[ünglichen] Sinn wieder… Indem ich dem Gemeinen einen hohen Sinn, dem Gewöhnlichen ein geheimnißvolles Ansehn, dem Bekannten die Würde des Unbekannten, dem Endlichen einen unendlichen Schein gebe, so romantisire ich es.   (334)

Wir werden sehen, dass auch Lovecraft ausgiebig von diesem Verfahren Gebrauch macht. Die Begegnung mit dem Übernatürlichen muss allerdings für den Romantiker nicht immer beglückend sein. Denn neben dem Wunderbaren steht gleichermaßen das Unheimliche als Kehrseite desselben Phänomens. Und so wie die Begegnung mit dem Wunderbaren beim Individuum Staunen, Hinwendung, Faszination, Rührung oder Sehnsucht hervorrufen kann, so reagiert es auf das Unheimliche gemeinhin mit Angst, Abwendung, Ekel/Abstoßung, Flucht und Verdrängung. Die Romantik hat bekanntlich großes Interesse am Unheimlichen gehegt, der Schauerliteratur (*gothic novel*) neuen Auftrieb gegeben und als so genannte »Schwarze Romantik« zur Etablierung der modernen Horrorliteratur beigetragen. Bis heute übt das Unheimliche auf viele Leser einen großen Reiz aus und eben diese Faszination für das Übernatürliche steht in romantischer Tradition. Lovecraft war sich dieser romantischen Tradition, in der er sich als Horrorautor befand, in hohem Maße bewusst und reflektiert die (romantische) Anziehungskraft des Unheimlichen in seinem Essay »Supernatural Horror in Literature«, auf den wir weiter unten genauer eingehen werden. Werfen wir zuvor einen Blick auf eine Passage aus einem Brief Lovecrafts an August Derleth aus dem Januar 1930. Hier schildert Lovecraft eine bestimmte Mentalität und Wirklichkeitswahrnehmung, die wir als romantisch bezeichnen können:

> Was meine Träume seit vierzig Jahren heimgesucht hat, ist ein Gefühl abenteuerlicher Erwartung, verbunden mit Landschaften, Architektur, und den Erscheinungsweisen des Himmels. Ich kann mich selbst als Kind von 2 1/2 Jahren auf der Eisenbahnbrücke von Auburndale, Mass. sehen, wie ich hinab auf die Geschäftsbezirke der Stadt schaue und dabei das Bevorstehen eines Wunders fühle, das ich weder vollständig beschreiben noch mir vorstellen konnte – und es gab keine Stunde meines späteren Lebens, in der verwandte Empfindungen gefehlt hätten. Ich wünschte, ich könnte meine Idee zu Papier bringen – das Gefühl des Erstaunens, der Befriedigung, die sich in obskuren Dimensionen verbergen und die nur in seltenen Augenblicken auf problematische Weise er-

reicht werden können durch das Erblicken alter Straßen, weit über Meilen seltsamen hügligen Landes, endlose Marmorstufen hinauf, die in Terrassen mit Balustraden enden. Merkwürdige Gedanken, die einen größeren Dichter als mich bräuchten, um ästhetisch effektiv umgesetzt werden zu können. (zit. n. Frenschkowski 95)

Romantisch ist an der hier geschilderten Sichtweise das Gefühl »abenteuerlicher Erwartung«, das die Betrachtung bestimmter Orte und Landschaften beim Subjekt auslöst. Wenn Lovecraft sehnsuchtsvoll auf die eigentlich prosaischen »Geschäftsbezirke der Stadt« hinunterblick und dabei das »Bevorstehen eines Wunders« erwartet, dann weist dies eine große Nähe zu Uhlands »Ahnen des Unendlichen in den Anschauungen« auf. Es ist jene romantische Stimmung, dass den Dingen ein übernatürliches Geheimnis innewohnt, die geweckt werden will. Eichendorffs schlafendes Lied kommt uns in den Sinn. Wichtig ist, dass Lovecraft dies im Jahre 1930 als Erwachsener nur sieben Jahr vor seinem Tod betont. Es handelt sich also um ein Gefühl, das ihn sein ganzes Leben lang nicht mehr losließ, wie er auch selbst feststellt (s. o.). Der Romantiker Lovecraft schildert denn auch typische Szenerien, die eine schauerlich-romantische Atmosphäre besitzen und die den Romantiker ›magisch anziehen‹: »das Erblicken alter Straßen, weit über Meilen seltsamen hügligen Landes, endlose Marmorstufen hinauf, die in Terrassen mit Balustraden enden«. Eben solche Szenen finden wir in Lovecrafts Texten wieder, wie wir am Beispiel von *The Silver Key* weiter unten sehen.

Ein Schlüsseltext für das Verständnis von Lovecraft als Romantiker ist sein Essay »Supernatural Horror in Literature«. Darin charakterisiert er den Leser von Horrorliteratur mit Eigenschaften, die in den Texten der Romantik auch den romantischen Individuen zugeschrieben werden: »[This reader has] a certain degree of imagination and a capacity for detachment from every-day life. Relatively few are free enough from the spell of the daily routine to respond to rappings from outside«[1]. Eine ausgeprägte Phantasiebegabung, die Fähigkeit zur (inneren) Distanzierung von der Alltagswelt und gleichermaßen eine Sensibilisierung für Offenbarungen des Übernatürlichen sind genuin romantische Eigenschaften, die der romantische Theologe Friedrich Schleiermacher (1768-1834) als »Sinn und Geschmack fürs Unendliche« (242) bezeichnet. Und hiermit unterscheiden sich die Leidenschaften der romantischen Horrorleser auch vom banalen »taste of the majority«, den Lovecraft geringschätzt. Der Reiz der Horrorliteratur besteht für Lovecraft in der Begegnung mit dem Unbekannten und Übernatürlichen; auch hier bewegt er sich auf den Pfaden der

---

1 Alle folgenden Zitate aus »Supernatural Horror in Literature« entstammen der Online-Fassung des Aufsatzes, hg. von. S.T. Joshi u. David E. Schultz: http://www.hplovecraft.com/writings/texts/essays/shil.aspx [letzter Zugriff 14.4.2018].

typisch romantischen Denkweise. Er leitet dies psychologisch aus der Jugendzeit des Menschengeschlechts her, als das Individuum sich einer Welt gegenüber-sah, die offenbar von übermächtigen Kräften regiert wurde: »The unknown... became for our primitive forefathers a terrible and omnipotent source of boons and calamities visited upon mankind for cryptic and wholly extra-terrestrial reasons, and thus clearly belonging to spheres of existence whereof we know nothing and wherein we have no part.« Auch wenn der Reiz des Unbekann-ten demnach so alt wie die Menschheit ist, so sei der Mensch doch auch im wissenschaftlichen Zeitalter noch von zahlreichen Mysterien und Wundern umgeben: »For though the area of the unknown has been steadily contracting for thousands of years, an infinite reservoir of mystery still engulfs most of the outer cosmos, whilst a vast residuum of powerful inherited associations clings around all the objects and processes that were once mysterious, however well they may now be explained.«

Die Tiefen von Zeit und Raum sind auch in der Moderne kaum erschlossen und bilden weiterhin »an infinite reservoir of mystery«. Mit großem Selbst-bewusstsein adelt Lovecraft die Horrorliteratur weiter, wenn er sie mit der Religion auf eine Stufe stellt. Während Letztere sich dem Wunderbaren zu-gewandt habe, sei es die Aufgabe der Horrorliteratur, sich den dunklen Seiten des kosmischen Mysteriums zu widmen: »Because our feelings toward the beneficent aspects of the unknown have from the first been captured and for-malised by conventional religious rituals, it has fallen to the lot of the darker and more maleficent side of cosmic mystery to figure chiefly in our popular supernatural folklore.« Angesichts der für den Menschen psychologisch so notwendigen Auseinandersetzung mit allen Aspekten des Übernatürlichen zieht Lovecraft das selbstbewusste Fazit: »With this foundation, no one need wonder at the existence of a literature of cosmic fear. It has always existed, and always will exist.« Die Qualität einer gelungenen Horrogeschichte bemisst sich für Lovecraft an folgenden Aspekten: »whether or not there be excited in the reader a profound sense of dread, and of contact with unknown spheres and powers; a subtle attitude of awed listening, as if for the beating of black wings or the scratching of outside shapes and entities on the known universe's utmost rim.« Auch dies steht in der romantischen Tradition, nicht nur in der allge-meinen Faszination für das Unbekannte. Vielmehr erinnert das ehrfurchtsvolle Lauschen auf Entitäten am Rande des Wahrnehmbaren an die romantische Sensibilität für das auf Erweckung wartende Wunder. Dass Lovecraft in sei-nen besten Geschichten dem Leser eben eine solche romantische Ahnung des Numinosen ermöglicht, stellt auch Frenschkowski fest: »Wo der Leser durch sie [Lovecrafts Geschichten] hindurch der rätselhaften Tiefe des Ozeans oder der Fremdartigkeit des Weltraums imaginativ ansichtig wird, gelingt Lovecraft die Evokation des Erhabenen und Unheimlichen« (60). Und er präzisiert, dass

Lovecrafts Erzählkunst darin besteht, die Wunder und Abgründe des Kosmos im Alltäglichen sichtbar zu machen:

> Die eigentliche schriftstellerische Begabung Lovecrafts liegt darin, das *Nahe* (vor allem die ihm vertrauten Städte Neuenglands) zum Träger des *Fernen* und *Fremden* zu machen. Vor seiner Haustür suggeriert Lovecraft dem Leser… erstaunlichere und erschreckendere Plätze als geringere Schriftsteller im Dschungel Afrikas, in der Karibik oder auf Mars und Venus.   (83)

Nach dem bisher Gesagten dürfte deutlich sein, dass es sich bei diesem Verfahren, das uns das Nahe fern oder fremd macht, um das Prinzip der Romantisierung handelt (s. o.).

The Silver Key – eine romantische Erzählung

Überprüfen wir nun exemplarisch den Einsatz romantischer Motive in der Lovecraft-Erzählung *The Silver Key*. Denn in ihr kommen romantische Elemente ganz besonders stark zum Ausdruck. *The Silver Key* wurde 1926 in der Zeitschrift *Weird Tales* veröffentlicht und gehört zum so genannten Traumlande-Zyklus, in dem Figuren im Schlaf die titelgebenden phantastischen Orte bereisen und dort Abenteuer erleben. In Lovecrafts Gesamtwerk stechen diese Geschichten hervor, da die Begegnung mit dem Übernatürlichen für die menschlichen Protagonisten in den Traumlanden oftmals keine grauenhaften Schicksale (Tod oder Wahnsinn) bereithält und das Übernatürliche zwar unheimlich, aber auch in höchstem Maße anziehend erscheint. Die Traumlande haben somit insgesamt einen weniger starken Horrorcharakter, sondern erzeugen eine märchenhafte und – wie wir sehen werden – romantische Atmosphäre.

Die Hauptfigur in *The Silver Key* ist Randolph Carter, der in verschiedenen Lovecraft-Erzählungen auftaucht. Hier begegnet er uns als ein Romantiker, der als Kind und junger Mann der Alltagswelt durch nächtliche Reisen in die Welt der Wunder zu entkommen sucht, mit 30 Jahren jedoch den Zugang zur Traumwelt verliert. Mit eben dieser Schilderung der Lebensumstände beginnt die Erzählung:

> When Randolph Carter was thirty he lost the key of the gate of dreams. Prior to that time, he had made up for the prosiness of life by nightly excursions to strange and ancient cities beyond space, and lovely, unbelievable garden lands across ethereal seas; but as middle age hardened upon him, he felt these liberties slipping away little by little, until at last he was cut off altogether.   (428)

Die Reise zu fremden und fernen Städten, betörenden Gärten und ätherischen Meeren erscheint im Sinne des Wortes als eine traumhafte Möglichkeit für ein romantisches Subjekt. Mit großer Trauer denkt der auf die Alltagswelt zurückgeworfene Carter dementsprechend auch an die Begegnungen mit dem Geheimnisvollen und Phantastischen zurück: »No more could his galleys sail up the river Oukranos past the gilded spires of Thran, or his elephant caravans tramp through perfumed jungles in Kled, where forgotten palaces with veined ivory columns sleep lovely and unbroken under the moon« (ebd.). Die beiläufige Erwähnung von Orten wie Oukranos oder Kled, die dem Leser unbekannt sein dürften, verstärkt nur den romantischen Reiz, den die hier evozierten Orte auch auf diesen ausüben können. Bereits zu Beginn der Erzählung wird also auch unsere Sehnsucht nach dem Wunderbaren geweckt.

Die erste Hälfte der Erzählung wird bestimmt von Carters Auseinandersetzung mit seiner unbefriedigenden Situation als Romantiker. Es wird deutlich, dass die Einflüsse der rationalistisch-materialistisch orientierten Erwachsenenwelt für den Verlust seiner Traumfähigkeit – und damit der Auslebung seiner romantischen Ader – verantwortlich sind:

> He had read much of things as they are, and talked with too many people. Well-meaning philosophers had taught him to look into the logical relations of things, and analyse the processes which shaped his thoughts and fancies… Custom had dinned into his ears a superstitious reverence for that which tangibly and physically exists, and had made him secretly ashamed to dwell in visions. Wise men told him his simple fancies were inane and childish… (ebd.)

Hier wird ein spannungsvoller Gegensatz aufgebaut, der typisch für die romantische Weltsicht ist, denn natürlich sind es gerade die anerkannten Autoritäten der irdischen Welt (»well-meaning philosophers«; »wise men«), die sich irren, indem sie Carter auf die empirischen Fakten verweisen und seine Träume als kindischen Eskapismus verurteilen. Typisch romantisch müssten somit genau diese Philister ihre Weltsicht anpassen, denn gerade ihnen und nicht den Träumern fehlt das Verständnis für die Vielschichtigkeit des Kosmos. Carter versucht in der Folge, sich anzupassen und die Ratschläge anzunehmen, allerdings ohne Erfolg: »So Carter had tried to do as others did, and pretended that the common events and emotions of earthy minds were more important than the fantasies of rare and delicate souls. He did not dissent when they told him that the animal pain of a stuck pig… in real life is a greater thing than the peerless beauty of Narath with its hundred carven gates and domes…« (429). Der Romantiker, der sich der schlummernden Wunder bewusst ist, kann sich eben nicht mit dem Prosaischen zufriedengeben, vielmehr kommt die romantische Sehnsucht immer wieder zum Vorschein, wenn ihn die ästhetischen Erscheinungen unserer Welt an die überirdischen Wunder erinnern, die er nun verloren hat: »He walked impassive through the cities of men, and sighed because no vista seemed fully real; because every flash of yellow sunlight on tall roofs... served only to remind him of dreams he had once known, and to make him homesick for ethereal lands he no longer knew how to find« (431). Ähnlich der in Zweifel gezogenen Weisheit der Autoritäten kehrt sich auch hier die alltägliche Wahrnehmung um, denn das vermeintlich Reale wie die US-Ostküstenstädte erscheint Carter irreal (»no vista seemed fully real«).

Nachdem der Romantiker demnach den Zugang zum Wunderbaren verloren hat, auf das Alltägliche zurückgeworfen wird, obwohl ihn weiterhin übernatürliche Ahnungen plagen, wird er zum Décadent, der durch extreme Genüsse den verlorenen Zugang zum Phantastischen wiedergewinnen **möchte**:

> So, Carter bought stranger books and sought out deeper and more terrible men of fantastic erudition; delving into arcana of consciousness that few have trod, and learning things about the secret pits of life, legend, and immemorial antiquity which disturbed him ever afterward. He decided to live on a rarer plane, and furnished his Boston home to suit his changing moods; one room for each, hung in appropriate colours, furnished with befitting books and objects, and provided with sources of the proper sensations of light, heat, sound, taste, and odour.   (ebd.)

Zu dieser okkulten, ästhetizistischen anti-bürgerlichen Einstellung passt auch der zynische Humor, den Carter entwickelt und mit dem er der vermeintlichen Sinnlosigkeit und poetischen Armut des Alltags begegnet:

> Once in a while, though, he could not help seeing how shallow, fickle, and meaningless all human aspirations are, and how emptily our real impulses contrast with those pompous ideals we profess to hold. Then he would have recourse to the polite laughter they had taught him to use against the extravagance and artificiality of dreams; for he saw that the daily life of our world is every inch as extravagant and artificial, and far less worthy of respect because of its poverty in beauty and its silly reluctance to admit its own lack of reason and purpose. In this way he became a kind of humorist, for he did not see that even humour is empty in a mindless universe devoid of any true standard of consistency or inconsistency.   (429)

Glück erfährt der exzentrische Romantiker hierdurch jedoch nicht, im Gegenteil, sein Leben versinkt in Passivität und Lähmung, die lediglich von kurzen

Erinnerungen an die Traumlande unterbrochen werden. Selbst den Freitod zieht er als letzten Ausweg in Erwägung:

> But these horrors [occult studies] took him only to the edge of reality, and were not of the true dream country he had known in youth; so that at fifty he despaired of any rest or contentment in a world grown too busy for beauty and too shrewd for dreams. Having perceived at last the hollowness and futility of real things, Carter spent his days in retirement, and in wistful memories of his dream-filled youth. He thought it rather silly that he bothered to keep on living at all, and got from a South American acquaintance a very curious liquid to take him to oblivion without suffering. (432)

Carter ist am Tiefpunkt seiner Agonie angekommen. Die Rettung naht für ihn durch seinen Großvater, der ihm im Traum erscheint und ihn auf den titelgebenden silbernen Schlüssel verweist, den Carter anschließend findet und der ihm das visionäre Träumen wieder ermöglicht: »His dreams were meanwhile increasing in vividness… They were calling him back along the years, and… were pulling him toward some hidden and ancestral source« (433). Die Geschichte geht nun in den finalen dritten Teil über, in dem Carter sein Elternhaus aufsucht, »[to] go into the past and merge himself with old things« (ebd.).

Im Hinblick auf die Verwendung romantischer Motive ist insbesondere Carters Ankunft von großem Interesse, da Lovecraft hier auf zahlreiche Topoi der romantischen Landschaftsdarstellung zurückgreift. So erreicht Carter das Haus am frühen Abend, d. h. in der Zeit des Zwielichts. Die Zeit des Sonnenuntergangs wird in der romantischen Landschaftsdarstellung in Literatur und Malerei häufig verwendet, da dies eine Zeit ist, in der sich Gegensätze begegnen und ineinander übergehen (Tag/Nacht, Hell/Dunkel, Heute/Morgen, Subjekt/ Umwelt etc.). Das abendliche Zwielicht eignet sich somit in hohem Maße als Stimmungselement für Situationen, in denen sich das Übernatürliche offenbaren kann. So auch im Falle Carters, vor dessen Augen sich die Landschaft im Abendlicht in eine romantische Szenerie ›verwandelt‹: »Afternoon was far gone when… he paused to scan the outspread countryside golden and glorified in the slanting floods of magic poured out by a western sun. All the strangeness and expectancy of his recent dreams seemed present in this hushed and unearthly landscape« (434). Die verzauberte Landschaft ist in ein geheimnisvolles Zwielicht getaucht, in dem sich Carters Traumerfahrungen spiegeln können: »Shadows thickened around him, for the night was near. Once a gap in the trees opened up to the right, so that he saw off across leagues of twilight meadow… pink with the last flush of day, the panes of the little round windows blazing with reflected fire« (ebd.). Die romantische Verschmelzung der Gegensätze findet im Falle Carters auch in einem ganz unmittelbaren Sinne statt, denn an diesem Ort scheinen zuerst die Jugenderinnerungen des alten Carters Realität anzunehmen: »Then, when he was in deep shadow again, he recalled with a start that the glimpse must have come from childish memory alone, since the old white church had long been torn down to make room for the Congregational Hospital« (ebd.). Anschließend verschwimmen die Grenzen zwischen Erwachsenem und Kind noch stärker und wir haben den Eindruck, dass es nun der kindliche Carter ist, von dem uns der Erzähler berichtet:

> Randolph Carter stopped in the pitch darkness and rubbed his hand across his eyes. Something was queer. He had been somewhere he ought not to be; had strayed very far away to places where he had not belonged, and was now inexcusably late. …He was not sure he had his little telescope with him, and put his hand in his blouse pocket to see. No, it was not there, but there was the big silver key he had found in a box somewhere. Uncle Chris had told him something odd once about an old unopened box with a key in it, but Aunt Martha had stopped the story abruptly, saying it was no kind of thing to tell a child whose head was already too full of queer fancies.   (435)

Die Erzählung verweilt einige Abschnitte lang beim jungen Carter und berichtet von dessen kindlicher Sehnsucht nach dem Phantastischen, bis die Erzählung sich wieder dem Erwachsenen zuwendet, der nunmehr verschwunden sei: »Carter's relatives talk much of these things because he has lately disappeared« (437). Diese spannungsvolle Vermischung der Zeitebenen erscheint im Kontext der Romantik als ein reizvolles Spiel mit der Aufhebung der Gegensätze. Eben dies kommentiert auch der Erzähler zuletzt, der uns darauf hinweist, dass der alte Carter zwar als verschwunden gilt, er jedoch nicht an dessen Tod glaube – mit folgender Begründung: »There are twists of time and space, of vision and reality, which only a dreamer can divine; and from what I know of Carter I think he has merely found a way to traverse these mazes… He wanted the lands of dream he had lost, and yearned for the days of his childhood. Then he found a key, and I somehow believe he was able to use it to strange advantage« (ebd.). Hier wird noch einmal mit der Autorität des Erzählers bestätigt, dass ganz im romantischen Sinne verschiedene Zeiten, getrennte Räume sowie Traum und Realität nicht als absolute Gegensätze zu verstehen sind. Romantikern wie Carter gelingt eben das Kunststück, diese Grenzen aufzuheben und der Sehnsucht zu folgen und in die Traumwelt einzugehen. Literarisch löst Lovecraft dies auf eine für den Leser sehr spannende Weise, indem er Carter nicht mehr auftreten lässt, aber von Gerüchten spricht, die ihn in den Traumlanden verorten. Indem der Protagonist nun aus der Alltagssphäre verschwunden ist, der sich auch der Leser zugehörig fühlt, und an jene Orte entrückt wird, die dem Leser nur als verheißungsvolle Namen bekannt sind, wird auch dessen Sehnsucht geweckt, Carter ins Reich der Phantasie zu folgen:

> It is rumoured in Ulthar, beyond the river Skai, that a new king reigns on the opal throne in Ilek-Vad, that fabulous town of turrets atop the hollow cliffs of glass overlooking the twilight sea wherein the bearded and finny Gnorri build their singular labyrinths, and I believe I know how to interpret this rumour.   (438)

Die Betrachtung von *The Silver Key* macht deutlich, wie stark diese Erzählung klassische Topoi der romantischen Weltanschauung enthält. Letztlich handelt es sich um die typische Geschichte eines Romantikers, der zuerst einen Zugang zum Wunderbaren besitzt, diesen verliert und auf Abwege gerät, die ihn fast das Leben kosten, bis er zuletzt erneut Kontakt mit dem Übernatürlichen herstellen kann und sogar in das Reich der Poesie (Traumlande) überwechselt. Eine ähnlich geartete Handlung finden wir u. a. in E. T. A. Hoffmanns *Der Goldene Topf*, eine Erzählung, die dem Romantikkenner Lovecraft sicherlich bekannt sein dürfte. Wie einleitend erwähnt, finden sich romantische Motive auch in Lovecrafts Horrorgeschichten, wie in einem Folgeartikel gezeigt werden soll. All dies zusammen kann hoffentlich dazu beitragen, die vorherrschende Lesart Lovecrafts als Rationalist und Materialist zu relativieren. Durch diese Untersuchung wird hoffentlich auch Frenschkowskis Desiderat eingelöst: »Insofern interpretiert Lovecrafts Mythologie seine bewusste, atheistische und materialistische Philosophie nicht nur, sondern entgrenzt und relativiert sie auch (wie eine dekonstruktivistische Lektüre zeigen kann).« (96)

Bibliographie

Eichendorff, Joseph v. *Sämtliche Werke des Freiherrn Joseph von Eichendorff. Historisch-kritische Ausgabe.* Begr. v. Wilhelm Kosch & August Sauer. Hg. Hermann Kunisch, Helmut Koopmann u. a. Bd. I.1. Stuttgart: Max Niemeyer, 1993ff.

Eilmann, Julian. *J.R.R. Tolkien – Romantiker und Lyriker.* Essen: Oldib Verlag, 2016

Frenschkowski, Marco. »H.P. Lovecraft. Ein kosmischer Regionalschriftsteller«. In: *H.P. Lovecrafts kosmisches Grauen.* Hg. Franz Rottensteiner. Frankfurt a. M.: Suhrkamp, 1997. 60-104

Lovecraft, Howard Philips: »The Silver Key«. In: *The Complete Fiction of H.P. Lovecraft.* New York: Race Point Publishing, 2014. 428-438

---. »Supernatural Horror in Literature«. Hg. S.T. Joshi & David E. Schultz. http://www.hplovecraft.com/writings/texts/essays/shil.aspx [Letzter Zugriff 14.4.2018]

Mosig, Dirk W.: »H.P. Lovecraft – Mythenschöpfer«. In: *H.P. Lovecrafts kosmisches Grauen.* Hg. Franz Rottensteiner. Frankfurt a. M.: Suhrkamp, 1997. 162-173

Novalis. *Schriften. Die Werke Friedrich von Hardenbergs.* Hg. Paul Kluckhohn & Richard Samuel. Bd. 2. Hg. Richard Samuel, Hand-Joachim Mähl, Gerhard Schulz. Stuttgart, 1960

Schleiermacher, Friedrich Ernst Daniel. »Über die Religion. Reden an die Gebildeten unter ihren Verächtern«. In: *Schleiermachers Werke.* Hg. Otto Braun & Johannes Bauer. Bd. 4. Neudruck d. 2. Aufl. Leipzig: Scientia Verlag, 1967. 207-399

Uhland, Ludwig. »Über das Romantische«. *Ludwig Uhland. Dichtungen, Briefe, Reden.* Hg. Walter P.H. Scheffler. Stuttgart: J.F. Steinkopf Verlag, 1963

Die Welt der Deryni und ihre Entstehung

Friedhelm Schneidewind (Mannheim)

Die Romane und Geschichten von Katherine Kurtz um die zauberfähigen Deryni gelten als Höhepunkte der historischen Fantasy, ihre Autorin als eine der Erfinderinnen dieses Subgenres. In rund 20 Büchern geht es um den Konflikt von Kirche und Magie (oder zumindest magisch erscheinender Kräfte) und um Probleme, die es für Menschen mit »Besonderheiten« oder Auffälligkeiten in der Gesellschaft geben kann. Exemplarisch werden anhand dieser Problematik aber auch viele andere Aspekte behandelt. Obwohl die Geschichten in einer mittelalterlichen Welt spielen mit einer Art Magie, sind sie in vielen Punkten leicht übertragbar auf unsere Welt und sogar unsere Zeit – und das ist von der Autorin beabsichtigt und macht einen Teil des Reizes aus.

Da die Reihenfolge des Erscheinens der Deryni-Romane nicht mit dem darin beschriebenen historischen Ablauf übereinstimmt, habe ich sie im Literaturverzeichnis in der chronologischen Reihenfolge angegeben und diese auch in einer Zeitleiste dargestellt.

Die Autorin

Katherine Irene Kurtz wurde 1944 in Coral Gables (Florida) geboren. Sie hat einen akademischen Grad in Chemie (BS) und einen in englischer mittelalterlicher Geschichte (MA), studierte ein Jahr Medizin und ist ausgebildete Erikson-Hypnotiseurin. Mehrere Jahre arbeitete sie als technische Schreiberin für das Los Angeles Police Department. Sie lebt mit ihrem Ehemann Scott MacMillan seit 1986 in Irland.

Kurtz bezeichnet sich als Christin mit großer Affinität zu jener Spiritualität, die sie in den Deryni-Geschichten manchmal aufscheinen lasse (Kurtz, *Deryni-Tales*, 25). Nach eigenen Aussagen träumte Katherine Kurtz 1964 die Grundstory zur Deryni-Saga und machte daraus ein Jahr später eine Geschichte[1]. 1970 erschien der darauf basierende Roman *Deryni Rising*, der sofort zum Bestseller wurde; seither ist Kurtz freiberufliche Schriftstellerin. Es folgten bisher 16 Romane, mehrere Bücher mit Geschichten und Essays sowie mit dem *Codex Derynianus* eine Art Lexikon. Seit 1978 gibt Kurtz die *Deryni-Archives* heraus, eine Zeitschrift mit Storys von Fans; die ihrer Meinung nach besten versammelte sie 2002 in einer Anthologie. Ab und zu schreibt Kurtz auch andere

---

1   Am 16.10.1964, niedergeschrieben auf 2 Karteikarten, daraus wurde die Geschichte »The Lords of Sorandor«, veröffentlicht 1986 im Sammelband *The Deryni Archives* (dt. 1991: »Die Herren von Sorandor« in *Die Deryni-Archive*).

Fantasy-Romane und mit Deborah T. Harris gemeinsam den *Adept-Zyklus*, in dem sich Krimi und Fantasy mischen.

Natürlich will Kurtz mit ihren Romanen und Geschichten unterhalten, sie hofft aber auf mehr:

> I've always said that the first job of an author is to entertain, to tell a danged good story; but if I can also catalyze an eagerness to learn things that will help a person grow as an individual, that's even better, it's icing on the cake. When all is said and done, if I could be remembered for one thing, it would be that I made my readers think, and enjoy doing it, and that I left their lives richer than they would have been if they'd not read my work. I don't aim to change people's minds, but I do try to open them.
>
> (Kurtz, *Deryni-Tales* 6)

Dieser aufklärerische Ansatz wird schon in den ersten Romanen deutlich und von Buch zu Buch erkennbarer, auch werden im Subtext immer mehr Themenbereiche angesprochen, so etwa die Auseinandersetzung mit anderen Religionen und Lebensentwürfen, und das Plädoyer für Toleranz wird immer stärker. Dies alles, ohne dass Spannung oder Qualität leiden.

> I was brought up to judge people for who they were as individuals, not by their religion or the color of their skin or other superficial characteristics over which they had no control, but I was also aware that blanket discrimination was still very much with us. (If discrimination based on sexual preference existed when I was growing up, I was not aware of it, but it had become so by the time I was laying out the background of the Deryni; and thus, the Deryni also became a vehicle for talking about homosexual issues, as well as religious and racial ones.)   (Kurtz, *Deryni-Tales* 25)

In mindestens zwei Belangen erinnern Kurtz und ihr Werk an Tolkien und Mittelerde: Zwar erfindet Kurtz keine eigenen Sprachen, und ihr geografischer wie zeitlicher Horizont sind erheblich enger[2], aber die Welt der Deryni wird seit inzwischen fast 50 Jahren kontinuierlich ausgebaut, immer detaillierter ausgearbeitet und beschrieben. Wie Tolkien legt Kurtz Wert darauf, dass sie die Geschehnisse weniger erfinde als vielmehr erforsche (vgl. Kurtz, *Deryni-Archive*

---

2   Der beschriebene geografische Raum ist nicht viel größer als die Britischen Inseln, auch wenn vor allem in den neuesten Büchern weitere Gegenden angesprochen werden. Und auch wenn Kurtz' Zeitleiste (im *Codex Derynianus*) kurz vor Christi Geburt beginnt, spielen sich die Hauptereignisse zwischen 900 und 1130 ab.

9), und sogar ihre Sekundärliteratur wird in die Geschichte eingebaut, auch hierin Tolkien ähnlich oder auch Joanne K. Rowling mit den »Schulbüchern« von Harry Potter.[3] Durch Kurtz' großzügigen Umgang mit Fan-Fiction und die Zusammenarbeit mit vielen interessierten und kreativen Menschen gewinnt das Deryni-Universum darüber hinaus immer neue Aspekte und wird wohl noch auf Jahre hinaus Stoff für Geschichten liefern.

Die Geschichte(n) und die Geschichte hinter den Geschichten

Katherine Kurtz erzählt ihre Geschichten in einer unserem Mittelalter nachempfundenen Welt:

> Sie werden sie wahrscheinlich wenigstens etwas als vertraut emp-finden, weil Gwynedd und seine benachbarten Königreiche im groben Parallelen zu England, Wales und Schottland im zehnten, elften und zwölften Jahrhundert aufweisen, was die Kulturstufe, den technologischen und technischen Entwicklungsstand, die Vergleichbarkeit der gesellschaftlichen Struktur sowie den Einfluß einer mächtigen mittelalterlichen Kirche angeht, deren Tätigkeit in das Leben fast jedes Menschen hineinwirkt, ob von hoher oder niedriger Geburt. Der Hauptunterschied, abgesehen von historischen Persönlichkeiten und Örtlichkeiten, besteht darin, daß Magie funktioniert; die Deryni sind nämlich ein Geschlecht von Zauberern.   (Kurtz, *Deryni-Archive* 9)

Die Deryni zeichnen sich durch vererbbare besondere Kräfte aus, die je nach Auffassung als Magie, Zauberei oder gottgegeben bezeichnet und betrachtet werden. Von manchen werden die Deryni als besondere Menschen, als Rasse oder sogar als eigene Menschenart betrachtet, anders als alle anderen Menschen. Dies hat natürlich Konsequenzen für den Umgang mit ihnen und auch für die Einschätzung sogenannter »Halb-Deryni«.

Die Geschichte in dem Land, in dem später die elf Königreiche und viele andere kleine Reiche liegen, unterscheidet sich in den ersten Jahrhunderten nach Christus, so weit ersichtlich, nicht sonderlich von der Geschichte der

---

3   Kurtz' Lexikon *Codex Derynianus* wurde in seiner ersten Ausgabe (1998) angeblich 1126 fertiggestellt; um die Unterschiede zur zweiten Auflage von 2005 zu erklären, entspricht diese angeblich einer ergänzten Version von 1130 – dies wird in einem in der Welt der Deryni angesiedelten wissenschaftlichen Vorwort erläutert. Es gibt auch »wissenschaft-liche« und kunsthistorische Untersuchungen aus der Welt der Deryni aus unserer Zeit, etwa in den *Deryni-Tales*.

britischen Inseln in unserer Welt. Spätestens mit dem Auftauchen der Deryni im 3. Jahrhundert aber entwickelt sie sich anders. Im 9. Jahrhundert gibt es neben Gwynned, das von den nicht-derynischen Haldane-Königen beherrscht wird, mehrere andere Königreiche und kleinere unabhängige Länder mit Deryni-Herrschern und teils sehr unterschiedlichen Kulturen. So wird im Königreich Bremagne Französisch gesprochen, die Menschen von Meara erinnern an die schottischen Highlander. Das mächtigste Reich neben Gwynned ist Torenth, anders als Gwynned nicht von Rom christianisiert, sondern von Byzanz, und daher mit einer orthodoxen Kirche, deren Hochsprache Griechisch ist – und die bei aller Toleranz darauf achtet, dass sich in hohen Kirchenämtern nicht viele Deryni finden. Hier gibt es Minarette und Moscheen und leben Muslime sowie Menschen mit schwarzer Hautfarbe, als »Mohren« bezeichnet, die oft mit Krummschwertern kämpfen. Muslimische und schwarze Deryni bekleiden nicht selten hohe Ämter, etwa als Botschafter, oder beherrschen gar ihre eigenen Länder, so der Emir von Nur Hallay und der Khan von R'Kassi. Wie der Paddischah von Torenth werden sie gemeinhin als Könige bezeichnet. In den Ländern, in denen die (weißen oder schwarzen) Muslime die herrschende Schicht stellen, leben Muslime und Christen, Schwarze und Weiße, Deryni und Nicht-Deryni friedlich zusammen – die »Mohrenkriege« sind Jahrhunderte her. Es gibt berühmte Akademien, in denen Deryni geschult werden. Besonders die Heilkräfte der Deryni werden geschätzt – und diese nutzen keineswegs nur den Herrschenden. In Gwynned ändert sich dies alles, als 822 torenthische Deryni das Land erobern und eine brutale Tyrannei errichten; »normale Menschen« gelten ihnen weniger als Vieh.

> … es läßt sich keine allgemeine Deryni-Feindlichkeit vor dem Jahr 822 nachweisen. In diesem Jahr drang der derynische Prinz Festil, jüngster Sohn des Königs von Torenth, von Osten ins Land ein, und es gelang ihm, die Herrschaft der Haldane-Könige überraschend zu stürzen, die gesamte Königsfamilie der Haldanes – mit Ausnahme des zweijährigen Prinzen Aidan, der dem Morden entging – zu massakrieren… Willkür und Machtmißbrauch seitens hoher derynischer Kreise wurden zunehmend offenkundiger und führten schließlich im Jahr 904 zum Sturz des letzten Festil-Königs durch andere Deryni und zur Restauration der früheren menschlichen Linie von Herrschern in der Person von Cinhil Haldane, einem Enkel Prinz Aidans.   (Kurtz, *Deryni-Archive* 13)

Dies ist die Zusammenfassung von *Camber von Culdi*, dem ersten Roman der »frühen Deryni-Trilogie«. Diese Trilogie und die um die »Erben von Sankt Camber« schildern die 25 Jahre nach der Restauration. Der Deryni-Graf Camber von Culdi als treibende Kraft schafft es, in den Haldanes derynigleiche Kräfte zu wecken, die allerdings als gottgegebene Eigenschaft der Könige ausgegeben werden. Leider ist der neue König ein zwar wohlmeinender, aber kein guter Herrscher: Als Mönch erzogen, ist er unglücklich, nicht mehr Priester sein zu dürfen, und versäumt es, die Vorbehalte gegen die Deryni zu bekämpfen. Im Gegenteil, er überlässt die Macht gierigen Deryni-Hassern.

> Unglücklicherweise gab man der Deryni-Magie als solcher, nicht dem falschen Verhalten und der Habgier einer Handvoll einzelner, die Schuld an den Übeln des Interregnums. Zudem versäumten die neuen Herrscher keine Zeit, kaum daß man die Restauration bewerkstelligt hatte, ehe sie die Ziele, wenn nicht gar die Methoden, ihrer vorherigen Herren übernahmen... Binnen lediglich weniger Jahre gerieten die in Gwynedd gebliebenen Deryni politisch, gesellschaftlich und religiös in die Isolation; die neuen Herren scheuten keinen nur irgendwie erdenklichen Vorwand, um den zuvorigen Herrschern jeden Einfluß zu nehmen und sich ihren Reichtum anzueignen... Nur das vollständige Verleugnen der eigenen Kräfte und Fähigkeiten mochte einem Deryni noch das Überleben sichern, und selbst dann lediglich unter strengster Überwachung.   (Kurtz, *Deryni-Archive* 13)

Die meisten Deryni, die den Pogromen, dem »Deryni-Holocaust«[4], entgehen, fliehen in andere Länder, einige verbergen sich im Untergrund. Manchen gelingt es, ihre wahre Identität zu verheimlichen, oft wissen ihre Nachkommen nichts von ihrer Herkunft und ihren Kräften, gelten vielleicht als begabt im Umgang mit Tieren oder Wunden oder haben das »Zweite Gesicht«. 200 Jahre später hat zwar die Anti-Deryni-Stimmung nachgelassen, die Kirche allerdings bleibt bei ihrer rigiden Auffassung. »Der späte Deryni-Zyklus« und »Die Geschichten von König Kelson« erzählen vom Kampf des jungen Königs Kelson gegen die antiderynischen Kräfte in Kirche und Gesellschaft. Nachdem er die letzte Nachfahrin der festilischen Usurpatoren und den König von Torenth dank seiner derynischen Kräfte geschlagen hat, erzwingt Kelson trotz Kirchenspaltung, Bürgerkrieg und Reichsbann, trotz Verrat und Attentaten am Ende die Aufhebung der antiderynischen Gesetze der Kirche und schafft dauerhaften Frieden und Freundschaft mit den seit Jahrhunderten feindlichen Ländern Meara und Torenth.

    Die Romane schildern dies alles aus der Sicht von Gwynned, es gibt aber keine einfache Schwarz-Weiß-Zeichnung, weder in den internen Konflikten Gwynneds – immer finden wir vernünftige, moralisch akzeptabel handelnde

---

4   Diesen Begriff verwendet Kurtz mehrfach; er wird im englischen Sprachraum häufig auch in anderen Zusammenhängen als der Judenverfolgung benutzt.

Personen auf beiden Seiten, wie auch das Gegenstück – noch bezüglich der anderen Länder. Je später die Romane geschrieben wurden, desto differenzierter sind sie in dieser Hinsicht. Und es gibt Kurzgeschichten von Kurtz, die die Ereignisse aus der Sicht der Gegner beleuchten, wie es in einem Vorwort heißt: »told from the other side, the point of the view of the bad guys – who aren't really bad guys, of course; they're simply on the opposite side« (Kurtz, *Deryni-Archive* 165).

Und die auf der »richtigen« Seite handeln häufig auch zumindest fragwürdig. So betrügt König Donal Haldane seine Frau, um einen männlichen Erben mit garantierter Deryni-Abstammung zu zeugen, und der Camberische Rat denkt ernsthaft darüber nach, dieses Kind zu ermorden – beides natürlich zum Wohle des Staates.

Neben Adligen spielen oft Mönche, Bauern oder Bergvölker eine wichtige Rolle; nicht selten sieht man die Ereignisse gespiegelt in deren Wahrnehmung. Häufig wird die schwierige Rolle der Frauen beleuchtet, die dynastischen Zwecken dienen und daher Kinder am laufenden Band gebären müssen (viele sterben bei der Geburt oder kurz danach), oft mit einem nicht geliebten Mann. In den späteren Romanen und Geschichten tauchen auch Deryni mit anderem religiösen Hintergrund auf. Die »alte Religion«, die in Gwynned vor dem Christentum verbreitet war, wird nur noch selten ausgeübt, meist vermischt mit derynischen Praktiken. Wo der Himmelsvater aber häufiger verehrt wird, werden dessen Anhängerinnen und Anhänger oft verfolgt.

Einer der weisesten und klügsten Deryni-Lehrer ist ein muslimischer Prinz aus den Ländern im Osten. Gab es in früheren Jahrhunderten noch »Mohrenkriege«, so entwickeln sich im Lauf der Jahrhunderte schließlich Handels- und diplomatische Bande. Die bedeutendsten Deryni- und Weisheitsschulen im 10. und 11. Jahrhundert liegen in R'Kassi, einem Königreich, in dem Muslime und Christen, Schwarze und Weiße, Deryni und Nicht-Deryni friedlich miteinander leben.

Der Deryni-Bischof Arilan studiert zwar den Talmud und geht als junger Priester bei einem Rabbi in die Lehre, Juden spielen allerdings in Gwynned sonst kaum eine Rolle. Kurtz begründet dies so:

> When the concept of the Deryni universe first began to take shape, with a gifted people persecuted because they are different, I found myself drawing conscious parallels with the discrimination and persecution historically experienced by the Jews of our own world-also a persecuted people set apart by factors not readily apparent, many of them forced to live secret lives... Not all my readers recognized this parallel between the Deryni and the Jews, because some of them asked about the apparent absence of Jews in Gwynedd – though when I told them what my intention had

been-that, in a sense, the Deryni were the Jews of Gwynedd – they
saw it.   (Kurtz, *Deryni-Tales* 25f.)[5]

WAS aber sind sie nun eigentlich, diese Deryni?

Wirklichkeit, Wahrnehmung und Wahn

In den ersten Romanen erscheinen die Fähigkeiten der Deryni tatsächlich wie Magie: Ausgebildete Deryni können »Gedanken sehen«, »Lügen erkennen« bzw. »Wahrheit lesen« und Schlaf und Schmerzen unterdrücken, viele können anderen Personen ihren Willen aufzwingen, manche ihnen sogar ohne deren Wissen posthypnotische Befehle erteilen (»einen Bann auflegen«) bis hin zu Mordbefehlen gegen die besten Freunde. Viele können mit Gedankenkraft Pfeile lenken und Schlösser öffnen, einige wenige können heilen, und mit Hilfe spezieller Rituale und Portale können Deryni teleportieren. Besonders Befähigte können sogar die Gestalt anderer Menschen annehmen, und in Torent, wo die »Magie« allgemein akzeptiert ist, sorgen speziell dafür ausgebildete Deryni für das passende Wetter. Das Liebesleben eines Paares kann, wenn beide Derynikräfte haben, dadurch sehr positiv beeinflusst werden, kommt es doch über die körperliche Vereinigung hinaus zu einer geistigen Verschmelzung und einem intimen Band, das über alle Verbindungen hinausgeht, die Nicht-Deryni möglich sind.

In den *Deryni-Archiven* erläutert Kurtz, dass vieles, was den Menschen in diesem Quasi-Mittelalter als Magie erscheine und von manchen Deryni als von Gott gegebene Kräfte interpretiert werde, heute als außersinnliche Wahrnehmung oder paranormale Phänomene angesehen würde, wie Telepathie, Telekinese und Teleportation. Viele moderne Errungenschaften würden den abergläubischen Menschen der mittelalterlichen Feudalgesellschaft wie Magie vorkommen – das entspricht Clarkes Drittem Gesetz: »Jede weit genug entwickelte Technologie ist von Magie nicht zu unterscheiden« (Clarke 37).[6]

---

5   Dieser Vergleich ist nur in historischer und soziologischer Sicht sinnvoll: in der Verfolgungssituation, darin, dass beide leicht zu erkennen sind (männliche Juden an der Beschneidung, Deryni an ihrer Reaktion auf bestimmte Drogen), auch in der Auffassung zumindest mancher Deryni, ein »ausgewähltes Volk« zu sein. Ein Unterschied ist allerdings gravierend: Judentum ist eine Religion, Derynitum eine biologische Eigenschaft. Jude oder Jüdin kann man werden – oder auch dem Judentum entsagen (auch wenn die kulturelle Prägung bleiben mag). Deryni ist man, oder man ist es nicht. Man kann es weder aus freier Entscheidung werden noch die Fähigkeiten endgültig ablegen.

6   Magie im weitesten Sinne bezeichnet nach geläufiger Definition alle Praktiken, die dazu dienen, den Verlauf von Ereignissen auf »übernatürliche« Weise zu beeinflussen. Ob etwas als Magie betrachtet wird, kommt also darauf an, wieweit man die Mechanismen und Zusammenhänge der Welt als natürlich oder nicht (aner)kennt. Der berühmte Schriftsteller und Wissenschaftler Sir Arthur C. Clarke beschrieb 1962 in seinem Buch *Profiles of the*

Der Gebrauch der meisten derynischen Fähigkeiten muss erlernt und ge-
übt werden, und diese werden über die Geschlechtschromosomen vererbt.[7] Die
Deryni sind sich der biologischen Grundlagen natürlich nicht in wissenschaftlicher Weise bewusst; einige erahnen bestenfalls die Erbgänge oder zumindest,
dass es Regeln gibt, und manchmal gibt es Angst vor der Abschwächung der
Fähigkeiten: »Of course, we don't know how the blood gets diluted, down the
generations« (Kurtz, *King Kelson's* 257). Deryni bezeichnen sich selbst mal als
Volk, als Stamm, als Rasse, als Art, als Gattung ... ohne dass diese Begriffe
klar definiert wären. Im modernen Sinn sind alle falsch: Deryni sind Menschen
wie alle anderen mit einer besonderen vererbten Befähigung, die unterschiedlich ausgeprägt sein kann. Dabei spielt es keine Rolle, ob jemand »Voll-« oder
»Halb-Deryni« ist; dennoch werden den »Halb-Deryni« meist weniger Fähigkeiten zugesprochen, und als »Halbblut« gelten sie vielen Deryni als weniger wert.

In muslimischen Ländern und jenen mit gemischter Religion ist Derynitum
so wenig ein Problem wie in den meisten christlichen Ländern in und um
Gwynned. Dort aber kam es nach der Machtübernahme der menschlichen
Könige zur Restauration:

> In der nun völlig Menschen unterstellten Kirche verlagerte sich
> während nicht einmal einer Generation die politische Begründung
> der Deryni-Feindlichkeiten zu deren philosophischer Rechtferti-
> gung, so daß man die Deryni schließlich als an und für sich böse
> einstufte, als Brut des Teufels, die möglicherweise sogar außerhalb
> jeder Rettung durch die Kirche stand – denn es konnte doch wohl
> keine rechtschaffene und gottesfürchtige Person solche Dinge tun,
> wie die Deryni sie taten, also mußten die Deryni Handlanger des
> Satans sein.   (Kurtz, *Deryni-Archive* 13)

Sogar eigene Orden zur Bekämpfung der Deryni-Ketzerei werden gegründet,
mit Großinquisitor und Folterknechten. Viele weltliche Adlige gewinnen an
Macht, indem sie Kirchenfürsten werden. Beim Konzil von Ramos 918 werden
alle Deryni-Heiligen entheiligt und nachträglich exkommuniziert, zuvorderst
natürlich Sankt Camber; ihre Anbetung wird untersagt. Ein Beispiel für die
Kirchenjustiz: Einmaliges Anrufen von Sankt Camber wird mit Auspeitschung
bestraft, im Wiederholungsfall wird die Zunge herausgerissen, das Schreiben

---

Future: An Inquiry into the Limits of the Possible zunächst nur ein »Gesetz«, eine zweite
Regel wurde zwei Jahre später in der französischen Ausgabe als »zweites Gesetz« bezeichnet. Das veranlasste Clarke, diese Aussage in der ersten Überarbeitung seines Buches
1973 selbst als zweites Gesetz zu bezeichnen und das berühmt gewordene dritte Gesetz
zu formulieren: »Any sufficiently advanced technology is indistinguishable from magic.«

7 Zu den biologischen Hintergründen, möglichen Erbgängen und Konsequenzen für Ver-
   erbung und Fortpflanzung s. Schneidewind, *Heiler*.

des Namens führt zum Abhacken der Hand. Mitglieder vom Orden St. Cambers werden lebendig verbrannt (*nach* Auspeitschung und Herausreißen der Zunge). Den Deryni wird die Ausübung kirchlicher Dienste bei Todesstrafe untersagt, es kommt zu Folterungen, Kreuzigungen, Verbrennungen. Schon der Versuch, sich zum Priester weihen zu lassen, zieht den Tod auf dem Scheiterhaufen bei lebendigem Leib nach sich. Und Deryni sind leicht zu enttarnen: Die Droge *Merascha* macht sie hilflos und wird zum bevorzugten Folterwerkzeug der Inquisitoren. Diese Praktiken lassen im Laufe der Zeit zwar nach, gehen aber nie ganz verloren und werden immer wieder neu belebt.

Kurtz schildert nicht die Kirche als verdorben, brutal, korrupt; es sind einzelne mächtige Mitglieder, die sie auf diesen Weg führen, und von Beginn an stellen sich manche Tapfere diesen entgegen, wenn auch erfolglos. Im Laufe der Jahrzehnte verfestigt sich der Glaube an die teuflische Natur der Deryni in Volk und Kirche; selbst eine Berührung durch sie könnte unheilbringend sein, ja zur ewigen Verdammnis führen. Immer wieder gibt es aber Geistliche, die aus Nächstenliebe oder Toleranz auch Deryni unterstützen. Schließlich gelingt es, viele Bischöfe und Priester, die ehrlich vom Glauben an die Verdammnis der Deryni beseelt sind, vom Gegenteil zu überzeugen: weil »rechtschaffene«, gläubige Deryni sich durch jahrzehntelanges vorbildliches Verhalten als Priester und Bischöfe einen entsprechenden Ruf und Vertrauen erwerben und dadurch, dass manche über die Heilfähigkeit verfügen, die 200 Jahren lang niemand mehr beherrschte. Dies überzeugt viele Gläubige: Denn wenn Jesus ein Heiler war, Heilen also eine gottgegebene Fähigkeit ist, wie könnte sie dann Deryni zu eigen sein, wenn diese verdammt wären? (Glücklicherweise gelingt es, von der Idee abzulenken, sie könne auch ein Werkzeug der Versuchung sein, vom Teufel verliehen …) Trotzdem erweist es sich als schwierig, das »einfache Volk« von seinen Überlieferungen zu kurieren und ihm die neuen Glaubenssätze zu vermitteln; es dauert Jahrzehnte, ehe die Deryni überall wenigstens einigermaßen akzeptiert sind.

Riten, Religion und rechtes Handeln

Die Kirche in Gwynned erinnert an die Kirche unseres Mittelalters, auch im Glauben an die direkte Wirkung von Gebeten, Heiligenverehrung, Weihungen und Ritualen. Die meisten der derynischen Rituale in Gwynned sind an kirchliche Rituale angelehnt, bis hin zu Latein als »Hochsprache« (in Torenth, von Byzanz christianisiert, ist es Griechisch). Sogar viele der Anrufungen und Floskeln sind identisch, oft wird auf die Bibel Bezug genommen, geleitet werden die Rituale meistens von Kirchenmännern oder in Klöstern geschulten Frauen.

Meist werden Gott oder die Dreifaltigkeit angerufen, manchmal auch Maria oder St. Camber. Für Schutzbanne oder -kreise werden die vier Evangelisten und noch öfter die vier Erzengel Michael, Gabriel, Raphael, Uriel/Ouriel an- bzw. herabgerufen. Weniger Gläubige ziehen hierfür meist die vier Elemente oder die Winde (Windrichtungen) heran; nur einmal erwähnt Kurtz einen »atheistischen« Derynimeister. Die griechisch-orthodoxen Deryni in Torenth haben ähnliche Rituale. Es wird kein Deryniritual auf muslimischer Basis beschrieben oder gar ein gemischtes, doch da viele gut geschulte Deryni ihre Ausbildung in R'Kassi erhalten haben, dürfte es Ähnlichkeiten geben, und mit den Erzengeln haben wohl auch die muslimischen Deryni keine Probleme. Für viele Priester unter den Deryni genießen die derynischen »magischen« Rituale die gleiche »Heiligkeit« wie kirchliche, etwa das der Wandlung oder der Priesterweihe; durch die Verwendung christlicher Floskeln und Anrufungen stellen sie das für sich auch sicher. Es gibt aber auch Rituale, die sehr viel weltlicher ablaufen, gerade unter Nichtgeistlichen, hier werden gerne die Elemente angerufen.

Vor und nach der Verfolgung der Deryni durch die Kirche erkannte diese viele derynische Rituale als wirksam an, insbesondere das »Duellum arcanum« als »Gottesurteil«. Wenn ein Haldane beteiligt war, galten dessen Kräfte als Erbe seiner königlichen Weihe, der Salbung. Die Heilkraft als für die meisten Menschen edelste und wichtigste Kraft der Deryni wurde vor dem Konzil von Ramos als göttliche Gabe interpretiert, Heiler und Heilerinnen genossen höchstes Ansehen. Der Gabrieliten-Orden war als Heilerorden von höchster Bedeutung auch für die kirchliche Lehre. Er wurde nach der Restauration zerschlagen, alle Heilkräfte gingen verloren, später aber war das Argument der Heilkraft als göttliche Gabe mit ausschlaggebend für die Aufhebung der Beschlüsse von Ramos.

Mit der ethischen Bewertung der derynischen Kräfte ging die Kirche, solange sie diese akzeptierte, ganz pragmatisch um, analog dem Umgang mit Waffen: Es kam darauf an, was man damit anrichtete!

Und so sehen es auch die meisten Deryni. Die üblichen ethischen Probleme haben sie mit anderen Menschen gemein; bei Herrschern kommen spezielle hinzu, etwa wenn ein König Menschen hinrichten lassen muss aus Staatsraison, auch wenn er sie gerne leben ließe: »… killing women and children has always been bad business« (Kurtz, *In the King's* 262).

Vor allem in zwei Bereichen tauchen für Deryni besondere Fragen auf. Der erste ist nur indirekt von ihrer besonderen Begabung abhängig: die Schwierigkeit, als Deryni Geistlicher zu sein. Viele Priester werden ihres Amtes enthoben oder gar exkommuniziert, wollen aber dennoch als Priester tätig sein – und meistens entscheiden sie sich auch dafür, gemäß der Auffassung, dass man Priester für immer sei und dass Menschen diese Bindung an Gott nicht auflösen könnten. König Cinhil feiert deshalb auch nach Aufhebung seiner Mönchsgelübde weiterhin die Messe, wenn auch heimlich.

Sieht man von der Verdammung der Derynikräfte nach dem Konzil von Ramos ab, galt und gilt deren Anwendung im größten Teil der elf Königreiche und der umgebenden Länder als eine Art Werkzeug, wie das Wissen einer Ärztin oder die Waffenfähigkeiten eines Ritters, so dass nur selten wirklich ethische Probleme auftauchen. Es wird für Deryni dann schwierig, wenn sie ihre eigenen Kräfte als »böse« ablehnen. Meist aber wird bei der ethischen Bewertung der »Magie« nicht nach der Art der verwendeten Kräfte geschaut, sondern nach deren Verwendungszweck, ähnlich wie beim Einsatz von Waffen – oder dem Feuer, das wärmen, aber auch verbrennen kann.

Manchmal wird auch unter Deryni oder in der Kirche zwischen »schwarzer« und »weißer« Magie unterschieden, häufiger wird diese Unterscheidung aber im »gemeinen Volk« gemacht:

> »Kannst du mir kundtun, was's, dass ich ein Deryni bin, für dich bedeutet?« fügte er in aller Ruhe hinzu. »Daß Ihr … Ihr Euch mit Schwarzer Magie befasst«, kam es zu Ferris' eigenem Entsetzen über seine Lippen. [...] »Mit Magie, ja, deren Farbe indes ist eine Frage der jeweiligen Auslegung. Ich gebiete über einige ganz außergewöhnliche Fähigkeiten, Ferris, jedoch verwende ich sie ausschließlich im Namen der Gerechtigkeit.«
> (Kurtz, »Gericht zu Kiltuin«, in: *Deryni-Archive* 280)

Eine grundlegende Aussage über den Umgang mit Magie bzw. den besonderen Kräften der Deryni macht einer der Haupthelden der Deryni-Saga, Alaric Anthony Morgan, Herzog, Reichskanzler und König Kelsons Kämpe.

> »Mir stehen mehr Kräfte und andere Arten von Kräften zu Gebote … als den meisten Menschen, aber was ihren Gebrauch angeht, so muß ich dafür vor demselben König und demselben Gott Rechenschaft ablegen wie Ihr – und wie jeder Priester, jeder Bischof –, ebenso meinem eigenen Gewissen … Dieweil ich weit größere Fähigkeiten als andere Sterbliche besitze, ist mir eine weitaus größere Verantwortung aufgebürdet.« (Kurtz, *Erbe* 388)

Dies könnte Vorbild sein für die Aussage des modernen Superhelden Spiderman, dass große Macht große Verantwortung mit sich bringt. Doch es ist nur eine Grundaussage der meisten Ethiken, und somit zeigt uns Kurtz auch an dieser Stelle, wie nahe die Welt der Deryni der unseren ist. Wie in einem Brennspiegel, wie in einem Mikroskop sehen wir in dieser mittelalterlichen Welt viele unserer Probleme – und uns darüber zum Nachdenken anzuhalten, ist eines der Ziele der Autorin.

Bibliographie

I. Primärliteratur: Die Deryni-Texte von Katherine Kurtz

Anordnung chronologisch nach der Handlungszeit (nicht nach Erscheinungsdatum). Bei Redaktionsschluss (02/2018) lieferbare Bücher sind mit einer [1] gekennzeichnet, als Kindle-Edition erhältliche mit [2]. Die anderen sind in der Regel über Antiquariate erhältlich. Nicht alle Ausgaben konnten erfasst werden; es finden sich auf jeden Fall die ersten und letzten Ausgaben. Die Zitate stammen alle aus der jeweils frühesten Ausgabe.

The Legends of Camber of Culdi/Früher Deryni-Zyklus [903 – 918]:
Camber of Culdi. New York: Ballantine Books/Del Rey, 1976[2]
Camber von Culdi. München: Heyne, 1979/Thienemann, Stuttgart, 1998/Bastei-Lübbe, Bergisch Gladbach, 2000
Saint Camber. New York: Ballantine Books/Del Rey, 1978[2]
Sankt Camber. München: Heyne, 1980/Thienemann, Stuttgart, 2002/Bastei-Lübbe, Bergisch Gladbach, 2000
Camber the Heretic. New York: Ballantine Books/Del Rey, 1981[2]
Camber der Ketzer. München: Heyne, 1983/Thienemann, Stuttgart, 2002/Bastei-Lübbe, Bergisch Gladbach, 2000
The Legends of Camber of Culdi Trilogy: Camber of Culdi, Saint Camber, and Camber the Heretic. Kindle Edition, 2016[2]

The Heirs of Saint Camber/Die Erben von Sankt Camber [918 – 928]:
The Harrowing of Gwynedd. New York: Ballantine Books/Del Rey, 1989[2]
Das Martyrium von Gwynedd. München: Heyne, 2000
King Javan's Year. New York: Ballantine Books/Del Rey, 1992[2]
König Javans Jahr. München: Heyne, 2002
The Captive Kings = The Bastard Prince. New York: Ballantine Books/Del Rey, 1993[2]

The Childe Morgan Trilogy [1082 – 1106]:
In the King's Service. New York: ACE, 2003[1+2]
Childe Morgan. New York: ACE, 2006[1+2]
The King's Deryni. New York: ACE, 2014[1+2]

The Chronicles of the Deryni. Später Deryni-Zyklus [1120/21]:
Deryni Rising. New York: Ballantine Books, 1970/ACE, 2004[1+2]
Das Geschlecht der Magier. München: Heyne, 1978/1983/1985
Deryni Checkmate. New York: Ballantine Books, 1972/ACE, 2005[1+2]
Die Zauberfürsten. München: Heyne, 1978/1983
High Deryni. New York: Ballantine Books, 1973/ACE, 2008[2]
Ein Deryni-König. München: Heyne, 1978/1983
The Chronicles of the Deryni Series (3 Book Series). Kindle Edition, 2016[2]

The Histories of King Kelson. Die Geschichten von König Kelson [1123 – 1128]:
The Bishop's Heir. New York: Ballantine Books/Del Rey, 1984[2]
Das Erbe des Bischofs. München: Heyne, 1989
The King's Justice. New York: Ballantine Books/Del Rey, 1985[2]
Die Gerechtigkeit des Königs. München: Heyne, 1989
The Quest for St. Camber. New York: Ballantine Books/Del Rey, 1986[2]
Die Suche nach Sankt Camber. München: Heyne, 1989
King Kelson's Bride. New York: ACE, 2000[2]

The Deryni Archives. New York: Ballantine Books/Del Rey, 1986
Die Deryni-Archive. München: Heyne, 1991

Deryni Magic (A Grimoire). New York: Ballantine Books/Del Rey, 1991; Randolph, MA: Grey Ghost Press, 2005

»Imaginary History: A Genalogical Approach«. *The Work of Katherine Kurtz. An Annotated*
  Bibliography & Guide
  (Bibliographies of Modern Authors) Boden Clarke & Mary A. Burgess. Los Angeles: Borgo
  Press, 1993: 117-124

Katherine Kurtz als Herausgeberin:
  Deryni Tales. An Anthology. New York: ACE, 2002

Katherine Kurtz mit Robert Reginald:
  Codex Derynianus. Hardcover Limited Edition. Nevada City: Underwood Books, 1998
  Codex Derynianus II. Nevada City: Underwood Books, 2005

900	925	1075	1100	1125

Camber of Culdi: 903/04
Saint Camber: 905–907

Camber the Heretic: 917/18
The Harrowing of Gwynedd: 918
King Javan's Year: 921/22

The Bastard Prince: 928

In the King's Service: 1082 – 1092

Childe Morgan: 1093 – 1096

The King's Deryni: 1099 – 1106

Deryni Rising: 1120
Deryni Checkmate + High Deryni: 1121
The Bishop's Heir: 1123/24
The King's Justice: 1124
The Quest for St. Camber: 1125
King Kelson's Bride: 1128

II. Sekundärliteratur

The Eleven Kingdoms: Poster Map of the Deryni World. Randolph/Mass: Grey Ghost Press, 2003

Clarke, Arthur C. *Profile der Zukunft. Über die Grenzen des Möglichen.* München: Heyne, 1984

Clarke, Boden & Mary A. Burgess. *The Work of Katherine Kurtz. An Annotated Bibliography &*
  Guide (Bibliographies of Modern Authors). Los Angeles: Borgo Press, 1993

Reginald, Robert. »Derynian Dreams: The Fantasy Worlds of Katherine Kurtz«. *Xenograffiti:*
  Essays on Fantastic Literature. Los Angeles: Borgo Press, 1996; Wildside Press/
  Kindle Edition, 2011

Rosenberg, Aaron, Ann Dupuis & Melissa Houle. *The Deryni Adventure Game.* Randolph,
  MA: Grey Ghost Press, 2005

Schneidewind, Friedhelm. »Heiler und Ketzer. Kirche, Gott und Magie in der Welt der
  Deryni«. *Götterwelten. Phantastik und Religion. Tagungsband 2006.* Hg.: Thomas Le
  Blanc & Bettina Twrsnick. Schriftenreihe und Materialien Bd. 97. Wetzlar: Phantastische
  Bibliothek Wetzlar, 2007. 112-145

Sturm, Thomas F. *Die Geschichte von König Kelson. Dritte Deryni-Trilogie. Eine Zyklen-*
  rezension. Altheim: Sonnenring, 1989

The Voice of Nature in Middle-earth through the Lens of Testimony

Andoni Cossio (Vitoria-Gasteiz)

Introduction[1]

It is well-known that J.R.R. Tolkien had a distaste for allegory and symbolism in his works: "There is *no* 'symbolism' or conscious allegory in my story" (L 262). Yet he appreciated applicability: "That there is no allegory does not, of course, say there is no applicability. There always is. ...there is I suppose applicability in my story to present times" (262). Following this last line of thought, the intention of this paper is to analyse how Tolkien, by use of the genre of testimony through the character Treebeard in *The Lord of the Rings*, generated as a by-product a political applicability which endows the Ents with a powerful voice to speak on behalf of nature and trees.

Tolkien was against a technologically overdeveloped world, being very protective of trees and nature: "I am (obviously) much in love with plants and above all trees, and always have been; and I find human maltreatment of them as hard to bear as some find ill-treatment of animals" (L 220); and as he himself stated in a letter to the editor of the *Daily Telegraph*: "In all my works I take the part of trees as against all their enemies" (419). This could also be seen in his daily life; in a letter, Tolkien criticised the foolish behaviour of a neighbour who was eager to have a huge poplar hewn, as it kept her house and garden in shadow and supposedly could fall on it (321). Tolkien considered these reasons unfounded and claimed: "Every tree has its enemy, few have an advocate" (321). In fact, this incident seemed to trigger a change, as his biographer Humphrey Carpenter signals: "But the poplar had already been lopped and mutilated, and though he managed to save it now, Tolkien began to think about it" (199). Possibly, because of these kinds of unfortunate personal experiences he severely denounced the unnecessary abuse of trees and gave them a voice.

He brought into being the Ents, colossal walking trees with human form, as the guardians of the forests, heralded by Yavanna in her warning to Aulë in *The Silmarillion*: "'Now let thy children beware! For there shall walk a power in the forests whose wrath they will arouse at their peril'" (42). Looking at the

---

1　This essay has been completed under the auspices of the Predoctoral funding for non-doctoral Research Staff Training awarded by the Basque Government and of the research group REWEST, funded by the Basque Government (IT-1026-16) and the University of the Basque Country (UPV/EHU).

etymology of the name, Tolkien himself claimed the name Ent came from their connection with stone and "From the Anglo-Saxon poem *The Wanderer*, 87: '*eald enta geweorc idlu stodon*', 'the old creation of giants [i.e. ancient buildings, erected by a former race] stood desolate" (L 445). Julian Evans explains that *ets* is the Hebrew word in the Old Testament for tree (4) and originally *ent* is an Anglo-Saxon word which means 'mighty person of long ago' or 'giant' (L 208). This last Anglo-Saxon etymology embodies Tolkien's concept of Ents to whom the reader may easily relate due to their anthropomorphism.[2] Andrea Denekamp argues on several occasions that the Ents have a different function: "they [the Ents] remain the voice of non-human nature" (5) indeed, an irate nature (8), offering a different perspective (24) and their creational intention was no other than to offer a rupture with humanity (5). Nevertheless, as Ignacio Abella argues, it can be easily perceived that the individual conscience of the Ents is what identifies them with humans (168) as well as their appearance. It is possible that we are not as closely bonded to nature as we used to be, thus the anthropomorphic form that Tolkien gave to the Ents, may further help humans empathise with the natural world.

In one of his letters, Tolkien resents that in an intended film adaptation of the LotR by the screenwriter Morton Grady Zimmerman, the latter is not concerned for trees. He also reveals the important part these play in his work: "I deeply regret this handling of the 'Treebeard' chapter, whether necessary or not. I have already suspected Z [Zimmerman] of not being interested in trees: unfortunate, since the story is so largely concerned with them" (L 275). In the mentioned chapter, which is the object of this study, the reader is provided with the narration of nature, an always forgotten side defended by no one.

In the 18th century with the rise of the English realist novel, a new type of fiction emerged in the form of diaries, personal narrations, which ultimately developed into a genre known as testimony. This genre typically comprises tales of human suffering that take place in the real world, seen in the 20th century in the testimonies of persecution of World War II; *The Diary of a Young Girl* (1947), also known as *The Diary of Anne Frank*, being representational and a well-known example. Testimony, though in Tolkien's case crafted from imagination and not real, is very much present in LotR through the character Treebeard. In this paper I will present the formal characteristics and critical approaches to the genre of testimony and take a look at its presence in the narration. I will argue that through this genre, though unconscious of its use, Tolkien may have wanted readers to be cognizant of the irresponsible destruction of trees, and what these life forms might have felt, creating a collective awareness that could prevent future ravages.

---

2   Joseph Loconte designates the Ents as "humanoid trees" (9).

The Concept and Genre of Testimony in Treebeard's Narration

Paraphrasing Javier Sánchez Zapatero, testimonies are first-person narratives which go against the established history, opposing the official version given by the ruling power (105), and the narrative events are recorded by the author of the testimony or a third person. Hugo Achugar explains that testimony occurs whenever a subject is deprived of its voice and has been marginalised (66; Sánchez Zapatero 104), in Giorgio Agamben's words: two characteristics which bestow authority upon the witness (158). Margaret Randall adds that the witness presents a perspective of an event that really took place and this person can be a participant, main or secondary actor of the events that are being described, or an external narrator who aims to transmit the story to a broader audience (33).

One of the words in Latin to refer to a witness is *testis* and implies the following: "*testis* from which our word 'testimony' derives, etymologically signifies the person who, in a trial or lawsuit between two rival parties, is in the position of a third party (**terstis*)" (Agamben 17), increasing the 'validity' of the narration, of which Treebeard is an excellent example.

Let us now turn to the question of who the primary author of the testimony is in the chapter "Treebeard" of LotR. According to the text, "Treebeard is Fangorn, the guardian of the forest; he is the oldest of the Ents, the oldest living thing that still walks beneath the sun upon this Middle-earth" (LotR 499). Fangorn is also the name of the place that he inhabits and takes care of, and he is labelled by Tom Shippey as a 'natural object' (132). This comes to show that he is understood not as part of the fauna but of the flora, hence an ideal vehicle for its representation. Brian Bates points out, that in the Middle Ages people conferred knowledge upon extraordinarily ancient trees (51), very true in Treebeard's case; a very learned individual who is the possessor of great wisdom. "Since Treebeard's memory reaches back to the earliest of times, he assumes the role of a guardian of memory with some authority" as Doris McGonagill (160) postulates. His longevity and knowledge grant him an outstanding perspective of past times and allow him to make the right decisions in the present, making him an adequate 'spokestree' to guarantee a future for nature.

Many scholars, as Elise Mckenna both when describing the novel LotR and Peter Jackson's movies, agree that the figure of Treebeard is intrinsically linked to the environment (230).[3] Liam Campbell describes Treebeard as a "waking force of nature" in Middle-earth (66); one of the mediums used by Tolkien to

---

3   The fact that the character Treebeard can be taken as a representative of nature's thoughts is a recurring and outstanding idea in Liam Campbell's *The Ecological Augury in the Works of JRR Tolkien* (38, 176, 199, 247).

express how sorry he was for nature's destruction (61) and also as an animated version of nature (79). In fact, there is an implicit ecological stance present in Tolkien's work, that of the Ents against the cruelties of a process of industrialisation,[4] which in Laura Crossley's words is a major theme in LotR (175).

The genre of testimony, in some cases, as Dominick LaCapra explains, is a tribute paid to the memory of loved ones (157). It is also a source of knowledge, as it reveals a parallel and hidden reality to readers (Sánchez Zapatero 103) and through its narrations the witnesses are able to save their experience and point of view, and thus themselves from oblivion (105).

It is also necessary to identify the transcriber. In the case of Treebeard, he is not a literate individual and therefore, Merry and Pippin are the media through which Frodo is able to keep record of the events experienced by this being. The hobbits, as well as nature, have been put aside in the history of Middle-earth, and the dissemination of the story by a marginalised individual in the official history is a responsibility bestowed on Frodo.

Treebeard's story, which was originally oral, was later narrated by Merry and Pippin to Frodo,[5] who wrote it down. Achugar defines this as the 'complex social subject' (63) constituted by the literate (transcriber) and the marginal subject (witness), which in this case is completed by the intermediaries. Still, it is quite clear that what Achugar names the 'solidary literate' (78) is in this case performed by Frodo, transcribing the story and trying not to alter the voice of the witness whose speech is independent from the transcriber's comments. Frodo highlights this need of objectivity when he cannot understand why Bilbo introduces an invented element into the story of the Ring: "'If you mean, inventing all that about a 'present', well, I thought the true story much more likely, and I couldn't see the point of altering it at all'" (LotR 40).

History is a construct of the ruling elites and testimony offers for the first time the unique chance of enabling the 'making of history' by anyone (Randall 35), not necessarily the ones in power. Before being dethroned Saruman is an authority in Middle-earth, something that may suggest that he has certain influence over the writing of the History of the territory. Saruman and his minions are a threat to Treebeard, Ents and trees in general as he is determined to tame nature and exploit it for his own personal benefit. At first, he makes use of Fangorn's natural resources for the improvement of both Isengard and

---

4   Therefore, fulfilling Yavanna's wish: "Would that the trees might speak on behalf of all things that have roots, and punish those that wrong them" (S 40).

5   The whole story told in LotR is the testimony of Bilbo Baggins, Frodo Baggins and, to a lesser extent, Sam Gamgee, compiled in the Red Book of Westmarch: "Tolkien was obliged to pretend to be a 'translator.' He developed the pose with predictable rigour, feigning not only a text to translate but behind it a whole manuscript tradition, from Bilbo's diary to the Red Book of Westmarch..." (Shippey 117), showing how much he believed it himself. Tolkien even refers to his work by this title: "I shall, if I get a chance, turn back to the matter of the Red Book and allied stories soon" (L 300).

his army's weapons. This abuse of natural resources exists in the Real World, Robert Harrison points out that in England land managers considered the woods to be the enemies of progress (100) in the same fashion as Saruman and thus justifying their exploitation.

The testimony in Treebeard's narration goes against the traditional history of Middle-earth in the sense that a new perspective is added as Andrew Light indicates: "What he [Treebeard] and the other Ents do is not simply care for the forest as much as they serve as a narrative device that allows part of nature to speak for itself" (154). In the traditional history of Middle-earth, nature and trees have not been able to express their views on their maltreatment as this narrative has mainly been concerned with the Great Wars and the deeds of the Free Peoples.[6] As Treebeard points out at the beginning of his testimony:

> "I have not troubled about the Great Wars," said Treebeard; "they mostly concern Elves and Men. That is the business of Wizards: Wizards are always troubled about the future. I do not like worrying about the future. I am not altogether on anybody's *side*, because nobody is altogether on my *side*, if you understand me: nobody cares for the woods as I care for them, not even Elves nowadays."   (LotR 472)

In this confession, Treebeard makes explicit his independence from the primary affairs of the people that inhabit Middle-earth, also implying that what he will narrate will go against mainstream history imposed by the governing civilisations.

Although Treebeard is a single individual this testimony under analysis is by no means personal. It could well represent the perspective of the other Ents and even, the symbolic opinion of 'normal trees' if these had the human capacity of speech. Sánchez Zapatero describes how Treebeard's voice represents the collective: "Gracias a su capacidad para reconstruir experiencias y hacer al lector sentirse en el lugar del otro, la experiencia individual adquiere un valor ético universal" ("Thanks to its capacity to reconstruct experiences and put the reader in the shoes of the other, the individual experience acquires a universal ethic value"; my transl.; 109). That is, readers are able to feel empathy for a being which is totally alien to them, to feel its suffering, sadness and comprehend its misfortune. Thus, allowing a greater understanding of the 'other's' life experience which makes them realise that their lives could have been similar (108f.). In his testimony, Treebeard portrays these feelings of despair when he narrates the carnage inflicted on the trees:

---

6   For instance, the second Defeat of Sauron (if his first surrender to Númenor taken as first), the Desolation of Smaug, the Quest of Erebor, the Battle of the Five Armies among others.

He and his foul folk (Saruman and his minions) are making havoc now. Down the borders they are felling trees—good trees. Some of the trees they just cut down and leave to rot—orc-mischief that; but most are hewn up and carried off to feed the fires of Orthanc. There is always a smoke rising from Isengard these days.
"Curse him, root and branch! Many of those trees were my friends, creatures I had known from nut and acorn; many had voices of their own that are lost forever now. And there are wastes of stump and bramble where once were singing groves."
…Skinbark lived on the mountain-slopes west of Isengard. That is where the worst trouble has been. He was wounded by the Orcs, and many of his folk and his tree-herds have been murdered and destroyed.   (LotR 474f.)

Frodo identifies so much with the testimony of Treebeard that despite being just a medium for his words it feels as if the Ent himself were speaking. In order to reach the goal of being a narration soaked with a moral message, testimonies should transmit the violence of the events that took place with extreme intensity (Sánchez Zapatero 119) as in this case. Myriam Jimeno clarifies that this collective understanding materialises mainly due to the sharing of the suffering that the testimony allows (173). This enables readers to place themselves in the witness's situation, empathise with the victims and hence, understand the problem better (173). The emotional bond and solidarity that this produces helps transfer the 'pain' that the witness suffers to the reader (178). As history tends to repeat itself, in this way, perhaps, the reader will not allow the barbarity told in the narrative to take place again in the future, generating a collective conscience in society:

> Se pretende que el infierno personal relatado se convierta en material para la reflexión de los lectores y adquiera, por tanto, dimensiones de universalidad que le hagan trascender de las coordenadas espaciales y temporales en las que se produjo y que le permitan convertirse en paradigma condenatorio aplicable a cualquier manifestación histórica similar. (Sánchez Zapatero 119)

> The intention is that the personal hell narrated, becomes material for the reader to reflect upon and thus, it acquires dimensions of universality that make it transcend spatial and temporal coordinates in which it happened, and that allows it to become a condemnatory paradigm applicable to any similar historical manifestation.   (my transl.; Sánchez Zapatero 119)

This universality is the intent and ultimate goal of Treebeard's testimony. It has a similar feeling and tone of some of the testimonies concerning World War II, specifically those which focus on the murder and burning of humans, demonstrating the applicability of the testimony in fantasy literature. In the passage above, trees are described as if they were humans, which helps the readers create a closer tie and understand their suffering. It recalls the events which took place in Oradour-sur-Glane, where on the 10th of June 1944, 207 infants were killed and burned as narrated by the journalist Héctor Rojas Herazo:

> Aquel es el saldo que el fuego… ha dejado de doscientos siete niños de la población francesa de Oradour. Yesas [sic] cenizas no han sido aventadas. Han sido dejadas allí, en el mismo sitio que las amontonara el invasor,… lo que hoy pudiera ser doscientas siete vidas para el amor, para la congoja o para la esperanza,… Esos niños no fueron reducidos a polvo porque ellos lo quisiesen. (391)

> That is the result the fire… has left of two hundred and seven children of the French town of Oradour. And those ashes have not been fanned. They have been left there, in the same place where the invader had piled them, … what today could have been two hundred and seven lives for love, for grief or for hope… Those children were not reduced to ashes because they wanted to.
> (my transl.; 391)

The situation described is as desperate as Treebeard's, and the focus is placed on the two passages about the loss of loved ones, a tenet of the testimony. At a certain moment in LotR, when Treebeard is parting from Celeborn and Galadriel he uses the expression "by stock or by stone" (981). This phrase that according to Shippey adds no meaning to the conversation but "works well for Fangorn, whose sense of ultimate loss naturally centres on felled trees and barren ground" (181). That loss is ultimately what the testimony aims to represent; the suffering of a being that would have not been able to voice nature's suffering.

Addressing now the reception of the testimonial narrations, this can only occur if the authors generate what Sánchez Zapatero calls the ethics of memory, by which readers should believe the narrated events as true (Sánchez Zapatero 111). At no moment are readers blindfolded; before tackling testimonies, readers make a literary pact with the narrator and accept that the texts in front of them are credible and authentic (110f.). Ergo, the narrator becomes an ethical and political messenger that should not conceal or omit details of the events that took place; instead, facts should be presented as they were (LaCapra 157).

In the case of Treebeard's testimony in LotR, the transcriber makes no attempt to verify the events first hand or to interview Treebeard personally, though they have a brief encounter in Isengard at the end of the book on Frodo's return journey (979-982). Consequently, Frodo, the narrator of the story, is forced to accept Merry's and Pippin's version of Treebeard's testimony. This certainly applies a kind of 'filter' to the events narrated and there is no suggestion in the text of any kind of alteration having taken place.

In this way, Frodo is similar to those historians, who prefer 'circumstantial spectators' rather than direct witnesses since they offer the high degree of objectivity and neutrality they are seeking (LaCapra 159). Both the circumstantial spectator and the direct witness are observers: the former suffers the consequences of the event, whereas the latter contemplates passively the action; Treebeard fulfils the role of the circumstantial observer and part of it may have been told by Skinbark. This distance is enhanced further thanks to the intermediaries Merry and Pippin, as they offer the necessary detachment to produce a narration which is closer to the truth, though readers must always bear in mind that purely objective truth is not always possible.

On Frodo's role as a transcriber it is said that the process starts in The Field of Cormallen: "Frodo and Sam learned much of all that had happened to the Company after their fellowship was broken" (LotR 955) and the subsequent recording process is foretold as well: "Frodo will have to be locked up in a tower in Minas Tirith and write it all down. Otherwise he will forget half of it" (956). Later in Rivendell, Bilbo also takes some notes when he hears the story from Merry and Pippin (986) yet Frodo is the one in charge of editing the material: "Collect all my notes and papers, and my diary too, and take them with you, if you will. You see, I haven't much time for the selection and the arrangements and all that. Get Sam to help, and when you've knocked things into shape, come back, and I'll run over it" (988). After going through so many filters which would make the narrative more objective, Frodo makes the final decision since Bilbo never has the opportunity to go through the material. Therefore, he is the sole faithful steward of Treebeard's tragic tale and the objective and truthful voice which lends credence to its transmission.

One must be aware that a testimony, in spite of containing historical truths, is always subjected to the fictionality of transforming those events into words (Sánchez Zapatero 116), providing the text with certain literary characteristics such as the organisation and editing of the discourse.

It is necessary to bear in mind that the original narrator, Treebeard, not the transcriber, is telling the events from his own memory and even if the story is real in a literary sense, the facts may be presented in a way in which they are slightly altered from reality (116). This effect is enhanced because the transcriber has not heard the story from the sufferer, but from a secondary source, heightening the effects of bad memory. This is not altogether negative, for in the testimony the portrayal of feelings and the empathy with which they engage the reader are more important than the exactitude of the events (118).

Moreover, to achieve that effect certain writers nowadays put aside veracity in favour of fictionality, to enhance the outcome of their account:

> La recurrencia a la construcción de mundos ficcionales concebidos como metáforas de presentes históricos concretos provoca que la realidad no se presente ante el lector como una reconstrucción efectuada e impuesta por el autor. Más bien, ésta surge como una multiplicidad que, más que aprehendida, ha [de] ser comprendida. En consecuencia, el uso de estos recuerdos basados en la creación y el artificio puede activar el valor reflexivo y cognoscitivo de los textos y, con ello, convertirlos en instrumentos válidos para potenciar el uso ejemplar de la memoria.　(Sánchez Zapatero 131-132)

> The recurrence to the building of fictional worlds conceived as metaphors of specific historic present causes that reality is not presented to the reader as a reconstruction executed and imposed by the author. Actually, it emerges as a multiplicity that, more than being grasped, has to be understood. As a consequence, the use of these memories based on the creation and artful device can activate the reflexive and cognitive value of the texts, and with it, turn them into valid instruments to boost the exemplary use of memory.　　　　　(my transl.; Sánchez Zapatero 131-132)

Even the objective genre of biography cannot save itself from some creative process where the writer uses the information with a particular and personal goal. This is the case with Simón Bolívar's[7] fictional reconstruction in Waldo Frank's novel *Birth of a World: Bolivar in Terms of His Peoples* (1951) whereby an altogether totally new perspective of the South-American dictator is offered, drawing him closer to the individuals he ruled over. As Randall explains, Bolívar's imaginary representation as crafted by Waldo Frank is considered to be testimonial (39) and consequently, should it not also be possible to consider fantastic literature's testimony as testimonial? As John Fowles narrates in *The French Lieutenant's Woman* (1969):

7　Simón Bolívar 'Libertador' (1783 Caracas, Venezuela - 1830 Santa Marta, Colombia) was the leader of the Spanish-American Independence. He wanted a united Spanish-America similar to the USA model. He founded the Republic of Bolivar (nowadays Bolivia). His approach to ruling countries did not please everyone, in particular the local oligarchies that ended up rebelling against him because of his dictatorial manners. Nonetheless, Waldo Frank provided in 1951 a new perspective of the leader showing him as benign to the ordinary people.

> But this is preposterous? A character is either "real" or "imagin-
> ary"? If you think that, hypocrite lecteur, I can only smile. You
> do not even think of your own past as quite real; you dress it up,
> you gild it or blacken it, censor it, tinker with it… fictionalise it,
> in a word, and put it away on a shelf—your book, your romanced
> autobiography. We are all in flight from the real reality. That is a
> basic definition of Homo sapiens.   (87)

From this it may be derived that the line between fantasy and reality is a thin one. Tolkien himself made a claim about how sub-creations can be part of reality: "the author if it is the supreme Artist and the Author of Reality, this one was also made to Be, to be true on the Primary Plane" (L 101). The intent in a novel or a testimony could be essentially the same; to transmit a discourse of those without a voice who go against the established history and which allows the possibility of reconstructing truth (Randall 39). Moreover, Tolkien, in the Andrew Lang Lecture on fairy stories, made the following claim hoping that in some way his readers may regard his mythology as close to reality: "'Every writer making a secondary world,' he declared, 'wishes in some measure to be a real maker, or hopes that he is drawing on reality: hopes that the peculiar quality of this secondary world (if not all the details) are derived from Reality, or are flowing into it'" (Carpenter 195). In fact, Tolkien said on Middle-earth: "imaginatively this 'history' is supposed to take place in a period of the actual Old World of this planet" (*Letters* 220).

   In spite of its real-life nature, one must bear in mind that the genre of a real testimony commonly makes use of fictional devices for its narration. Thus, fictionality should not invalidate Tolkien's narrative as a testimony. In a testimony, falsity is considered to invalidate it, whereas a novel is not discredited for having been invented and always preserves the "truths" narrated (Achugar 76). Acknowledging this claim, and considering the aforementioned evidence of Tolkien's hybrid, it can be derived that certain novels can include potential testimonies, as in the case of Treebeard's.

Concluding Thoughts

The previous section shows that Treebeard's narration meets all the required characteristics to be labelled formally a testimony. It also demonstrates that testimonies can be employed to great effect even in a fantastic setting such as Middle-earth, in order to denounce the ravaging of trees and destruction of nature. Testimony in fictional literature, no matter how fantastic, is an important moralising tool and LotR is a clear example of that through the words of Treebeard. The previous offers a new perspective without precedence: the one of nature, portraying its previously unexpressed suffering through the narrative. Moreover, the use of Treebeard's anthropomorphic shape, which helps draw the reader closer to the natural world, is a clever strategy to defend nature from human exploitation and create a collective conscience of its suffering.

Due to the great wisdom with which Ents are endowed, the final outcome may also come to tell the reader that "when forests are destroyed, it is not only an accumulated history of natural growth that vanishes. A preserve of cultural memory also disappears" (Harrison 62). This is because of the fact that myths and knowledge concerning forests, preserved by the Ents in the story, may be forgotten when the physical place has vanished.

However, it is also necessary to point out that the role of witness is not the only one played by Treebeard in the story. Both he and the Ents are active participants in the revolt against the tyrants who aim to reduce Middle-earth to ashes. The lack of any feasible alternative results in the rage for the felled and burned trees which is redirected towards socially helpful action: "we may help the other peoples before we pass away" (LotR 486). Rather than hold their ground and wait until Sauron or Saruman burst into their territory, they try to fight back: "the ents are thus marching to try to make a difference in an age when dark forces have risen and threaten the trees and the very ecology of Middle-earth" (Campbell 262).

Notwithstanding, the Ents will without a doubt pass away, and therefore, the trees' most sustainable, loyal and non-selfish servants will vanish and leave the future of the forests in the hands of Men. As Magdalena Mączyńska postulates: "the Fourth Age may either restore the respect for nature or strengthen the reverence for steel and machines" (130f.), much as in the Real World. A final question remains unanswered: will Aragorn's descendants, as our own, acknowledge the primordial importance of not only trees and forest, but of all kinds of life-forms, or will they fail for being as short-sighted as Saruman and Sauron?

Bibliography

Abella, Ignacio. *La Magia de los Árboles.* Barcelona: Integral, 1996

Achugar, Hugo. "Historias paralelas/ejemplares: la historia y la voz del otro." In: *La voz del otro: testimonio, subalternidad y verdad narrativa.* Eds.: Hugo Achugar & John Beverly. Lima/Berkeley: Latinoamericana Editores, 1992, 61-83

Agamben, Giorgio. *Homo Sacer III: Remnants of Auschwitz, the Witness and the Archive.* Transl.: Daniel Heller-Roazen. New York: Zone Books, 1999

Bates, Brian. *The Real Middle-earth: Exploring the Magic and Mystery of the Middle Ages, J.R.R. Tolkien and* The Lord of the Rings. New York: Palgrave Macmillan, 2003

Campbell, Liam. *The Ecological Augury in the Works of JRR Tolkien.* Zurich/Jena: Walking Tree Publishers, 2011

Carpenter, Humphrey. *J.R.R. Tolkien: A Biography.* Pb. ed. Boston/New York: Houghton Mifflin, 2000

Crossley, Laura. "Digital Perfection or, Will Middle-earth be the Death of New Zealand?" In: *How We Became Middle-earth. A Collection of Essays on "The Lord of the Rings."* Eds.: Adam Lam & Nataliya Oryshchuk. Zurich/Jena: Walking Tree Publishers, 2007, 169-183

Denekamp, Andrea. "'Transform stalwart trees': Sylvan Biocentrism in *The Lord of the Rings.*" In: *Representations of Nature in Middle-earth.* Ed.: Martin Simonson. Zurich/Jena: Walking Tree Publishers, 2015, 1-27

Evans, Julian. *God's Trees: Trees, Forests and Wood in the Bible.* Revised ed. Leominster: Day One Publications, 2015

Fowles, John. *The French Lieutenant's Woman.* London: Triad-Granada, 1977

Harrison, Robert. *Forests the Shadow of Civilisation.* Chicago/London: The University of Chicago Press, 1993

Jimeno, Myriam. "Lenguaje, subjetividad y experiencias de violencia." In: *Antípoda, Revista de Antropología y Arqueología* 5 (2007): 169-190

LaCapra, Dominick. *Escribir la historia, escribir el trauma.* Transl.: Elena Marengo. Buenos Aires: Nueva Visión, 2005

Light, Andrew. "Tolkien's Green Time: Environmental Themes in *The Lord of the Rings.*" In: *The Lord of the Rings and Philosophy: One Book to Rule Them All.* Eds.: Gregory Bassham & Eric Bronson. Chicago/La Salle: Open Court Publishing, 2003, 150-163

Loconte, Joseph. *A Hobbit, a Wardrobe and a Great War: How J.R.R. Tolkien and C.S. Lewis Rediscovered Faith, Friendship, and Heroism in the Cataclysm of 1914-1918.* Nashville: Nelson Books, 2015

Mączyńska, Magdalena. "On Trees of Middle-earth: J.R.R. Tolkien's Mythical Creation." In: *Representations of Nature in Middle-earth.* Ed.: Martin Simonson. Zurich/Jena: Walking Tree Publishers, 2015, 119-137

McGonagill, Doris. "In Living Memory: Tolkien's Trees and Sylvan Landscapes as Metaphors of Cultural Memory." In: *Representations of Nature in Middle-earth.* Ed.: Martin Simonson. Zurich/Jena: Walking Tree Publishers, 2015, 139-169

McKenna, Elise. "To Sex up *The Lord of the Rings*: Jackson's Feminine Approach in his 'Sub-creation.'" In: *How We Became Middle-earth. A Collection of Essays on "The Lord of the Rings."* Eds.: Adam Lam & Nataliya Oryshchuk. Zurich/Jena: Walking Tree Publishers, 2007, 229-237

Randall, Margaret. "¿Qué es y cómo se hace un testimonio?" In: *La voz del otro: testimonios, subalternidad y verdad narrativa.* Eds.: Hugo Achugar & John Beverly. Lima/Berkeley: Latinoamericana Editores, 1992, 33-57

Rojas Herazo, Héctor. *Obra periodística, 1940-1970. Tomo II: La magnitud de la ofrenda.* Ed.: Jorge García Usta. Medellín: Fondo Editorial Universidad EAFIT, 2003

Sánchez Zapatero, Javier. *Escribir el horror: Literatura y campos de concentración.* Barcelona: Montesinos, 2010

Shippey, Tom. *The Road to Middle-earth.* Pb. ed. New York: Houghton Mifflin, 2003

Tolkien, J.R.R. *The Letters of J.R.R. Tolkien.* Ed.: Humphrey Carpenter with the assistance of Christopher Tolkien. Pb. ed. New York: Houghton Mifflin, 2000

---. *The Lord of the Rings.* 50th Anniversary Edition. New York: Houghton Miffin Harcourt, 2004

---. *The Silmarillion.* Ed.: Christopher Tolkien. 7th pb. ed. London: Harper Collins Publishers, 2013

Discourses of Knowledge and Power: Invisibility and Seeing in *The Lord of the Rings*

Laura Selle (Berlin)

> *And with that, even as his eyes were lifted up to gloat on his prize, he stepped too far, toppled, wavered for a moment on the brink, and then with a shriek he fell. Out of the depths came his last wail* Precious, *and he was gone.*　　　　　　　　　(LotR 946)

Introduction

G ollum's fall into the depths of Mount Doom, after taking the Ring from Frodo, is a disappearance from sight, but it is decidedly non-magical.[1] Nevertheless, it is a vanishing which is paradigmatic for the way invisibility in *The Lord of the Rings* acts as a signifier of a subjection to Sauron's power: we do not see the process of Gollum falling—or, as a matter of fact, the actual disintegration of the Ring—and therefore see the subjugating effect of Sauron's power by means of the Ring without seeing its specific technologies. Indeed, there is a close interdependence between the Ring's power to make invisible and Sauron's power to dominate; it lies in the conceptualisation of that power, where power derives from a discourse of knowledge. The Ring does not only make its wearer invisible; it polices visibility and vision and, thus, controls the production of knowledge and creates effects of power. Furthermore, invisibility, as Yvette Kisor and Gergely Nagy suggest, signifies a loss of subjectivity not only by making the subject vanish from the community within the story but also by acting as a textual signifier of the subjection to Sauron's power (Kisor; Nagy, *Body*).[2] The Ring's power—and, by extension, the text—does not only hide the Ring-wearer, though, but also effectively Sauron himself, and the answer to the question of whether he really sees everything. Therefore, my approach in the following analysis will be a close reading of *The Lord of the Rings* in order to determine how invisibility and seeing work together within the story and specifically on a textual level to establish defining principles and technologies

---

1　Although, as my further argument will show, if invisibility is treated as a signifier, there is nothing magical about it whatsoever. For another perspective on the question of magic in Tolkien, see the chapter by Gergely Nagy in this volume.

2　For further discussions of invisibility in *The Lord of the Rings* with different approaches, see Kisor; Eaglestone.

in Sauron's discourse of power. Only then will I look at my findings from a Foucauldian perspective, specifically Foucault's concept of *Panopticism* as a social theory. Thus, I will argue that invisibility is not *a* power of the Ring but part of a larger discourse not of being unseen but, seemingly antithetically, of seeing.[3]

"horribly and uniquely visible": Visual Effects of the One Ring

Like other fictional devices—most prominently perhaps the cloak of invisibility in *The Song of the Nibelungs* or, more recently, the *Harry Potter* series as well as the Helm of Hades in classical mythology—the One Ring brings about invisibility not when possessed but when worn; becoming invisible is not just an ability, it requires a performance—an aspect I will come back to later. Thus, when the Ring is first introduced and used by Bilbo in *The Hobbit*, it is depicted as a simple artefact which grants magical invisibility whenever someone puts in in his finger. This corresponds with its effect witnessed by spectators in *The Lord of the Rings;* in fact, every time the narrative is focalised on a character watching someone put on the Ring, that person is simply described as 'vanishing.'[4] It also functions as the Ring's defining principle, even used by Frodo to reassure himself that he is holding the real Ring (LotR 133).[5] Accordingly, the foremost reason for any character to use the Ring is to escape unwanted eyes. We only experience other properties of the Ring when the narrative is focalised on the wearer himself, which is the case for seven out of nine instances of the Ring being used effectively.[6]

---

3   My strong textual focus on the discourse of seeing and invisibility makes my analysis and course of argument very different to Hugo Filipe Ramos's reading of *The Lord of the Rings* from the perspective of surveillance studies. While Ramos, too, applies Foucault's concept of Panopticism to elements of surveillance in Tolkien's work, his approach is more historical-technical and less text-based than mine, his main conclusion being that the application of surveillance studies to *The Lord of the Rings* is fruitful. In particular, Ramos does not observe the failure of Sauron's surveillance. See Ramos.

4   The word 'vanish' is often used as the initial description of what happens after someone places the Ring on his finger. In the case of the incidents on Weathertop and at Amon Hen, it only comes up in the later recollections of Sam (LotR 197) and Boromir (LotR 404), respectively.

5   At the same time, given that Isildur was able to cut the Ring off Sauron's hand we can assume that Sauron himself was visible while wearing it and likewise is Galadriel, who we know is wearing a ring of power (LotR 353-66).

6   I say 'used effectively' because of Tom Bombadil's immunity to all effects of the Ring, be it turning invisible himself or seeing Frodo, when he wears it (LotR 133). Indeed, nothing quite discloses the fact that the effects of the Ring are precisely that—effects—better than Tom's nonchalance towards it.

Strikingly, at least two of the most immediate effects of wearing the Ring are also visual ones.[7] Firstly, both Frodo and Sam experience a dimming of their eyesight when wearing the Ring at Amon Hen and at Cirith Ungol, respectively: Frodo sees "as through a mist" (LotR 400) and Sam observes that "all things about him now were not dark but vague; while he himself was there in a grey hazy world..." (LotR 734). While the Ring makes its wearer unseen, it also makes him unseeing or, more precisely, polices the things he sees.[8] A second effect of wearing the Ring directly contradicts these first observations. Whereas Aragorn tells the Hobbits that the Nazgûl "themselves do not see the world of light as we do" (LotR 189), Frodo experiences how, instead of being hidden from them after putting on the Ring on Weathertop, "their eyes fell on him and pierced him..." (LotR 195). Suddenly, the Nazgûl can see him and he can see them in return. Similarly, when Sam uses the Ring at Cirith Ungol, "he did not feel invisible at all, but horribly and uniquely visible..." (LotR 734). This evidence suggests that while making its wearer invisible to the eyes of most others, the Ring also makes him visible to both Sauron and the Ringwraiths. Thus, in the power of the Ring there seems to be a curious conflation of invisibility and the abilities to see and *be seen*. Consequently, the main power of the Ring does not seem to be making its wearer invisible but, rather, to police his visibility and vision.[9]

A look at Sauron himself reveals how intrinsically these magical properties are tied to the nature of his power. Indeed, the contradicting visual properties of the Ring are materialised in the depiction of Sauron. As Nagy observes, one of the techniques the narrator uses to represent Sauron in *The Lord of the Rings* is naming him. The name *Sauron* itself is an Elvish word meaning 'abominable' and thus unlikely to be his actual name (Nagy, *Body* 124). In fact, Sauron does not "use his right name, nor permit it to be spelt or spoken" (LotR 416) but is referred to by many names: from titles like "Dark Lord" or simply "the Enemy" to the metonymical "Dark Tower." Another term famously used in reference to Sauron is "the Eye." While the former all constitute more abstract characteristics or enforce Sauron's position as the main antagonist, the latter

---

7   For a further discussion of how the Ring changes sensory perception, see also Rawls; for other power technologies connected to the Ring, see Ramos esp. 141.

8   Indeed, Wodzak and Wodzak deliver a scientific argument for the way "that invisibility comes with at least partial blindness in Middle-earth, which agrees with our understanding of physics" (Wodzak and Wodzak 131f.).

9   While Frodo's visions on top of Amon Hen seem to be accurate depictions of what is happening in some distant places, the Ring also produces deceiving or deluding visions, even when it is not worn. Examples: the moment Bilbo asks to take a look at the Ring once more in Rivendell and transforms into a shadowy creature before Frodo's eyes (LotR 232); when Sam wears it and sees himself transformed into a "Hero of the Age" (LotR 901); when, a little later, Frodo takes back the Ring and, instead of Sam, sees a vision of an orc trying to steal it from him (LotR 912). Melanie Rawls gives further analysis of these visual effects. See Rawls 31.

is the only reference to Sauron which alludes to anything bodily or corporeal. After noting the discourse around visibility inherent to the Ring above, it does not come as a surprise that the bodily feature Sauron is represented by—or performs?—is an eye. Furthermore, while the Eye is referred to as "his" eye, "the Eye of Sauron" or "Eye of Mordor," it is most often used as a synecdoche for all that is Sauron; no other part of his physical body, let alone his whole form, is depicted as consistently in *The Lord of the Rings*.

Sauron's Physicality

There are differing opinions among critics as to whether or not Sauron possesses a body. Kisor assumes the existence of a body for the sole reason that Sauron must have one in order to wear, and thus wield, the Ring (Kisor 20, 24). Melanie Rawls and Nagy, on the other hand, are convinced that Sauron lost his body along with the Ring at the end of the second age (Rawls 30; Nagy, *Body* 123). Sauron is never depicted in his bodily reality; none of the characters ever see or describe him in terms of his appearance.[10] On a textual level, Sauron himself is invisible. At the same time, he is highly present and feared within the story—and not merely because he is the main antagonist. Where does he derive that power from?

To begin with, he has physical representations, most notably the tower of Baraddûr and, naturally, the Ring itself. Nagy notes how Sauron's strengthening "is always figured as a 'return' to his tower and its ,rebuilding'" (Nagy, *Body* 124). We see examples of that when the narrator tells us that "the Dark tower had been rebuilt… From there the power was spreading far and wide," (LotR 44) and when Gandalf tells Frodo that "he has indeed arisen again… and returned to his ancient fastness in the Dark Tower of Mordor" (LotR 51). During the Council of Elrond, the Dark Tower is used as a metonymy for Sauron several times (LotR 250-51). Another means of presence are his armies and the Nazgûl who are servants to his will to such a degree that they seem to be extensions to his power rather than individual agents—which I will come back to later. However, the threat they pose is prone to be an immediate threat for life and limb—they appear physically on various steeds and carry weapons—while

---

10 As I was reminded during the Tolkien Seminar in Augsburg, there is, of course, the issue of Gollum mentioning the Black Hand with its four fingers (LotR 641). While this may be regarded as an indication that Sauron still possesses a body, Gollum's speech is heavily metaphorical a lot of the time; he might well be referring to a more psychological impact: Gollum is talking of a traumatic experience, essentially saying that even with his maimed corporeality, Sauron still can torture. This reading is mirrored in the moment on the Field of Cormallen when, after the destruction of the Ring, a dark shape rises and "stretched out towards them a vast threatening hand, terrible but impotent" (LotR 949) before being blown away by the wind.

Sauron threatens on a more fundamental, omnipotent level. How does the reader—and the characters, as a matter of fact—know that Sauron, indeed, is there as an active player?

As his representation by the Eye suggests, Sauron is most present by looking. While an eye or a gaze themselves can bear great meaning or power, Nagy argues that it acts as a sign for Sauron in several ways:

> It is an *iconic* sign in the first place: the Eye is *physically like* Sauron, at least like all that is knowable of him for subjects in the signifying system of Middle-earth... It is also an *indexical* sign, since it is the source and cause of Sauron's most poignantly felt effect, his *gaze*, the horizon of his operation, knowledge and presence... Finally, the Eye is undoubtedly a *symbolic* sign for Sauron, as in his being called the "Great Eye," "Lidless Eye," "Eye of Barad-dûr," words to signify a supposedly non-linguistic reality; also as an emblem on banners and war gear. (Nagy, *Body* 125f.)

Keeping these multiple significations in mind, what is intriguing about the Eye is that even though it is extremely present in the text it, again, is very rarely *seen* in its physical reality. Following Nagy's differentiation of the Eye into different signs, the one that readers encounter most often is the *symbolic* sign. It is used as one of his many names, seen, as Nagy notes, as his emblem and it is present as an apprehended gaze;[11] Gandalf anticipates the Eye to look towards Isengard or Rohan after the fall of Saruman and the victory at Helm's Deep (LotR 589) and he expects Sauron to watch for signs after the Battle of the Pelennor Fields (LotR 879f.). In addition, since there seems to be no possibility for victory in openly challenging Sauron, the whole purpose of marching against Mordor is to "at all costs keep his Eye from his true peril" (LotR 879f.), i.e. drawn away from Frodo and Sam. Finally, when Gollum guides Frodo and Sam towards the Black Gate, he is in constant fear of the Eye, especially during the passage through the Dead Marshes (LotR 630). Both of them, in turn, encounter it as a lingering threat: at Amon Hen, Frodo *feels* the Eye looking for him (LotR 401), he *knows* it is searching for him through Galadriel's mirror (LotR 364) and both times Sam wears the Ring at Cirith Ungol, he *knows* it is searching for him, too (LotR 734, 898). Neither of them, however, encounters the Eye in its reality in those instances—only visions. In fact, contrary to my initial proposition, it seems that Sauron is most present not when he is looking, as Eaglestone argues (Eaglestone 76), but when there is fear of his surveillance.

---

11   While the gaze is part of the Eye as indexical sign for Nagy, I read it as symbolic, the reason for which will become clear in the course of my argument.

There is a strong visual presence in the image of the ever-watching Eye, which is therefore very poignantly depicted in Peter Jackson's film adaptation as a huge flaming eyeball on top of Barad-dûr. However, the text itself does not provide the reader with the same satisfaction of a strong visual representation. In fact, the reader has to wait until quite far into *The Fellowship of the Ring* to even get a glimpse of the Eye in a physical shape when Frodo looks into the Mirror of Galadriel: "In the black abyss there appeared a single Eye that slowly grew, until it filled nearly all the Mirror... The Eye was rimmed with fire, but was itself glazed, yellow as a cat's, watchful and intent, and the black slit of its pupil opened on a pit, a window into nothing" (LotR 364). Not only is this, incidentally, the first time the Eye is mentioned as a sign for Sauron at all, it is also the only time that it is *shown*, i.e. described in visual terms.[12] After this first encounter—for both Frodo and the reader—the Eye is never visually depicted again and, after all, it is not clear whether Frodo sees a true image or an imagination or vision of it in the first place.

Indeed, there is a stark discrepancy between the assumption and fear of Sauron's gaze and the evidence given for it by the text. He certainly knows a lot about the events in Middle-earth, no doubt thanks to his spies who gather information for him, chief among them the Nazgûl. According to Gollum, "they see everything, everything. Nothing can hide from them... And they *tell* Him everything. He sees, He *knows*" (LotR 630, my emphasis) but there is an ambivalence to his exclamation; he states both that the Nazgûl see and tell Sauron, and that Sauron sees himself. The crucial point in Gollum's observation, however, is the idea that Sauron *knows* which alludes to knowledge-producing practices. The Nazgûl are complicit in Sauron's discourse of power and instruments in his system of surveillance: He *sees* whatever his servants report back to him and therefore *knows*, instead of actually seeing himself. This discrepancy shows itself in other examples. As I mentioned above, it is true that at Amon Hen, Frodo *feels* that "there was an eye in the Dark Tower that did not sleep... A fierce eager will was there. It leaped towards him; almost like a finger he felt it, searching for him" (LotR 401). However, despite its search, it does not succeed in finding him. During their passage of the Dead Marshes, Frodo notices how "thin, so frail and thin, the veils were become that still warded it [the Eye] off" (LotR 630) and when Sam wears the Ring, he feels "the malice of the Eye of Mordor, searching, trying to pierce the shadows that it had made for its own defence, but which now hindered it in its unquiet and doubt" (LotR 898). It is notable, indeed, that in all three instances the Eye is invoked specifically but that even as close to Mordor, Sauron clearly does not see; apart from the

---

12   The "eye of the Dark Power" (LotR 47) is mentioned once before when Gandalf first talks to Frodo about the nature of the Ring but he does not speak about the symbolic sign of "the Eye."

pivotal scene at Mount Doom—which I will come to in a moment—he is never depicted as seeing in the text.

If the Ring neither grants its wearer invisibility, nor Sauron the ability to see, what powers does it possess then and how does it feature in its master's discourse of power? While the Ring as such is not invisible, it is notable for its simplicity and the stark contrast between the powers it is supposed to possess and how the text depicts them.[13] It is described as a weapon with massive powers, able to cause terrible damage and—if wielded by someone strong enough—to twist all good intentions into evil (LotR 61, 267). Gandalf and Elrond appear to have a comprehensive idea of what the Ring is capable of but they only ever allude to its specific powers. Even Sauron's powers when in possession of the Ring are not described in detail. Roberts contests a "certain vagueness" as to what the Ring might do in the wrong hands but, indeed, we never learn what it does in the "right," i.e. Sauron's hands, either (Roberts 62). Thus, the Ring's only visible power is its power of invisibility. However, even this property remains curiously invisible to the reader; as I mentioned above, the narrative is focalised on the person using the Ring most of the time. As a consequence, while vanishing from the sight of other characters, he does not disappear from the text. At the same time, the one thing that spectators *can* see with regard to the power of invisibility is the vanishing of the subject; in the moment the Ring exhibits its power, it simultaneously makes the subject—and, thereby, itself—invisible.

I would argue, therefore, that what we see with regard to the Ring's powers, is not the power itself but the effect, i.e. the disappearance of the subject. Indeed, the Ring is mostly depicted through its effects. Thus, when Gandalf first tells Frodo about the Ring as one of the Great Rings, he does not elaborate on its history, maker, or powers, but explains the effect it has on anyone who keeps or wears it for a long time: It would make him "permanently invisible" (LotR 46f.). Subsequently, the question arises of what kind of power the Ring actually possesses, since none of its powers in themselves are visible. What is at stake then, is not calling into question the power of the One Ring. Rather, I want to consider a different question: Does it matter if the Ring possesses any particular powers? And more importantly: Does it matter if Sauron sees or not? It seems that the main power of the Ring—for Sauron—is the exertion of power itself, the creation of an epistemic discourse of truth, and it is rooted in its technologies of surveillance.

---

13 As Adam Roberts observes, all other Rings of Power are set in with gems and precious stones, while the One Ring is a simple gold band. See Roberts 62.

The Panopticon

I n *Discipline and Punish*, Foucault develops Panopticism as a social theory of the effects of constant surveillance out of Jeremy Bentham's 18th-century design of the Panopticon: a prison which consists of a circular arrangement of cells for solitary confinement with a central watchtower from which a single watchman can surveil all inmates. Most importantly, however, they are—and have to be—unable to discern if they are being watched at any point in time (Foucault 200f.). There are strong parallels between the power of Sauron's gaze and Foucault's Panopticon in the "visibility that insists on a rigorous and universal power" (Chance 21). Sauron effectively establishes his own Panopticon in which his most physical representation is a watchtower, namely Barad-dûr, from which a watchman, the Eye, observes the inmates of a *ring* of cells, i.e. anyone under the power of the One Ring.[14] When Ramos speaks about "Sauron's Panopticon," he distinguishes between the Eye of Sauron as the main Panopticon and other means of surveillance—the Ring, the Palantíri, the Nazgûl—as "mini-Panopticons" (Ramos esp. 138-41).[15] However, I would argue that all these technologies combine into the absolute effect of Sauron's surveillance and, therefore, only together constitute his Panopticon, the Ring and the Nazgûl being vital aspects and effects, respectively, of its power.

Beyond the symbolic, Sauron's Panopticon works very much like Bentham's for several reasons. Most importantly, in order to be present and to exert power over his subjects, Sauron does not need to see. On the contrary, he needs to remain invisible for his power to work in the first place; he needs constant fear of surveillance in his subjects without proof of its absence. Just like the Panopticon, Sauron dissociates "the see/being seen dyad: in the peripheric ring, one is totally seen, without ever seeing; in the central tower, one sees everything without ever being seen" (Foucault 202). The fact that Sauron does not possess any known form greatly helps this. The subjugating power of the Panopticon is not in one's *actual* visibility but in the fear of being watched at any time. Sauron successfully creates that threat.

Secondly, by making the Ring-wearer invisible and dimming his sight, Sauron conforms with the Panopticon's dictum of making the one subjected to its power "the object of information, never a subject in communication" (Foucault 200). Both, Eaglestone and Judith Klinger emphasise the importance

---

14 Wodzak and Wodzak point out that not only Sauron, but also Saruman and Denethor "are all watchers in towers" by way of using the Palantíri. See Wodzak and Wodzak 141.

15 In her analysis of Peter Jackson's film adaptation, Cherylynn Silva also identifies Sauron's system of surveillance as a Panopticon, though an incomplete one because he "only observes one place at a time" (Silva 18). Incidentally, this is a crucial point the film misses and, therefore, not applicable to the book where the perceived threat of surveillance by Sauron and his servants is constant and absolute.

of a community or another to identify with or against in order to retain one's own sense of self and individuality, especially for the Ring-wearers (Eaglestone 76; Klinger 363–66). By making him invisible, the Ring separates its wearer from that community and thus "a collective effect is abolished and replaced by a collection of separated individualities" (Foucault 201). In addition, by making all of Middle-earth a potential object of his investigation, Sauron establishes himself as the only creator of knowledge and, therefore, truth. Silva identifies his invincibility as a truth (see Silva 16) and Wodzak and Wodzak observe something similar in the way Sauron "imposes his 'sight'" on Saruman and Denethor and thus "drives them to see the world as he wills it" (Wodzak and Wodzak 141). Seeing—or not seeing—become crucial technologies in Sauron's discourse of truth, where only the ability to see and be seen constitute the power to produce knowledge—knowledge essential to defeat Sauron.[16]

Thirdly, Sauron and his Ring produce just those "homogeneous effects of power" that are the ultimate goal of the Panopticon (Foucault 202). The case which best represents this is that of the Nazgûl. Sauron does not have to watch his Nazgûl constantly and their Rings do not make them invisible in the same way the One Ring does, because

> he who is subjected to a field of visibility, and who knows it, assumes responsibility for the constraints of power; he makes them play spontaneously upon himself; he inscribes in himself the power relation in which he simultaneously plays both roles; he becomes the principle of his own subjection. By this very fact, the external power may throw off its physical weight; it tends to the non-corporeal; and, the more it approaches this limit, the more constant, profound and permanent are its effects… (Foucault 203)

The Ringwraiths are so strongly subjected to his power that they themselves perform their subjection by enacting a kind of invisibility which makes them *unseen* but not wholly invisible to the eyes of others. Sauron's gaze "articulates power relationships in physical terms," (Nagy, *Subject* 65) making the Nazgûl inscribe his power onto their own bodies. As a consequence, what is invisible about them is not their whole form but their subjectivity; whenever they appear, the narrator notes their cloaks but when Gandalf confronts the Witch King at the gates of Minas Tirith, there is explicit mentioning of the gap between his cloak and the crown on his head (LotR 829). It is the same effect that Gandalf warns Frodo about in the very beginning (LotR 46f.). By contrast, when Sam

---

16 Silva identifies hope as a point of resistance against Sauron's proclaimed invincibility. Even though Frodo's task seems impossible, the members of the fellowship keep up their hope and root their continuing agency to support him in this hope. See Silva 16.

wears the Ring, everything about him turns invisible, including Frodo's sword Sting whose glow the orcs walking in front of him do not see (LotR 637). Thus, the longer a being is subjected to Sauron's discourse of knowledge, the more it becomes complicit in its own subjection.

"… in a *blinding* Flash": Sauron's Fall

S auron orchestrates a discourse where seeing means having knowledge and, therefore, power, and where being seen means being a subject of investigation but in which he himself ultimately fails to perform. By using the Eye as an iconic, indexical and symbolic sign, Sauron tries to materialise himself as an omnipotent and omnipresent agent of power in replacement of the physical body which he does not possess anymore. However, as I argued, Sauron never succeeds in seeing. Indeed, even the powerful Palantíri do not grant him the ability to actively see.[17] On the contrary, Aragorn has to show himself to Sauron in order to be seen (LotR 879) and even supposedly weaker characters like Pippin or Denethor make a somewhat conscious decision to look into a Palantír and be seen, while a mere piece of cloth is enough to shut Sauron's gaze out (LotR 592; 853).

The pivotal moment in which all his deceptions—and the unreliability of the text itself—are disclosed is the apparent failure of the quest when Frodo claims the Ring: It is then that "[Sauron's] Eye piercing all shadows looked across the plain to the door that he had made; and the magnitude of his own folly was revealed to him in a *blinding* flash" (LotR 946, my emphasis). Only in this moment of realisation, Sauron is finally depicted as unseeing and even though "the whole mind and purpose of the Power… was now bent with overwhelming force upon the mountain" (LotR 946) he is unable to interfere. Sauron's moment of realisation offers an insight into the power dynamics at play—not just within the story but also on a textual level. Before, the text was trying to deceive its readers regarding Sauron's ability to see and made them complicit in the assumption that he can, but during the climactic scene in the heart of Mount Doom, he is actively *blinded* in the wake of his ultimate loss of power. Without seeing, Sauron has no power and as soon as the truth about his blindness is disclosed, his discourse of knowledge crumbles.

In order to be freed from Sauron's subjugating power, it is not the watchman who needs to be overcome but the prison itself; only if the Ring is destroyed, the

---

17   In fact, when Frodo sees the Eye in Galadriel's mirror, there is an indication that he would have to actively show himself to be seen by it, too: "…and Frodo knew with certainty and horror that among the many things that it sought he himself was one. But he also knew that it could not see him—not yet, not unless he *willed* it" (LotR 364, my emphasis).

mere possibility of being watched will be obliterated. As long as it exists, there will be the fear of surveillance because "power has its principle not so much in a person as in a certain concerted distribution of bodies, surfaces, lights, gazes" (Foucault 202). Subsequently, the realisation of Sauron's blindness negates the power of the Ring in so far that even though Frodo does not become genuinely visible, he does suddenly become vulnerable to Gollum's attack—a vulnerability to an external force that no Ring-wearer had experienced previously. In the aftermath, a continued existence of Sauron and the Ring is impossible because the most important premise of their technologies of power is unveiled: Sauron cannot always see and the knowledge he has been producing is not the only possible truth.[18]

This finally lets me circle back to my initial assertions about Gollum's fall. His (manner of) disappearance does not just coincide with his reclaiming of the Ring, it is the logical consequence and final performance of Gollum's subjection to Sauron's power. He bites the Ring off Frodo's finger, stumbles over the edge and "he was gone" (LotR 946). After having been controlled by it for so long, he cannot be freed from the prison but, by inscribing in himself the power-relation of the Panopticon with a fatal finality, can only perish with it. In the light of the massive power effects associated with the Ring and its master, their demise is depicted extraordinarily quietly. The text does not provide us with a description of Gollum's fall or the unmaking of the Ring. We are shown the crumbling of the fortresses of Mordor and the text itself seems to rear up in highly visual descriptions of falling battlements, plumes of smoke and blazing fires as if to perform the visible and material reality of Sauron one last time. Ultimately, though, these moments end in relative calm and quiet: Gollum and the Ring are simply *gone*, the Nazgûl burst into flame and then *go out* and a *hush* falls on the fields of Cormallen (LotR 946-949). Bereft of its prerequisite after the watchman is removed from the tower, the whole prison—and all that was truly bound by its power—implodes.

Conclusion

As proposed in the introduction, invisibility in itself is not a power that the One Ring *grants* its wearer but a textual signifier of subjection in the discourse of knowledge orchestrated by Sauron. Within this discourse, the ability to see means the ability to produce knowledge and, therefore, to have power. To be invisible or to have one's vision policed means being subjected to

---

18 In a similar sense, Nagy accounts for Sauron's downfall with the fact that he never achieves to be a genuine centre of discourse and therefore does not manage to control meaning. See Nagy, *Body* 129.

surveillance and made an object of investigation. Therefore, invisibility in *The Lord of the Rings* is inherently a textual deception and never fully real(ised). Indeed, the text itself performs a variety of visual truths which turn out not to be real: Sauron cannot see, the Eye—which is highly present as a name, physical representation and function—is almost never shown or seen and the Ring-wearer does not gain true invisibility. Mostly, however, Sauron is proven not to be invincible and the falsification of this produced truth can finally lead to his defeat.

Bibliography

Chance, Jane. *The Lord of the Rings: The Mythology of Power.* University Press of Kentucky, 2001

Eaglestone, Robert. "Invisibility". In: *Reading* The Lord of the Rings: *New Writings on Tolkien's Trilogy.* Ed.: Robert Eaglestone. Continuum, 2006, 73-84

Foucault, Michel. *Discipline and Punish. The Birth of the Prison.* Transl.: Alan Sheridan. Vintage, 1995

Kisor, Yvette. "Incorporeality and Transformation in *The Lord of the Rings*". In: *The Body in Tolkien's Legendarium: Essays on Middle-earth Corporeality.* Ed.: Christopher Vaccaro. McFarland, 2013. 20-38

Klinger, Judith. "The Fallacies of Power: Frodo's Resistance to the Ring". In: *The Ring Goes Ever On. Proceedings of the Tolkien 2005 Conference: 50 Years of* The Lord of the Rings. Ed.: Sarah Wells, vol. 1, The Tolkien Society, 2008, 355-69

Nagy, Gergely. "A Body of Myth. Representing Sauron in *The Lord of the Rings*". In: *The Body in Tolkien's Legendarium: Essays on Middle-earth Corporeality.* Ed.: Christopher Vaccaro. McFarland, 2013, 119-32

---. "The 'Lost' Subject of Middle-earth: The Constitution of the Subject in the Figure of Gollum in The Lord of the Rings". *Tolkien Studies* 3 (2006): 57-79

Ramos, Hugo Filipe. "O Panóptico de Sauron: Poder E Vigilância No Senhor Dos Anéis de J.R.R. Tolkien [Sauron's Panopticon: Power and Surveillance in J.R.R. Tolkien's *Lord of the Rings*]". *Observatorio (OBS*) Journal* 7, no. 3 (2013): 129-52

Rawls, Melanie. "The Rings of Power". *Mythlore* 40 11, no. 2 (Autumn 1984): 29-32

Roberts, Adam. "The One Ring". *Reading* The Lord of the Rings: *New Writings on Tolkien's Trilogy.* Ed.: Robert Eaglestone. Continuum, 2006, 59-70

Silva, Cherylynn. "One Ring to Rule Them All: Power and Surveillance in the Film Adaptation of *The Lord of the Rings*". *The Undergraduate Review.* Bridgewater State University 2, no. 1, (2006): 15-20

Tolkien, J.R.R. *The Lord of the Rings.* 50th Anniversary Edition, HarperCollins, 2009

Wodzak, Michael A., & Victoria Holtz Wodzak. "Visibílium Ómnium et Invisibílium: Looking Out, On, and In Tolkien's World". *Tolkien Studies* 11 (2014): 131-47

Summaries of the German Essays

Romantic Worldbuilding in H.P. Lovecraft's Work

Julian T.M. Eilmann

H.P. Lovecraft is considered one of the grandmasters of modern horror literature who himself has created a literary cosmos in which human beings are encountering terrible cosmic entities with the frequent effect of ending up (firstly) mad and/or (later on) dead. In this article another side of Lovecraft is highlighted that presents the author as deeply rooted in the romantic tradition, an observation that may confuse those who understand Lovecraft as someone particularly promoting materialism and rationalism in his work. But despite this self-depiction as an anti-spiritualistic author, Lovecraft extensively deals with the fascination for the supernatural, wonderful and mysterious that surrounds and lures the human being—a genuine romantic motive. Especially Lovecraft's fantastic *Dreamland* cycle focuses on these romantic topoi. His story "The Silver Key" is a portray of a romantic individual, Randolph Carter, disgusted by the ordinary world, superficial human beings and sciences that only scratch on the surface of life. Instead, the adult Carter is driven by a strong romantic desire for the dreamland he had contact to in his youth. The text focuses on depicting Carters romantic longing that ultimately drives him towards escaping into the land of poetry—the Dreamlands—via the magical silver key. This ending of a romantic individual who longs for transcendence and thus leaves the ordinary sphere is a typical romantic narrative.

Apology of the Fantastic

Christian and Sophie Lemburg

In this paper, we investigate the role of worldbuilding for fantasy, its audience and its impact. The interaction with fantastic imaginary worlds and their specific secondary realities works similar to modern mental training. The specific creation of the fantastic secondary realities—the specifically fantastic worldbuilding—increases saturation, absorption, retention and repetition of the contents through saliency and use of familiar structures, resulting in a strong identification with these contents, which again leads to the creation of "tribes" and further development of the individual. The simulation of alternative actions in the context of a new framework with enhanced capabilities offers the opportunity to simulate alternative solutions to problems and to try out or train new alternative actions and roles in the imaginary world, resulting in new solutions to existing problems. These activities have training effects and may work as preventative measures. Furthermore, the specifically fantastic world-building forms a basis for identification, sense-making and finding answers in a context differing from the main social construct. In this way, fantasy creates mental potentials, individuals and groups which can be viewed as an "emergency reserve" or "innovation potential" in comparison to the main social construct. In short: fantasy prevents us from stagnating.

The World of the Deryni and their Creation

Friedhelm Schneidewind

T he American author, scholar and historian Katherine Kurtz (born 1944) has written more than twenty books introducing the "magical race" of the Deryni. In the world of the Deryni, magic and a pseudo Catholic Church lead a not always peaceful co-existence. This alternative version of the Middle Ages is considered a highlight of historical fantasy literature, and the imaginary society presented is used to mirror our real-world situation and poses numerous questions regarding ethics and religion.

Zusammenfassungen der englischen Aufsätze

Game of Thrones gesehen durch das Prisma der Tolkien'schen Theorie über »fairy stories«

Annie Birks

A ngesichts des Genres, der Reichweite und des weltweiten Erfolgs der *Game-of-Thrones*-Serie erscheint es für jeden Fantasy-Interessierten relevant und legitim zu untersuchen, ob die Serie die von Tolkien in seinem Essay *On Fairy-stories* aufgeführten Zutaten für eine gute »fairy story« enthält. Dieser Beitrag fragt danach, in welchem Ausmaß wir Wiedergewinnung, Flucht, Trost und allgemeine Anwendbarkeit in der Serie finden. Dafür werden Online-Kommentare der Fangemeinschaft, Presseartikel sowie die Ergebnisse einer 2015 durchgeführten Umfrage unter mehr als 2.000 Studierenden in der französischen Universitätsstadt Angers analysiert.

Die Geschichte der Frauen in George R.R. Martins Welt

Isabel Busch

Dieser Aufsatz zeigt auf, dass George R.R. Martin in seiner erschaffenen Phantasiewelt Westeros, die am prominentesten in den Romanen *A Song of Ice and Fire* erscheint, Hinweise auf seine Konzeption von Gleichberechtigung der Geschlechter bzw. Geschlechterungleichheit in dieser Welt durch seine Kriegerinnen gibt. Diverse Einzelfiguren und Figurengruppen aus Westeros, die als Kriegerinnen bezeichnet werden können, werden untersucht und in einen Gender-Kontext gestellt. Nach jedem Abschnitt, der sich mit solch einer Figur/Figurengruppe beschäftigt, wird ein potentielles Gegenstück für diese Kriegerinnen aus der realen Weltgeschichte aufgezeigt. Wie wir sehen, gibt es in Westeros einige Beispiele für eine wechselseitige Beziehung zwischen den jeweils variierenden Graden der Akzeptanz von Kriegerinnen und der Gleichberechtigung der Geschlechter. Es wird argumentiert, dass zumindest in Westeros Frauen eher dort einen egalitären Status genießen, wo es auch für sie akzeptabler ist, Waffen zu tragen. Wenn die möglichen historischen Vorbilder vorgestellt werden, wird ein entsprechender Vergleich gezogen.

Die Stimme der Natur in Mittelerde durch die Linse des literarischen Zeugnisses

Andoni Cossío

Dieser Essay untersucht die Verbindungen zwischen »realer Welt« und literarischen Sekundärwelten und will darlegen, wie Genres der »echten Welt« in der Phantastischen Literatur Verwendung finden können: etwa die Textsorte des *Zeugnisses*, das aus realistischen Teilstücken zusammengesetzt ist. Dies wird anhand einer Analyse des Zeugnisses des Baumhirten Baumbart gezeigt. Dafür wird der theoretische Hintergrund von Zeugnissen erläutert (Dominick LaCapra, Giorgio Agamben, Hugo Achugar, Javier Sánchez Zapatero, Margaret Randall, Myriam Jimeno). Anschließend werden die Eigenschaften aufgeführt und analysiert, die in der Erzählung von Tolkiens Werk und der Subkreation Arda vorkommen. Vordergründig streben Zeugnisse danach, denen eine Stimme zu geben, die durch die vorherrschenden Geschichts-Autoritäten übergangen worden sind; Baumbarts Zeugnis ist der Inbegriff einer solchen »vergessenen Geschichte«. Das Hauptanliegen eines Zeugnisses ist es, Aufmerksamkeit für bis dato verdeckte Perspektiven auf historische Ereignisse zu wecken. Baumbart geht jedoch noch einen Schritt weiter, indem er rebelliert und eine Revolution gegen Saruman anführt, der für die mutwillige Zerstörung vieler Bäume verantwortlich ist. Dieses einzigartige Zeugnis repräsentiert nicht nur ein Individuum oder eine Gruppe von Bäumen, sondern die Natur selbst (im weiten Sinne des Wortes) – d.h. sowohl die Welt von Arda als auch die »reale Welt«.

»Sub-creation« bei J.R.R. Tolkien und J.L. Borges

Natalia González de la Llana

Dieser Aufsatz nimmt eine vergleichende Analyse von J.L. Borges' und J.R.R. Tolkiens Konzept des Autors als Schreiber, als Vermittler vor. Als nicht-religiöser Mensch sieht Borges nicht Gott als Ursprung seiner Fiktion, sondern die Literatur der Vergangenheit. Für Tolkien hingegen ist der Künstler ein Werkzeug Gottes, der in seinen Werken ein Echo des Evangeliums erkennen lässt.

Ein solches Konzept des Autors als Vermittler macht die Originalität eines Werkes zu einem eher unwichtigen Merkmal und erlaubt einen Dialog mit anderen literarischen Texten, so dass Intertextualität zu einer essentiellen Basis der *sub-creation* wird. Sowohl bei Borges als auch bei Tolkien ist also das Umschreiben, die neue Interpretation von alten Erzählungen ein wichtiger Teil der schriftstellerischen Arbeit. Bei Borges geht es um die Auseinandersetzung mit unvergänglichen Themen, die stetig wiederaufgenommen werden. Tolkien möchte die Wahrheit hinter den Mythen aufdecken.

Dennoch stellt man, auch wenn diese zwei Autoren einige Parallelen in Bezug auf ihre Ideen über Autorenschaft und Schreibprozess aufweisen, auch Unterschiede in der Bedeutung oder Absicht fest, die sie an ihre Geschichten knüpfen. Borges' Verständnis der Welt als Chaos führt ihn zur neophantastischen Literatur (Fanfan Chens *mirror-discourse*), um die Irrealität des Universums darzustellen. Tolkien entwickelt im Gegensatz dazu seine Phantasie innerhalb des Rahmens des Wunderbaren (*dream-discourse*) in seinem Versuch, einen Zustand zu präsentieren, in dem Menschen der Schöpfung harmonisch gegenüberstehen.

»Worldbuilding« und Mythopoeia in zeitgenössischer Fantasyliteratur

Massimiliano Izzo

In seinem *Buch Imagining Worlds – The Theory and History of Sub-creation* behandelt Mark J.P. Wolf die Begriffe »Worldbuilding« und »Zweitschöpfung« als Synonyme. Der Terminus »Zweitschöpfung« wurde erstmals von J.R.R. Tolkien in seinem Vortrag *On Fairy-stories* verwendet, in welchem er unter anderem die Schöpfung von Mythen, oder Mythopoeia, erläutert. In dem Aufsatz beschreibt Tolkien Zweitschöpfungen als einen »Aspekt der Mythologie«, eine Kunst, die dem elbischen Zauber gleicht; als die Fähigkeit, eine sekundäre Welt zu erschaffen, die die gleiche Konsistenz wie die reale Welt aufweist. Tolkiens mythopoetische Zweitschöpfung stimmt jedoch nicht vollständig oder gar nicht mit dem weiterreichenden und detaillierteren Worldbuilding überein, besonders wenn dieses sich mit den Aspekten des alltäglichen Lebens auseinandersetzt wie etwa Ökonomie, Politik und Logistik. Tolkien war darauf bedacht, auf einer recht oberflächlichen, vagen Ebene des Worldbuildings zu verbleiben und Elementen, die außerhalb der mythologischen (und linguistischen) Dimension liegen, keine große Aufmerksamkeit zu schenken. Fantasyschriftsteller nach Tolkien haben stets angestrebt, eine Balance zwischen den beiden zu finden, so wie es Tolkien in *Der Herr der Ringe* schaffte. Unter denen, die in Tolkiens Fußstapfen traten, sind die Wege der Mythopoeia und des Worldbuilding bis auf wenige Ausnahmen stets auseinandergegangen. Auf der einen Seite gibt es Mythenschöpfer, die sich vom detaillierten Worldbuilding und der grandiosen epischen Welt des *Herrn der Ringe* entfernen. Am anderen Ende des Spektrums stehen zeitgenössische Autoren von epischer High Fantasy, die meist die Mythopoeia gegen einen mehr historisch ausgelegten Ansatz eintauschen, ihre Welten mit reichhaltigen Details ausstatten und eine ausgeprägte Entmythologisierung der phantastischen Elemente betreiben.

Dieser Aufsatz analysiert die Natur dieser Dichotomie zwischen Mythopoeia und Worldbuilding und zeigt mögliche Wege auf, wie Autoren diese Gegensätzlichkeit überwinden und Werke schaffen können, die beide Aspekte vereinen.

Armeen der Finsternis als Katalysator von Veränderungen und Verkörperung des Bösen

Franz Klug

J.R.R. Tolkiens Mittelerde ist der Schauplatz gewaltiger Konflikte zwischen den Freien Völkern und den despotischen Herrschern Morgoth und Sauron, die Armeen der Finsternis aus Drachen, Balrogs, Orks, Trollen und Nazgûl kommandieren. Die literarische Erschaffung dieser dunklen Kreaturen ist dem Prozess der *sub-creation* zuzuordnen, der Schöpfung von Sekundärwelten, wie sie Mark J.P. Wolf in seinem Buch *Building Imaginary Worlds* (2016) behandelt. Der vorliegende Aufsatz beschäftigt sich mit der semantischen und etymologischen Betrachtung der von Tolkien geschaffenen Armeen der Finsternis und untersucht dabei auch die zugrundeliegenden mythologischen Themen und Konzepte. Tolkiens Werk beeinflusste auch spätere Phantasiewelten wie etwa das *Warhammer*-Universum oder George R.R. Martins *Lied von Eis und Feuer* (als HBO-Serie:

A Game of Thrones). Genauso wie in Tolkiens Welt begegnen wir auch in diesen Sekundärwelten verschiedenen Armeen der Finsternis. Wie diese Armeen erschaffen wurden und inwiefern sie in Verbindung zu Tolkiens ursprünglichen Schöpfungen stehen, ist ebenfalls Thema dieses Aufsatzes. Sowohl Tolkiens Armeen der Finsternis als auch die düsteren Heerscharen aus *Warhammer* und *A Game of Thrones* lassen sich als Verkörperung des Bösen definieren. Ein Schwerpunkt dieser Abhandlung besteht darin, diese Verkörperung des Bösen hinsichtlich ihres theologischen und ethischen Sinngehalts zu untersuchen. Da das Böse direkt in das Geschick seiner phantastischen Sekundärwelten eingreift, gilt es des Weiteren festzustellen, inwiefern sich diese jeweiligen Armeen der Finsternis als Katalysatoren der Veränderung auf ihre Sekundärwelten auswirken. Insgesamt soll die Betrachtung der Ursprünge dieser Armeen, ihrer Rolle als Verkörperung des Bösen und ihrer katalysatorischen Wirkung einen Einblick in die Konstruktion und Intention solcher Armeen der Finsternis geben.

Zur Konstruktion des Phantastischen durch Dialog in Tolkiens Erzählkosmos

Timo Lothmann, Arndt Heilmann, Sven Hintzen

In dieser Studie werden die Dialoge einer repräsentativen Textsammlung aus dem Mittelerde-Legendarium näher betrachtet, um das funktionale Potential von Dialog im Allgemeinen und dessen Einfluss auf Weltbildung im Besonderen zu untersuchen. Zu diesem Zweck werden korpusanalytische Werkzeuge aus der Linguistik mit einem kognitiven Ansatz kombiniert.

Der für die Studie zusammengestellte Korpus umfasst Tolkiens *Das Silmarillion*, *Der Hobbit* sowie *Der Herr der Ringe*. Alle Texte wurden annotiert und in der Folge unter anderem einer automatisierten Wortart-Analyse unterzogen. Eine Beispieldiskussion konzeptueller Metaphern rundet den Methodenkatalog ab. Als Ergebnis der darauf aufbauenden quantitativen und qualitativen Analyse hervorstechender sprachlicher Merkmale in ausgewählten Beispielen dialogischer Interaktion (z.B. der Dialog zwischen Smaug und Bilbo in *Der Hobbit*) tritt zutage, dass Dialoge deutliche Unterschiede in Aufbau und Funktion innerhalb des Korpus aufweisen. Die gefundenen Muster führen schließlich zu einer funktionsbasierten Klassifizierung der Dialoge in vier Haupttypen: *bantering* (Plaudern), *personalising* (Personalisierung), *story-propelling* (Vorantreiben der Erzählung) und *historicising* (Historisierung). Diese Typen werden in der vorliegenden Studie mit dem Ziel modelliert, die Vielfalt der Stile und der Inhaltsdimensionen von der Mikro- bis zur Makroebene abzudecken. Bedeutsam ist, dass das zugrundeliegende systematische *Foregrounding* in den

Dialogen jeweils einen eigenen Beitrag zur Dichte der Weltbildung und der Erzählkohärenz leistet.

Ein Ziel dieser Studie ist es, zu einem insgesamt besseren Tiefenverständnis der Konstruktion der Tolkien'schen phantastischen Welten zu gelangen. Das dargelegte Modell von Dialogtypen ist dahingehend angelegt, dass es auch für Studien von Dialog in fiktionaler Literatur über Tolkien hinaus nutzbar ist. Aus dem Zusammenhang von Dialog als einem vielseitigen und strategisch verwendeten Mittel ergibt sich ein hohes Potential für experimentelle Folgestudien mittels Eye-Tracking.

Auf der Suche nach Individualität und fundamentaler Realität in Neil Gaimans *Neverwhere*

Magdalena Mączyńska

Neil Gaiman zeigt in *Neverwhere* eine dunkle und komplexe Vision Londons. Es besitzt ein merkwürdiges und unterirdisches Doppel, welches zwar unauflöslich mit der überirdisch gelegenen Stadt verbunden, jedoch gleichzeitig gänzlich eigen ist. Als ein Ort für Ausgestoßene, die nicht an der Konformität der Hauptstadt teilhaben möchten, offenbart sich die Unterseite dem Protagonisten Richard Mayhew ungewollt als sowohl gefährlich wie auch verlockend. Als er die Parallelstadt betritt, ist er sich der Konsequenzen seiner Entscheidung nicht bewusst. Schnell erkennt er, dass es keine leichte Aufgabe ist, die Regeln zu verstehen, die diese andere Dimension beherrschen, da die Unterscheidung zwischen dem, was real und nicht real ist, verschwimmt. Schließlich begreift Richard, dass Unter-London auf eine unbestimmbar beunruhigende Weise gefährlich ist, da es die felsenfest verankerten Normen und Überzeugungen durchbricht und damit die Vortäuschung falscher Tatsachen zersprengt. Indem die Unterseite die tiefliegenden Ebenen von Richards Wesen berührt, legt sie seinen Charakter offen. Unter-London verstärkt seine Eigenschaften, egal, ob gut oder schlecht. Richard, der danach strebt, in die alltäglichen Dimensionen Londons zurückzufinden, findet sich auf der Suche nach seiner Individualität. Unter-London verändert Richard, indem es ihm seine Wünsche und sein Verlangen offenbart. In *Neverwhere* erschafft Neil Gaiman einen Protagonisten, der gezwungen ist, sich der anderen, alternativen Stadt zu stellen und seine Meinungen und Vorurteile neu zu bewerten, da diese durch den Kontakt mit dem Unbekannten zerstört werden. Richard muss sein Leben und seine Prioritäten neu ordnen, als er versteht, dass Unter-London authentischer und zugleich zugänglicher ist als seine eintönige Existenz in London.

Dieser Essay befasst sich mit Neil Gaimans Roman *Neverwhere* und der sekundären Welt, die der Autor erschafft, seiner Struktur und Verbindung zur primären Welt sowie dem Verständnis von Realität, mit dem sich der Protagonist auseinandersetzt. Zusätzlich wird Richard Mayhews physische als auch metaphysische Reise durch Unter-London beleuchtet.

Eine Welt zweitschöpfen: Von der Künstlichkeit zum Artefakt

Marguerite Mouton

Die Diskussion über »Worldbuilding« scheint oft ein künstliches Schaffen zu implizieren. Dieser Text soll diese Annahme in Frage stellen, indem Tolkiens Briefe, insbesondere die vom 7. bis 8. November 1944, im Detail betrachtet werden. Der Essay untersucht, in welchem Sinne eine sekundäre Welt die Strukturen der primären Welt teilt – so wie man solche Strukturen etwa auch im Neuen Testament findet. Die Welt, die Tolkien erschuf, verdient es nicht, als »künstlich« bezeichnet zu werden, da sie die Erfahrungsstruktur der realen Welt enthält. Jedoch bleibt sie ein Artefakt, welches die Bedingungen für solche Erfahrungen bereitstellt.

Keine Magie bei Tolkien: Den repräsentationalen Kriterien des Realismus widerstehen

Gergely Nagy

Obwohl in der theoretischen wie generischen Kritik von Fantasy »Magie« immer ein bedeutender Begriff war, spielt er in Tolkiens Mittelerde und seinen eigenen theoretischen Schriften eine relativ geringe Rolle. Während er sein Legendarium entwickelte, entfernte Tolkien allmählich die meisten seiner früheren »magischen« Ideen und transformierte sie in Manifestationen der theologischen Hierarchie Mittelerdes in den literarischen Texten und der Faszination der Kunst in *On Fairy-stories*. Tolkiens Mittelerde-Texte und das *Silmarillion* von 1977 enthalten daher keine Magie im traditionellen kultur-historischen Sinn. Dies ist ein Aspekt von Tolkiens spezifischer Art der systematischen mythopoetischen Praxis im Gegensatz zu den ideologisch aufgeladenen repräsentationalen Kriterien des Realismus: Ein Gegenstück zur Ideologie des Realismus ist etwas, das die literarische Phantastik (auf jeden Fall Tolkiens Variante) möglich macht.

Dekonstruktion des »historischen« Hintergrunds in Tolkiens Vorwort zu *Farmer Giles of Ham*

Łukasz Neubauer

Tolkiens sorgfältige Arbeit, die Welt von Arda zu kreieren, war ein lebenslanger Prozess, dessen Elemente immer noch (wieder)entdeckt, analysiert und diskutiert werden. In der Tat begründet Arda mit der mittelalterlichen Substruktur und den oft impliziten, aber erkennbaren christlichen Untertönen eine der bemerkenswertesten Errungenschaften der Weltenschöpfung in der gesamten literarischen Welt. *Farmer Giles of Ham* unterscheidet sich zwar sehr von Tolkiens Werken über Mittelerde, insofern die Hauptfunktion darin liegt, seinen eigenen Kindern etwas narrative Unterhaltung zu bieten. Außerhalb des Mittelerde-Kanons gelegen, ist es überdies in seiner strukturellen Integrität und Nachhaltigkeit deutlich weniger ausgebildet. Jedoch überrascht es wenig, dass die Mechanismen und Themen, die Tolkiens andere fiktionale Werke kennzeichnen, nicht völlig abwesend sind. Trotz seines konzisen Charakters und ironischen Tons ist die Geschichte von Ægidius Ahenobarbus reich an solch typischen Tolkien'schen Kennzeichen wie die Kartierung der geographischen Konturen und der Gebrauch unterschiedlicher linguistischer Register. Schließlich ist *Farmer Giles of Ham* vielleicht etwas überraschend ziemlich konsistent – ungeachtet der zahlreichen Anachronismen – darin, den »historischen« Hintergrund der Legende »möglicherweise nach den Tagen König Coels, doch vor Arthur oder den Sieben Königreichen der der Engländer« (siehe Vorwort FGH) einzuordnen. Dieser Beitrag untersucht diese »historischen« Fundamente der Narrative Tolkiens mit einer besonderen Betonung der Rolle und Funktion seines pseudo-historischen Vorworts zu dieser Geschichte.

Transmediales Worldbuilding und Medienkonvergenz

Helmut W. Pesch

Der Begriff Worldbuilding hat in jüngerer Zeit mit der medialen Verwertung von Werken, welche die Wertschöpfungskette eines erfolgreichen Produkts verlängern, einen neuen Stellenwert gewonnen. Die damit verbundene Fokussierung auf den Hintergrund des Werkes wird in der Literaturkritik durchaus zwiespältig diskutiert. Tolkiens Werk gilt als ein Musterbeispiel des Worldbuilding, was ihm in der kritischen Akzeptanz keinesfalls zum Vorteil gereichte. Sein Roman *The Lord of the Rings* ist mit Karten, Abbildungen und Paratexten bereits multimodal angelegt und erfordert einen in der Deutung von Zeichensystemen versierten Leser. Aus seinen jahrelangen Vorarbeiten wurde posthum eine Menge an nicht- oder nur teilweise kanonischen Texten veröffentlicht. Dies findet bei der Verfilmung eine Parallele im Überdesign von Materialien, die nur ansatzweise Verwendung finden. Hinzu kommen partizipatorische Aspekte wie Fanfiction, von den Rechteinhabern mit einer prekären Mischung aus Toleranz und Misstrauen gesehen, da sie sowohl die Deutungshoheit als auch die ökonomische Kontrolle über das geistige Eigentum infrage stellen. Dabei ist unklar, inwieweit solche sekundären und tertiären Texte noch Teil der Storywelt sind. Dies gilt auch für parallele Narrative wie die Fiktionalisierung des Autors in Romanen. Die Spannung zwischen kohärenten Storywelten und den heterogenen kreativen Werken des transmedialen World-building, bei denen vom Pastiche bis zur ironischen Brechung und ästhetischen Umwidmung alles möglich ist, wirft auch die Frage auf, inwieweit die Deutung von Fantasy als postmodernes Spiel innerhalb begrenzter Parameter noch halt-bar ist. Als ein kulturelles Phänomen sind Tolkiens Figuren und Themen längst Allgemeingut geworden und haben damit auch gemeinschaftsstiftende Funktion gewonnen. In diesem Sinne sind alle, die an diesem Diskurs teilnehmen, ein Teil von Mittelerde.

Wie unterscheidet man eine Zweit- von einer Erstschöpfung? Eine Leibniz'sche Erklärung einer Unterscheidung von J.R.R. Tolkien

Jan Levin Propach

Die Architektonik der Metaphysik Leibniz' findet in diesem Beitrag Verwen-dung, um das Verhältnis zwischen Erst- und Zweitschöpfung – Begriffe, die Tolkien verwendet – zu klären und zu bestimmen. Sie eignet sich nicht bloß, weil Leibniz wie Tolkien selbst in einer christlich-theistischen Tradition steht, sondern auch, weil er wie Tolkien davon ausgeht, dass die Wirklichkeit eine zweifache Struktur aufweist. Sie ist nicht nur etwas Konkretes, sondern sie ist primär etwas Gedachtes. Während menschliche Zweitschöpfungen wie Fiktionen durch einen endlichen Intellekt gedacht werden und daher stets unvollständig bleiben müssen, sind Gottes Fiktionen für Leibniz vollständig bestimmt, wenngleich es sich bei ihnen um unendlich fein strukturierte ge-dankliche Gebilde handelt. Vollständig bestimmt sind diese dennoch, weil der unendliche göttliche Intellekt sie denkt. Eine der Grundthesen des Theismus ist, dass alles ontologisch radikal von Gott allein abhängt. Deshalb werden in diesem Beitrag menschliche Fiktionen als unvollständige Teile vollständiger göttlicher Fiktionen betrachtet. Weil allerdings die göttlichen Fiktionen durch den sie denkenden Intellekt geeint sind, findet sich dieses Moment der Einheit in jeder guten Fiktion. Darin liegt auch der Grund, wieso sie etwas mit uns als Lesern zu tun haben. Es erscheint zwar so, als erzählten sie von »weit entfernten« Welten, in Wirklichkeit handelt es sich jedoch um eine einzige Wirklichkeit, deren Einheit darin gegründet ist, dass Gott das Gesamte der Wirklichkeit denkt.

Ausgangspunkte durch fremde Reiche – Literarische Weltschöpfungen bei Tolkien, Jordan und Williams

Patrick Schmitz

Die Analyse von Struktur und Eigenschaften literarischer Welten in der Fantasyliteratur ist zweifelsohne von entscheidender Bedeutung. Die packenden Welten in diesen Werken entsprechen einem der Puzzleteile, die die Faszination ausmachen. So identifizieren sich zahlreiche Leser*innen nicht nur mit Protagonisten wie Bilbo, Rand oder Simon Schneelocke, sondern auch mit fiktiven Schauplätzen wie Hobbingen, Emondsfeld oder Erchester. Aufgrund des Umstandes, dass diese Handlungsräume sowohl den Erstkontakt zwischen Leserschaft und fiktionaler Welt ermöglichen, als auch gleichzeitig Ausgangspunkt für die späteren Reisen der Charaktere in die fremde Sekundärwelt sind, sollte gerade diesen einführenden Orten und den mit ihnen verbundenen Kulturen eine zentrale Bedeutung im Rahmen einer Analyse eingeräumt werden.

Die vorliegende Studie untersucht detailliert ebendiese Räume aus Tolkiens Werken über Mittelerde, Robert Jordans Serie *Das Rad der Zeit* sowie Tad Williams' *Die Saga von Osten Ard*. In diesem Rahmen wird die Struktur dieser Schauplätze analysiert und vor dem Hintergrund der Konzepte der Fremdheit und Vertrautheit u.a. aus Tolkiens eigenen Schriften verglichen. Darüber hinaus wird mithilfe der Ergebnisse von relevanten Studien u.a. von Ekman und Methoden u.a. von Harshav herausgestellt, auf welche Weisen der literarische Weltenbau genutzt wird, um eine Schwelle zwischen anfänglichem Fokus auf Vertrautheit und späteren Verfremdungsstrategien zu erzeugen.

Diskurse von Wissen und Macht: Unsichtbarkeit und Sehen in *Der Herr der Ringe*

Laura Selle

In *Der Herr der Ringe* wird das Verleihen von Unsichtbarkeit vielfach als die Haupteigenschaft des Einen Rings dargestellt: Wenn ein Ringträger den Ring ansteckt, wird es unsichtbar. Wie dieser Beitrag darlegt, gehen jedoch viel mehr Effekte mit dem Tragen des Rings einher und Sauron selbst ist in einen weit größeren Diskurs von Unsichtbarkeit und Sehen verwickelt. In der Tat besteht eine enge Wechselbeziehung zwischen der Macht des Rings, Unsichtbarkeit zu verleihen, und Saurons Macht zu herrschen. Sie liegt in der Konzeptualisierung dieser Macht, wo diese durch einen Wissensdiskurs produziert wird. Der Ring macht seinen Träger nämlich nicht nur unsichtbar; er kontrolliert Sichtbarkeit, aber auch Sehvermögen und infolgedessen die Produktion von Wissen und kreiert dadurch Machteffekte. Unsichtbarkeit ist als ein solcher Effekt nicht nur ein Verlust von Subjektivität, sondern auf der Textebene auch ein Signifikant der Unterwerfung in einem durch Sauron inszenierten Wissensdiskurs. Innerhalb dieses Diskurses bedeutet Sehen die Fähigkeit, Wissen zu produzieren und, infolgedessen, Macht zu haben. Unsichtbarkeit oder die Einschränkung des eigenen Sehvermögens bedeuten dagegen, Überwachung ausgesetzt und ein Untersuchungsobjekt zu sein. Im *Herrn der Ringe* ist Unsichtbarkeit dabei grundsätzlich eine textuelle Täuschung und nie vollständig real(isiert). Der Text selbst legt eine Vielzahl visueller Wahrheiten dar, die sich letztlich als nicht real erweisen: Sauron kann nicht sehen, das Auge – welches als Name, physische Repräsentation und Funktion sehr präsent ist – wird beinahe nie gezeigt oder sichtbar gemacht und der Ringträger erlangt niemals wahre, vollständige Unsichtbarkeit. Vor allem jedoch wird Saurons Unbesiegbarkeit widerlegt und die Falsifizierung dieser produzierten Wahrheit kann endlich zum Sieg über ihn führen.

Der Ansatz dieses Beitrags ist ein close reading des *Herrn der Ringe,* um festzustellen, wie Unsichtbarkeit und Sehvermögen innerhalb der Geschichte und speziell auf der Textebene zusammenarbeiten, um entscheidende Prinzipien und Technologien in Saurons Machtdiskurs aufzustellen. Die dadurch erlangten Beobachtungen werden dann in eine Foucault'sche Perspektive gerückt und insbesondere mit Foucaults Konzept des Panoptizismus als Sozialtheorie in Verbindung gebracht. Unsichtbarkeit wird damit nicht als *eine* Kraft des Rings behandelt, sondern als Teil eines größeren Diskurses – nicht der Unsichtbarkeit, sondern, scheinbar antithetisch, des Sehens.

Satirische Weltschöpfung: Von Brobdingnag nach Tralfamadore

Ross Smith

Der Beitrag an satirischem Worldbuilding zu westlichem Gedankengut in den letzten drei Jahrhunderten durch Werke von Swift, Wells, Zamyatin, Huxley, Orwell, Vonnegut und anderen Autoren war tiefgreifend und beständig. Niemand hat eine beißendere Kritik des Totalitarismus geschaffen als Orwell in *1984.* Es gibt keine bessere Diskussion moderner Ängste über Genmanipulation als *Schöne neue Welt*, nur wenige Romane über die Grauen des Krieges, die so bewegen wie Vonneguts *Schlachthof 5*. Liliputanische, Brobdingnagische, Swift'sche und Orwell'sche Konzepte, Kreaturen wie die Yahoos, Houyhnhnms, Eloi und Morlocks sowie paradigmatische Figuren wie Lemuel Gulliver und der Große Bruder sind zentraler Teil der europäischen und amerikanischen Kultur geworden. Dieser Essay diskutiert die Evolution von literarischem Worldbuilding zu satirischen Zwecken und identifiziert die vorrangigen ethischen und sozialen Probleme, die von den betreffenden Autoren angeprangert werden, und berücksichtigt auch J.R.R. Tolkiens und C.S. Lewis' Beiträge zu diesem faszinierenden und unterhaltsamen Subgenre.

Eukatastrophe und Tolkiens Weltschöpfung: Eine theologische Lektüre

Guglielmo Spirito

»Ich habe abgeschlossen, indem ich gesagt habe, dass die Auferstehung die größtmögliche ›Eukatastrophe‹ im bedeutendsten aller Märchen war…« (übersetzt aus Brief 89 an Christopher Tolkien, 7./8.11.1944), »die großartigste und allesumfassendste *Eukatastrope, die nur denkbar ist*« (FS 104). Meine Absicht ist es, die *Eukatastrope* als Kostprobe der Wahrheit darzulegen: »nicht nur der plötzliche Blick auf die Wahrheit hinter dem scheinbaren Anankê unserer Welt, sondern auch ein Blick, der wirklich ein Lichtstrahl durch die Spalten des Universums um uns ist«, wie Tolkien sagt (L 89). Ich möchte erläutern, dass es genau diese *Spalten* sind, die eines der mächtigsten Elemente in Tolkiens Weltschöpfung sind. Um die Tiefen des Tolkien'schen Neologismus und dessen Konsequenzen in der von Tolkien erschaffenen Welt zu verstehen, werde ich das Wagnis eingehen und die *Theologie* als hermeneutisches Werkzeug verwenden.

Fokalisierung und Weltschöpfung

Allan Turner

Für viele gehört die (literarische) Weltschöpfung ausschließlich zum Fantasy-Genre. In diesem Artikel wird jedoch behauptet, dass sie auch in anderen Gattungen eine wichtige Rolle spielt, z.B. im historischen Roman, wo dem Durchschnittsleser meist weder der Handlungsort noch die zeitgenössische Situation hinlänglich vertraut sind, so dass sie ihm durch den Text vorgestellt werden müssen. Für die kognitive Linguistik findet die zwischenpersönliche

Kommunikation statt, indem sich der Mensch in Wechselwirkung zwischen seinen Vorkenntnissen und seinem Gegenüber ständig neue konzeptuelle Welten zusammenstellt und ausbaut (s. Joanna Gavins, *Text World Theory*). Dabei hilft die menschliche Fähigkeit, sich in die Lage eines anderen hineinzudenken, was die wichtige Rolle der Fokalisierung in Erzählungen erklärt: Stellvertretend für den Leser entwickelt eine Person in der Handlung durch ihre Wahrnehmungen eine zusammenhängende Textwelt. Dieser Vorgang wird am Beispiel der historischen Romane *Waverley* (1814) und *Rob Roy* (1817) von Walter Scott veranschaulicht. Darin schafft der Autor durch die Augen eines Fokalisierers, jeweils eines jungen Engländers mit wenig Welterfahrung, die detaillierte und differenzierte Kulisse eines Schottlands im Umbruch, wo nicht nur Hochland und Tiefland, Katholik und Protestant, sondern auch die alte, feudale Ordnung und das neue kapitalistische (aber friedliche) Zeitalter im Gegensatz zueinander stehen.

Formen von Rassismus als Facetten des literarischen Weltenbaus in der Fantasyliteratur

Nilüfer Ulusoy-Schmitz

Die Wechselwirkungen zwischen Tolkiens Erfahrungen im Ersten Weltkrieg und seiner literarischen Tätigkeit sind von zahlreichen Autoren hinreichend untersucht worden. Neben diesen Erfahrungen wirkte sich selbstverständlich auch der historische und soziale Kontext auf das Verfassen seiner Werke aus. So ergaben sich in Europa und auf der ganzen Welt Trennungsbewegungen zwischen Kulturen, die mitunter auch auf rassistischem Gedankengut basierten. Inwiefern dieser Rassismus bzw. diese Abgrenzungsgedanken in verschiedenster Ausprägung eine Rolle in Tolkiens Werk spielen, wird im Rahmen der vorliegenden Studie untersucht. So wird z.B. das Verhältnis unter den Hobbits vor dem Hintergrund aktueller Rassismusforschung eingeordnet. Auf diese Weise soll erarbeitet werden, welche Rolle Fremdenfeindlichkeit, Vorurteile etc. zur Tiefe der Schöpfung von literarischen Welten beitragen. In einem zweiten Schritt sollen die Erkenntnisse mit dem Stellenwert des Rassismus in weiteren Werken der Fantasyliteratur verglichen werden. Zu diesem Zweck werden die Werke Rowlings und Rothfuss' hinzugezogen. Schließlich soll geklärt werden, in welcher Hinsicht der Gegensatz zwischen Eigen- und Fremdidentität zur Konstruktion literarischer Welten in der Fantasyliteratur beiträgt.

Zwischen Räumen und Welten mit den »Eld Green« und den »Kyn Folk«

Christine Vogt-William

Dieser Aufsatz untersucht das Konzept der Weltschöpfung in die Fantasy-Trilogie *The Kynship Chronicles* (2005-2007) des indigenen nordamerikanischen Schriftstellers und Literaturwissenschaftlers Daniel Heath Justice. Nach den Prinzipien von ›Genealogy‹ und ›Kinship‹ in der literarischen Weltschöpfung (Wolf) werden die Trilogie und Tolkiens *The Lord of the Rings* einander gegenübergestellt, um die generischen und textuellen ›Kinships‹ beider Werke zu beleuchten. Ein wesentlicher kritischer Aspekt des Aufsatzes ist die literarische Darstellung indigener Völker in beiden Texten. Diese werden postkolonialen und dekolonialen Analysen unterzogen, wobei das ›decolonization imperative‹ für Werke der Fantasyliteratur ein wichtiges Merkmal für das Verständnis von ›Genealogy‹ und ›Kinship‹ bildet. Dabei wird Justice' kritischer Standpunkt gegenüber der Darstellung des kulturellen Anderen in von europäischen Fantasyschriftstellern verfassten Werken eingehender betrachtet. Es werden Ansätze zu dekolonialen Dialogen zwischen den britischen und den indigenen nordamerikanischen kulturhistorischen Kontexten eruiert, die diesen Werken zugrunde liegen. In diesem Sinne sollen das Lesen und das Verfassen von Werken der Fantasyliteratur Diskussionsgrundlagen ermöglichen, wobei Leser mit unterschiedlichen kulturellen Hintergründen die asymmetrischen Machtstrukturen und -operationen, die in der Primary World wirken, erkennen und hinterfragen können, um somit eine ›clarity of vision‹ (FS 57f.) zu erlangen. Solch eine ›clarity of vision‹ geht mit Mark Wolfs Behauptung einher, dass die Betrachtung von literarischen Weltschöpfungspraktiken im Fantasy-Genre Veränderungen in Weltanschauungen bewirken kann (193).

Reviews / Rezensionen

Lisa Coutras
Tolkien's Theology of Beauty. Majesty, Splendor, and Transcendence in Middle-earth

New York: Palgrave Macmillan, 2016, 279 pp.

Starting point and centre of Coutras's study are the theological implications of Goodness, (transcendental) Beauty, and Truth in Tolkien's work. The theological framework for such an approach is provided by the seven volumes of *The Glory of the Lord: A Theological Aesthetics* by the Swiss Catholic theologian Hans Urs von Balthasar (1905-1988). The choice of this frame of reference is, to some extent, arbitrary since we have no evidence that von Balthasar's publications were known to Tolkien. However, since von Balthasar's writings are considered to be in accordance with Catholic orthodox teaching, he can thus be seen simply as an exemplary representative of a tradition that goes back, via Saint Thomas Aquinas, to Saint Augustine of Hippo.

Coutras's focus may be on Christian theology, yet she starts her study proper with an informed overview of the scholarly debate concerning Tolkien's pagan elements and the central importance of beauty in his work as a means to bring goodness and truth into our world and thus break the spell of evil enchantment. The close connection between 'beauty inside and outside', i.e. physical beauty as a reflection or at least indication of 'inner beauty' (aka virtue) has been discussed before (e.g. Honegger. 2005. 'Zur Phänomenologie von Gut und Böse' in Thomas Honegger et al. 2015. *Eine Grammatik der Ethik*, 67-88), and Coutras covers this ground competently and in depth. She not only consults the *Catechism of the Catholic Church* (always a good idea when talking about matters Catholic), but also considers important thinkers such as St. Bonaventure and, of course, von Balthasar, whom she links indirectly to Tolkien via Louis Bouyer, a close friend of the former and colleague of the latter. Coutras further explores the theological ramifications of the relationship between beauty and goodness, which has become complicated through the effects of the Fall that led to the loss of the original unity of Beauty, Goodness, and Truth. Thus, while human creativity is able to bring forth beauty and still partakes (at least partially) in divine beauty, it is at the same time limited and tainted by human corruption. This 'theoretical' chapter also makes use of some of C.S. Lewis's works in order to understand Tolkien's concept—which is a good idea since Lewis was always more explicit in matters of religion than his friend.

Coutras then continues her study with an investigation into the importance and function of myths in the context of exploring the human condition in Tolkien's work. She follows largely the argument presented in 'On Fairy-stories' and highlights Tolkien's identification of the Incarnation as "myth to be actualised within historical reality" (35). Coutras has obviously not used Flieger and Anderson's critical edition of the text since she gives no indication that she is aware that this important argument was, most likely, not yet present in the original lecture (1939) and appeared only in the revised version published in 1947. Likewise, the poem *Mythopoeia*, referred to by Tolkien himself in *On Fairy-stories* and easily accessible in print or on the net, should have been at least mentioned in this context since it contains the essence of Tolkien's thoughts on this subject. Nevertheless, Coutras's argument that Tolkien's 'holistic' view of (pagan) myth as reflecting imperfectly (due to the Fall) the original union of truth and beauty remains valid. She then concludes by relating these findings to the views found in von Balthasar, who, like Tolkien, also stresses the fact that transcendental beauty is conveyed by the entire form and cannot be broken down into individual parts.

This pattern of discussing a theologically relevant concept and its implementation in Tolkien's work, and then presenting parallels or analogues in von Balthasar's œuvre, continues throughout the following chapters. Thus, we find an analysis of the central symbolism of light in both Tolkien (cf. Flieger's *Splintered Light*) and von Balthasar, with the latter arguing that "creation's passive character as reflection is necessarily linked to an active splendour", which is very close to Tolkien's "the light of being reflects the radiance of holiness derived from the light of Ilúvatar, the absolute Being" (57). Furthermore, the relationship between body and soul is discussed on the basis of the easily accessible publications by Tolkien on that topic (*History of Middle-earth*), but without considering the important 'Fragments on Elvish Reincarnation' in Michaël Devaux (ed). 2014. *J.R.R. Tolkien, l'effigie des Elfes.* Further chapters analyse the relationship between words/language and creative power/primal reality, the question of Good and Evil (here I missed the two books edited by Paul E. Kerry, which contain several relevant essays), and discuss heroism and suffering with a focus on the story of Túrin Turambar. While Coutras's observations on the fate of Túrin are coherently argued, there is at least one important aspect missing: the question of Free Will and Providence, which would have been especially relevant for the discussion of Morgoth's curse (pp. 162, 178). Coutras mentions divine providence on page 181, but does not explore its implications for Túrin's fate, and the style of her conclusion (p. 182) must be characterised as preaching rather than scholarly discourse.

The book concludes with an exploration of men and women, or rather male and female principles in Tolkien. It gives a good overview of feminist criticism of Tolkien's work so far, yet runs the (methodological) danger of mixing different categories of sources. Literary (and other) scholars have to be careful not to conflate an author's personal opinions, as found in his diaries or letters, with the ideas and contents found in his or her literary works. The fact that an author expresses an opinion in a letter does not automatically entail that this opinion is to be found in his or her literary texts. Luckily, in Tolkien's case there seems to be a considerable congruence between his (semi-)private expressions of opinions and those found in his literary works, so that the conflation of the different categories is not too harmful.

The more theoretical part is followed by two case studies: Galadriel as a representative of the transcendental feminine, and Éowyn as Tolkien's take on the shield-maiden motif. Both chapters are cogently argued and the argument well-put.

In conclusion it can be said that Coutras is often able to provide new insights thanks to looking at Tolkien through the lens of von Balthasar. This works best, in my opinion, in the chapter undertaking a close reading of the story of Lúthien. At other times the establishment of parallels to von Balthasar is a bit mechanistic and when Coutras 'forgets' it, as in her chapter on Éowyn, it is no great loss. The study does not always cover all the relevant secondary literature (I have pointed out just some of the publications that could and maybe should have been included), and the language sometimes shifts into a 'preaching mode'. This may come with the territory covered, but it struck me as inappropriate for a scholarly study. All in all, however, Coutras's study is worth reading, her grasp of Tolkien's 'theology' sound, and her case studies illuminating.

Thomas Honegger

Markus May, Michael Baumann, Robert Baumgartner, Tobias Eder (Hrsg.) Die Welt von *Game of Thrones*. Kulturwissenschaftliche Perspektiven auf George R.R. Martins *A Song of Ice and Fire*

Bielefeld: transcript 2016 (= Edition Kulturwissenschaft 121), 400 S.

D as aktuelle HBO-Flaggschiff *Game of Thrones* ist mittlerweile zum popkulturellen Phänomen avanciert, die Serie fasziniert gleichermaßen Massenpublikum und Kritiker der gehobenen Feuilletons, wie es im Klappentext des hier zu besprechenden Buches heißt. Unter der Herausgeberschaft von Markus May, Michael Baumann, Robert Baumgartner und Tobias Eder, erschienen im Bielefelder Transcript-Verlag, präsentiert es die Ergebnisse einer Tagung vom November 2015, die ganz im Zeichen von *Game of Thrones* bzw. *A*

Song of Ice and Fire stand. Das Werk versammelt 23 Beiträge unterschiedlicher Disziplinen, die sich mit Martins *secondary world* und deren Serienumsetzung auseinandersetzen. Die bislang vor allem literatur- und medienwissenschaftlich geführte Diskussion um *Game of Thrones* soll mit vorliegendem Band erweitert werden, Interdisziplinarität ist ebenso das erklärte Ziel der Herausgeber wie das Herausstellen einer Bedeutung der Martin'schen »Fantasy in der Krise« (S. 14) als mögliche Antwort auf »Kontingenzerfahrung als... zentrale[r] Signatur der Moderne« (S. 14). Entsprechend bunt gemischt präsentiert sich der akademische Werdegang der Beiträgerinnen und Beiträger – für die Thematik klassische Disziplinen wie Germanistik, Mediävistik und Filmwissenschaft stehen neben Artikeln musik- oder politikwissenschaftlicher Provenienz.

Analog zur Tagung präsentiert sich der Inhalt nach acht Themenslots geordnet. Der erste Abschnitt befasst sich mit Familienpolitik und dynastischen Fragen in Westeros und will unter anderem einen Blick auf die großen handlungsbestimmenden Konflikte werfen, da diese weitgehend aus Spannungen innerhalb der und zwischen den mächtigen Familien resultierten. Stefan Donecker befasst sich etwa mit genealogischen Aspekten, und Anja Müller untersucht die Löwensymbolik des Hauses Lannister.

Der zweite Teil thematisiert Kulturgeographie und Geopolitik. Ausgehend von der Erkenntnis, dass kulturelle Ideologien stets aus der Bestimmung eines Verhältnisses des Eigenen hin zum Fremden entstehen, befasst sich Igor Eberhardt mit dem Topos Norden in *Game of Thrones*. Hierfür stellt er zunächst den Norden als Imaginationsraum des Monströsen vor, um dann für die Serie festzustellen, dass die unwirtliche Region neue Heldenfiguren produziert, die von sozialen Außenseitern zu Streitern wider die aus dem Norden kommende Gefahr werden. Mario Grizelj will anschließend Alteritätsdiskurse in *Game of Thrones* untersuchen, schreibt allerdings eher eine kulturwissenschaftliche Einführung in den Alteritätsbegriff, wobei seine eigentliche Fragestellung etwas in den Hintergrund zu geraten droht.

Im dritten Teil, der Religion und Mythen in den Fokus stellt, diskutiert Rainer Emig sehr lesenswert den Zusammenhang von Religion und Macht, während Dominik und Marco Frenschkowski sich religionswissenschaftlich mit Feuer und Eis befassen. Johannes Rüster unterzieht den Glauben an die Sieben einer theologischen Analyse.

Der vierte Abschnitt thematisiert soziale Fragen und Genderaspekte. Hier untersucht Hans Richard Brittnacher mit Barbaren und Bastarden »Figuren des Hybriden« und kommt zu dem plausiblen Schluss, dass es gerade jene Gestalten sind, die der Dekonstruktion einer moralisch verkommenen Gesellschaft dienen. Corinna Dörrich befasst sich anhand realhistorischer Beispiele des europäischen Mittelalters mit dem Rittertum in Westeros, und Felix Schröter fokussiert weibliche Figuren in Videospieladaptionen des Epos.

Der nachfolgende Slot untersucht Ethik, Moral und Politik, greift also wesentliche Grundelemente auf, von denen sich Martins Werk nährt. Michael Baumann thematisiert unter Rückgriff auf die Überlegungen Max Webers die Herrschaftsstruktur in Westeros, Christoph Petersen zeigt mithilfe einer frühneuzeitlichen politischen Theologie Legitimationsstrategien einer Regentschaft Daenerys' auf und Peter Seyferth sucht anhand eines politikwissenschaftlichen Verständnisses von Realismus nach einer »realistischen Fantastik« in *Game of Thrones*. Der sechste Abschnitt des Buches ist mit »Archiv und Medienreflexion« überschrieben. Obwohl aus den einleitenden Sätzen der Herausgeber klar wird, worauf man damit hinaus möchte, wirken die zugehörigen Beiträge inhaltlich doch nicht wirklich zusammengehörig. Hier findet sich einer der stärksten Texte des Bandes: Christian Weng bietet nicht nur eine auch für den musikalischen Laien verständliche Analyse des *Main Title* der Serie, sondern ebenso eine gelungene Einführung in die generellen Funktionsweisen von Filmmusik. Daneben befasst sich Robert Baumgartner mit der Sexualität in *Game of Thrones* und Matthias Langenbahn thematisiert das »Fechten als Strukturelement«. Anschließend geht es siebtens um Übernatürliches innerhalb der erzählten Welt, wenn sich Tobias Eder mit den *White Walkers* als Phänomenen des Fremden auseinandersetzt und Markus May sehr kenntnisreich nach der Funktion von Rätseln und Mystifikationen fragt.

Der letzte Slot stellt – passend zum interdisziplinären Ansatz – die Transmedialität in den Fokus. Die hier versammelten Beiträge von Franziska Ascher, Maria Kutscherow, Simon Spiegel und Tobias Unterhuber setzen sich mit Adaptionen von Martins Romanreihe auseinander. Das geschieht durchweg auf hohem Niveau – der Artikel von Spiegel zu den »Sexpositions« und der von Ascher zu Videospiel-Umsetzungen seien hier hervorgehoben. Insbesondere Aschers Vorschlag eines Konzepts des Agonalen als Analyseheuristik scheint bemerkenswert. Allerdings wird an dieser Stelle des Bandes dessen Anlage als etwas inkonsequent entlarvt. Wenn es extra einen Slot zu medialen Adaptionen der Bücher gibt, impliziert dies, dass in den anderen Abschnitten auch nur (oder zumindest zum großen Teil) die Romane untersucht werden. Das ist aber nicht der Fall: Die HBO-Serie – und damit die mit Abstand wichtigste Adaption – ist mindestens genauso Gegenstand der vorangegangenen Beiträge wie die Buchreihe. Dass ein Großteil der Artikel allenfalls marginal zwischen Serie und Büchern unterscheidet, tut ihrer Qualität indes keinen Abbruch, da dort zumeist Fragen verhandelt werden, die für beide Umsetzungen gleichermaßen Gültigkeit besitzen. Nichtsdestotrotz wirkt das Einführen eines extra für mediale Adaptionen vorgesehen Slots unter diesen Umständen etwas befremdlich. Verstärkt wirkt dieses Befremden noch, wenn schon der Titel des Buches nicht zwischen Romanen und Serie unterscheidet.

Bei aller beschworenen Interdisziplinarität sind viele der Beiträge doch wieder literaturwissenschaftlich motiviert, und auch ein deutlicher Bezug zu Gegenwartsproblemen mag sich bei einigen Texten nicht wirklich erschließen (Ausnahmen: die Artikel von Christoph Petersen und Rainer Emig). Nichtsdestotrotz haben die Herausgeber hier einen überaus lesenswerten Beitrag vorgelegt, der durchaus geeignet scheint, den wissenschaftlichen Diskurs um Martins Werk ein gutes Stück voranzutreiben. Da das Werk aber durchweg deutschsprachig angelegt ist, ein Großteil jenes Diskurses dagegen in englischer Sprache geführt wird, bleibt abzuwarten, ob der Band sich zu einem Standardwerk etablieren kann. Zu wünschen wäre es ihm auf jeden Fall.

Jan Niklas Meier

Tolkien Studies: An Annual Scholarly Review, Vol. XIII

Morgantown, West Virginia Univ. Press, 2016, 324 pp.

Tolkien Studies 13 is the second volume with the new paperback look and I am slowly getting used to it since, after all, the content is the main thing—or so I tell myself. Although issue 13 carries the burden of the 'unlucky' number, it does not disappoint and provides an impressive array of very readable essays.

Simon J. Cook opens the paper section with 'The Cauldron at the Outer Edge: Tolkien on the Oldest English Fairy Tales.' This essay can be seen as a companion piece to Cook's earlier paper published in *Tolkien Studies* 12 (2015). This time, Cook looks at Tolkien's discussion of two marginal elements in *Beowulf*, i.e. the Heathobard story and the celebration of Scyld Scefing. Cook posits Tolkien's interpretation of these elements, as found in his 'Beowulf: The Monsters and the Critics' and the posthumously published commentary on *Beowulf*, within the framework of the preceding and contemporary discourse of *Beowulf* criticism. According to Cook, Tolkien not only establishes the vital function of the monsters for the meaning and artistic balance of the poem, but he also points towards the tragic dimension encountered in the tragedy of Ingeld and Freawaru, merely alluded to in *Beowulf*, yet like many of the other digressions and intertextual allusions, adding to the depth of the poem. He also discusses Tolkien's composition of 'King Sheave' (ca. 1937) and shows how Tolkien endeavours to provide, by means of a fictional text, the lost background to the only fragmentarily surviving allusions in the extant works such as *Beowulf*. The second part of the essay looks at historical and mythical analogues such as the motif of two people from enemy tribes/families falling in love with each other, examples of which would be Ingeld and Freawaru, the god Frey and the giant-daughter Gerdr and, I may add anachronistically, Romeo and Juliet. Some of these elements found at the outer edge will, according to Cook, re-occur in *The Lord of the Rings*. However, I am a bit wary of connecting Arwen and Aragorn to this specific instance (i.e. Ingeld and Freawaru). The overall contextualisation of *The Lord of the Rings* as belonging to a world that is merely accessible through the shadowy allusions, however, is convincing and in the tradition of Shippey's 'Beowulfian depth' argument.

Cook's piece is followed by Paul Acker's 'Tolkien's *Sellic Spell*: A Beowulfian Fairy Tale', which provides an insightful and clearly structured discussion of how Tolkien conceived his *Sellic Spell* in order to achieve his aim of providing the lost folk tale behind the first part of *Beowulf*. Acker shows that he does so by, for example, omitting the historicising and individualising references (thus the individualised concrete 'Hrothgar' becomes the more general and generic 'the King of the Golden Hall') and by placing the tale in a generic folk-tale setting: 'Once upon a time... in the North'. On the one hand, Acker tracks down the most likely sources of inspiration, which are, among others, Lang's treatment of the *Völsunga saga* and his preface in the rare Large Paper edition of *The Red Fairy Book*, where he apologises for turning the story of Sigurd back into a fairy tale. On the other hand, he puts *Sellic Spell* into the context of the scholarly discussion of the topic (esp. Chambers) and shows how Tolkien uses the freedom of re-writing the first part of *Beowulf* to answer some scholarly queries, such as 'Why did Beowulf allow Grendel to kill Hondscio before stopping him?' and to bring the storyline more into harmony with his own ideas of what a fairy tale should be.

John D. Rateliff, in his 'Pagan and Christian in *The Fall of Arthur*', provides a competent and stimulating discussion of those elements that Tolkien introduced with the aim of making the story of Arthur compatible with his legendarium. Rateliff takes Tolkien's statement about the Arthurian legends from the letter to Milton Waldman (L 144) as his starting point and systematically discusses the three major objections: 1) the Arthurian legend is British, not English; 2) it is too lavish, fantastical, incoherent, and repetitive; and 3) it is explicitly Christian. Rateliff's observations on why the inclusion of Christianity proves disruptive to a sub-created world (p. 50) are especially perceptive and, as far as I know, the first sustained treatment of the problem (see now also Claudio Testi's study *Pagan Saints in Middle-earth*). The second part of the essay examines how Tolkien tried to address these problems. The 'British' nature of Arthur and the clearly 'English' (or Saxon) identity of his foes meant that he could rise to prominence only at a time when the ruling elite was no longer Anglo-Saxon (i.e. English). It is therefore no surprise that the first prominent re-telling of Arthur's life is that of Geoffrey of Monmouth (ca. 1136) with the new Norman elite as its primary audience. Tolkien, by taking a more or less historical Arthur, could not ignore these basic facts and retained the enmity between Arthur and the Germanic ancestors of the English, though he re-wrote the Anglo-Saxon conquest in two other scenarios, as Rateliff points out: the 'invasion' of the Shire under Marcho and Blanco, and the re-settlement of Calenardhon by the Rohirrim (see also DeForrest's paper in the same volume of *Tolkien Studies*). The fantasy elements, however, are greatly reduced in *The Fall of Arthur* and Tolkien adds Lancelot's journey into the west (in the *imram* tradition), thus introducing a possible link to his legendarium. The incorporation fails, however, mostly due to the undeniable presence of the Christian religion, which makes a re-interpretation of the Arthurian legend "an inappropriate foundation on which to build the Matter of Middle-earth" (p. 59).

The Fall of Arthur is also the topic of T.S. Sudell's 'The Alliterative Verse of *The Fall of Arthur*' and continues the Arthurian theme. Sudell gives a potted introduction to the different forms of alliterative verse (Sievers's five types), the history of alliterative poetry in English, and the challenges and problems an author encounters when attempting to write alliterative poetry in Modern English. The bulk of the paper consists of a competent and knowledgeable discussion of the different metrical types Tolkien used in *The Fall of Arthur*, his application of different alliterative patterns (crossed alliteration, trans-verse alliteration), and the influence of phonology and dialect on both metre and alliteration. In an appendix, Sudell gives the metrical analysis of every line found in *The Fall of Arthur* as well as some interpretative tables. The essay is of great value for the study of the poem and a further step would be to place Tolkien's achievement in *The Fall of Arthur* within the larger context of his corpus of alliterative poetry, as outlined by Tom Shippey in his 2013 essay 'Tolkien's Development as a Writer of Alliterative Poetry in Modern English' (in Julian Eilmann and Allan Turner (eds.). 2013. *Tolkien's Poetry*, 11-28) which, unfortunately, Sudell does not seem to be familiar with.

Dennis Wilson Wise's 'Book of the Lost Narrator: Rereading the 1977 *Silmarillion* as a Unified Text' aims at countering the prevalent opinion that the 1977 *Silmarillion* is, for better (Nagy) or worse (Kane), a 'problematic' text full of internal inconsistencies and a 'composite text' rather than a 'unified text'. Wise points out that, in contrast to other posthumous publications such as *Unfinished Tales* and the volumes of *The History of Middle-earth*, the 1977 *Silmarillion* has achieved a canonical status that sets it apart. This motivated Wise to reread *The Silmarillion* as a unified text and to construct a possible narrator, whom he characterises as a poet of great rhetorical skill and high moral seriousness, comparable to the Greek historian and philosopher Xenophon. The essay, though well-written and argued, is in its present form nothing more (nor less) than a stimulating *jeu d'esprit*. In my mind, the argument would have gained greater force if Wise had connected his discussion to the parallel phenomenon found in Biblical studies where we have canonical texts and, in the Catholic tradition, the teachings of the Church Fathers, next to non-canonical apocrypha (nota bene: some of the Catholic canonical texts, such as the Old Testament *Book of Judith*, are considered apocryphal in the Protestant tradition). I would have found a discussion within such a framework more fitting and a finer differentiation into various levels of 'canonicity' helpful to strengthen Wise's argument.

Jeremy Painter's '"A Honeycomb Gathered from Different Flowers": Tolkien-the-Compiler's Middle-earth "Sources" in *The Lord of the Rings*' can be seen as a companion piece to Wise's preceding paper, though the subject of the analysis is not the narratorial unity of *The Silmarillion* but the relationship and effect of the putative source-traditions constituting the narrative called *The Lord of the Rings*. Taking Tolkien's translation conceit as his starting point, Painter identifies three main narrative strands which he connects to the putative manuscript traditions of the Red Book of Westmarch. These three strands are discernible not only by means of the different point-of-view characters, but also – and this is the main argument of the paper—by means of themes and motives typical for each. Painter identifies the three main strands as those centred around Merry, Pippin, and Frodo and Sam, and assigns them the sigla H (Holbytla), P (Periannath), and Æ (Ælfwine = Elffriend), respectively. Æ features prominently metaphysical themes (elves) and is characterised by calendrical timekeeping, whereas H focuses on the motifs and rituals of Rohan, often subtly changing the presentation of events to suit the Rohirrim culture. Thus H 'unhorses' the enemies (or omits any mention of horses) and makes a point of transforming the heroes into riders (even the dwarf Gimli). P, then, seems to follow Aragorn's career to the throne of Gondor and is concerned with matters Gondorian. Moreover, it often presents competing loyalties. Painter's paper is, like Wise's before, another *jeu d'esprit*, yet it is well argued and makes even the expert reader engage with new interest with a text s/he knows seemingly so well. As an aside I have to mention a minor mistake and what I would call an 'oversight', respectively: First, Jean Froissart is not an "Italian historian" (p. 136), but French (born ca. 1337 in Valenciennes—and his major works are all in French). Second, trying to find textual evidence for his thesis, Painter at least once overlooks other important elements that do not fit (or stand in ironic contrast to) his argument. Thus, he argues (correctly) that the 'horse theme' occurs prominently in Éomer's preparation for the Rohirrim's 'last stand' on a hillock during the Battle of the Pelennor Fields when he plants his banner showing a white horse (p. 137-38)—with all the Alfredian (and Chestertonian) allusions this may evoke. However, quoting this instance of equine heraldry, it would have been equally important to point out that for their last stand the Rohirrim actually *get off their horses* and form an Anglo-Saxon shield-wall— implying that when things get tight the 'Anglo-Saxons on horseback' revert to their original infantry style of fighting (as I have discussed in Thomas Honegger, 'The Rohirrim: "Anglo-Saxons on Horseback"? An Inquiry into Tolkien's Use of Sources.' In Jason Fisher (ed.). 2011. *Tolkien and the Study of His Sources: Critical Essays*, 116-132).

Michael Potts's '"Evening-Lands": Spenglerian Tropes in *Lord of the Rings*' is a contribution to the exploration of one of the most influential interpretations of the growth and decay of cultures and civilisations: Oswald Spengler's *Der Untergang des Abendlands* (German original 1918/1922; English transl. 1926: *The Decline of the West*). Spengler's ideas and tropes soon became widely known and influenced even those who had never read his book. The most important motif for our purpose is Spengler's idea that human societies follow a universal cycle of growth and expansion, which is then followed by stasis and decline. The youthful cultures are, according to Spengler, characterised by an agricultural lifestyle and a general population growth since the citizens see themselves primarily as reproductive beings. This changes with the maturation of culture into civilisation, which shows a de-population of the landscape, a growth of the cities, and an accompanying self-perception of their citizens as intellectual beings. Potts then traces this 'philosophy of history' in Tolkien's *The Lord of the Rings*, with Gondor and its major city, Minas Tirith, as the prime example of an 'aged civilisation' in a state of decline—which is contrasted to the youthful agricultural society of the Shire and the expanding and dynamic realm of the Rohirrim (although if the reader cares to do some research into the history of the Rohirrim in Rohan, s/he will find out that they have not really been ex-panding for the last few centuries). The argument is nevertheless convincing, not least since Spengler's view is (at least partially) based on older models, such as the succession of the ages (from Golden to Silver to Iron etc.) or the related *mundus senescit* topos (see Dirk Wiemann's '*Mundus senescit*: Tolkien and the Allure of Medieval Nostalgia.' *Hither Shore* 8 (2011): 24-38), which are likely to have influenced Tolkien, too. I see Potts's main contribution in showing another actualisation of an important motif—and not so much in his attempted refutation of Patrick Curry's more eco-critical approach as presented in *Defending Middle-earth* (1997), and which has been developed further in his later essays (see Patrick Curry. 2014. *Deep Roots in a Time of Frost. Essays on Tolkien*). Overall, Potts's paper makes stimulating and interesting reading and adds to the better understanding of Tolkien's contemporary intellectual milieu.

Like Potts, Matthew M. DeForrest in his 'J.R.R. Tolkien and the Irish Question' aims at elucidating certain aspects in Tolkien's work by means of looking at potential parallels and analogues in contemporary history. Starting from a possible Irish etymology of *Forgoil*, a term used by the Dunlendings for the Rohirrim, he explores potential parallels and analogies to the troubled relationship that has existed for centuries between Britain and Ireland. Much of the essay is a lesson in early 20th-century history, and though the parallels between Tolkien's Dunlendings and the Irish are not that compelling, there are sufficient indications that Tolkien's characterisation of the relationship between the dispossessed Dunlendings and the usurping Rohirrim, and the possible peaceful solution of the problem, is, if not partially inspired by the 'Irish Question', then at least applicable to the problem.

The enjoyable volume concludes with the substantial sections on 'Book Reviews' and 'The Year's Work in Tolkien Studies 2013'.

Thomas Honegger

Julian T.M. Eilmann
J.R.R. Tolkien, Romanticist and Poet

Zürich/Jena: Walking Tree Publishers, 2017, Pb., 474 S.

Mit diesem Band legt *Walking Tree Publishers* die englische Übersetzung der 2016 auf Deutsch erschienenen Dissertation von Julian Eilmann vor, mit der dieser in Jena bei Thomas Honegger promoviert wurde. Dies bereichert die englischsprachige Tolkienforschung, indem geeignete Werke aus anderen Originalsprachen verfügbar gemacht werden, ohne den ursprünglichen Kontext – in diesem Fall: Dissertation an einer deutschen Universität – unsichtbar werden zu lassen. Bei der vorliegenden Monographie ist dies umso erfreulicher, ist sie doch die erste Monographie, die sich ausführlich mit der Frage danach beschäftigt, ob sich in Tolkiens Werk eine romantische Geisteshaltung zeigt oder zumindest wesentliche Züge einer solchen erkennbar sind. Darüber hinaus wird mit der Lyrik Tolkiens eine Textgattung untersucht, die bis vor wenigen Jahren in der Tolkienforschung eher unterrepräsentiert war – mit der Aufnahme von diversen Aufsätzen von Julian Eilmann, die in überarbeiteter Form Eingang in diese Dissertation gefunden haben.

Der deutsche Kontext der Untersuchung Eilmanns zeigt sich schon zu Beginn, wenn er im Einleitungskapitel die Fragestellung vor dem aktuellen Forschungsstand erläutert und legitimiert, da in der bisherigen deutsch- und englischsprachigen Sekundärliteratur nur sehr wenige Titel zu finden sind, die sie bearbeiten. Für seinen starken Fokus auf die deutsche Romantik als Hintergrundfolie für die Lektüre Tolkiens führt er deren zentrale Bedeutung für die Definition des Romantischen an. Eine methodische Fundierung findet auf der Basis von Göran Hermeréns Studie *Influence in Art and Literature* und einer auf Ziolkowski zurückgehenden Unterscheidung zwischen romantischem Einfluss und Nachleben der Romantik statt. Ein solches Nachleben diagnostiziert Eilmann in Tolkiens Werk.

Auf dieser Grundlage widmet sich der Verfasser im vier Kapitel umfassenden ersten Hauptteil der Frage nach Tolkien als Romantiker. Hierzu führt er an, aufgrund welcher romantischen Charakteristika von einer romantischen Geisteshaltung Tolkiens gesprochen werden könne. Grundlage dafür ist das

mit Safranski skizzierte Wesen der (deutschen) Romantik, dessen Kern in der
Sehnsucht nach dem Unendlichen besteht. Eine romantische Poetologie, die
als ein »window into the Infinite« zusammengefasst wird und mit dem Traum
einer neuen Mythologie sowie einer Wieder-Verzauberung der Welt zusammen-
hängt, schlägt sich in der Phantastiktheorie Tolkiens nieder, insbesondere in
dem von ihm in *On Fairy-stories* dargelegten Aspekt des »regaining of a clear
view«, d.h. der *Recovery*.

Es folgt das ausführlichste Kapitel des Bandes, das sich mit der romantischen
Phantastik des 19. und frühen 20. Jahrhunderts auseinandersetzt. Eilmann greift
auf Werke von Lord Dunsany, Kenneth Morris und George MacDonald sowie
Cosmo von Wehrstahl zurück und analysiert im vierten Kapitel romantische
Motive in Tolkiens Werk wie die Bedeutung von Ästhetik und Poesie, die
Sehnsucht nach dem Wunderbaren und Transzendenten, die sich gerade bei
Eriol zeigt, geschilderte Transzendenzerfahrungen (verbunden mit veränderter
Wahrnehmung), Naturerfahrung und Nostalgie bzw. Heimweh. Dabei stehen
die frühen Werke, also seine Gedichte aus den 1910er- und 1920er-Jahren und
das *Book of Lost Tales* im Vordergrund; aber auch *Smith of Wootton Major*
wird ausführlich besprochen. Mit diesen Parallelen und rezipierten Werken
ergänzt Eilmann den starken Fokus auf die deutsche Romantik in der Exposition des Bandes und erleichtert sicherlich die Rezeption seiner These in der
angelsächsischen Forschung.

Der zweite und kürzere Hauptteil untersucht, wie sich in der späteren Lyrik
Tolkiens unterschiedliche romantische Motive – wie die Transzendenzerfahrung
– niederschlagen. Zunächst plädiert Eilmann dafür, die in den Werken Tolkiens
eingebetteten Lieder und Gedichte auch als eigenständige Werke zu analysie-
ren, bevor er sie zunächst als Teil der kulturellen Kommunikation Mittelerdes
schildert. Als solche fungieren sie als Volkslieder, Gelegenheitsdichtung und
Wanderlieder. Anschließend kommt der Zusammenhang von Liedern, Poesie
und Magie in Mittelerde in den Blick, der sich besonders in der schöpferischen
Kraft der Poesie sowie bei den Figuren Tom Bombadil und Lúthien Tinúviel
ausdrückt, aber auch im poetischen Transzendenzerlebnis Frodos am Fluss
Nimrodel. Zuletzt gelingt es Eilmann zu zeigen, dass die vorab am *Lord of
the Rings* herausgearbeiteten Ergebnisse auch auf die Lieder und Gedichte im
Hobbit zutreffen, was insbesondere für den Zusammenhang zwischen einer
kollektiven Liedtradition und der individuellen künstlerischen Produktion gilt.

Der Band wird abgeschlossen mit einer kurzen Skizze des »big picture«, die
sehr passend mit einer kurzen Analyse von *Bilbo's Last Song* endet.

Die Dissertation Julian Eilmanns kann sehr empfohlen werden, da sie
eine bis dato kaum bearbeitete Lücke der Tolkienforschung auf überzeugende
Weise schließt. Sie gibt Zeugnis seiner tiefgehenden Kenntnis des Œuvres
Tolkiens sowie der Romantik und seiner Fähigkeit zu einer präzisen Lektüre
des Originaltextes. Hinzu kommt seine eigenständige Auseinandersetzung mit

der übrigen Tolkienforschung, die jedoch an einigen wenigen Stellen – wie bei der Diskussion zu *On Fairy-stories* oder Magie in Tolkiens Werk – noch umfassender hätte berücksichtigt werden können. Seine Argumentation für die romantische Geisteshaltung Tolkiens und wie sie sich in seiner Poetologie sowie seinen Liedern und Gedichten finden lässt, überzeugt durchweg, sodass sie ein gelungenes Plädoyer für die Verortung Tolkiens in der romantischen Phantastik darstellt. Insbesondere in Verbindung mit dem von Julian Eilmann gemeinsam mit Allan Turner herausgegebenen Band *Tolkien's Poetry* stellt sie darüber hinaus einen wichtigen Beitrag zur Tolkienforschung dar, dadurch dass die oft wenig beachtete Lyrik Tolkiens in ihrer Bedeutung für das Gesamtverständnis des Werks ausführliche Beachtung findet.

Barbara Krüger

Tolkien Studies: An Annual Scholarly Review, Vol. XIV

Morgantown, West Virginia Univ. Press, 2017, 300 pp.

It is encouraging to see that the former *via regis* to understanding Tolkien's work, i.e. the *interpretatio mediaevalis* as established by Tom Shippey, Michael Drout, or John Ryan, is still used. H.L. Spencer joins the illustrious company with his well-researched essay 'The Mystical Philology of J.R.R. Tolkien and Sir Israel Gollancz' in which he explores Tolkien's relationship with the medieval and Shakespeare scholar Sir Israel Gollancz. Gollancz was the founding secretary of the British Academy, and as such the dedicatee of Tolkien's famous British Academy lecture 'Beowulf: The Monsters and the Critics', even though Tolkien did not mention his name once in his lecture. Spencer knowledgeably discusses the thematic overlaps, the differences in style, and also the competition between the two scholars, who both edited *Sir Gawain and the Green Knight* (Tolkien & Gordon 1925; Gollancz (posthumously) 1940) and shared a predilection for many of the same Middle English texts. This makes Spencer's 'parallel lives' of these two academics an important contribution to putting Tolkien into the wider academic context and I hope we will see further research in this area.

Christopher Gilson's essay 'His Breath Was Taken Away: Tolkien, Barfield and Elvish Diction' takes once more a look at the relationship between the creation of Tolkien's private languages and mythology, and Owen Barfield's linguistic philosophy. Gilson, by means of a detailed analysis of some elements of Tolkien's nomenclature which was developed for his personal mythology, is able to show convincingly how Tolkien's deep thinking about language and myth predates his acquaintance with Barfield's theory. The fellow Inklings' ideas about the ancient semantic unity come only later into Tolkien's view and then reinforce and influence his own ideas on the matter.

Sound and meaning are, to some extent, also the subject of 'Could Gollum Be Singing a Sonnet? The Poetic Project of *The Lord of the Rings*'. Kathy Cawsey's informative and illuminating analysis of the use of poetic forms in Tolkien's work is a welcome contribution to a field of research that has seen as yet few substantial publications—the most recent one being Julian Eilmann and Allan Turner's 2013 volume *Tolkien's Poetry*. It is therefore all the more enjoyable to find Cawsey's essay both very readable and clearly presented with well-chosen examples. She shows convincingly how Tolkien used poetic forms, and deviations from that norm to impart meaning. Thus, he privileges medieval and non-modern forms and avoids, for example, the 'canonical' iambic pentameter. Furthermore, to take the titular question 'Could Gollum Be Singing a Sonnet?', Cawsey argues that Gollum is indeed singing a warped and perverted sonnet—a poetic 'insider joke' since Tolkien thus gives the highest form of modern English poetry to one of the lowliest creatures in his epic.

Somewhat more speculative though still tied to a close reading of the texts is Eleanor R. Simpson's discussion of Tolkien's (*avant la lettre*) anti-speciesist portrayal of nature ('The Evolution of J.R.R. Tolkien's Portrayal of Nature: Foreshadowing Anti-speciesism'). She discusses numerous instances of interactions between non-human beings (e.g. animals, trees) and humanoid beings (e.g. hobbits, humans, elves) and though there seems to be, as a rule, a progression from *The Hobbit* to *The Lord of the Rings* with the non-human beings gaining greater independence and agency, we also have exceptions to this rule. Thus, for example, the eagles, who were independent protagonists in the earlier work, have been reduced to little more than literary devices in the later epic. In this context, I was also wondering what to make of the mountain ravens (e.g. Roäc) in *The Hobbit* or the Crebain in *The Lord of the Rings*, neither of which is mentioned by Simpson. And although her essay takes a somewhat limited approach to a clearly circumscribed topic, it would have been desirable to link it more closely to larger issues—as the author does only tentatively towards the end when she connects it to Tolkien's project of re-enchantment. Furthermore, the placement within the larger discourse of Tolkien's eco-critical stance would also be desirable (cf. Liam Campbell. 2011. *The Ecological Augury in the Works of JRR Tolkien*; Patrick Curry. 2014. *Deep Roots in a Time of Frost. Essays on Tolkien*; Matthew Dickerson and Jonathan Evans. 2006. *Ents, Elves, and Eriador. The Environmental Vision of J.R.R. Tolkien*; and Martin Simonson (ed.). 2015. *Representations of Nature in Middle-earth*).

The Fall of Arthur is one of the more recent posthumous works by Tolkien that has attracted the attention of a growing number of scholars since its publication (see, most recently, the essays by Rateliff and Sudell respectively, in *Tolkien Studies* 13). Leonard Neidorf, then, gives us a reading of Tolkien's fragmentary take on the Arthurian legend as a piece of literary criticism ('J.R.R. Tolkien's *The Fall of Arthur*: Creation from Literary Criticism'). Neidorf argues that Tolkien's poem reflects his conviction that in order to make the Arthurian legend work, it must be purged of its numerous internal contradictions and incongruencies. Thus, Tolkien decided to re-write it in a semi-historical setting and within a heroic framework, re-casting the key characters accordingly. He therefore gives us a war-like, heroic Arthur and Gawain, a seductive and 'fay' Guinevere, and a lust-driven Mordred. This allows Tolkien to disambiguate the tale and divest it of some of the troubling elements that it had acquired through the centuries (such as the incestuous origin of Mordred, the courtly love relationship between Lancelot and Guinevere, and Gawain's womanising). Similar challenges were encountered by John Milton, who gave up his plans for an Arthurian epic poem in favour of what became *Paradise Lost*, and Lord Alfred Tennyson, who persevered and gave us *The Idylls of the King*. A comparison between the approaches of these authors and Tolkien's would have shed further light on the latter's choices, but in the end, it does not detract from the deserts of Neidorf's well-written and stimulating essay.

The two concluding essays of *Tolkien Studies* 14 ('Visualizing the Word: Tolkien as Artist and Writer' and '"Akin to my own Inspiration": Mary Fairburn and the Art of Middle-earth') are a testimony to editors' luck since they complement each other in an ideal way. The first, by Jeffrey MacLeod and Anna Smol, takes a more general look at Tolkien's view of the visual arts and how it influenced his writing, especially where we have visualisations of scenes and landscapes. The authors thus explore Tolkien's 'painterly style' (Rosebury) and set it in relation to some contemporary artistic theories (esp. A.H. Munsell's colour theory). In a further step, they also look at Tolkien's calligraphy and, most importantly, at his thoughts and comments about visual and literary art in connection with sub-creation. The last point involves a re-evaluation of the infamous Note E in 'On Fairy-stories' where Tolkien seemingly rejects the use of visual art for the purpose of sub-creation. Based on their research, MacLeod and Smol argue that Tolkien was not per se against the use of visual art for sub-creation but advocated a balance of word and image, so that the image would neither dominate nor render obsolete the verbal description. Such an attitude explains Tolkien's predilection for the minimalist illustrations by Cor Block or Pauline Baynes, which were suggestive and left a lot to the imagination of the audience—something that, by contrast, cannot be said of Peter Jackson's movies.

Tolkien's search for the perfect illustrations for his epic *The Lord of the Rings* is also the theme of the article by Paul Tankard, which reads almost like a concrete illustration of the more general and abstract concepts discussed in the preceding essay. Tankard sketches the exchange of letters, notes, and pictures between Tolkien and the artist and illustrator Mary Fairburn. Apart from providing insights into a hitherto neglected episode of the Professor's biography and a flashlight onto Mary Fairburn's life, we also get to know more about Tolkien's evaluation of drawings/paintings as art in itself and as art functioning as illustrations for his works. He thus valued Pauline Baynes' drawings for his shorter and more light-hearted works, such as *Farmer Giles of Ham* or *Smith of Wootton Major*, yet thought her style not suitable for the more elevated and noble matter of works like *The Lord of the Rings*. Although Mary Fairburn was never officially commissioned with the illustration of Tolkien's epic, it is fascinating to see that her visions of Middle-earth obviously found favour with Tolkien.

The volume concludes with a note by J.M. Silk in which he knowledgeably explores the connections between the Sindarin word/name 'Arien' (maiden of the sun) and the English name 'Daisy', and Giovanni Costabile's note on the intertextual parallels and their implications between the pear-stealing episodes in Augustine's *Confessions* and Tolkien's 'The New Shadow' respectively. These are followed by the substantial sections with 'Book Reviews' and 'The Year's Work in Tolkien Studies 2014'.

Thomas Honegger

Claudio A. Testi
Pagan Saints in Middle-earth

Zürich/Jena: Walking Tree Publishers, 2018, Pb., 196 S.

In dem vorliegenden Band unternimmt einer der bedeutendsten italienischen Tolkienforscher, Claudio Testi, den Versuch, eine Frage zu klären, die in der Tolkienforschung schon lange sehr kontrovers diskutiert wird: Ist sein Werk grundlegend paganen oder christlichen Charakters? Während manche Autoren wie Joseph Pearce sehr dezidiert davon sprechen, Tolkiens Werk sei nur mit Rückgriff auf den christlichen und näherhin katholischen Hintergrund des Autors zu verstehen, betonen andere wie Catherine Madsen oder (moderater) Ronald Hutton, das Werk sei nicht christlich und trage deutliche pagane Züge. Testi stellt diesen Perspektiven seinen eigenen synthetischen Zugang gegenüber, den er in der These zusammenfasst: »Tolkien's world is not Christian but Pagan; therefore his work is fundamentally Catholic.« (vii)

Diese These entwickelt er ausführlich in zwei Teilen von je drei Kapiteln in dieser Monographie, die die englische Übersetzung eines 2014 erschienenen italienischen Bandes ist, der wiederum auf einem 2013 in *Tolkien Studies* publizierten Aufsatz aufbaut. Testi setzt sich mit einer Fülle von Sekundärliteratur auseinander, wobei vor allem die italienische und englischsprachige Tolkienforschung im Blick sind (in eigener Sache: auch Aufsätze aus *Hither Shore* werden rezipiert). Der Band dient damit nicht nur der thematischen Auseinandersetzung mit den unterschiedlichen Perspektiven und der Erläuterung der eigenen These, sondern gibt auch Zeugnis von der italienischen Tolkienforschung.

Nach verschiedenen Vorworten (zu den unterschiedlichen Ausgaben und von Verlyn Flieger) folgt eine Einführung in die Fragestellung und den Aufbau des Bandes. Anschließend bespricht Testi im ersten Teil die unterschiedlichen Perspektiven, d.h. er stellt zunächst die Ansätze vor, die Tolkiens Werk als dezidiert christlich deuten wie insbesondere Joseph Pearce, Stratford Caldecott, Peter Kreeft, Ralph Wood u.a. Dabei weist er auf die Schwachstellen dieses Ansatzes hin wie die Verwechslung von Allegorie und Anwendbarkeit mit Exemplifizierung und Interpretation oder die Folgerung einer vollständigen Entsprechung aufgrund einer partiellen Ähnlichkeit. Im zweiten Kapitel geht es um die Ansätze, die Tolkiens Werk als pagan kennzeichnen (neben Madsen und Hutton können Patrick Curry und in Italien Gianfranco de Turris genannt werden). An diesen kritisiert Testi unter anderem, die Bedeutung jener Texte, in denen die Verbindung zwischen dem Legendarium und dem Christentum deutlich wird, werde vernachlässigt, oder geschichtlicher Paganismus werde mit »Tolkien'schem« Paganismus verwechselt. Beide Ansätze werden der gesamten Breite des Werks Tolkiens nicht gerecht. Als dritte Perspektive führt er jene Autoren an, die keine eindeutige Position beziehen und eher von einem widersprüchlichen »Universum« ausgehen. Die richtigen Beobachtungen dieses Ansatzes greift er in seinem eigenen Vorschlag eines synthetischen Zugangs auf, der einer solchen dialektischen Lektüre eine analogische Unterscheidung verschiedener Ebenen vorzieht. Diese basiert auf der strikten Unterscheidung zweier Gesichtspunkte und begrifflicher Ebenen: der scholastischen Unterscheidung zwischen Natur und Gnade.

Der zweite Teil dient dazu, diesen von Testi vorgeschlagenen synthetischen Zugang zu erläutern. Hierzu nennt er im vierten Kapitel zunächst kurz diese beiden Ebenen, erläutert, was er unter »pagan« versteht – nämlich im weiten Sinne all jene, die keiner abrahamischen Religion angehören –, und skizziert die von ihm vorgeschlagene Synthese. Dies nimmt er im fünften Kapitel ausführlich auf, wenn er anhand insbesondere der philologischen Texte Tolkiens die poetischen und hermeneutischen Prinzipien bespricht. So plädiert er beispielsweise dafür, *Beowulf* illustriere die Harmonie zwischen paganen und christlichen Kulturen wegen der beiden unterschiedlichen Ebenen von Natur und Offenbarung. Des Weiteren untersucht er, wie diese Prinzipien in Tolkiens Zweitschöpfung umgesetzt werden, indem er u.a. nach natürlicher Theologie und religiösen Riten in Tolkiens Werk fragt, aber auch die ausgedrückte Geschichtsphilosophie und das Verhältnis von Schicksal und Vorsehung berücksichtigt.

Im sechsten Kapitel widmet sich Testi der Frage des katholischen Charakters des Werks Tolkiens, wozu er zunächst erläutert, was er unter »katholisch« versteht, nämlich insbesondere das Prinzip der Harmonie von Natur und Gnade zu vertreten, und schließlich ausführt, wie Tolkiens Werk als »fundamental katholisch« verstanden werden kann.

Der Band schließt mit einer kurzen Zusammenfassung von Testi, worin er die Besonderheit seines Ansatzes pointiert ausdrückt, bevor ein Schlusswort von Tom Shippey, in dem dieser sich sehr lobend über den Ansatz Testis äußert, diese Monographie abrundet.

Grundsätzlich ist es sehr zu loben, dass diese Monographie in ihrer englischen Übersetzung nun den Ansatz Testis eines synthetischen Zugangs zur Frage nach dem paganen oder christlichen Charakter des Werks einer weiteren Leserschaft zugänglich macht. Denn in der Tat ist Testis Argumentation sehr gut begründet sowie nachvollziehbar und überzeugt gerade dadurch, keine einseitige Position zu beziehen oder einfach von Widersprüchen auszugehen. Gleichwohl kann kritisiert werden, dass Testi ein recht enges Verständnis von Katholizismus voraussetzt, indem er insbesondere katholische Theologie de facto mit der Theologie Thomas von Aquins gleichsetzt. Ein Beispiel dafür ist seine Behandlung des Themas Vorsehung und freier Wille, wo der Autor weder modernere theologische Ansätze noch die allgemeine philosophische und theologische Diskussion über das Verhältnis von freiem Willen, Vorsehung und Gottes Allmacht berücksichtigt. Dies mag vielleicht oder sehr wahrscheinlich sogar den Besonderheiten des italienischen Diskurses geschuldet sein, könnte jedoch die Rezeption seiner These in anderen Diskursgemeinschaften einschränken, die Theologie und Philosophie mit weniger ausführlichem Rekurs auf den Aquinaten betreiben. Nichtsdestoweniger kann die Lektüre dieses Bandes jedem und jeder empfohlen werden, der oder die an dieser kontroversen Frage interessiert ist und darüber hinaus einen Einblick in die italienische Art der Tolkienforschung gewinnen möchte.

Thomas Fornet-Ponse

Our Authors

Annie Birks, Ph.D., teaches English language, literature and translation at the Université Catholique de l'Ouest, Angers, France. Her long-lasting interest in J.R.R. Tolkien and C.S. Lewis, together with her doctorate on *La Rétribution dans l'oeuvre de J.R.R. Tolkien* (Université Paris-Sorbonne), have led to articles and lectures on these two authors.

Isabel Busch, M.A., studied Modern English Language and Literature, Comparative Literature and Modern History at Rheinische Friedrich-Wilhelms-Universität Bonn and at University College Cork. She is currently a PhD student working on a dissertation on *Concepts of Gender in the Modern English Fantasy Novel*. Furthermore, she works in a managing and researching capacity at the Haus der FrauenGeschichte, Bonn. Her research interests include: fantasy literature, gender studies, English literary and cultural history (especially Tudor-era). busch@hdfg.de.

Andoni Cossío received his MA in Comparative Literature and Literary Studies from the University of the Basque Country with a dissertation on the role and symbolism of forests, woods and trees in Tolkien's *The Hobbit* and *The Lord of the Rings*. He has been awarded a Predoctoral funding for non-doctoral Research Staff Training scholarship by the Basque Government to work on his Ph.D. dissertation on the role of trees and forests in Tolkien's works. He has presented papers on Tolkien at international conferences, and has been involved in the organization of four International conferences on the Inklings (2015-18). He teaches English at Spain's state university UNED. andoni.cossio@ehu.eus

Julian Tim Morton Eilmann, Dr. phil., StR., Magister Artium in History, German Philology and Literature, Arts History (Aachen/Nottingham), currently works as a grammar school teacher for German, history and film in Aachen. His dissertation (2016, Jena) *J.R.R. Tolkien: Romanticist and Poet* was placed on the shortlist of "German Fantastic Award" 2017. His research focus lies on Tolkien's poetry and the romantic tradition in modern fantasy literature. Since many years, he publishes papers on Tolkien and, in 2013, the essay collection *Tolkien's Poetry* together with Allan Turner. julianeilmann@web.de

Natalia González de la Llana studied Literary Theory and Comparative Literature and received her Ph.D. from the Complutense University in Madrid after winning research scholarships for stays at La Sapienza University Rome and Humboldt University Berlin. She has worked at the Romance Language

Departments of the Universities of Münster and Aachen, where she currently teaches and researches. Her interests include fantastic literature, children's and youth literature, creative writing, or the relationships between literature and religion.
natalia.llana@ifaar.rwth-aachen.de

Arndt Heilmann is a Ph.D. student of English Linguistics at RWTH Aachen University. His research foci are translation process studies, psycholinguistics and corpus studies. He mainly is interested in quantitative assessment and statistical analysis of linguistic phenomena and their effect on physiological measures, such as eye-tracking and keystroke-logging data, but also on functional linguistic theories. In his Ph.D. project he investigates the influence of expertise on translation processes and products.
arndt.heilmann@ifaar.rwth-aachen.de

Sven Hintzen is an MA candidate of English Studies at RWTH Aachen University. He currently works as a student assistant at the department of English Linguistics. His research interests are in translation studies and in cognitive and systemic-functional approaches to metaphor.
sven.hintzen@rwth-aachen.de

Massimiliano Izzo is a passionate reader of high fantasy, speculative fiction, and all sorts of mythological stuff. His previous contributions to Tolkien studies ('Recurrent Patterns of the Fall in Tolkien's legendarium' and 'In Search of the Wandering Fire: Otherworldly Imagery in "The Song of Ælfwine"') were presented at the 2016 and 2017 Tolkien Seminars in Leeds and have been published in the conference proceedings.
massimorgon@gmail.com

Franz Klug is studying English and Art at Friedrich Schiller University Jena and Bauhaus University Weimar. Since 2016, he has been working as a student assistant for English Medieval Studies.
franz.klug@uni-jena.de

Christian Lemburg, Dipl. Psych., is working as consultant and negotiator in the software industry. His interest in Tolkien is built on a fascination with the imaginary worlds of fantasy and science fiction literature from a psychological perspective.
christian@lemburg.net

Flora Sophie Lemburg finished school 2017 at St. Ursula Gymnasium in Aachen. Currently, she studies English Philology and Philosophy at Georg-August University in Göttingen.
sophie@lemburg.net

Timo Lothmann, Dr. phil., is a post-doc researcher and lecturer of English Linguistics at RWTH Aachen University. He has also taught at the universities of Münster and Paderborn. His research interests include cognitive approaches to language, reading and translation processing, pidgin and creole languages, early English poetry, and J.R.R. Tolkien's oeuvre. He lays particular stress on interdisciplinary perspectives. Recent publications comprise a metaphor approach to the *Beowulf* dragon and an analysis of Tolkien's concept of Faërie as a framework for the blending of story rooms. He currently focuses on fields of application of conceptual metaphor and blending theory.
timo.lothmann@ifaar.rwth-aachen.de

Magdalena Mączyńska, MA, graduated from the University of Opole. Having completed her studies in the English language and literature, she submitted her Master's thesis on J.R.R. Tolkien's mythopoeia and the writer's creative use of mythical themes present in Norse, Finnish and Celtic mythologies. She has attended international conferences and has published articles about British and American fantasy literature, which is her major area of research. Her Ph.D. thesis focuses on the works of Tolkien, Marion Zimmer Bradley and Philip Pullman.
magdalena_m9@tlen.pl

Marguerite Mouton recieved her Ph.D. in comparative literature and literary theory from the University Paris 13 (France), where she taught French literature, before teaching at the University of Cergy-Pontoise. Her thesis, to be published by Classiques Garnier Editors, is entitled: The "Deep Enchantments" of the Epic: Highlighting a New Epic Model with regard to the Powers of Imagination in the Works of Victor Hugo and J.R.R. Tolkien (*Notre-Dame de Paris* and *La Légende des siècles*, *The Book of Lost Tales*, *The Lays of Beleriand* and *The Lord of the Rings*).
marguerite.mouton@laposte.net

Gergely Nagy, Ph.D., is an independent scholar who taught at the University of Szeged, Hungary, for 15 years. He wrote his dissertation on the 1977 *Silmarillion* and its basis in textuality, but even prior to that, argued in several articles and papers that textuality and the network of (fictional) texts is central to Tolkien's representation (and thus creation) of culture. He also published papers on Malory and Chaucer, and at the University of Szeged, taught courses on medieval English literature, 20th century fantastic literature and film (including Tolkien, Harry Potter, and science fiction), and 20th century popular music. He has been the

member of the *Tolkien Studies* editorial board from the periodical's inception, and in the early 2000s, he was instrumental in creating the Hungarian Tolkien Society.
bwglamorak@gmail.com

Łukasz Neubauer received his Ph.D. in English Philology from the University of Łódź. He is a researcher and lecturer at the University of Koszalin, Poland, where he teaches courses on Tolkien, Old English literature and Arthurian romances. Apart from his publications dealing with various medieval as well as Christian influences and resonances in *The Lord of the Rings*, he has also written papers on *The Battle of Maldon*, *Beowulf*, *Hêliand*, Icelandic sagas and the so-called "beasts of battle" trope in, particularly but not exclusively, Old Germanic poetry. He is also a member of the British branch of the International Arthurian Society and a conceptual coordinator of the annual Medieval Fantasy Symposium in Mielno-Unieście, Poland.
lukasz_neubauer@poczta.onet.pl

Helmut W. Pesch, Dr. phil., studied English Philology, History of Art and Classical Archaeology. His doctoral dissertation, published in 1981, was the first scholarly study of fantasy as a literary genre in Germany. As a former editorial director of e-publishing and crossmedia exploitation he was involved in the conception and realisation of cross- and transmedia projects. He is also known as an author and translator and an expert on Tolkien's invented languages.
mail@helmutwpesch.de

Jan Levin Propach studied Catholic Theology and Philosophy at LMU Munich and the Munich School of Philosophy. He is a Teaching and Research Assistant at LMU Munich and the University of Augsburg and doing his Ph.D. about Leibniz', Lewis', and Plantinga's theories of possible worlds. As a member of the German Tolkien Society he is interested in the relationship between fantasy literature and philosophy.
jan.propach@kthf.uni-augsburg.de

Patrick Schmitz studied English and History at RWTH Aachen University. After working in Cologne and Aachen, he currently works as a teacher at a school in Nideggen. He is a member of the German Tolkien Society and has given presentations on topics such as violence in fantasy literature. His current work is focused on literary worldbuilding.
patrick.schmitz1@rwth-aachen.de

Friedhelm Schneidewind studied Biology and some terms Computer Science. He is currently working as teacher at Berufsbildungswerk Neckargemünd and as a free-lance teacher especially for media design, as author of several lexicons

and several books on mythology, phantastic literature and Tolkien, as well as journalist, editor, publisher and musician. 2016 he published *Das neue große Tolkien-Lexikon*.
www.friedhelm-schneidewind.de

Laura Selle, B.A., is a scholar of Comparative Literary Studies and English Studies, currently enrolled in the master's program for gender studies at the Humboldt-Universität Berlin. Her research interests lie at the intersection of literature and popular culture with an analytical approach firmly rooted in intersectional queer feminism.
laura@selle-jena.de

Ross Smith is the author of *Inside Language: Linguistic and Aesthetic Theory in Tolkien* (Walking Tree Publishers, 2011). He has published numerous articles in leading academic journals on matters of translation, language invention and lingustic aesthetics, particularly in relation to J.R.R. Tolkien and other 20th century mythopoeic authors. He has a degree in English from the University of Edinburgh and is a member of the Chartered Institute of Linguists.
rosstranslations@gmail.com

Guglielmo Spirito is a Conventual Franciscan Friar working and living in Assisi. In Rome he got his Ph.D. in Theology with specialisation in Spirituality at the *Antonianum*. Since 1994, he is professor at the Theological Institute of Assisi and at the Pontifical Faculty of Saint Bonaventure in Rome. He gave courses of Theology in Canada, Croazia, Romania, Russia, Mexico, Lebanon and Kenya, and lectures on Tolkien in England, Germany, France and Canada. On J.R.R. Tolkien he had published essays, articles and books as well as several papers with Walking Tree Publishers and in *Hither Shore*.
fraguspi@gmail.com

Allan Turner, Ph.D., was until recently lecturer in English at the Friedrich-Schiller-Universität, Jena. He now lives in retirement in north-eastern England, trying to find his way in a post-Brexit world. His main interests within Tolkien studies lie in the fields of stylistics and translation.
allangturner@aol.com

Nilüfer Ulusoy-Schmitz studied English and French at RWTH Aachen University. After working in Aachen, and Alsdorf, she currently works as a teacher at a school in Mönchengladbach. She is a member of the German Tolkien Society and is interested in the role of racism as well as in the function of orientalism in fantasy literature.
niluefer.ulusoy@rwth-aachen.de

Christine Vogt-William, Ph.D., studied English, German and Psychology at the University of Essen, Germany, where she received her MA in English Literature and Cultural Studies. She completed her doctoral thesis at the University of York, England, as a Marie Curie Gender Graduate Fellow. From 2008 to 2010, she was a Visiting Scholar at the Department of Women's Studies at Emory University, Atlanta, Georgia, USA. On returning to Germany, she taught at the Universities of Münster and Freiburg, and from April 2014 to March 2017, she taught literary and cultural studies as an Interim Professor for Postcolonial and Gender Studies at the English and American Studies Department, Humboldt University, Berlin. In 2018, she held a 1-year postdoc fellowship from the Chancengleichheitsprogramm at the University of Augsburg. Besides her research interests in canonical, postcolonial and diasporic Anglophone literatures with a leaning towards intersectional readings of race and gender, she is an avid fantasy and science fiction reader.
cvogtwilliam@yahoo.com

Unsere Autor*innen

Annie Birks, Ph.D., unterrichtet Sprachwissenschaften, Literatur und Übersetzung an der Université Catholique de l'Ouest in Angers, Frankreich. Ihr langjähriges Interesse an J.R.R. Tolkien und C.S. Lewis hat, vereint mit ihrer Doktorarbeit *La Rétribution dans l'oeuvre de J.R.R. Tolkien* (Université Paris-Sorbonne), zu Artikeln und Vorlesungen zu diesen beiden Autoren beigetragen.

Isabel Busch, MA, studierte Anglistik, Komparatistik und Neuere und Neueste Geschichte an der Rheinischen Friedrich-Wilhelms-Universität Bonn und am University College Cork. Sie arbeitet derzeit an einer Dissertation zu Gender-Konzepten im modernen englischen Fantasy-Roman. Sie arbeitet zudem als Geschäftsführerin und wissenschaftliche Mitarbeiterin im Haus der FrauenGeschichte in Bonn. Ihre Forschungsinteressen beinhalten: Fantasy-Literatur, Gender Studies, englische Literatur- und Kulturgeschichte (speziell Tudor-Ära).
busch@hdfg.de

Andoni Cossío erlangte seinen MA in Comparative Literature und Literary Studies von der University of the Basque Country mit einer Dissertation über die Rolle und den Symbolismus von Wäldern und Bäumen in Tolkiens *Der kleine Hobbit* und *Der Herr der Ringe*. Ihm wurde von der Baskischen Regierung ein Dissertationsstipendium gewährt. Er hat Vorträge über Tolkien auf internationalen Konferenzen gehalten und war an der Organisation von vier internationalen Konferenzen beteiligt, die sich mit den Inklings beschäftigt haben (2015-2018). Er unterrichtet Englisch an der spanischen Universität UNED. andoni.cossio@ehu.eus

Julian Tim Morton Eilmann, Dr. phil., StR., Magister Artium in Geschichte, Germanistik und Kunstgeschichte (Aachen/Nottingham), ist seit 2008 Gymnasiallehrer für Deutsch, Geschichte und Literatur (Film) in Aachen. Seine Dissertation (2016, Uni Jena) *J.R.R. Tolkien – Romantiker und Lyriker* kam 2017 auf die Shortlist des Deutschen Phantastikpreises. Seine Forschungsschwerpunkte liegen auf Tolkiens Lyrik und der Romantiktradition der modernen Phantastik. Seit vielen Jahren hält er Vorträge und veröffentlicht Aufsätze zu Tolkien. 2013 hat er zusammen mit Allan Turner den Sammelband *Tolkien's Poetry* publiziert. julianeilmann@web.de

Natalia González de la Llana, Dr. phil., hat Literary Theory und Comparative Literature studiert und ihren Doktortitel von der Complutense University in Madrid erhalten. Forschungsaufenthalte brachten sie an die La Sapienza Universität Rom und die Humboldt Universität Berlin. Sie hat für das Institut der Romanischen Sprachen an den Universitäten von Münster und Aachen gearbeitet, wo sie momentan unterrichtet und forscht. Ihre Interessen reichen von Phantastischer Literatur, Kinderliteratur und Jugendliteratur, kreativem Schreiben bis zur Beziehung zwischen Literatur und Religion. natalia.llana@ifaar.rwth-aachen.de

Arndt Heilmann ist Doktorand der Englischen Linguistik an der RWTH Aachen. Seine Forschungsschwerpunkte sind Translation Process Studies, Psycholinguisitics und Corpus Studies. Er ist vor allem interessiert an quantitativen Studien und statistischer Analyse von linguistischen Phänomenen und ihren Auswirkungen auf physiologische Bereiche wie etwa eye-tracking und keystroke-logging Daten sowie an funktionellen linguistischen Theorien. In seinem Doktoratsprojekt untersucht er den Einfluss von Expertise auf Übersetzungsprozesse und -produkte. arndt.heilmann@ifaar.rwth-aachen.de

Sven Hintzen ist ein Masterkandidat der English Studies an der RWTH Aachen. Er arbeitet momentan als studentische Hilfskraft am Institut für Englische Linguistik. Seine Forschungsinteressen sind Übersetzung sowie kognitive und system-funktionale Ansätze an Metaphern. sven.hintzen@rwth-aachen.de

Massimiliano Izzo ist begeisterter Leser von High Fantasy, Spekulativer Fiktion und allerart anderer mythologischer Dinge. Seine früheren Beiträge zur

Tolkienforschung („Recurrent Patterns of the Fall in Tolkien's legendarium" und „In Search of the Wandering Fire: Otherworldly Imagery in *The Song of Ælfwine*") wurden 2016 und 2017 auf den Tolkienseminaren in Leeds vorgestellt und in den Tagungsbänden veröffentlicht.
massimorgon@gmail.com

Franz Klug studiert Englisch und Kunst an der Friedrich-Schiller-Universität Jena und der Bauhaus Universität Weimar. Er arbeitet seit 2016 als studentische Hilfskraft für die Englische Mediävistik.
franz.klug@uni-jena.de

Flora Sophie Lemburg hat im Wintersemester 2017/2018 ein Studium der englischen Philologie und Philosophie an der Georg-August Universität in Göttingen begonnen.
sophie@lemburg.net

Christian Lemburg, Dipl. Psych., arbeitet als Berater und Verhandler in der Software-Branche. Sein Interesse an Tolkien beruht auf einer Faszination für die imaginären Welten der Fantasy- und Science-Fiction-Literatur aus einer psychologischen Perspektive. Er ist Vorstandsmitglied der Deutschen Tolkien Gesellschaft.
christian@lemburg.net

Timo Lothmann, Dr. phil., ist ein Post-doc-Forscher und Dozent für Englische Linguistik an der RWTH Aachen. Er hat außerdem an den Universitäten in Münster und Paderborn unterrichtet. Seine Forschungsinteressen umfassen kognitive Ansätze an Sprache, Literatur und Übersetzungsprozesse, Pidgin und Kreolsprachen, frühe englische Poesie und J.R.R. Tolkiens Œuvre. Er legt einen besonderen Schwerpunkt auf disziplinübergreifende Perspektiven. Seine aktuellen Publikationen thematisieren einen Metapher-Ansatz zum Drachen in *Beowulf* und eine Analyse von Tolkiens Konzept von Faërie als ein Rahmen für die Verschmelzung von story rooms. Er fokussiert sich momentan auf Anwendungsfelder von konzeptueller Metapher und Theorieverschmelzung.
timo.lothmann@ifaar.rwth-aachen.de

Magdalena Mączyńska, MA, erhielt ihren Abschluss von der Universität von Opole. Sie studierte Englische Sprache und Literatur und verfasste ihre Masterarbeit über J.R.R. Tolkiens keltische Mythologien. Sie hat an internationalen Konferenzen teilgenommen und Artikel zur britischen und amerikanischen Fantasy-Literatur verfasst, da dies ihr zentrales Forschungsfeld ist. Ihre Doktorarbeit betrachtet die Werke von J.R.R. Tolkien, Marion Zimmer Bradley und Philip Pullman.   magdalena_m9@tlen.pl

Marguerite Mouton bekam ihren Ph.D. in Vergleichender Literaturwissenschaft und Literaturtheorie von der Universität Paris 13, Frankreich. Dort unterrichtete sie französische Literatur, später auch an der Universität von Cergy-Pontoise. Ihre Abschlussarbeit trägt den Titel: The "Deep Enchantments" of the Epic: Highlighting a New Epic Model with Regard to the Powers of Imagination in the Works of Victor Hugo and J.R.R. Tolkien (*Notre-Dame de Paris and La Légende des siècles,* The Book of Lost Tales, The Lays of Beleriand *and* The Lord of the Rings).
marguerite.mouton@laposte.net

Gergely Nagy, Ph.D., ist unabhängiger Wissenschaftler, der 15 Jahre an der Universität von Szeged, Ungarn, gelehrt hat. Er schrieb seine Dissertation über das 1977er *Silmarillion* und dessen Basis in Textualität und hatte schon zuvor in mehreren Essays argumentiert, dass Textualität und das Netzwerk von (fiktionalen) Texten ein zentraler Punkt von Tolkiens Repräsentation (und dadurch Kreation) von Kultur sind. Er hat außerdem Artikel über Malory und Chaucer verfasst sowie Kurse über mittelalterliche englische Literatur wie auch über Phantastische Literatur, Film und Popmusik des 20. Jahrhunderts gegeben. Er ist schon seit deren Beginn im Herausgebergremiums der *Tolkien Studies* und war maßgeblich an der Gründung der ungarischen Tolkiengesellschaft beteiligt.
bwglamorak@gmail.com

Łukasz Neubauer erhielt seinen Ph.D. in Englischer Philologie von der Universität von Łódź. Er ist Forscher und Dozent an der Universität von Koszalin, Polen, wo er Kurse über Tolkien, altenglische Literatur und Arthurische Romanzen gibt. Neben seinen Publikationen, welche sich mit verschiedenen mittelalterlichen und auch christlichen Einflüssen und Resonanzen in *Der Herr der Ringe* beschäftigen, hat er außerdem Artikel über *The Battle of Maldon, Beowulf, Hêliand,* Isländische Sagen und die Figuren der sogenannten "beasts of battle" in vor allem, aber nicht ausschließlich, altdeutscher Poesie verfasst. Er ist außerdem Mitglied der britischen Sektion der International Arthurian Society und ein Koordinator des jährlichen Medieval Fantasy Symposium in Mielno-Unieście, Polen.
lukasz_neubauer@poczta.onet.pl

Helmut W. Pesch, Dr. phil., studierte Anglistik, Kunstgeschichte und klassische Archäologie und promovierte 1981 mit der ersten deutschsprachigen Dissertation über Fantasy als literarisches Genre. Als ehemaliger Lektor und Programmleiter für E-Publishing und crossmediale Verwertung war er selbst an der Konzeption und Umsetzung cross- und transmedialer Projekte beteiligt. Er ist auch bekannt als Autor, Übersetzer und Experte für Tolkiens Kunstsprachen.
mail@helmutwpesch.de

Jan Levin Propach hat Katholische Theologie und Philosophie an der LMU München und der Hochschule für Philosophie München studiert. Er ist wissenschaftlicher Mitarbeiter der LMU München und der Universität von Augsburg und verfasst seine Doktorarbeit über die verschiedenen Theorien von Leibniz, Lewis und Plantinga über mögliche Welten. Als Mitglied der DTG interessiert er sich sehr für die Beziehung zwischen Fantasy-Literatur und Philosophie.
jan.propach@kthf.uni-augsburg.de

Patrick Schmitz studierte Englisch und Geschichte an der RWTH Aachen. Aktuell arbeitet er als Lehrer an einer Schule in Nideggen. Er ist Mitglied der DTG und hat Vorträge z.b. über Gewalt in der Fantasyliteratur gehalten. Sein momentaner Arbeitsfokus ist literarische Weltenschöpfung.
Patrick.Schmitz1@rwth-aachen.de

Friedhelm Schneidewind studierte Biologie und einige Semester Informatik. Er ist Berufserprober im Berufsbildungswerk Neckargemünd und tätig als freier Dozent im Medienbereich, als Autor, u.a. mehrerer Lexika und Sachbücher zu Mythologie, zu Phantastischer Literatur und zu Tolkien, als Journalist, Herausgeber, Verleger und Musiker. 2016 erschien von ihm *Das neue große Tolkien-Lexikon*.
www.friedhelm-schneidewind.de

Laura Selle, B.A., ist vergleichende Literaturwissenschaftlerin und absolviert derzeit an der Humboldt-Universität Berlin ein Masterstudium in Gender Studies. Ihre Forschungsinteressen liegen im Spannungsfeld von Literaturwissenschaft und Populärkultur mit einem intersektionalen, queer-feministischen Analyseansatz.
laura@selle-jena.de

Ross Smith ist der Autor von *Inside Language: Linguistic and Aesthetic Theory in Tolkien* (Walking Tree Publishers, 2011). Er hat zahlreiche Artikel in führenden akademischen Zeitschriften zu Themen wie Übersetzung, Spracherfindung und linguistische Ästhetik, besonders in Verbindung zu J.R.R. Tolkien und anderen mythopoetischen Autoren des 20. Jahrhunderts, veröffentlicht. Er hat einen Abschluss in Englisch von der University of Edinburgh und ist Mitglied des Chartered Institute of Linguists.
rosstranslations@gmail.com

Guglielmo Spirito, Prof. Dr. theol., ist ein Franziskaner-Mönch und arbeitet und lebt in Assisi. Hier erhielt er seinen Ph.D. in Theologie mit einer Spezialisierung in Spiritualität am Antonianum in Rom. Seit 1994 ist er Professor am Theologischen Institut von Assisi und an der Päpstlichen Fakultät St. Bona-

ventura in Rom. Er hat Theologiekurse in Kanada, Kroatien, Rumänien, Russland, Mexiko, Kenia und dem Libanon gegeben sowie Vorlesungen zu Tolkien in England, Deutschland, Frankreich und Kanada gehalten. Er hat zahlreiche Essays, Artikel und Bücher über J.R.R. Tolkien verfasst und einige Artikel bei Walking Tree Publishers und im *Hither Shore* veröffentlicht.
fraguspi@gmail.com

Allan Turner, Ph.D., war bis 2014 Dozent für Englisch an der Friedrich-Schiller-Universität in Jena. Er verbringt seinen Ruhestand im nordöstlichen England und versucht, sich in einer Post-Brexit-Welt zurechtzufinden. Seine zentralen Interessenfelder in der Tolkienforschung liegen in den Bereichen Stilistik und Übersetzung.
allangturner@aol.com

Nilüfer Ulusoy-Schmitz studierte Englisch und Französisch an der RWTH Aachen. Sie unterrichtet momentan an einer Schule in Mönchengladbach. Sie ist Mitglied der DTG und interessiert sich für die Rolle von Rassismus sowie die Funktion von Orientalismus in der Fantasyliteratur.
niluefer.ulusoy@rwth-aachen.de

Christine Vogt-William, Ph.D., hat Englisch, Deutsch und Philosophie an der Universität Essen studiert, wo sie ihren Master in Englischer Literatur und Kulturwissenschaften erworben hat. Sie schrieb ihre Doktorarbeit an der University of York in England als ein Marie Curie Gender Graduate Fellow. Sie war 2008-2010 Visiting Scholar am Department of Women's Studies der Emory University, Atlanta, Georgia, USA. Zurück in Deutschland unterrichtete sie an den Universitäten Münster und Freiburg und war Vertretungsprofessorin für Postcolonial & Gender Studies an der Humboldt Universität. 2018 hatte sie ein Post-doc-Stipendium des Chancengleichheitsprogramms der Universität Augsburg. Aktuell arbeitet sie an ihrem zweiten Buch über das biologische Zwillingsdasein in anglophoner Literatur.
cvogtwilliam@yahoo.com

Siglenverzeichnis

Die Schriften von J.R.R. Tolkien werden im Text jeweils ohne Angabe des Verfassernamens mit den folgenden Siglen zitiert. Die jeweils benutzte Ausgabe findet sich im Literaturverzeichnis.

AI:	The Lay of Aotrou and Itroun
ATB:	The Adventures of Tom Bombadil and other Verses from the Red Book / Die Abenteuer des Tom Bombadil und andere Gedichte aus dem Roten Buch
AW:	Ancrene Wisse and Hali Meiðhad
B:	Die Briefe von J.R.R. Tolkien
BA:	Bilbos Abschiedslied
BB:	Baum und Blatt
BGH:	Bauer Giles von Ham
BL:	Beren and Lúthien / Beren und Lúthien
BLS:	Bilbo's Last Song
BMC:	Beowulf: The Monster and the Critics
BT:	Blatt von Tüftler
BUK:	Beowulf: Die Ungeheuer und ihre Kritiker
BW:	Die Briefe vom Weihnachtsmann
CH:	The Children of Húrin
CP:	Chaucer as a Philologist
EA:	The End of the Third Age (History of Middle-earth 9). Auszug
EW:	English and Welsh / Englisch und Walisisch
FA:	The Fall of Arthur
FC:	Letters from Father Christmas
FGH:	Farmer Giles of Ham
FH:	Finn and Hengest
FS:	On Fairy-stories
GD:	Gute Drachen sind rar
GN:	Guide to the Names in the Lord of the Rings
GPO:	Sir Gawain and the Green Knight, Pearl, and Sir Orfeo
H:	The Hobbit / Der Hobbit / Der kleine Hobbit
HB:	The Homecoming of Beorhtnoth Beorhthelm's Son
HdR:	Der Herr der Ringe
HdR I:	Der Herr der Ringe. Bd. 1. Die Gefährten
HdR II:	Der Herr der Ringe. Bd. 2. Die Zwei Türme
HdR III:	Der Herr der Ringe. Bd. 3. Die Rückkehr des Königs / Die Wiederkehr des Königs
HdR A:	Der Herr der Ringe. Anhänge
HG:	Herr Glück
HH I/II:	The History of the Hobbit
HL:	Ein heimliches Laster
KH:	Die Kinder Húrins
L:	The Letters of J.R.R. Tolkien
LB:	The Lays of Beleriand (History of Middle-earth 3)

LN:	Leaf by Niggle
LotR:	The Lord of the Rings
LotR I:	The Fellowship of the Ring. Being the first part of The Lord of the Rings
LotR II:	The Two Towers. Being the second part of The Lord of the Rings
LotR III:	The Return of the King. Being the third part of The Lord of the Rings
LotR A:	The Lord of the Rings. Appendices
LR:	The Lost Road and other Writings (History of Middle-earth 5)
LSG:	The Legend of Sigurd and Gudrún
LT 1:	The Book of Lost Tales 1 (History of Middle-earth 1)
LT 2:	The Book of Lost Tales 2 (History of Middle-earth 2)
MB:	Mr. Bliss
MC:	The Monsters and the Critics and Other Essays
ME:	A Middle English Vocabulary
MR:	Morgoth's Ring (History of Middle-earth 10)
My:	Mythopoeia
NM:	Nachrichten aus Mittelerde
OE:	The Old English Exodus
OK:	Ósanwe-Kenta
P:	Pictures by J.R.R. Tolkien
PM:	The Peoples of Middle-earth (History of Middle-earth 12)
R:	Roverandom
RBG:	The Rivers and Beacon-hills of Gondor
RGEO:	The Road Goes Ever On (with Donald Swann)
RS:	The Return of the Shadow (History of Middle-earth 6)
S:	Silmarillion
SD:	Sauron Defeated (History of Middle-earth 9)
SG:	Der Schmied von Großholzingen
SGG:	Sir Gawain and the Green Knight / Sir Gawain und der Grüne Ritter (Essay)
SK:	The Story of Kullervo
SM:	The Shaping of Middle-earth (History of Middle-earth 4)
SP:	Songs for the Philologists
SV:	A Secret Vice
SWM:	Smith of Wootton Major
SWME:	Smith of Wootton Major Essay
TB:	On Translating Beowulf
TI:	The Treason of Isengard (History of Middle-earth 7)
TL:	Tree and Leaf
ÜB:	Zur Übersetzung des Beowulf
ÜM:	Über Märchen
UK:	Die Ungeheuer und ihre Kritiker. Gesammelte Aufsätze
UT:	Unfinished Tales
VA:	Valedictory Address
VG 1:	Das Buch der Verschollenen Geschichten 1
VG 2:	Das Buch der Verschollenen Geschichten 2
WJ:	The War of the Jewels (History of Middle-earth 11)
WR:	The War of the Ring (History of Middle-earth 8)